LOVE HERO

CREATING TRUE LOVE IN THE MODERN WORLD

ANDREW BARCENAS

DEDICATION

July 3, 2022
Abbey,

These last couple of years have graced me with some beautiful lessons. Miracles don't come around that often, unicorns come out just when we think they don't exist; dreams are sometimes a snapshot of reality; and your heroes are sometimes the ones you're trying to be a hero for. I learned those lessons because you are truly an anomalous miracle to me. You are a unicorn. You escaped from a dream into reality. I've never called anyone my hero before. But you are my hero. In many ways, for many reasons.
You have the most compassionate heart for life I've ever met.
You're astoundingly beautiful, as we can all see in that white dress.
You love intentionally through every love language.
You have the ability to access the purity, innocence, joy,

*and excitement of a child, and it's one of the most
magnificent things I've ever seen.
You are wise beyond your years.
I vow to recognize your wisdom and humble myself to
correct my flaws when wisdom finds them.
I vow to recognize God's grace in your love because
grace is not something we deserve or earn—it is a gift.
I vow to prize you as such, not take you for granted,
and find my way back to reality if I do.
I promise to protect you from harm. To tenderly hold
and care for your heart, soul, and mind as my own and
lift them above me in high water. To be brave to scout
the house when we hear sketchy noises.
And when whatever wounds come to find you, I vow to
hug you, cuddle you, hold you, and kiss you until
healing also finds you.
I promise to always respect and treat you as a strength,
ally, complement, and to be proud of your presence. I
will follow you into battle during clumsy, silly, and
awkward moments.
I will love and accept everything you are and support
everything good and holy you aim to be.
I vow to love you whether we have a name of wealth or
a penny to our name; to love you in tragedy and in the
ideal; to love you in all your forms, through all my
days.
Today, a journey of continually redefining what
marriage means to us begins. So, may we love and
connect with one another beyond what any legal
institution could ever dream of demanding.
Today we leave behind whatever broken legacies lie in
our history or in our DNA and bring only the blessings.
It is the honor of my life to write a new legacy
with you.
Above all, and most importantly, I vow to see you and*

*love you through the eyes of God. To be the best channel
of His unfathomable for you. To speak His love when
you can't hear it, to be His hands so you can feel it, and
to carry His presence so you always remember.
Though I have loved you and carried you with me long
before time and space permitted it, as you'll come to find
more about in the coming days (I wrote her letters years
before meeting her), and today I finally meld my being
and soul to yours.
You are the greatest secret I will always keep.*

Your loving husband,
Andrew

*My hope for you, dear reader, is that you dedicate yourself to building a
love like this.*

CONTENTS

Love Hero

CREATING TRUE LOVE IN THE MODERN WORLD

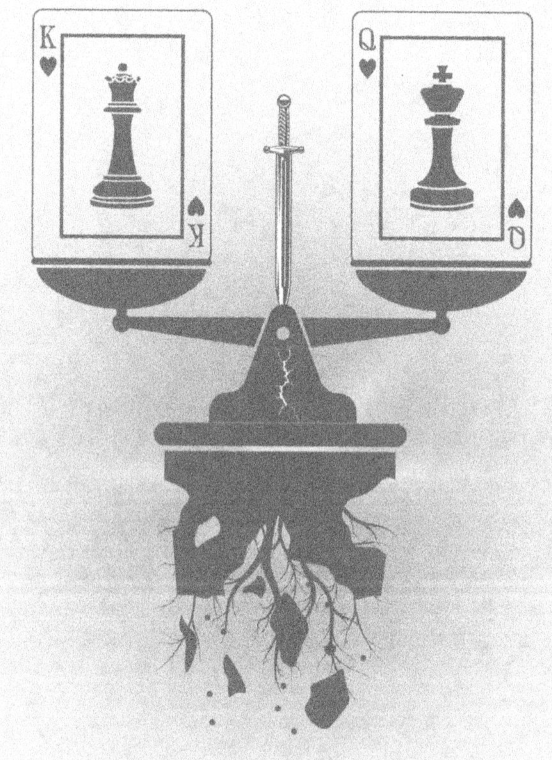

ANDREW BARCENAS

INTRODUCTION

Of all the relationship books out there, you've perhaps picked up the only book in existence that reverse engineers the myth-like concept of "true love." The fundamental question this book answers is, "What would an actionable blueprint of true love look like in the modern world?"

Indeed, this isn't a general book about relationships. It's not about what makes relationships succeed, how to date better, or "keeping the spark alive." No, those books already exist, and I value your time too much to whip off a tablecloth to reveal something you've already seen.

This book is about exposing a hidden, narrow path, threading the needle, and speaking a secret never uttered before. Straying from this path, you'll undoubtedly find broken relationships. You'll also find relationships that *work just fine*. Yes, you read that right; nobody needs to abide by all the principles in this book to have a *functional* relationship.

But if what you seek is a treasure so sacred that it seems only those handpicked by God or the whims of the universe receive it, then you've found the map. This treasure is usually only ever stumbled upon. I aim to create a map so clear that you can advance straight to it.

THE MAP

Romance and dating don't have a long history. The reason we don't have obvious, well-mapped paths to creating true love is that we've only had the freedom to choose who to love for a couple of centuries. Outside that window, humans have never really been "free" in their mate selection. Relationships were predetermined and transactional —purely chosen for convenience, mutual family benefit, access to resources, or bloodline preservation.

Not only have we recently gained the freedom to select our mates and love, but our modern world has dismantled most mating cultures and traditions built on that freedom. Any established dating and relationship paths are fragmenting as a new world emerges.

So, if you're dating and feel you're in muddy waters, *it's because you are.* If you can't see a path that leads to a superb partner to create true love with, it's because *there isn't one.* Not one we can point to, anyway. And if you're in a relationship, struggling to find a way forward, it may very well be because society's relationship foundations are crumbling around you.

With this acknowledgment of murky waters and unclear paths, we come to another uncomfortable truth. If there's no obvious path many can point to, it means there are no perfect guides. There are *no experts on modern relationships and love who can tell us exactly what to do.* There are only theories, cultural trends, human tendencies, helpful data, and people somewhat familiar with those things.

If there really were experts out there, we wouldn't be buying and rummaging through books like this. We'd know precisely which books and authors had *the* correct answers. This lack of "expertise" stems from the fact that "right answers" often differ from person to person, and no one is an expert on our own circumstances except for us. No one is coming to save us. Nor *can* they.

From this moment on, dear reader, you need to be critical of any theory, influencer, video, author, doctor, therapist, coach, and any situational advice people preach. In this book, I give you a map and a compass, but where you go—straight, left, right, or even backward—is entirely up to you.

Unless the advice already aligns with one's understanding of reality and love, blindly accepting and using it will most likely waste one's time and resources. That's because when we're just doing what we're told, actions rarely flow from our hearts—the core of who we are. Creating true love isn't dependent on performing a set or flow of specific actions, but entirely on how the core identities of people intermingle.

Identity formation will be a focus in this book because the fleeting treasure of true love requires every ounce of autonomy and willpower we have. Autonomy has two Greek roots: *auto*, meaning self, and *nomos*, meaning law or rule. So, autonomy is the ability to self-govern or self-rule—to be able to choose our path.

While this book provides a map and compass, the world is constantly changing, and so are the candidates we can create true love with. That means the path to creating true love is continually in flux, and it always will be.

No one can show us exactly where to go because the trees move—new obstacles come and go. Grasses overgrow. The sun, moon, and stars spin around us hour by hour. Spooky noises and wild variables emerge. And the rain transforms the landscape. A map is ultimately a tool to navigate all the possibilities; it's not a bus to the destination. Hence, the importance of autonomy and identity.

If you're looking for an easier way to get what you "deserve," I assure you, the "true love" you think exists... *does not*. True love is a treasure that doesn't bargain. It doesn't trade, it doesn't make exceptions; it has no favorites, and it owes *no one*. It requires blood, sweat, tears, and a particular type of death. No one is spared. The faint of heart will wander, grow weary, and complain. They will search to no avail.

If you're reading this section in the aisle of a bookstore or reading a preview, before you buy this book, decide whether true love is *really* something you'd do anything for. Not everyone is ready for the truths within these pages. Since we'll be directly threatening ego and personal pride in this book by consistently pushing for development and embracing multiple points of view, it may naturally spark anger, denial, and defensiveness.

This book is titled *Love Hero* because only those who fully embrace self-sacrifice and aspire to the highest ideals have what it takes to create true love. The target audience of this book is the people yearning for the love of legends; those who will walk through trial and fire to touch and keep a piece of paradise. Only they will feel true love graze their skin like sunlight and resurrect a legend lost to time.

Continuing my transparency, while I strive to develop a universal, first-principles framework for true love, I draw many principles from a Christian worldview and speak through that lens occasionally. Throughout the book, I encourage readers to reframe my language to fit their own lens. If one prefers the universe or probabilities instead of God, great.

Ultimately, every principle I share uses this question as its backbone: "Does this increase the likelihood I'll create a more beautiful love?" If you can accept that and test every principle I share under that lens, we'll get along *just fine*.

My Predisposition

Since autonomy and identity are focal points throughout this book, we'll increase ownership over our lives and, therefore, our power to control our romantic outcomes. While I'll apply therapeutic, consulting, and mentoring philosophies as needed, I'll primarily leverage my coaching expertise to support this endeavor.

Therapy aims to heal, restore functionality, promote normalcy, do deep work, and cope with stress, anxiety, and trauma. While it's a crucial discipline, it also predisposes one to a mindset in which healing is *always* in progress. Meaning that there is always something to fix, and total healing from conditions and diagnoses may never be achieved.

Consultation is advice, opinion, and answer-giving—very black and white. "Things are the way they are; this is what's worked in the past, so this is the calculation." *Mentorship* is of a similar vein, where mentees aim to retrace the paths to success others have taken.

Coaching takes the perspective that clients are whole and powerful. Clients are experts in their own lives, and they can *either* overcome their obstacles and achieve their goals outright *or learn* the skills, tools, knowledge, and characteristics needed to do so. Meaning, anything is possible, and there's *always* a way forward with coaching.

My predisposition throughout this book is genuine hope and faith in you. I firmly believe that *you* have control over your own destiny. You're not perfect by any means, but you have who you are and the obstacles separating you from who and where you could be. So, I invite you to believe you have the power to move forward. Be bold and free enough to dream without judging yourself.

You're an amazing, capable human being. Humans can build skyscrapers, create alternate realities, compose transcendent music, design autonomous systems, facilitate cross-continental communication and travel, and invent shake weights.

Don't get caught up in not having the best income, attractiveness, humor, charisma, or living space. You can learn, grow, adapt, and utterly transcend the boundaries that resemble any box or condition. A beautiful future awaits beyond the horizon of what we understand our limits to be.

CALL TO ADVENTURE

Adopting the principles in this book may be the most challenging thing you've ever done. We're about to test your grit and resilience to discomfort because you may very well learn that you hold dear some obstacles to true love. *Chapter 1* summarizes the state of society and its obstacle-like implications for the dating and relationship landscape.

Society's condition is relevant because it's home to all who make up the world of relationships. It's home to us, the person we may be with, the people we'll date, the person we may want to spend the rest of our lives with, or the person to whom we've already committed our lives.

And despite whatever feelings of hopelessness, frustration, and confusion society breeds in us, it's *not* an inescapable condition that dooms our relationships. It's not a posture of the world against us. Nor is it pout-time. It opens the door to a beautiful challenge and quest, and it's time to rise to the occasion.

1

THE MODERN LANDSCAPE OF ROMANTIC RELATIONSHIPS

Understanding the state of society is fundamental to this book's goal because, regardless of our relationship status, we're being subconsciously influenced by the world around us. A clear understanding of its influences helps us define our challenges and address them.

The influences collaborating on the disaster that is the modern relationship landscape can be summarized by five factors: (1) political developments, (2) the food industry, (3) the pharmaceutical industry, (4) media and AI technologies, and (5) cultural shifts.

As I begin, I'd like to clarify a few points. First, this chapter *over-simplifies* society's state and omits counterarguments. Second, I'm not declaring that these forces are evil or malicious. I'm not about to drop the hottest conspiracy theory of *"Who's Out to Get You in 2026 and Beyond."* If they have any desire, it's not as deep as screwing us over. It's simply about money and power. If it takes screwing us over to get those, fair enough. But it's not a personal vendetta or anything.

I also don't think it's fair to speculate which influence is the source of it all. It's probably safe to assume that all these influences are mutually responsible and rely on each other to stay in power and sway society's trajectory.

Let's begin.

Political Developments

The divisive political landscape of the Western world derives much of its nature from the human survival response. Modern economic inequality is at an all-time high, and emotional and physical well-being are in the dumps. Many people endure daily stress, pain, and fear regarding their basic human needs.

When one's reality is a continual crisis, every waking moment is about survival, and the amygdala remains continually active. The *amygdala* is the brain region that processes threats and fear. While it's handy in zombie apocalypses, it's also active when we're struggling to put food on the table, can't afford a place to live, have no supportive community to belong to, or are under a crushing amount of debt. It's active when we feel like our backs are against the wall.

When a society ruminates in survival mode, its culture and politics warp, and it classifies any conflict or opposing view as an explicit threat. So, instead of civilized discourse over differences, we'll engage one another with intense conflict or disassociation. Fight-or-flight.

Politicians have *every* incentive to feed into this primal soap opera. It's terribly easy to recruit for a cause if *survival* depends on it. Running for governor to fix all the roads may gain us some traction. But if we're running to fund universal healthcare, it'll flatline the opposition. Survival is the most basic human instinct and value. If people are actively bleeding out, they won't care to discuss street improvements.

We can also imagine how useful it'd be to get people to identify with specific policies or ideologies. They're more likely to support policies and politicians that reflect parts of their identities and fight opposing forces to preserve themselves.

The attachment of identity to perspectives concerning race, sex, socioeconomic status, sexual orientation, religion, gender, and disability status is what we refer to as *identity politics*. Identity politics is inherently polarizing because identity is *existential* and draws on our energy and instincts for survival.

Survival instincts shut down the brain regions responsible for cognitive empathy and reasoning, making us largely blind to anything other than protecting ourselves from harm.[i] There's no instinct to listen to and consider others' feelings when they're swinging knives at us. When identity politics becomes part of a society's culture, it inherently divides the society. That includes individuals in or seeking romantic relationships.

Though identity politics prides itself on the ideals of justice and human benevolence, it *doesn't* promote societal unity or happiness. It spikes anxiety and puts people on the edge of rage and hate toward opposing views, which naturally discourages joy, peace, and open-mindedness. When identity politics runs amok, people would rather form militias than peaceful, diverse-minded communities.

As militias form, identity politics encourages people to view their opposing forces as responsible for their troublesome circumstances. And as that sense of victimhood brews across society, it becomes commonplace and even trendy for individuals to claim "conditions" that define them as underprivileged, abnormal, oppressed, or in an unfair position.

Privilege and oppression *do* exist. A harsh truth of life, though, is that fortunate and unfortunate circumstances find both the deserving and undeserving. It is simply the human condition, and there isn't always a rhyme or reason to it. Yet there are two responses to misfortune.

The *resilient response* takes control, responsibility, and ownership of one's life by reframing misfortune as a challenge in one's story. It turns tragedy into opportunities for learning and growth or a source of inspiration and wisdom for others. One takes responsibility not necessarily in the way that they believe the tragedy that befell them is their fault, but in the way that they claim power over what their circumstances look like now and going forward, *despite* the horror. In a trauma context, this is referred to as *survivor mentality*.

Conversely, a *victim response* absolves one of ownership and responsibility for one's unfavorable circumstances by placing the blame on other parties. Victimhood is the default response to misfortune because taking responsibility for circumstances we didn't entirely cause is counterintuitive. Nevertheless, serious repercussions happen when we *don't* take ownership of our circumstances.

Victim mentalities deprive us of power, autonomy, and resilience. When we relinquish responsibility and ownership, we *also* relinquish power and control. Without total ownership, we have no direct authority, and without authority, we cannot change our circumstances.

Highlighting this issue is essential because *victimhood directly inhibits true love.* An unwavering state of victimhood requires that we be accommodated, served, and kept at the center of attention. That strangles true love for two reasons.

First, anyone whose first instinct is to be accommodated, served, and the focus of attention *doesn't* have the instinct to think about others first. That includes their partner. Their instinct will be to competitively compare themselves to their partner in a manner that asks, "Who should do more to accommodate the other's condition?" They become competitors from different tribes of identity who view each other through a fight-or-flight lens.

Second, since victimhood fosters low autonomy, it reduces people's control over the trajectory of their lives and over their romantic endeavors. They aren't eager to outgrow their flaws or alter their circumstances to improve their relationships because they don't believe they can.

I'm *not* saying we, as a society, shouldn't help or show compassion for people just because they should completely own their circumstances. Nor am I saying that we shouldn't seek and recognize opportunities where we can treat our fellow man and woman with more grace and fairness. I *am* saying it's vital to recognize that when society and culture teach us that external forces control our circumstances, they *also* teach us to leave the power to change those circumstances *outside* of ourselves.

If this world is ever going to reach an equilibrium of peace, well-being, and prosperity, it won't come through guilt-tripping, shaming external forces, or flexes of moral superiority. It'll come through invitations and gestures of exemplary goodwill and love, and well-intended accountability.

Odds are, if we suffer from anything, it's what has historically been called *the human condition*. That condition includes periodically suffering physically, mentally, emotionally, and socially. Since not everything has a rhyme and a reason, not everything needs to be classified as a "condition."

I acknowledge there are horrific traumas that leave holes in people's beings and sabotage and puppet-master their relationships. No one knows for sure what makes people more or less naturally resilient to traumatic experiences or more or less likely to embrace a "normal" life. But there's no question—they *can* thrive.

My wife scores a 7/10 on the Adverse Childhood Experiences (ACE) test, and she's one of the healthiest people I know. Another friend of mine also scored a 7, and he inspires me to aim higher every day. They're both *rock stars* somehow.

I say somehow because compared to 0, an ACE score of 4 increases the likelihood of attempted suicide by 1,220%, depression by 460%, and lung disease by 390%, and the likelihoods rise with each escalating score. To really hit this home for you, someone with a score of 4 or more has a life expectancy *20 years shorter* than someone who scores 0.[ii]

Yet whether you're healed, healing, or part of the 83% of people who won't score higher than 3, I'll be treating you as a resilient and fully viable candidate to create true love, and my invitation to hope and dream remains the same.

Open your eyes to dream and pursue the possibilities. Even if you *are* a victim, you're free to switch your role. You can dare to leave victimhood on hold, play the hero, expand your power and resiliency, and return to victimhood's familiar security whenever you need.

Overall, regardless of the origin of humanity's peril in meeting basic needs, the modern political climate fosters a culture that emphasizes a victim mindset, fight-or-flight responses, competitive self-interest, low ownership, and low autonomy. All are debilitating for individuals, society, and the relationship landscape.

But that's just an appetizer.

An Upset Tummy

Humanity is well-acquainted with food scarcity. Only in the last century or so have we largely solved the problem of starvation. We essentially solved it by processing food, extending shelf life, and mass-producing carbohydrates. Strategic food distribution would *completely* resolve the issue.

For the first time in human history, *more people are dying of overeating than are dying from starvation*. In 2022, 2.5 billion people were overweight,[iii] and in 2024, an estimated 673 million people suffered from malnutrition.[iv]

The standard processed-foods diet prioritizes *profits* and *survival* over health. Processed foods serve health very poorly. Our bodies are designed to extract energy and nutrients from whole foods that grow directly in the ground or from animals that eat those foods.

Whole foods not only contain more valuable nutrients and help us feel full, but they also require much more effort to extract energy. *That's a good thing.* When we eat whole foods, our bodies expend energy breaking them down, then absorb and use the surplus energy.

Imagine eating 100 calories of whole foods. Your body expends 20 calories to break them down, leaving a net intake of 80 calories. But when we eat processed, refined, or modified versions of whole foods, we don't have to spend nearly as much energy because they're *already* partially broken down.

So, suppose we consume 100 calories of processed food. A large Oreo cookie, perhaps. In that case, our bodies might expend only 10 calories breaking it down, leaving us with a net absorption of 90 calories. Although both types of food may be labeled as 100 calories, one leads to greater fat storage and weight gain, poorer metabolic health, and poorer overall physical health.

Processed foods also impact our mental well-being. There are essentially four big chemicals in the body associated with feelings of well-being: oxytocin, endorphins, dopamine, and serotonin.

Oxytocin is a bonding chemical released when we connect deeply with someone or engage in physical touch. Babies emit this stuff off their heads like spa diffusers, which is why if you smell their heads, it's pleasant. Lil' homies have hacked your system to get you to sacrifice yourself for them in a house fire before you even know it.

Exercise releases feel-good *endorphins*, most noticeably during runner's high. They have natural pain-relieving capabilities. *Dopamine* is the pleasure chemical that's released when we eat sugar, do a line of unstoppable cocaine, experience sexual euphoria, gamble, win a game, or complete a goal.

Serotonin is subtler but vital to mental well-being. Its levels rise when we exercise, laugh, and eat a meal. The kicker is that the gut— our intestines—*produces some 95% of the serotonin in the entire body.*[v] We refer to the gut as the *microbiome*. It's a lovely little community of various bacteria living together in harmony.

These bacteria prize diversity, respect each other's uniqueness, and prefer to maintain their differences. As a result, they adhere to their specific diets and benefit from particular foods entering their cozy community. Compared to neighboring bacteria, one may not enjoy breaking down cherries, but they go nuts for pistachios. The other neighboring bacteria might enjoy beans, greens, tomatoes, potatoes, or sage, and be happy to leave cherries alone.

The more kinds of food we eat, the greater the diversity of bacteria in our guts. This microbiome diversity probably has more benefits than we're aware of. Still, we know that a diet focused on processed foods *significantly* reduces the diversity of the foods we consume and, consequently, the diversity of our microbiome.

Processing breaks down foods into simple base ingredients, like enriched unbleached wheat flour or high fructose corn syrup, which are then used as core ingredients in food products. The problem is, as you might guess, only one or two types of bacteria benefit from this, and their utopian idea of diversity and equality goes down the toilet.

The more diverse a microbiome is, the more smoothly it functions and the better it fulfills its responsibilities. While it has an incredible list of responsibilities, serotonin production and its significant role in mental health are of utmost importance.

When a processed-food diet is the standard for a society, people absorb more calories, gain weight, and harm their guts. That reduces their serotonin production and harms their mental health and emotional stability. This reduces the likelihood that healthy relationships form because healthy minds and individuals tend to build them.

There's much more I could say, but that's a snapshot of the food industry's effect on the dating and relationship world. Well, I suppose if you care about not getting sick or infected, you might also care that, according to UCLA, *the gut hosts 70% of the immune system*, which fends off disease.[vi]

Cue the pharmaceutical industry.

The Popping Pills Game

The pharmaceutical industry works like any other business: it sees a need and provides a solution. The need they see is human illness, and they offer immediate short-term solutions. They capitalize on the human preference for convenience over significant change.

They're not *stopping* anyone from solving the roots of their problems and improving their health and lives; they're just not necessarily *encouraging* people to think long-term about their well-being. Which makes sense. If they *actually* solved root problems, they'd lose customers. Corporations have a duty to their shareholders to keep and grow their businesses. Losing customers isn't part of their plan.

One clear example of exploiting humanity's preference for convenience is the readily available prescriptions for antidepressants. Instead of prescribing lifestyle changes that effectively treat depression, like exercise,[vii] pro-pharmaceutical Western medicine most commonly treats depression with drugs called SSRIs—Selective Serotonin Reuptake Inhibitors.

SSRIs essentially function by *prolonging* feelings of well-being rather than *inducing* feelings of happiness. They target the serotonin chemical we discussed earlier in the gut. Well-known SSRIs are Prozac, Zoloft, Paxil, and Lexapro. Tragically, and much to the dismay of the pharmaceutical industry, some of their drugs reduce the richness of gut bacteria and the gut's ability to produce serotonin.[viii]

Together, the food and pharmaceutical industries set the stage for chronic physical and mental illness. They conceptually team up in a way where processed food worsens bodily function and reduces serotonin production, and pharmaceuticals shove those problems under a luxurious Persian rug. This creates a complacent standard in which society copes with persistent health problems instead of promoting real healing. Ultimately, that damages society and the landscape of relationships.

Let's continue to turn up the volume.

News, Social Media, and the Dawn of Artificial Intelligence (AI)

News and social media amplify all other destructive societal forces. If you think the news's main purpose is to inform you, *you're wrong*. Their primary aim is to elicit a survival response from the amygdala to gather listeners. News media caters to negative content because it captures and retains human attention.

Amygdala stimulation is a subconscious "addiction" present in every human being, and many industries, including the news media, take advantage of this. If a driver on the other side of the road waves us down and we come to a stop, roll down our window to give them a listen, and they tell us a fluffy bunny is grooming a beaver 300 meters ahead, we may or may not be happy we gave them the time of day.

If they waved us down to say there's a domino effect of giant trees falling on the road headed this way, that's another story. Our subconscious addiction to pertinent survival information will snort that crack all day long, and we'll whip our arses around in the other direction!

When the news media isn't exploiting our fundamental survival instincts to influence us, social media exploits our tendency to compare ourselves with others. In psychology, this mental comparison with others uses what are called reference points. *Reference points* serve as litmus tests for human aspirations of success, satisfaction, and happiness. There are positive and negative results.

Our reference points tell us whether we've reached one of those aspirations, depending on how well we fare *compared to others*. If my neighbor is having sex 5 times a week and I'm only having sex once, then shoot, that person is a sex god, and I'm an undesirable dweeb! If my coworker is driving a $90,000 sports car while I'm still driving my mother's old 1992 Corolla, then I must be a miserable failure with little worth!

FOMO, Fear of Missing Out, is a modern term that frames reference points. It's a mental exercise comparing our reality to what could have been or what could be. Whatever metric of comparison one can use, we use it. We compare what we're doing or have to what others are doing or have. This is irrespective of whether we have any context of others' circumstances.

Throughout history, we've run these comparisons and beaten ourselves up. Before the constant bombardment of social media in our lives, there were mainly magazines at grocery stores or commercials beckoning us to a more beautiful and successful life. Or maybe we saw a nice horse out on our walk, realized we don't have one, and our success meter frowned.

Nowadays, unfortunately, we can sit at home, scroll on our phones, and see beautiful people doing beautiful things all the beautiful time! While much of it is an edited façade and thus a radically unfair comparison, we compare ourselves anyway. Regardless of how aware we are and no matter what chants and affirmations we tell ourselves, by the time we see something to compare ourselves to, actual mental damage has already been done.

One piece of evidence for this is a recent study by Boston University. It found that the more one scrolls on social media through the typical myriad of doctored and perfected images, the more likely they'll want to undergo cosmetic surgery.[ix]

In short, *media technology has not only amplified the intensity and unfairness of each comparison but also exponentially increased the number of reference points we encounter daily.* Without a doubt, this robs us of joy, fosters insecurity, deepens division, and ultimately harms society's prospects for relationships.

Finally, AI is only beginning to disrupt human life. It has already triggered a cascade of job losses,[x] instilled a worldwide sense of suspicion and distrust of what's real online, and disrupted the way we relate and communicate with one another.

Concerning the latter, AI language learning models (LLMs) such as ChatGPT, Gemini, Claude, and Grok are freely available to create responses to emails and text messages without personal effort. This omits the development of critical thinking ability and emotional intelligence that real life and relationships with other human beings require.

Studies have shown that unguarded use of these tools adversely affects learning outcomes[xi] and cognitive development[xii] because users tend to prioritize convenience. Sitting with a problem, thinking about what to say or do, and saying or doing the wrong thing and learning from it aren't convenient. Waving a magical prompt and watching the problem go away *is*. While AI can be a powerful tool for productivity, it can also be detrimental to mental fitness, which is foundational to human connection.

Then, of course, there is the dawn of AI companions. They're already available, and we're approximately 85% of the way toward having video-live AI entities that can engage in natural, long-term, context-aware voice conversations, simulate empathy and connection, and satisfy sexually explicit requests onscreen likely without limit or objection. They'll be highly accessible and low-cost.

This will create a hypnotizing convenience for humans, and I suspect it'll be an even more devastating drug than pornography by orders of magnitude. While it'll undoubtedly pierce loneliness for some and befriend the unbefriended, it'll also drive many others to isolate from human relationships. It'll be even wilder as these virtual AI companions interface with real-world humanoid robots.

I can confidently say that no one, myself included, is ready for the disruption that AI will bring to this world in the next decade, let alone the next two. It'll gift a bounty of miracles, but as countries around the world fail to place guardrails on the race toward artificial general intelligence (AGI) for the means of world dominance, it'll leave no time for humans to adapt.

Soon, it'll be as if we're sticking our fingers into a river to test the water, not knowing that it's well enough to pull us in and fully consume us.

And on that existential note, we'll look at our societal shift away from centuries of tradition and the aftermath of the sexual revolution.

Cultural Shifts: Detaching from Judeo-Christian Ethics

We can summarize the sexual revolution as the 1960s-1970s social movement that liberated sexual experience from the exclusive clutches of reproduction and marriage. Marriage, traditionally a long-term, monogamous relationship between men and women, has several origin stories.

Throughout history, it has been a cornerstone for thriving families and societies. The West's origin story of monogamous relationships traces back to Christianity. According to Christian lore, the dawn of humanity came at the hands of an intelligent Creator. In the Bible's ancient Hebrew text, this Creator/God is frequently assigned a masculine identity. Hence, for simplicity and consistency, I'll also refer to the Christian God as "He."

God created the first two humans, Adam and Eve. Male and female. He made them in His own perfect image, and they were charged as romantic life partners and caretakers of the Garden of Eden. They were only given one rule: "Don't eat the fruit from this very specific tree."

I guess it was an impossible rule because they disobeyed and gobbled that fruit down almost immediately as God turned around. As they fell from perfection and creation's ideal, they were banished from the garden, and life began to decay and become increasingly imperfect. Time passed, they had children, and among them occurred murder, aging, war, human sacrifices, lying, cheating, and more.

Then, some 3,500 years ago, the stone tablets with the Ten Commandments were given to the ancient nation of Israel. These tablets served as a written assignment to exemplify what it would look like if this "one true God" were the king of a nation and of humanity.

As is part of any king's rule, his word is law, and what he says goes. He builds and destroys social structures according to his sense of fairness and justice. How he rules his kingdom tells you a lot about who he is. The establishment of the Ten Commandments, also known as *the law*, is no different.

A core teaching in Christianity holds that the law is a transcript of God's character. This aligns well with the biblical odyssey, as it focuses on God's mission to redeem all of humanity to its original, perfect identity, made in God's image and character. Israel simply served as the world's invitation to that redemption by exemplifying what it meant to accept it.

When the Judeo-Christian God gave them His commandments, He essentially offered them a prototype version of humanity's redemption. Whoever partook in His commandments of character partook in the redemption of His image.

Since I'm not trying to take you to church, I'll stick to how this pertains to culture. This set of laws outlining the prototype version of God's rule is what we'd call the dawn of Judeo-Christian ethics. These ethical guidelines established a standard for how people should interact with one another and conduct their lives.

While most of these laws were based on preexisting moral principles, such as Babylon's Code of Hammurabi, they were adapted and innovative enough to guide the ancient nation of Israel into its safest, justest, freest, and most prosperous era. Breaking these laws resulted in consequences including fines, public shaming, execution by stoning, and communal excommunication.

One might wonder how implementing a restrictive list of rules would lead to greater prosperity and freedom. While all laws offered some measure of moral progress, the one obviously relevant to romantic relationships and the sexual revolution is the seventh law, which opposes extramarital affairs. That law reveres the creation story of marriage, which pairs one man with one woman as the ideal, and prohibits hedonistic dominance.

Hedonism is the philosophy that values pleasure above all else. In pure hedonism, with no guardrails restricting pleasure, there'd be free-for-all horn dogs everywhere. And while unrestrained desire may sound appealing to some, unchecked pleasure has side effects, most of which harm society.

For starters, these laws came at a time in history when women had little power, few resources, and little to no rights. Men reserved most of these perks for themselves. As you'd expect, these circumstances made women highly dependent on men. But any law binding a woman to a man to form a single unit would classify the woman as an extension of the man, granting her co-ownership of his resources, access to his power, and the benefits of his rights.

Without marriage's law-based accountability, even if a man had the innate sense to honor the woman he impregnated and their child, what happens when there are no gates on his sex drive, and he impregnates another woman? Who then shall he honor? Which woman shall he give more attention and love to? How will the women compete for his attention? What happens when a third woman enters the picture?

When we're left to our own devices and driven by desires for pleasure, we fall into untamed dominance hierarchies governed by the *Principle of Unequal Distribution*. These concepts explain why CEOs command significantly higher multiples than the lowest-paid workers and why only a select few musicians produce the majority of mainstream music. Those at the top of the hierarchy—the winners—accumulate an unequal distribution of resources and privilege.

In the untamed ancient hierarchy of mating and reproduction, the strongest and most intelligent males would accumulate the most resources. They would push and shove their way to the best land, shelter, and resources, because they could undo most anyone who got in their way. Females would then flock to the males with the most resources, safety, and strength. Not just one or two females. Maybe not just three.

Yet the God of Israel wanted to support a better alternative for humanity. It included a system where the nation's strength and security didn't rest on military might but on its God. It introduced a deal in which people received abundant resources, land, and security in exchange for modeling the prototype version of human redemption: embodying God's character and law.

This deal or "covenant" radically transformed the nation's way of life. An abundance of resources means there's no need to compete with others aggressively. With plentiful land and safety, seeking the strongest mate is no longer a life-or-death issue.

With a divine-power-supported standard of one woman per one man, meaningful companionship and rewarding intimacy became more accessible. Though not completely eliminated, the sexual dominance hierarchy was tamed—and with that, they found a certain freedom.

Oliver Glanz, professor of Old Testament theology at Andrews University in Michigan, explains that the God presented in the Old Testament is a God of freedom. According to his study, the Hebrew God was the first god not to be narcissistic. Most ancient human origin stories, such as the Babylonian *Enuma Elish* and Sumerian *Atra-Hasis Epic*, tell tales of gods creating humans as servants and grunt workers. Whereas the Hebrew God is mainly present for the enjoyment, care, and benefit of His creation.

Humanity's biblical creation account presents several arguments in support of this. First, God creates man in His own image in Genesis 1:26. To create something in one's own image is to be happy sacrificing centralization on oneself. Second, He gives Adam and Eve *authority* over all living things in the Garden of Eden. Both demonstrate how the Hebrew God enjoys giving others control and a sense of freedom.

Third, it's curious that the text admits Adam is lonely even in the presence of a perfect God. In response, the Hebrew God said, "It is not good for man to be alone..." Hence, He created Eve, a being other than God with whom Adam could share experiences. Again, He shares the spotlight.

Genesis 1-3 highlights an idealistic example for those created in the image of God. *That ideal demands the sharing of control, power, and the spotlight.* This is extraordinarily significant in a time when the patriarchal model of society dominated. Essentially, all power and control resided in men, fathers specifically.

So, even if they didn't use it, the nation of Israel possessed the necessary philosophical tools to transcend from the human-snaring sexual dominance hierarchy, patriarchy, and hedonism. Those tools rested in their scriptures—the written law of God's image and the transcription of His character. There, a new force would guide their mating decisions: the freedom to choose *whom* they would love.

Now, this standard of locking two people together in an inescapable, permanent, everlasting marriage for a lifetime, forever and ever, might seem miserable to some; much less sing the name of freedom. However, the whims of pleasure and desire are no gracious masters. Nor do they proclaim the name of freedom.

Pleasure and desire operate on the dopamine reward system. As we've covered, we get hits of dopamine when we win, complete a goal, use certain drugs, orgasm, or eat sugar. While brilliant for motivating one to fulfill their desires, dopamine is also the *bedrock of addiction*.

The person going from relationship to relationship seeking honeymoon-phase highs, the swinging gold digger, the undisciplined wandering eye, and the porn addict are *all* ruled by the whims of pleasure and desire. In all these cases, an unquenchable thirst disrupts a soul at peace because pleasure is *literally* based on a system designed to work *against* us. Our bodies adapt to pleasure highs. What satisfied us last time often feels like a haunting void. So, we're either pushed to up the ante or sit in misery, denying our urges. This dynamic makes addiction recovery particularly grueling and turns the pursuit of euphoria into a losing game.

It is here that we come to an immutable truth of the human condition: *running from one master only lands one in the hands of another, and we either choose a master, or a master inevitably finds us.* Either way, a master always rules. Some will make us an apprentice, others will make us a slave.

Israel's new master and mission of character empowered them to seek love *beyond* mere pleasure and survival. I mean, you can practically imagine if resources, riches, power, fertility, safety, and pleasure didn't control your every move. What would be the next thing you'd look for? It probably centers around the idea of character.

Obviously, this new direction didn't suddenly mean character was the *only* thing that mattered in mate selection. Naturally, yes, we'd want a face we're happy to lie next to and a body motivating us to keep on bumpin'. But since mating took on a more lifelong nature, we'd better be *bloody sure* our partners can contribute to our life goals and don't drive us up the wall. So, regardless of what other societal influences remained, Israel's new focus on character governed its identity, relationships, and way of life.

Perhaps the best part of this focus was that it leveraged the dopamine system productively. Establishing an identity based on the image of their God technically set a goal. Goals involve progressive steps, habits, and actions that release dopamine.

Truthfully, identity is built through habits and actions; it's something mandating proof. If we don't go on runs, we're not runners. Not writing is to sacrifice the identity of a writer. Just as identity can die with habits that die, so too could the image-of-God identity. In fact, when the Israelite God tells His people to "keep" His commandments, He uses the word *shamar*. This is the same word God uses to charge Adam with the responsibility of caring for the Garden of Eden. He charges Adam to protect and guard it, as if it were something precious and alive that could wither and die.

The commandments weren't a mangy list of no-fun rules meant for grounds of judgment. They were a philosophy and an identity of living character, where not "keeping" a commandment was to let the character of their God pass away. Forgetting to nurture this living, redemptive image meant letting that identity die and resume the burdens of basic needs.

What worthier, more fulfilling, and more rewarding goal is there than to raise a kind and goodhearted child? To see our plants bear fruit or to witness our work and art enhance other people's lives? And to keep, guard, and enliven a philosophy that causes life itself to flourish?

But to put it bluntly, humanity has rarely done a satisfactory job of honoring the image of God. There's a reason many today have a sour taste of Christianity in their mouth. There's a reason Gandhi said, "If it weren't for Christians, I'd be a Christian."

Part of it is that people treat it as an inanimate object to be emulated rather than the living, moving, conscious structure it is. Now, to avoid this becoming a theology book, I'm going to bypass all the semantics of the image of God. I do, however, want to steer us toward recognizing the structure Christianity has provided Western society.

Despite humanity's flawed imitation of God's identity throughout history, it has still provided a critical structure. Plenty of ideological structures have come and gone throughout history, and some have proved better than others. Looking back, we can say Joseph Stalin's Soviet communism and Adolf Hitler's fascism weren't winning structures.

An overbearing structure eventually suffocates those living within it, leading them to resent the structure and consider abandoning it altogether. However, with too little structure, you get the Wild West. No one knows what's going on; there's no consistency to work with, and there's little sense of right or wrong since everything is relative. It's fun for a day or two until it becomes a fully realized chaotic nightmare.

Here's the central point of this entire section: *since structure keeps chaos at bay, societies that deconstruct their foundational structures unleash chaos.* It doesn't matter *what* the structure is. Abruptly resetting how an entire society functions will unleash chaos and confusion. Removing pillars of a society's culture is like pulling blocks out of a Jenga set, elevating instability. In the Western world, the structure we're steadily uncoupling from is Judeo-Christian ethics and standards, and we're handing the reins of sovereignty to self-interest, pleasure, greed, and power.

But what chaos am I referring to? Well, let's take some time to zoom in on how the cultural abandonment of Judeo-Christian marital ethics has affected American society. In the name of freedom from cultural judgment and the pursuit of pleasure, we've released sexual experiences from the clutches of marriage and granted them to the masses with no religious expectations or strings attached.

In 1960, only 5% of all U.S. births belonged to women out of wedlock. Since 2008, well after the 1960s-1970s sexual revolution, it has remained relatively stable at approximately 40%.[xiii] In tandem, the rate of U.S. single-parent households has been rising steadily for decades, reaching 23% in 2018.[xiv]

Children of single-parent households have poorer outcomes on almost every metric imaginable: mental health, physical health, academia, poverty rates, suicide rates, graduation rates, employment rates, and the rates of delinquent behavior like drugs and alcohol abuse, and crime.[xv] The cultural shift is *not* benefiting children.

In the 1980s, only 6% of 40-year-olds in the U.S. were never married. In 2021, that number was 25%, representing a near 5% increase every 10 years.[xvi] If that trajectory holds, in 25 years, half of the U.S. population will have never been married by age 40.

Tragically, this means Americans are having less sex. Well, possibly. I mean, they're indeed having less sex, but the verdict on whether it's related to marriage is still not clear. There are studies, surveys, and polls showing more sex for married people, and some declaring that singles have more sex. Based on the six sources I examined, the ratio is approximately 4:2, with married individuals leading. It seems more of a matter of opinion at this point.

On all accounts, though, married people *should* have more sex. They don't have to spend time finding a sexual partner, so they should have better sexual access. Ideally, established emotional intimacy should strengthen their attraction and sense of security. They also know each other's cues and non-verbal communication. There's not as much fear or anxiety around rejection, and there's more freedom to be curious, take risks, and experiment sexually. It's totally fair game to try out those firefighter-holding-puppies and princess Leia fantasies.

Assuming married couples stay married, they probably won't experience the same droughts that occur when cohabitating couples split and are between relationships. Hence, the possibility of more sex. Which is a spectacular highlight in life when done well!

One study reported that having sex once a week improved happiness more than earning an extra $50,000/year.[xvii] That's basically like earning $1,000 each time you have sex once a week! What a gig, you little hustler, you! Lower sexual activity is also associated with increased mortality, which is the likelihood of death.[xviii] So, as a direct rebuttal to the gym teacher in *Mean Girls* (2004), and not to be dramatic, but if you don't have sex, *you will die*. Being married may help.

Let's look at some other benefits. According to OHSU, sex benefits women by lowering blood pressure, strengthening the immune system, elevating self-esteem, decreasing anxiety and depression, increasing libido, providing natural and immediate pain relief, improving sleep and heart health, closer intimacy with a sexual partner, and "overall *stress reduction*, both physiological and emotional."[xix]

It's also worth noting that *cortisol*, the hallmark hormone of stress and anxiety, breaks down elastin and collagen. Both are essential for maintaining youthful-looking skin, among other aesthetic and functional benefits.[xx] Sex can also give women a fuller head of hair due to increased production of estrogen.[xxi] Men share in many of these aesthetic and health benefits.

As it stands, men and women would be healthier and better off if they had more sex. Perhaps this is partly why married couples also live, on average, 2 years longer than unmarried people.[xxii]

On a different note, the cultural shift away from Judeo-Christian ethics has also contributed to the loneliness epidemic. According to the U.S. Surgeon General, as many as half of American adults report "experiencing measurable levels of loneliness," increasing their risk of heart disease, stroke, dementia, and premature death.[xxiii]

Probably the most significant predictor of health outcomes in life is the number of close social connections we have. People lacking close connections have a *greater* risk of premature death *compared to someone who smokes 20 cigarettes a day.*[xxiv]

As traumatizing and damning as unhealthy churches have been for people, healthy churches have long been an opportunity for belonging and community. But I'd say we're more likely to get invited to a rave at the supermarket than to a healthy church or other proper place of consistent belonging these days. And as suffocating and oppressive as unhealthy marriages have been for some, healthy marriages have long provided opportunities for long-term security, intimacy, companionship, and friendship.

Though this *is* an oversimplification, and it's *not* the only factor affecting Western civilization, the abandonment of Christian culture in America doesn't appear to benefit children, women, or men. Evidence actually suggests it's contributing to the *destruction* of society and the landscape of romantic relationships.

Few things are entirely good or bad, though. There are certainly *positive* trade-offs from this culture shift. Now, LGBTQ+ people have the freedom to form meaningful, intimate, long-term relationships. We also have less stigma around divorce, which loosens the grip of those who'd trap and abuse others in marriages and starve them of love.

My goal here is *not* to imply that everyone needs to be Christian and honor its values, or even that the Christian foundation is the best there is. Nor am I implying we should go back to the "glory days." I'm all for transitioning to a better society and world, whatever the path. But where we're going isn't better than where we've been. The data makes that *quite* clear.

I'm urging us to examine the consequences of removing the pillars on which Western society, particularly American society, was built. By sacrificing the Judeo-Christian ethical foundation, we've given up a key piece of the puzzle for stable, worry-minimized lives and lifelong love. Fluctuating expectations and dissensus have replaced it, making the search for true partnership feel especially disorienting.

Throughout history, societal shifts in cultural values have manifested through protests, revolutions, and civil wars, resulting in the deaths of millions of people and the fall of empires. So, I'd say chaos flooding into the world of relationships is only to be expected. It's just important to know that's where we are.

Next, we'll explore how feminism has reshaped the romantic landscape—sometimes championing human progress and equality, sometimes complicating the creation of true love.

Inevitable Cultural Shifts: Ripples of Feminism

Feminism is the movement aimed at empowering women to attain political, economic, social, and personal equality with men. There have been several waves of feminism since about the 1850s, each wave focusing on different issues. In addition to life-changing rights, equality has shifted women's roles in families, households, and relationships.

Women are no longer limited to traditional motherhood or housework; they can pursue higher education, build careers, and experience the autonomy, power, and independence that long eluded them. In relationships, this egalitarianism fosters a stronger sense of shared power, enabling more direct communication and greater mutual respect. It also promotes richer intimacy and satisfaction, as well as the sharing of household duties, thereby supporting relationship stability.[xxv] And if relationships, marriages with children in particular, don't work out, there's less stigma around divorce and more welfare support.

Yet, regardless of all feminism's good reinvention of society, it isn't unique in the way that it's excluded from the *Trade-off Principle: when you gain one thing, you inevitably lose another; or when one thing increases, another decreases.* For example, while social welfare *successfully* aids vulnerable and abused domestic parties in need, that safety net *also* serves as an *incentive* for other parties to abandon relationships and families. Since they'll be fine on their own, there's no urgency to address their problems or refine ways to support their family systems. That places the domestic fallout on broader society, which has to step in to support.

Societies have a long history of reinventing themselves, guided by the belief that their ideas of progress and wisdom are superior to those of previous eras. But change, more often than not, brings unwanted and unforeseen consequences. It can lead to cycles like "Weak people create bad times, bad times create strong people, strong people create good times, and good times create weak people."

Sometimes, we really do possess the best pieces of science, wisdom, or way of being for a given issue or system, and changing course wouldn't represent progress. All fallen empires of the past once enjoyed a golden age that eventually crumbled when changing ideals and new leaders emerged.

If you believe anything in the world has gone awry in the past few decades or even the last couple of years, then you *certainly* don't believe that all reinvention is good reinvention. Things *can* and *do* get worse, even when we cumulatively aspire to become better. Not all progress is good progress.

Like I've mentioned and named, I fully believe there are beautiful things resting under feminism's wing. I *also* believe certain reinventions and branches of feminism have ultimately been unhelpful and not embodied progress. The most problematic or regressive shifts for society and relationships that I see are: (1) pursuing equality to the extent of attempting to dissolve the differences between men and women, (2) prioritizing freedom, independence, and individualism at almost any cost, and (3) the vilification of male expression of masculinity.

Pursuing equality is all well and good, but it becomes regressive when we assert that two different things are in fact the same thing. Two things can be of equal value even if they aren't the same thing.

Theists would argue that God designed men and women differently to complement one another. To say they are the same is to oppose their Creator. Those with an evolutionary mindset would claim that men and women evolved differently over thousands or millions of years. To deny those differences is to insult nature's elegant solutions for human flourishing.

There are numerous books that summarize the differences between men and women in psychological and physical functioning. *Men Are from Mars, Women Are from Venus, Why Men Don't Listen, and Women Can't Read Maps,* and *The Essential Difference: Male and Female Brains* are modern, insightful resources that highlight noticeable averages in sex-based uniqueness. They address qualities such as memory, communication, social skills, spatial navigation, fine motor skills, and emotional intelligence.

While we don't have to frame these differences as excuses or use them to discriminate, they're important elements of context. Claiming that men and women are the same ignores timeless wisdom and credible data. It also sets society up for disappointment, misunderstanding, conflict, and division, and is ultimately regressive.

One of several such sex differences Western society has attempted to ignore is covered by Louise Perry in her book, *The Case Against the Sexual Revolution.* Perry tactfully argues that erasing sex differences does a disservice not only to society but *especially* to women.

Taking an evolutionary psychology approach, she acknowledges that men's sexual behavior has always hinged on the aspiration to spread their genetic material as far and wide as possible to ensure the survival of their genes. This is thought to lead to qualities such as casual promiscuity, "catching feelings" less easily, and a higher sex drive. They can, in theory, pass on their genes as many times as they want.

Women, however, evolved to be much more cautious in their sexual behavior. Passing on their genetic material is limited by their ovulation cycle, a 9-month pregnancy, successfully giving birth, and personally sustaining the baby's survival in the months after. As childbearers, they're *forced* to heavily invest and sacrifice for their offspring. Therefore, the female nature of heightened choosiness makes sense. Their prioritization of mutual emotional availability and commitment functions as an evolutionary insurance policy for long-term stability and safety.

In the sense of evolutionary psychology, the sexual revolution actually caters *more* toward men as it prioritizes their instincts more than women's. Even though women may still carry the underlying instinct to seek emotional commitment and be sexually cautious, modern hookup culture teaches them to ignore their instincts and intuition, adopt men's wiring to become the same—"equal"—and make sex casually accessible. Pursuing equality to the extent of undoing evolutionary or intelligently designed differences *isn't* progress.

The second regressive misstep by mainstream feminism is the narrative that women should prioritize freedom, independence, and individualism above all. Multiple points highlight this as a poor value.

First, prioritizing freedom and individualism is fundamentally *incompatible* with women and humanity as a whole. The reality is that to prioritize freedom and independence above all else, one *must* oppose motherhood because it demands external support and is a woman's most limiting form. What she consumes, where she goes, what she can do, and the risks she takes are all limited by pregnancy and the dependency her baby has on her even after birth. Having an obligation to the well-being of children throughout their lifetimes is just part of being a parent. There's no way around this reality, and as a result, the feminist narrative of "freedom and individualism" completely sidesteps the issue.

Perry herself describes this sidestep as an "anti-natalist streak" that excludes mothers from feminist conversation. She notes that motherhood is considered in *fewer than 3%* of journal articles, text-books, and papers on modern gender theory[xxvi] because the ratio-nality of individualism crumbles when it encounters motherhood.

The truth is, this narrative carries an underlying value that's fairly anti-mother, which is, in a way, anti-baby. To lobby against babies is to be anti-human, for without babies, humanity ceases to exist. *Any philosophy that values and supports the extinction of humanity is not one to hold in high regard.*

It's not that freedom and independence are bad things for women —far from it. Freedom and independence are *vital.* But the second reason their prioritization is a poor value is that they're ultimately *currency* to a fulfilling life, not the *definition* of one. They're useful *tools* that let us choose what to build our lives around. But a hammer is not a project, and currency is meaningless if it's never exchanged for what one needs or desires. Tools and currencies are ultimately limited in that they cannot fulfill in and of themselves.

One such example of this truth is the limited impact the *tool* of wealth has on happiness. When money generously covers basic needs, approximately \$165,000 of yearly household income in 2026 dollars, money has a negligible effect on happiness.[xxvii]

It certainly makes sense because, at some point, excess monetary freedom becomes unusable. It's literally impossible to *use* \$1 trillion. We could certainly buy assets until that money was gone, but we couldn't live in all the houses we bought, drive all the cars we purchased, or live all the possible experiences we could buy. We frankly couldn't live long enough to *use* it.

Similarly, while it would be amazing to take six months of vacation a year and live in luxury hotels around the world, we'd find similar, if not greater, levels of happiness and fulfillment by using our freedom to prioritize growing a garden, cuddling with our pets, and building a family. Beyond meeting basic needs, *quality relationships*[xxviii] *and a sense of purpose*[xxix] *are the two most significant contributors to happiness and fulfillment.*

The mainstream feminist narrative takes the currencies and tools of freedom and independence and exalts them as *endmost objectives,* thereby undermining their purpose and distracting from meaningful things. It's *good* to be free to choose to be a single working woman or a married mother, and attain fulfillment however one wants. It's *not* good to idolize freedom and demonize its exchange for commitment, obligation, and accountability.

Paradoxically, despite all the freedoms, independence, rights, and privileges women have gained over recent decades, women's happiness has actually been trending *down*.[xxx] In fact, it is *married mothers,* perhaps, the *least* independent, who report the highest levels of happiness among women.[xxxi]

On the one hand, it's genuinely good that everyone, *including women*, gains meaningful "independence currency" before entering relationships and building families. It limits their susceptibility to exploitation, manipulation, and abuse. The most successful marriages and long-term mating relationships are established between the ages of 28 and 32,[xxxii] and those who have received at least a bachelor's degree.[xxxiii] By that age and lived experience, people are more likely to be mature and settle into effective coping mechanisms, conflict management skills, and reasonable self-sufficiency. These things help people build and maintain healthy relationships.

On the other hand, Sylvia Ann Hewlett cautions that the ideal years for career building and, therefore, independence, overlap seamlessly with the prime years of childbearing and family building.[xxxiv] Meaning, as independence and dual-income households become the norm, progression through family-based life stages stalls and can easily be misconstrued as a lower priority. Labels get avoided, engagements are delayed and prolonged, and marriages get put off or foregone completely.

No perfect solution exists for this trade-off. The time dedicated to developing one's career and independence cannot be dedicated to building a family, and vice versa. Combined with factors such as the economic and housing climates, the rates of relationships, marriages, fertility, and births in Western countries have reached all-time lows.

At the very least, the new dual-income household standard has been challenging for parents, particularly mothers, who *want* to be present with their children. For some reason, they'd rather do that than spend 40 hours every week accumulating tax dollars for a government that burns much of their hard-earned money on ridiculous budgets, corruption, and war. Some also don't appear to want to generate revenue for a company that'd replace them in 4 days. They'd rather cherish each moment, raising their children to build a better world and thriving in a proven, multi-millennia-old model of human purpose and fulfillment.

Unfortunately, once dual-income households become the societal norm, entities of power that benefit from mass human labor have no reason to reduce a workforce that fuels their addiction to greed and power. Dual-income households used to be a way to get *ahead*. Now, on average, it's typically the only way to keep heads above water. There's no going back, and even if we wanted to, most families could hardly afford a single-income household nowadays.

Finally, the last clear regressive shift I'll name is the vilification of male expression of masculinity. This vendetta is brought on by *extreme* feminism, which has bled into Western culture over time and developed something of a misandrous theme—the hate of men. I'll merely introduce this shift since I come back to it in a few pages.

The short version is that with the help of negativity-biased media algorithms, misogyny and misandry have become more common. Misogyny has clearly been inflamed in recent years, as trends show a significant increase.[xxxv] Misandry itself remains virtually unstudied, though one need only browse social platforms to find misandrous comments and content with similar rhetoric.[xxxvi]

In fact, considering the unpleasant developments we've covered in this chapter, it'd be extremely *counterintuitive* and *odd* if misandry were *not* on the rise. As world conditions worsen, people simply tend to be nastier with one another.

Nevertheless, from what I read, hear, and see in online media, a feedback loop of hateful culture between men and women has embedded itself within the Western relationship landscape. The regressive point here is that *any* hate and broad vilification of groups of people is unhelpful in establishing a better, more positive land-scape for relationships.

To conclude, feminism's impact on the landscape of relationships is extraordinary. With many desirable benefits came undesirable and unavoidable trade-offs in relationships. Together, those trade-offs (1) create a basis for societal confusion and conflict, (2) discourage family formation, which has historically been a cornerstone for human meaning and fulfillment, and (3) usher in a divisive mutual hostility between men and women.

Still, there are other factors disrupting the relational dynamics humanity is familiar with. Though we mourn the turbulence spousal relationships have endured, we've almost entirely forgotten about the village.

Inevitable Cultural Shifts: The Dissolution of Village Mentality

Something we seldom think about is the evolution of our definition of family. The *nuclear family* is the idea that couples and their dependent children are the basic units of a society; mom, dad, and kids, all in a house. It definitely wasn't always that way, though. For most of human history, grandparents, aunts, uncles, cousins, and even friends formed intimate communities and functioned as the basic units of society.

Villages raised children, and they once fulfilled many of the roles people now expect from their relationships. Maybe cousin Buckner had the best sense of humor, so we'd go to him if we wanted to laugh or feel happy. Perhaps if we needed intellectual stimulation, we'd talk to Dad. When we wanted empathy and understanding, we'd confide in our grandmother, Betty. For sex, we'd go to our spouse. Spouses weren't the embodiment of all these roles, though.

As the Industrial Age began, resources became increasingly plentiful, and women started to approach equality with men. Couples could move away from their village communities. Moving away from our funny cousin Buckner, we found a void of humor. Without our usual source of empathy, we found a void of compassion. With the dissolution of the village, we found a village-shaped void and desired to fill it. We still do.

Presently, depending on the current state of our villages and the degree to which we allow their uprooting, we may very well seek a village *in* a spouse. It's become commonplace to expect potential mates to be the complete village: attractive, good at sex, empathetic, intellectually stimulating, nurturing, hardworking, supportive, our best friends, excellent conversationalists, well-resourced, etc.

Human potential is probably about the same as it's always been, but now we have higher expectations for mates than ever before. That can be challenging to meet. If one doesn't have a village, they may hope their partner will be it in its entirety. Or they'll delegate any roles their village doesn't handle to their partner.

The main takeaway from this culture shift is that we face different circumstances than our predecessors. We look for "whole packages," while our ancestors didn't. If our ancestors had the exact expectations we do, they may well have had similar difficulty finding mates.

Therefore, when we compare ourselves with previous generations and eras, it's helpful to realize that circumstances were different and that people in those eras sought different things. Demands and needs change.

At last, our exploration brings us to one final stop. Villages aren't the only things falling apart. It seems men are too.

Inevitable Cultural Shifts: The Crisis of Men

The point of this section isn't to make fruitless comparisons between men and women. Instead, it's to say men are half of the heterosexual pair, and being in crisis severely affects their mating potential. This hurts everyone, including women.

Women face their own share of troubles that men will never know. Not only is every danger more intense for women, but men will never face pregnancy and birth, fluctuating emotions and energy levels due to hormone cycles, or be primarily seen as a sexual object. They deal with a minefield of emotionally unavailable and immature men, frequent sex-based power imbalance and prejudice, workplace harassment, and heavy expectations of falling into feminine roles, identities, appearances, and stereotypes. And while the list of women's challenges doesn't end there, a little-known crisis is unfolding among men that's devastating the relationship world.

Perhaps the most daunting part of this crisis is the world's abysmal financial state. The difference between men's and women's handling of the modern economic disaster is perhaps a matter of *hope*. Women have always carried the hope of finding security in a resource-rich provider when they couldn't provide for themselves, and they still do. Men have never been instilled with that hope. Women tend to avoid pairing with poorly-resourced men. That's hypergamy at work.

Hope, of course, has been a force that determines life and death throughout history. The book *Man's Search for Meaning* by Viktor Frankl is a good example of this. Frankl writes about the fate of those who gave up hope in concentration camps during the Holocaust. With broken spirits, nothing pushing them to survive, they ultimately perished. Both men and women have the same capacity to overcome financial disaster, but men haven't been socialized with the same hope.

So, what does this disaster look like? I'm sure you've seen it before. It's pretty hard to miss! It's the outrageously unsustainable wages versus the cost-of-living ratio. Over the past few decades, wages have fallen behind inflation.

Inflation happens every year. From 1960 to 2022, inflation has "officially" averaged around 3.8% per year.[xxxvii] Meaning, if the dollar loses 3.8% of its value, you'll want a 3.8% raise to afford the life you've *been* living. If you don't get that raise, you're technically getting a pay *cut*.

Inflation reduces the purchasing power of money. While wages have somewhat kept up with headline inflation, asset prices have skyrocketed over the last 50 years. The median price of a house in 2022 was $440,300. Adjusting for inflation to 2022 dollars, the median home price in 1972 was $189,500. We're paying more than *twice* as much as someone buying a home in 1972.

From 1972 to 2025, college tuition rose by more than 2,000%.[xxxviii] College graduates of 2023 also left with 500% more debt than students in 1970.[xxxix] Rent, groceries, and mortgage rates present their own inflation challenges.

While the disaster continues to escalate, men's ability to cope with it has waned. The number of traditional repetitive-action jobs in factories and manufacturing has dwindled significantly due to automation and government policy. Even when those traditional male jobs remain, their value and wages don't increase because they're susceptible to automation.

Projections indicate that men will continue to experience economic decline because they're falling behind in education, which limits their access to higher-paying careers. Among college degrees earned in 1972, men outnumbered women 56.5% to 43.5%. In 2019, women outnumbered men 57.5% to 42.5%, and that gap is only widening.[xl] For various reasons, men are choosing not to enroll in higher education.

Richard Reeves estimates that by 2030, for every *one* STEM job we create—Science, Technology, Engineering, and Math—we'll create *three* HEAL jobs—Health, Education, Administration, and Literacy. Statistically, men prefer STEM, and women prefer HEAL.

The ways most men used to meet the financial demands of life either no longer exist or are significantly less efficient, and most new job-creation opportunities won't favor men's preferences. Furthermore, the educational system that increases earning potential isn't producing as many male students, resulting in the female-led gender education gap.

Amid falling behind, men have few helpful role models for what it means to be a successful man in the modern world. Previously, one could follow in their father's footsteps in manufacturing and provide for their family. That's no longer the case.

Women's entry into the workforce didn't make their previous homemaker role obsolete. A career path is perfectly acceptable, but so is the traditional role of being a mother at home, which includes caregiving, child-rearing, and household management, among other responsibilities. So, the cultural examples of female success have actually *expanded* and diversified.

Men have experienced no cultural change in their definition of success as providers, and their pool of examples has shrunk since their fathers' footsteps are no longer readily replicable. Social media features the majority of male role models as fitness influencers, world-famous actors, eccentric personalities, or entrepreneurs of the hottest new companies. Unfortunately, those examples aren't highly replicable either.

Of course, traditional professions such as doctors, lawyers, and engineers still hold prestige. But they're not advertised like the roles on social media, which don't require 8+ years of grueling study and student loan bondage. This famine of role models exacerbates the male crisis by making it harder for males to find meaning and purpose.

Finally, young men are the most affected demographic in the loneliness epidemic.[xli] Men are stereotypically associated with lone wolf mentality, but modern developments have transformed that stereotype into a real problem. While no one can summarize all the causes perfectly, I believe some significant roots of the issue are: (1) the cultural vendetta against "toxic masculinity" and (2) various technologies. Here, we resume the conversation about the vilification of male expression of masculinity.

Given the long history of the patriarchy's exclusive relationship with power, anything resembling masculinity became prey in the age of feminism. The #MeToo movement of 2017 was a potent snapshot of the righteous revolt against toxic masculinity—male abuse of power. Women all over the world shared their survival stories of sexual assault and called for men drunk on power to be held accountable and face justice. It served as a *much-needed* societal call for women to be heard and respected.

Since the movement normalized calling out men, other movements emerged from its shadow and took it to another level. Eventually, it became normal and *trendy* to criticize and shame masculine behavior publicly, primarily through social media. These shamed behaviors ranged from *legitimate* concerns about toxicity to discomfort with creepiness to annoying, unwanted attention to dramatic disgust at missing wishlist items.

The trend ingrained itself into Western culture to the point that it instilled men with mass fear and hesitation around initiation, which persists to this day. If men approach women, they could very well become the next subject of public shaming for trying to initiate a romantic connection. This shaming practice aligned with the Western cultural trend of teaching men to be as small as possible, so as not to disturb, cause trouble, or do anything that might make others uncomfortable.

When we analyze chivalrous behaviors, we find that they're all rooted in masculinity. Opening the door or pulling out and pushing in a chair for someone takes control away from them, as now they can't do those things for themselves. The one volunteering to walk closest to the street takes the most risk, as if the other person were more fragile. Offering a coat attempts to override independence by solving the other's problem. Paying for dinner provides for someone else as if they need someone else taking care of their needs. All these practices stem from a position of power, control, and assertiveness.

So, while movements like #MeToo are necessary for justice and accountability against masculine abuse, going too far into a vengeful war on masculinity with almost zero tolerance for its male expression can lead to unintended consequences. Namely, the elimination of chivalry and the promotion of a culture that encouraged and pressured men to make themselves as small as possible.

As the pressure chamber of society forced men to shrink, their approaches to women dwindled. They seldom put themselves out there, formed fewer romantic relationships, and lost a key resource for creating friendships and socializing.

Social flourishing is just one of those differences between men and women. Women can typically make friends wherever they go without much effort. Men don't share that experience and often lack the natural social skills that women possess. A whopping 15% of men report hav*ing no close friends.*[xlii]

Many men default to socializing and establishing new friendships by participating in plans their girlfriends/spouses make. However, if men aren't getting into relationships with women, they not only lack their companionship but also the accompanying socialization. And a lack of romantic relationships is precisely what we're seeing for young men. In a 2019 study, 63% of young men and 34% of young women aged 18 to 29 were single.[xliii]

For various reasons, young women are *increasingly* choosing not to pair with young men. One reason is that society has not yet caught up with feminism's accomplishments regarding more equal earnings. Yet the prevailing standard is that women seek men who earn more than they do. So, since women essentially earn the same amount as men, every woman *can't* find a man who earns more than she does. It's mathematically *impossible*.

This issue is likely to become more significant in the future. Since women earn the majority of higher-education degrees, they may well earn *more* than men. In some cities, young women aged 25-34 are *already* out-earning their male counterparts.[xliv]

Technology and feminist culture pair together in a peculiar way to form another reason. A couple of decades ago, women could only choose from the men in their daily lives. Now, with social media and dating apps in the mix, the "options" at their fingertips extend to the foreign, sculpted, wealthy prince with a silver tongue and a personal photographer.

Modern women raised in the golden age of feminism were told to reach for the stars and that they were beautiful no matter what they looked like. They received every incentive and scholarship to succeed, and they regularly heard chants of "Girl Power," "Boss Babe," and "Strong Independent Woman!" A powerful and consistent wave of societal support tells women they can have it all, and social technology gives them the means to pursue it. Of course, old toxic messages still float around today: "a woman only belongs in the kitchen" or "a woman's value is just her body."

During the same period, young men were raised in a culture with a vendetta against masculinity. Society essentially told young men to sit down, aim at eye level, take their ADHD medication, and not complain; they're in a patriarchal society, so everything goes their way, and they don't need a hand because they have an unfair advantage as men—even if they don't feel like it. And any frustration, fear of rejection, or hardship they experience, the mainstream message is to suck it up and face the truth: *It's your fault. You just weren't good enough. Be better.*

Obviously, both messages present a stark contrast and will lead to different expectations and beliefs among men and women. Those who are told they're small, unwanted, and useless will live in a sobering reality, where withdrawal and decay are reasonable temptations. Those told they deserve the stars no matter what will have no problem asking for the moon. There are only so many moons, though, which means many women will compete over a small number of men.

A well-covered and now archived study published by *OkCupid* stated that women rate 80% of men as below average in attractiveness.[xlv] People speculate why they removed the survey from public view, since it was merely data. I suspect it fueled the already-intense conflict between Western men and women. Obviously, it's not great for their business as a dating app. They're trying to bring people together, not burn the bridges between them.

If the data from *OkCupid* is accurate, and we assume all women want an average attractive man or better, that leaves all women with only 20% of males. Five women fighting over one man's attention. Tinder data paints a gloomier picture, showing that women swipe right on 5% of men, while men swipe right on 47% of women.[xlvi]

Another data point: a two-part study over about two decades examined the sexual activity of young men and women ages 18-24. Part one examined 2000-2002, and part two examined 2016-2018. Sexual inactivity increased among young men, from 18.9% to 30.9%—about a third of males—and increased for young women, from 15.1% to 19.1%—about a fifth of females.[xlvii]

What we're seeing in the Western world is that more women are competing for and expressing interest in fewer men. Cultural shifts, technological developments, and media agendas have all aligned to create an exceptionally slim mating pool for women. Meaning fewer and fewer men qualify for dating and mating opportunities in the eyes of women.

So, what's left for the modern man? A lonely existence. Few care to know about their problems, and even fewer are willing to show compassion. To cope with their isolating and disenfranchising reality, they find camaraderie among internet alpha-male, manosphere, anti-feminist, misogynist, or red-pill communities and influencers. They either start or further form harmful habits around technologies that simulate the joys of life, like pornography or video games. All of which further isolates them from women.

Those who are unable to cope adequately give in to the temptation to withdraw entirely from society and life. Concerning society, two in five working-age men with only a high school diploma are out of the workforce.[xlviii] As for life, three out of four suicides and overdoses are men.[xlix] Just in the last 10 years, the suicide rate for young men aged 15-24 has increased 26%, and 31% for men aged 25-34.[l]

To sum it all up, the crisis confronting men is composed of five key factors: (1) diminished hope to overcome the modern financial climate, (2) declining economic power due to traditional male jobs disappearing and falling behind in education, (3) a fading core sense of identity and purpose as providers, (4) a shrinking pool of quality role models, and (5) profound loneliness.

Again, the purpose of this section is to *see* young men, not to present justifications for pity parties or say their lives are harder than women's. Women have their own struggles; I'm simply not an authority on that. And, *suffering isn't a competition*. It's just pertinent to know that many young men aren't doing well, and it's enough to put the relationship world in crisis.

When a significant proportion of men are ineligible for relationships, that means an equal number of women are excluded from long-term and fulfilling relationships. That results in an increasing number of lonely people, which is detrimental to society's overall health and functioning.

The Perfect Storm

While the crisis of men is enough to put the world of relationships in shambles, there's more going on, as we've covered. We've had radical political installations, the abrupt destruction and transformation of foundational cultures, dietary Armageddon, technological hurdles, a refocus on hedonism, and pharmaceuticals shoving problems under the rug. Artificial intelligence has its own barrage of punches waiting to settle on relationships. Still, this is the hand we're dealt as we establish or nurture long-term relationships today. We have to create true love in the middle of this clusterduck.

My emphasis in closing this chapter is this: *since society is the mold that shapes all people, the blame for the landscape of relationships lies mostly in the bigger picture of society.*

When women and men get unpleasant propositions, rude gestures, failed expectations, or bad experiences from each other, it's easy to blame the opposite sex for all their relationship issues. Blaming the nearest visible "bad guy" is the natural choice.

Thus, many men and women have made each other scapegoats for their problems, and are now fighting a proxy war against one another. If you've ever heard phrases like "Men are stupid and trash," or "Where are all the good men?" or "You have to work twice as hard for a woman who is half the woman your grandmother was," these are symptoms of minds fighting that war. These are the words of people who've dug in their heels, abandoned negotiations for long-term relationships, and leaned into hostility.

But there's far more beneath the surface, as we've just uncovered. This war is a misallocation of time and resources. Our issues should be with the structures that shape the people we're disenchanted with, and our grace and compassion should be with those who are scapegoated as the origin of our relationship woes. Our beef should be with the cookie-cutter, not the cookies.

The state of society and the scapegoating of the opposite sex form the bulk of the odds stacked against the creation of true love in the modern world. These are odds that even non-single hearts and minds face, and being aware of them is vital to preserving the delicacy of true love. Because as miraculous as the creation of true love is, its preservation is equally marvelous. Society and its obstacles do not discriminate between newly formed and longstanding love. They sow seeds of warring conflict all the same, and even flourishing gardens have weeds trying to bring ruin.

Those of us aspiring to create true love must defy impossible odds and refuse to let the state of the world shape our romantic destiny; we must peer through eyes of grace to see the hearts of our beloved hidden within those whom society brands as our adversaries. These are tasks fitting for a hero.

So, what's going to happen next is we're going to carefully examine this war, our role in it, and ready ourselves to overcome it.

You're going to need to suit up.

PREPARING FOR
MATING NEGOTIATION

We just finished outlining how the world has changed and how it has created an obstacle-ridden landscape for relationships. These obstacles receive little to no blame for the chaos they instigate between men and women. Instead, each sex blames the other for their troubles. The default perspective is that the opposite sex just hasn't adjusted properly to the new world —they're not doing something they should, and their roles should change.

So, let's go back to the beginning, to where this disparity in role distribution first began, and progress from there. This conflict began when the patriarchal model of society showed that its mandatory subscription could be optional. Again, patriarchy is a model of society where men hold most of the power and privilege. Regardless of how one feels about it, the patriarchal model was an elegant solution to a persistent list of needs: (1) resource accumulation, (2) household maintenance, (3) child rearing, and (4) familial safety.

As a man in a power and role-balanced relationship, I'm going to explain this as objectively as I can. Going down that list, people need resources for survival. That could involve using land to produce them, hunting and foraging, or trading labor or other resources for them. Less labor-intensive white-collar desk jobs didn't exist until about the last century, so obtaining resources required grunt labor. Retaining those resources meant being present around the homestead as much as possible to protect the family from robbery or injury.

Grunt labor and the need for protection would typically elect men as better candidates for resource acquisition and protection. On average, they have larger bone structure and more muscle mass. This male allocation to grunt work remains true, given that 90% of blue-collar workers—those engaged in intensive physical labor—are male.[i]

If men couldn't trade for something, they were less susceptible to exploitation because they could more readily go out and get the resources themselves. That makes men the obvious choice to be the public voice and chief advocate for the family, holding most of the social power. It's Trade 101: supply and demand. If you've ever played *Settlers of Catan*, you understand that when people need your resource more than you need theirs, you can leverage their desperation to serve your desire, and exploit your way to merciless game board domination.

Resources also needed to be managed and preserved. Since resource acquisition took the most time and energy, a significant portion of household logistics and child rearing required time and energy from another party. Hence, women contributed to those needs.

Anyone would be hard-pressed to find a better solution in the old world. It was the most benevolent solution that men and women could *mutually* devise. I say mutually because it was humankind versus plague, infection, famine, starvation, dehydration, strangers, and other nations. When people are dropping like flies from plague, or everyone is dying of starvation, no one is thinking about how they wish they were more included in the workforce so they could be strong and independent. Any discrepancies we have about inequality today were out of sight and out of mind because humanity had *much* bigger problems.

That is, until the old world passed away and our most primal threats were absolved. *Then* women could give special attention to how they were denied autonomy and excluded from the control and power that ran society.

For starters, if women could gather resources just as well as men, they wouldn't need a man to be their voice and advocate for them. The ratification of the 19th Amendment in 1920, which allowed women to vote, affirmed their ability to advocate for themselves. The Equal Pay Act of 1963 ensured that women receive the same pay as men for performing the same job at the same workplace, promoting fair access to resources.

Title IX made sex-based discrimination illegal in education programs. This empowered women and other underrepresented communities in education to further equalize access to high-paying, higher-education-gated careers. In tow, wherever you want to draw the line, the patriarchy became an *optional* model.

Women's newfound autonomy to navigate society enabled them to renegotiate the distribution of roles in the home, marriage, and family. One could now interpret any resistance to negotiation as the patriarchy's oppression. Minimizing someone's power to impact change and have control solely based on a superiority complex is the very definition of oppression. But if the patriarchy was ever to be seen as anything other than an ideal human solution, it wasn't until *after* the Industrial Revolution and the achievements of feminism in the past century.

It's important to honor the true nature of oppression. Patriarchy *can* be a healthy thing. A woman might not *want* to work 40+ hours a week, and instead want to spend time with her children and manage the household. She might want to leave the resource gathering and social advocacy up to her man, and want and trust him to make all the best decisions for everyone's well-being. That *isn't* oppression. That's what we'd call a role distribution that two adults consent to. It's an *optional* subscription.

Since it became optional, many men and women have negoti- ated the balance of time, energy, and duty at home and with their families. Time isn't proving to be an ally in these negotiations, however.

Each sex now finds itself in a conflict at a stalemate, plagued with unmet expectations, grandiose propaganda, entitlement, finger-pointing, and mutual vilification. They've effectively abandoned the mating negotiation table. Neither will give an inch because they think they're already being asked for too much and that the other side should provide more. What's left is often a mutual trade of bitterness and resentment.

To get a glimpse of the rift this conflict has created, in 2022, a whopping 57% of single Americans were *uninterested* in committed relationships or even casual dates—*the majority. Only 13% of singles were actually interested in establishing long-term committed relationships.*[ii] In other words, most people in the dating field are out to play games, and only about *one in ten* single people are actively looking for a love story.

Why is everyone uninterested and checking out? Well, let's process that. The tectonic cultural shifts occurring in the Western world have blurred expectations and standards for both sexes.

With gender roles and expectations more or less abolished, women should pursue men and ask them out just as much as men do them, but that's not happening. Who should pay the bill now, since both men and women can provide for themselves? Who is writing the rules now? Who *should* write the rules? Or should there be no rules? Who should we listen to?

Too many opinions are considered legitimate on the internet, and too many contradicting influences are overloading minds. Radical perspectives, which are the loudest, get the most airtime and attention. The result is a societal lack of consistent relationship standards and etiquette and gender roles, inducing an utter mating negotiation nightmare. *We tore down the old ways of mating negotiation and replaced them with dyssynchronous fragments, inconsistent frameworks, and random theories.*

Essentially, as a starting point, people are disinterested because they don't even know what they're supposed to be negotiating for.

Without a baseline of rules, everyone has to negotiate every single minuscule detail, and it becomes overwhelming. It discourages people from engaging at all. Psychology refers to this phenomenon as *choice overload*: too many options can lead to indecisiveness.

People prefer simple exchanges to elaborate negotiations. When roles are clearly defined, it's simple to determine compatibility and negotiate. Open-season roles and expectations produce the opposite result.

Besides widespread confusion about relationship roles, other factors discourage mating negotiation. One such problem is the apparent degradation of the dating pool, where partners are becoming less valuable. By that, I mean that if people could choose something about their partner, they would choose a specific way. Take beauty, for example. If one could determine whether their partner would be beautiful or unattractive, they would choose for them to be beautiful.

Beauty is highly regarded as a universal human value. Unfortunately for humanity, this is one of the metrics we have declined in just within the last century. According to Shafee Hassan, a structural engineer and anthropologist, people are becoming less attractive over time due to "modern diets, sleeping patterns, pollutants, and orofacial habits creating a greater inequality" between attractive and unattractive faces.[iii]

The authors of *Jaws: The Story of a Hidden Epidemic* reveal that something as simple as mouth breathing during youth can stunt the growth of the jaw—a key facial feature. This includes mouth breathing during sleep. Chewing soft foods also negatively affects jaw and facial development. As we've discussed, our diets have become more processed with time. Consumers can opt for apple juice and fruit puree pouches instead of hard fruit like whole apples.

We have routine exposure to toxic chemicals, such as PFAS, food dyes, preservatives, and pesticides, and we regularly consume microplastics. We're working longer hours to keep up with inflation, are more stressed out, and many depend on drugs for sleep that don't even deliver high-quality rest. Symmetrical facial formations, which we've consistently equated with attractiveness, may be rarer, meaning we have become less attractive as a species recently.

Additionally, on the attractiveness front, humans are becoming increasingly larger, thanks to the food issues we discussed in *Chapter 1*, and the fact that we're living more sedentary lifestyles. According to the National Institute of Health, over 2 in 5 adults are overweight.[iv] Estimates predict that over half of adults will be obese by 2030.[v] The World Health Organization conceptualizes obesity as "abnormal or excessive fat accumulation that presents a *risk to health.*"[vi]

Hear me out. While the prevailing social narrative is "fat is less attractive," the narrative *should* be *"unhealthy is less attractive."* Being obese or somewhere on the path to obesity *doesn't lessen anyone's value as a human being.* It does, however, hurt their value in the relationship market. Thinking purely mathematically, being obese decreases the *likelihood* that one will be an overall asset in a life partnership.

Author of *Rich Dad Poor Dad*, Robert Kiyosaki, defines an asset as anything that puts money in one's pocket—an overall contributor to economic prowess. He defines a liability as anything draining money from one's pocket. A car is an example of a liability because it doesn't make any money. It simply drains one's resources for payment plans, maintenance, insurance, and fuel costs.

If we're wise in building a future, we consider the asset and liability qualities in our partners, both financially and otherwise. Partners with excellent social skills would be an asset for navigating social gatherings. Those with distinguished careers would be significant financial assets. A partner with a rocking body would be an asset for great sex and adventure. Individuals with exceptional communication skills would be valuable assets for parenting and relational peace. A considerate partner would be an asset for romance and caregiving.

Those with substantial school debt may be a financial liability. Shout out to my homies. Partners with zero social skills would be a liability for social embarrassment. A partner with a bland personality would be a liability for romance and relationship longevity. You get the picture.

Now, please stick with me as we breeze through the "liability" obesity poses. To be clear, this isn't about shaming or dehumanizing obese people or those nearing that point. If this serves as a call for some to pursue health more intentionally, wonderful. But if anyone's going to be mad at anyone, they should probably direct their anger toward those who entice others to nestle onto a fast track toward a shorter lifespan and poorer quality of life.

Obesity worsens the longevity of relationships, as well as financial, lifestyle, and offspring outcomes. By relationship longevity, I mean a partner's premature death could shorten the relationship. The University of Oxford found that moderate obesity shortens lifespan by 3 years and severe obesity can shorten life expectancy by 10 years.[vii]

Financially, "Adults with obesity in the United States compared with those with normal weight experienced higher annual medical care costs by $2,505 or 100%, with costs increasing significantly with class of obesity... The effects of obesity raised costs in every category of care: inpatient, outpatient, and prescription drugs."[viii]

Excess body fat can impede participation in life and increase the likelihood of abnormal body function, such as diabetes, cardiovascular disease, sleep apnea, or sexual dysfunction. On the mental health front, obesity is associated with "significant increases in lifetime diagnosis of major depression, bipolar disorder, and panic disorder or agoraphobia."[ix]

Then, of course, we want our children to be healthy, active, social, laughing, and happy kids. Much of our health is determined by the genes our parents pass on to us. So, if we want healthy kids, it'd be beneficial to our kids if we mated with a healthy partner.

Healthy partners may not only have solid baseline genetics but may also be maximizing their epigenetic health. Epigenetics is the study of how lifestyle affects gene expression. For example, mothers who exercise during pregnancy can directly influence their children's muscle mass, bone density, and overall health: "Benefits for offspring are observable related to body weight and composition, cardiovascular health, and nervous system development."[x] So, maximizing means they'll intentionally manage their behavior and environment to have a positive impact on how their genes function and pass on to their children.

In sum, obesity can be a liability because it negatively affects (1) mental health, (2) bodily function, (3) lifestyle, (4) sexual function, (5) offspring health, and (6) overall quality of life.

My message and challenge to anyone struggling with weight or obesity is not to lose weight, but rather to *pursue health*. We'll cover what that means throughout the book. If you have any shameful emotions around weight, I invite you to transform them into a conviction to leave poor health behind.

Regardless of where we are on our health journey, we should *all* possess a sense of urgency to consider how we can add value to our partners' lives and minimize the liabilities we pose for them. This increases our value in the relationship market and enhances relationship stability. That *is* aspiration-worthy. That *is* a good value to have.

Aside from health and beauty, another reason for the declining interest in relationships is the widespread mentality that *they're temporary*. There are multiple possible origins of this mentality, but the most significant are probably (1) choice overload, (2) failed role-model relationships, and (3) statistical disloyalty.

Dating apps put an overwhelming number of relationship candidates at everyone's fingertips. Option overload can lead people to feel a heightened sense of self-value and to believe that there's always a better option out there. Living with this type of mentality will keep a person single and uncommitted for life. Why commit to someone if there are other, better options?

Second, everybody knows someone with divorced parents or has even lived through the drama of divorce themselves. Enough divorces have happened to convince us that relationships don't last forever. If we examine the divorce rate among public figures, there are few reliable examples of healthy relationships.

To top it all off, cheating is becoming more common. From 1990 to 2010, infidelity among wives increased by 40%. Though some say they still cheat less than men, who have about a 20% infidelity rate versus women's 13% rate.[xi] Voices of authority on the topic of infidelity, like Dr. Wednesday Martin, don't always share the same sentiment, however.

In her book *Untrue: Why Nearly Everything We Believe About Women, Lust, and Adultery is Wrong and How the New Science Can Set Us Free,* she elaborately supports her distinct belief that women are *more* likely to cheat than men. Whatever the case, *humans* give in to the whims of desire, and it's probably fair to say that both sexes exhibit similar levels of loyalty or disloyalty.

The perceptual and statistical risk of being cheated on can certainly affect one's willingness to put their heart on the line. It simply doesn't encourage the emotional, social, and energetic investments required to form long-term committed relationships.

Lastly, I'll just remind us all that, for many reasons, emotional stability is at an all-time low among the public. Economic inequality, political unrest, and cultural friction are at all-time highs. The normalization of dual-income households over the past few decades has significantly increased daycare attendance among children under 3, disrupting a critical period for attachment security, learning emotional regulation, and anxiety coping skills—a recipe for anxious generations.[xii]

In summary, as we examine the dissonance between men and women and their navigation of our new world, it's clear why so many mating negotiations fail and why relationship interest is so low. Not only does each sex hold the other largely responsible for the state of society, but they're developing doubts that the people they're supposed to be negotiating with are even worth the risk or effort.

And if people *do* engage in negotiations, they don't even know *how* they're supposed to negotiate or *what* they're supposed to be negotiating with or for. Not only is the end goal unclear, but the path is undefined. That leads to confusion, frustration, indecisiveness, and conflict. Mating negotiation is utterly broken, leaving Western society's men and women stuck in a state of perpetual conflict.

That's all about to change.

A Change of Heart

The Arbinger Institute presents a distinctive philosophy on conflict resolution in *The Anatomy of Peace: Resolving the Heart of Conflict*. It's not only beneficial for the workplace, friendships, and family, but it's also an invaluable resource for intimate relationships. A brief synopsis and application of this philosophy will provide a perfect starting point for addressing the conflict-ridden tone of mating negotiations.

The Anatomy of Peace teaches us that the posture of our hearts is the most crucial aspect of conflict resolution. There are only two postures: a peaceful heart and a hostile heart. A *hostile heart* sours every action and ignites fiery bitterness in those around us. A *peaceful heart* prevents escalation and promotes wholesome interaction.

Imagine one partner asks the other to make dinner. They may fulfill the request, but do it with a resentful attitude. They slam the food down in front of their partner and storm away. Not a pretty picture, right? It'd be better if they expressed their dire exhaustion and *denied* them while maintaining a genuine positive demeanor.

One posture—a hostile heart—will invite bitterness, frustration, fiery interaction, and conflict. The other—a peaceful heart—may allow room for those, but most likely, it'll invite understanding, compassion, and cooperation, and reduce the potential for conflict. *The posture of the heart is more foundational to conflict and its resolution than our actions are.*

Each posture views people in a specific way. A peaceful heart views others as people with genuine feelings, thoughts, concerns, and fears that are just as real as our own. A hostile heart views others as objects to blame.

Meaning, a hostile heart *dehumanizes* people. Of course, it's an inhumane action to dehumanize people. Deep within our hearts, we're convinced we shouldn't treat people as objects. When we deny that conviction, we deny our own humanity, and therefore, dehumanizing other people dehumanizes us. But we can't have that now, can we? If only... we had... an *excuse*. If we had *justifications* to dehumanize people, we could maintain our judgments and humanity *and* dehumanize them! Huzzah!

These justifications allow us to distance ourselves from those we're dehumanizing, leaving us as the only reasonable human beings in the conflict. We exaggerate the differences between them and us to create as much of a "human versus object" dynamic as possible. *Table 1* shows that there are four justifications: *Entitlement, Image Preservation, Superiority, and Inferiority.* Each carries unique messages, perspectives, and feelings.

Entitlement	Superiority
<u>Core Message:</u> I'm more deserving than others <u>Exaggerated Differences:</u> • I'm praiseworthy, they're misguided • I'm a victim, they tear me down • I'm undervalued, they're unthankful <u>Perspective on the World:</u> • Prejudiced • Unfair • Indebted to Me <u>Corresponding Feelings:</u> • Cheated • Grudgeful • Entitled	<u>Core Message:</u> I'm better than others <u>Exaggerated Differences:</u> • I'm superior, they're inferior • I'm important, they're not • I'm right, they're wrong <u>Perspective on the World:</u> • In need of me • Flawed • Ruthless <u>Corresponding Feelings:</u> • Restlessness • Annoyance • Contempt
Image Preservation	**Inferiority**
<u>Core Message:</u> I want others to see me a certain way <u>Exaggerated Differences:</u> • I'm unadmirable, they're critical • I'm faking, they're exposing me • I'm hiding, they're watching <u>Perspective on the World:</u> • Treacherous • Watching me • Judgmental <u>Corresponding Feelings:</u> • Distressed • Overburdened • Fearful	<u>Core Message:</u> I am less than others <u>Exaggerated Differences:</u> • I'm insignificant, they're vital • I'm disadvantaged, they're blessed • I'm cursed, they're fortunate <u>Perspective on the World:</u> • Neglects me • Difficult place • Out to get me <u>Corresponding Feelings:</u> • Hopeless & Bitter • Envious • Sorrowful

Table 1: Summaries of Justifications for Dehumanization

Once we justify hostile hearts, we invite others to the same, creating a *hostile feedback loop*. In this loop, their actions affect us, so we retaliate to affect them, and they retaliate in return. The only way out of this feedback loop is to regain a peaceful heart.

That requires that we (1) acknowledge our dehumanizing justifications, (2) reset to a peaceful headspace outside of the vicinity of conflict, (3) reevaluate the conflict from another perspective, and (4) apply our new convictions and learning.

Following our new convictions will preserve our peaceful hearts. Denying our new convictions will once again lead us down a dehumanizing path and the hostile feedback loop with no conflict resolution in sight. A steady flow of high stress and hostility awaits us there.

That's the extent of our synopsis. The reason we covered this is that we cannot dehumanize the people we're in relationships with. *True love is a creation by two human beings.* Hostile hearts that turn humans into objects prevent that.

Now, I'm going to ask you some questions, and you'll need to pause after each one to give them serious thought and take notes. This is for singles and non-singles alike. You're about to receive what's essentially an asynchronous coaching session about keeping a peaceful heart toward the opposite sex.

A Change of Heart Coaching Exercise

First, think of a frustration with the other sex you'd like to resolve. Maybe it's a behavior you strongly dislike.

- "What impact(s) does this frustration have on your life?"

Remember, the posture of our hearts is the most critical aspect of conflict resolution. When we are at peace, we view people as people. When we're hostile, we view people as objects to blame. A hostile heart elicits actions that invite the very behavior we are fighting against. A peaceful heart motivates things to go well.

Let's identify the posture of your heart.

- "What thoughts do you have about these people when they stir up your anger or emotions?"
- "What kind of person do you wish they would be instead?"
- "What's the difference between the two of you?"
- "If they represented the world, how does the world feel about you?"
- "What words could they say that would make you happy?"

A hostile heart requires us to view others as objects, and that requires justification. It requires us to exaggerate the differences between them and us. Looking at the four dehumanizing justifications,

- "Which justification do you think is closest to the way you feel about this situation?"
- Or more directly, "Which justification do you think you're using to view the other party not as a person?"

Once you recognize your justification, I invite you to take your mind to a space where you can revisit a peaceful heart. You can choose your destination, but here are some options: a *favorite memory*, a *place that's safe and sacred to you*, an *activity* that makes everything else fall away, or a *person*. Take your time basking in that space, fully experiencing your emotions, surroundings, and energy, and let scenes play out. Really soak it in. Pause here to do that, and once you're done, answer these questions:

- "What emotions do you experience in that peaceful space?"
- "What are you grateful for in this memory, place, or person?"
- "How quiet are your heart and mind there?"
- "What sorts of colors are around you?"
- "What message does this space have for you?"

- "How would you describe who you are in this mindful moment?"

Take a few deep and slow breaths.

Let's reevaluate your situation from a fresh perspective, perhaps a bird's-eye view, and close the exaggerated differences between you and them.

- "How are you both similar in your desires and goals?"
- "Who is this other party when they're being their best selves?"
- "If you were to be an outsider observing your conflict, what do you see that you didn't see before?"
- "Why do you think someone should take their side?"
- "What do you need to learn about their approach to the conflict?"
- "What do you think they admire about you?"
- "How are you contributing to their exaggerated differences?"
- "What have you missed that they caught?"
- "How is this party a strength for you?"
- "What is inspiring about them?"

Take some notes to *summarize your reevaluation and takeaways,* then design an *action* using these questions:

- "What is your heart convicting you to do now?"
- "What do you hope to learn about yourself through this action?"
- "How can you view this as a challenge?"
- "How can you make sure you continue to view them as a person and not an object?"
- "What does it look like to have a peaceful heart while they turn down your peaceful invitation and embrace a hostile heart?"

- "What actions are you willing to commit to, and what kind of accountability do you need to set up for yourself to make sure you fulfill these actions?"

This exercise walks through the most fundamental skill of conflict management: shifting the posture of the heart. It changes our convictions of action and how we treat other people. How we treat others will affect how they treat us. That's the feedback loop.

So, as you chart a new course of harmony with those you desire to create relationships with, it's my invitation that you come down from the edge, whatever assumptions you're tempted to jump to. Unclench your fists, whatever anger you harbor. Sit down to look the other sex in the eyes and listen to them earnestly, regardless of how much you have to say. Consider other points of view, no matter how much blame you want to cast.

Come back to the capsized negotiation table and place it upright before you get older too quickly and miss out on years of good sex or become unable to have children; before you get so lost in bitterness that you never find your way back; before you lose hope or live with life-ruining regrets; and before you burn more bridges and alienate wonderful opportunities.

Embrace a peaceful heart. Be bigger than you are now, and be the hero true love demands.

A Call for a Hero

We must again acknowledge that these last two chapters oversimplify the state of society and relational dynamics between men and women for brevity's sake. I overlooked some perspectives, left out rebuttals and counterpoints, and some cultural shifts and context are missing.

Nevertheless, here's the prophesied literary abomination run-on sentence your high school English teacher warned you about: In summary of understanding the relationship world, if you wreak havoc on everyone's gut, get them cracked out on antidepressants, add identity politics, shift society toward hedonism, emphasize dominance hierarchies, chip away at the cultural foundation upholding how society functions, experience inevitable turbulence of human progress, all under the megaphone amplification of social media and news media pushing divisive agendas, you get an extraordinary band of unsynchronized and overall burdened people making up much of the relationship candidates and participants of society who don't know how they're supposed to negotiate for companionship and are discouraged from thinking it's all worth it. *That* is where we are.

We live in a society and time primed to *prevent* the creation of healthy individuals and healthy relationships. This is clear not only through what you've read so far, but from what so many people's modern dating experiences are.

My goal in reviewing history and ancient ideas isn't to call everyone back to old values, but to provide context and make us aware of society's condition and trajectory, and how they shape relationships and their candidates. It's a shitty situation, and *no one* is coming to save us.

If you've felt called out, offended, or felt friction at any point while reading this book, and you're still here, *good*. That means you probably have what it takes to be the hero not only in your love story but in your life. A hero is only a hero when they contend with unyielding difficulty, absorb excruciating blows, and experience loss. Heroes sacrifice all for the sake of extending grace and life to others. They use their final breath to snatch victory from the jaws of defeat, gain their lifeline of strength from a single ray of sun, and stand against impossible odds with tears of courage in their eyes.

If you picked up this book feeling defeated or angry, gather yourself and your breath, and do not back down. If you have to consider that your villain stands in the mirror, do not break your gaze. Stand up to your opposition because if you want true love, you must become the hero you need and were always meant to be.

Again, it's vital that you avoid the trap of victimhood. Regardless of whether a situation isn't your fault, *the amount of ownership you take over your current situation is directly proportional to the power and agency you have to change it.* Part of being a hero is taking on more responsibility than is warranted. If you want an extraordinary love story, you'll have to push beyond the limits you perceive and the expectations you think you're supposed to uphold.

Even if this book doesn't directly lead you to meet the love of your life, I can absolutely promise a few things: You'll learn profound things about yourself, discover brilliant relationship philosophy that doesn't exist *anywhere* else, grow to love more profoundly, and cultivate your desire to love.

Upon experiencing those, your relationship life will never be the same. You'll make some life-changing decisions, setting your *future* relationship up for success, strengthen your *current* relationship beyond what you thought possible, or conclude that *ending* your relationship is the next best course of action.

From here on, the outcome of your relationship life is entirely in your hands. I include questions and exercises throughout the book because *you* are the expert of your own life. *You* will decide what is best for your life and what chapters you'll live going forward. *You* will choose which words lift off these pages and into action. And *you* will direct what the main character in your story does and who they become.

The relationship you dedicate yourself to long-term is the *single most impactful* decision you can *ever* make. Your financial future, mental, emotional, spiritual, and physical well-being, lifespan, friendships, career, and even the well-being of your potential children depend on it. Relationships determine our quality of life. This book exists so readers dedicate themselves to creating the best possible relationship.

As we exit our evaluation of the modern relationship landscape with a peaceful heart and take a seat at the negotiation table, we're going to clarify where in the air the rules for mating negotiation are. They're impossible to pin down entirely, but we can track them and navigate negotiations tactfully.

Lock in, and charge your stance. We're about to take flight.

3

NEGOTIATING WITH MATE-SELECTION THEORIES

Mating negotiations are experiencing a bit of a "Tower of Babel" moment. The Tower of Babel is a story in the Bible that took place after the Hebrew God sent the worldwide flood and delivered Noah and his family to safety on the ark. As civilization sprang forth once again through those saved on the ark, God created the rainbow as a symbol of His promise that He would never again flood the earth.

Not everyone believed that promise, though. So, they began building a tower unto the heavens as a surprise flood contingency plan. The Hebrew God didn't appreciate that, so He sabotaged their communication. Tower builders began speaking different languages. Doomed to miscommunication, they abandoned the project and went their separate ways.

Similarly, abandoning the old world fragmented our primary "languages" of mating negotiation, leaving multiple languages active simultaneously. So now, if people don't immediately realize they speak the same way, they struggle to communicate and understand each other, and give up on any love-building projects.

This chapter explains multiple theories of mate selection—why people pick the mates they do. With *no* common language or overlapping mate-selection theories, people quickly disperse, and no negotiation takes place. If people *do* operate under the same theories/languages of mate selection, then they engage in mating negotiation and have a conversation about whether they're mutually interested.

Sometimes we don't like the deals proposed to us. And sometimes others don't like what we're offering. They didn't have what we wanted to select, and/or we didn't have what they wanted to select. So, negotiations fail, and we go our separate ways.

If both negotiators find the terms favorable, they successfully negotiate and establish a relationship. In short: **Step 1** — *Speak the same language,* AKA operate under similar mate-selection theories. **Step 2** — *Have a conversation go well,* AKA mutually favor/select what each offers. And **Step 3** — *Commit to an ongoing exclusive conversation,* AKA successfully negotiate a deal, ensuring long-term value exchange in the form of a relationship. That's mate selection in a nutshell.

Theories of mate selection also qualify as *theories of mating consistency.* Although we rarely think of it this way, people in relationships consistently choose to be with their partners every day. They're *selecting* to devote energy to their current partner rather than a new one. This makes every theory useful to *both* single and non-single people.

In brief, these theories explain how single individuals choose a partner and how couples decide to stay together. By the end of the chapter, you'll conceptualize your personal *mate-selection strategy,* which is the unique *bundle* of mate-selection theories one uses to negotiate for relationships.

Uniqueness in Mating Negotiation

Every relationship expert you've ever heard, every piece of romantic advice you've received, and every article of love you've read—they're all based on points of view, mate-selection theories, and data much less complex than you. Sometimes it feels convenient and enlightening to fit ourselves into boxes, but if we want to live life to its fullest and create true love, a box will never suffice.

The importance of this box lesson became abundantly clear to me during my 2020 online dating process. Of course, you had your personality-type-test lovers on there, and it was trendy to know your attachment style according to attachment theory.

On a suburban walk, one of my dates shared how her attachment style affected her dating process, and we explored what my attachment style was for conversation's sake. I checked off almost *all* the characteristics of an *avoidant* attachment type.

I had plenty of deep friendships, wasn't lonely, had high self-esteem, was independent, held back from being exceptionally sweet and thoughtful, and didn't let the women I dated get too close. We could share vulnerable information, yet a deep connection with me would somehow remain out of reach. The theory seemed to really resonate with her, but I wasn't so sure about it and mostly shrugged it off in my mind. I was *looking* for a life-partner. *Why would I be avoidant?*

Sure enough, a week or two later, I met my future wife, held absolutely *nothing* back, and developed a deep connection with dope-ass chemistry. After our second date, I closed off all other dating connections and wished them the best.

Avoidant attachment type was one way to look at my scenario. My *real* type in attachment theory was *secure*, even though my behavior might have appeared otherwise. The reality was actually that I'd make profound subconscious calculations, and conclude: "This ain't it, Chief. You're not my wife." Then, I'd avoid fostering a connection with those women because I didn't want them to fall in love with me only for me to break their hearts later. This was all while doing my best to be open-minded about "making something work."

Boxes are recipes for misinterpretation. They can be functional and comfortable, but if we want our love lives to thrive, we must take

the insight they provide and *move on*. If there is a secret to love, it's
that *there is no secret*. Everyone must find their own way and put the
pieces together for themselves.

The truth about mate-selection theories is that *all of them and
none of them are true*. Everyone uses these theories to some extent,
both consciously and unconsciously. We can be fluent in them or
possess nearly no understanding of them. Yet just because we can't
understand or don't like specific theories, it doesn't mean other
people don't or shouldn't use them.

As I summarize these theories, note that this isn't an exhaustive
list of all mate-selection theories. It's simply a collection of the most
commonly used ones throughout Western society. Some don't even
have official titles or creators.

Nevertheless, this is where a living, breathing map to true love
begins to take shape. We're about to turn a light on in a very dark
room.

Hit the switch.

Attachment Theory

This theory proposes that the quality of the bond children share with
their primary caregiver determines how they'll bond and engage in
intimacy in other relationships throughout life.

Today, there are four accepted forms of attachment: (1) secure, (2)
anxious-resistant, (3) avoidant, and (4) disorganized-disoriented. The
last three are insecure attachment types.[i]

Secure attachment develops when a child forms a healthy
emotional bond with their caregiver during early childhood. Their
caregiver provides a stable environment with consistent expectations,
is reliable, loving, always returns, and refrains from neglect and
abuse. Pretty simple.

Say, however, a primary caregiver is busy and decreases their
engagement with their child. A child may exhibit extreme behaviors
to get attention, such as amplifying their emotions and screaming. It's

not that they're crazy—usually, it's the only way they know how to communicate their need for attention and validation that their caregiver is still there for them. They're looking for signs of security.

As they repetitively ask for signs and attention, they come across as needy. It's also normal for babies with this insecure attachment type to simultaneously seek comfort from their caregiver and push them away in an attempt to punish them for their feelings or treatment. This is the anxious-resistant attachment type, also known as *anxious ambivalent*.

Next, let's say someone excessively ridicules or punishes a child for his or her explosive energy and emotions. They may learn that suppressing their feelings is the best way to get by, appease their caregiver, and preserve their relationships. Hence, they grow up learning not to voice their emotions, which is a recipe for miscommunication, vulnerability avoidance, and the prevention of meaningful connection. This is the *avoidant-attachment* type.

Last, we have the *disorganized-disoriented* attachment style. It's called disorganized because children "fail to develop an organized strategy for successfully coping with separation distress."[ii] Separation means something as simple as a mother walking out of the child's line of sight. Will she return? Will she not? How might the child answer that question based on previous experience?

Children with a disorganized attachment style are *unpredictable* in their coping strategies. Once they encounter stress, they can socially withdraw, attempt to control with aggression and hostility, or manipulate caregivers with overly affectionate, sweet, or pleasing behaviors. Individuals with this attachment style are at higher risk of developing dissociative and borderline personality disorders.

In summary, attachment theory suggests that the main bond we form with our primary caregiver during childhood serves as a prototype for the bonds we establish later in life. If we have a secure attachment with our caregiver, it'll predict secure outcomes for our future relationships. If we form insecure attachments, we're more likely to face significant relationship challenges.

To help us apply attachment theory, *Table 2* summarizes how each attachment style tends to function in a relationship. So, knowing their functions, let's go over some helpful pieces of advice.

For starters, we *shouldn't* use our attachment styles as excuses for our struggles to maintain a healthy relationship or for being single. Research indicates that approximately 30% of people change their attachment style over time.[iii] That's merely the passing of time, *not intervention*.

If we're hyper-vigilant about recognizing and addressing the challenges of our insecure attachment, we'd yield healthy, functional relationships quite effectively. For example, if we're an avoidant person who feels like fleeing during an argument, we might force ourselves to stay. Or if we're an anxious-resistant person who feels clingy and needy, we might defy our discomfort and let go.

Another way to build a healthy relationship as an insecure type would be to pair with someone with a secure attachment style, because they're flexible with the needs of insecure types. If their partner wants to be alone, they can give them space. If their partner wants to be close, they can be close. If their partner wants to be vulnerable, they can be vulnerable. Or if their partner wants to take vulnerability slowly, they can.

When insecure styles mix, they often form poor combinations. An anxious-resistant type isn't ideal for an avoidant type. One partner smothers, chases, and closes the space between them during stressful times, while the other instinctively avoids them and creates distance. One would be quick to vulnerability while the other resists it and finds it uncomfortable. One would exaggerate emotions, and the other would suppress them. Both would exhibit highly unattractive or hurtful behaviors to the other and likely kill their connection.

If two anxious-resistant types pair up, they'll probably amplify each other's negative emotions, insecurities, and crises since neither of them has healthy emotional regulation. They might both shut down, refuse to communicate, fight over validation, and lack clear boundaries, making it easy for them to hurt each other.

Finally, if two avoidant types get together, neither will initiate vulnerability or emotional intimacy. They might ghost each other because they're too comfortable alone and don't care to close the gap. It's completely unpredictable when you include disorganized attachment types in the mix, so I'll skip giving an example for them.

Secure	Anxious-Resistant
• Positive view of self. • Comfortable with intimacy and vulnerability. • Happy to be alone or close. • Healthy and balanced emotional regulation. • Healthy boundaries. • Significant other is a plus, yet the world does not revolve around them. • Anxiety response is to leverage coping and problem-solving skills and to communicate effectively. • Cooperative, trusting, empathetic, compassionate, and flexible in relationships.	• Highly insecure view of self. • Quick to trust, be vulnerable, and cling to intimacy. • Fear of being alone, abandonment, and a need to be close. • Poor emotional regulation, leading to mood swings. • Poor sense of physical and emotional boundaries. • Significant other is a main source of self-worth. • Highly anxious. Anxiety response is to shut down or cling. • Downplay people's red flags. • Seek constant validation.
Avoidant	**Disorganized**
• Hyper-positive view of self. • Fearful and uncomfortable with trust, vulnerability, and emotional intimacy. • Very comfortable being alone. • Partitioned emotional regulation, where emotions get suppressed. • Strich and high boundaries that prevent people from getting close. • A significant other is not needed, as they are hyper-independent. • Anxiety response is to shut down, detach, or flee. • Can be dismissive and avoid communication or asking for help. • Focus on flaws.	• Inconsistent view of self and others. • Inconsistent desire for intimacy. • Inconsistent desire to be alone. • Difficulty regulating emotions or even feeling emotions. • Inconsistent physical and emotional boundaries. • Inconsistent desire for a significant other as they both seek and avoid connection and attention. • Anxiety response is unpredictable: clinginess, fleeing, manipulative, etc. • Lack empathy, fear others, and recreate dysfunction in relationships. • Can easily feel suffocated or abandoned.

Table 2: Attachment Styles in Relationships

If it's helpful to know, research shows the distribution of attachment styles is about 59% secure, 25% avoidant, 11% anxious-resistant, and 5% disorganized.[iv] This varies by nation, generation, and the time period in which the research was conducted.

I encourage you to further explore attachment theory on your own time to become better acquainted with how you form bonds with others!

Masculine-Feminine Theory

Home to some of the most controversial takes in relationships, we have the masculine-feminine theory. Its controversial nature stems from its stance on what it means to be a man or woman. This is one of the two leading theories of mate selection that ruled the old world.

Given people's sensitivity to this topic, here's a friendly reminder that, regardless of how we feel about each theory, it's essential we understand them because they help us understand others and the world around us. Whether we *subscribe* to and use a theory meaningfully is an entirely personal matter.

So, without further ado, the masculine-feminine theory is a philosophy dating back to humanity's earliest origin stories. It has fundamentally integrated itself into reality through the structures of language, religion, and *archetypal* descriptions of human experience.

Archetypes are recurrent symbols or typical examples of a person or thing. Think mythology, legends, old Disney narratives, the Chinese Taoist symbol, or the cross of Christianity.

Figure 1: Taoist Yin and Yang Symbol

The black-and-white Taoist symbol dates back about 2,400 years, and it represents a philosophy that a meaningful life walks the line between twin serpents: *Yin and Yang—chaos and order*. According to Dr. Jordan Peterson in his book, *12 Rules for Life*, walking the line is to have "one foot firmly planted in order and security, and the other in chaos, possibility, growth, and adventure." The two halves also represent the masculine and the feminine.

In the biblical creation story of Adam and Eve, many translations state that God took Adam's "rib" and created Eve from it. Since no other texts use the Hebrew word "hassela" to mean "rib," but instead "side," a better translation would be "side." As in two distinguished halves, engraving a complementary dynamic in the masculine-feminine archetype—neither being superior nor inferior.

For millennia, this theory has ascribed specific characteristics, traits, and "energies" to each sex. While *not exclusive* to either sex, they're imposed on them as generalized expectations based on observed behavioral preferences and perhaps even primordial design. And regardless of anyone's reluctance to admit it, there *is* some serendipitous and amusing accuracy behind their stereotypes.

The first thing that comes to mind as I examine *Table 3*'s list of traits is that my wife is a devoted student of chaos. She'll get 9 hours of sleep, stay in bed on her phone too long, get up, panic that she's not ready, apply her makeup as quickly as possible, rush to make her coffee, skip breakfast, look for her misplaced keys and phone... all while rushing me as I wait by the door.

As wild as that all is, it's not what chaos means within the masculine-feminine framework. According to Dr. Peterson, since patriarchy was the dominant model of control and power throughout history, it's well-associated and accepted that order is represented by the masculine. The feminine complement is lesser known. It's chaos that throws order off-kilter, bringing change.

Women have long influenced men with their presence. Throughout history, a woman expressing disappointment might have made a man second-guess himself. But getting the juiciest love-making session of his life after doing something she liked *programmed* him to *want* to make more woman-pleasing decisions. Men may not be naturally agreeable or flexible, but they'll voluntarily wrap themselves around a woman's pinkie for the right price. Chaos brings its own power for change.

Another archetypal example is that the feminine is the receptive party, and the masculine is the go-getting, assertive party. According to @datepsych, a cognitive and behavioral neuroscience research account on X, 77% of single women aged 18-30 wish they were approached more, and 86% of them want men to "make the first move." Though that preference isn't absolute, it is definitely the majority.

Masculine	Feminine
Order	Chaos
Analysis/Logic	Intuition
Focused	Playful
Assertive	Receptive
Independent	Collaborative
Intellect	Senses
Protect	Nurture
Control	Freedom
Active	Passive
Hard	Soft
Consuming	Creative
Doing	Being
Aggressive	Tender
Self-concern	Compassion
Boundaries	Vulnerable
Stable	Flexible
Competition	Cooperation
Talking	Listening
Outcome	Process

Table 3:: Summary of Masculine and Feminine Traits

People also associate the masculine with hardiness and the feminine with softness. On a biological note, average males have higher bone density and more muscle mass per pound than average females. Psychologically, men are on average more wired for competition and aggression than females.

Masculinity is associated with independence. Society expects men to take care of themselves and be self-sufficient. It's less common for men to share their feelings, ask for help, or be unfamiliar with a lone-wolf mentality.

Women can regularly huddle in the restroom together, share all their emotions and thoughts, cry together, go dancing at the club together, sleep and cuddle together—no one bats an eye. It's expected for women to be collaborative and have a pack mentality.

I could go on, but you get the point. There's unmistakable evidence that masculine and feminine traits often correspond to a particular sex. Though that's not to say the sexes should stay in their own lanes. It's normal and, in fact, *desirable* to possess some qualities of one's opposite domain.

In this theory, the philosophical goal for couples is to strike a *collective* balance and walk the line between both sides. Because when there's an imbalance, it's easy for things to feel off. For example, if the masculine exercises total control over the feminine by never letting her be social, dictating all her activities, having sex only when *he* wants to, or never letting her make any pivotal decisions—that feels off. He's treating her more like a doormat than a partner.

Anyone operating at the extreme of their sex's domain will feel off. Because anyone having a balanced interaction with them requires that they operate at the complementary extreme. Someone in total control needs someone in complete surrender, and no one with self-respect is willing to be a doormat.

It can feel equally off, if not even more off, for one to embody the extreme in their *counterpart's* domain. "Feeling off" means abnormal, uncomfortable, unattractive, strange, off-putting, cringy, silly, cheeky, or simply different. The specific impression all depends on the person. This phenomenon is how we get terms like Karens and gaydar. *Karens* are ladies who publicly act like steroid-juiced monsters, and *gaydar* is the intuitive alarm sounding off when men trudge too far into femininity, raising curiosity about their non-straight sexuality.

Healthy and successful relationships result from a *balance* of masculine and feminine principles. Complementation negates competition. That minimizes conflict and promotes a cohesive, *effective* partnership because there's no lapse in collective ability.

Every trait shines in its own time and can only be seen as a weakness or flaw when misused or mistimed. For example, hot-tempered Huxley is more likely to wreck the kids than to correct their behavior. Doormat Darcy won't be our fearless leader in the hour of need. That doesn't mean aggression or the ability to hold our tongue will never be needed, though.

One of the fundamental tenets of my thriving marriage has been sharing definitions of what it means to be a man and a woman, and covering all our masculine and feminine bases. The man is physically strong, stable, determined, orderly, assertive, somewhat rough, analytic, and competitive.

The physical labor and upkeep of the home fall on me, and I take our dog out at night so she's not walking alone with a 17-pound teddy bear. Perhaps, unconventionally, I'm tidier than she is, and I'll sometimes organize her closet. I bring order to our finances because she'd rather not.

Masculine hardiness is vital to the stability of our relationship. I'm often stoic and slow to frustration, anxiety, and anger, yet I offer a concerned, listening ear to assess which issues warrant urgent attention and response. I call her to stability because two chaotic, panicking souls do no one any good. Working out to become physically strong is a means to bring safety and security to our marriage.

Abbey excels in empathy, caregiving, intuition, thoughtfulness, inclusion, nurturing, tenderness, and creativity. She has an impeccable sniffer and a playful spirit I absolutely cherish. I'm cautious not to extinguish the beauty in her femininity and in her playful innocence lest I suffocate a quality that brings me a soothing, life-giving joy.

Feminine physical beauty is something she guards and highly values, partly because I do too. Her daily quick-and-easy 49-step beauty routine is a testament to this. If one of us is going to work, it's going to be me—especially when we have kids. She has also recently taken up traditional, practical feminine arts, such as sewing, crocheting, and embroidery.

Despite our mutual agreement on masculine-feminine expectations, we're also both extremely flexible. While Abbey attended graduate school and I focused on my writing projects and small business, she didn't do a single load of laundry for about two years. I also did 95% of the grocery shopping and most of the cooking. I still do all the dog bathing, grooming, food prep, and maintenance.

Abbey is an assertive communicator and decision-maker who sometimes struggles to let go of control. She's extremely confident, capable, and competitive in her academics and profession. The point is that we agree about all of this—*what a man and a woman are and what they can be.* It's a vital component of relationship success that's rarely talked about.

Since the relationship landscape is more discombobulated, pessimistic, and unhappy with the results modern gender doctrine produces, it's worth asking whether we're forcefully adopting doctrines that are less natural and more painful and divisive than traditional definitions of men and women.

The fact of the matter is that society still *loves* to elevate people who embody domains perfectly. Worldwide sensations like Zendaya, Selena Gomez, Taylor Swift, and Shakira all embody femininity, and they're worshiped because of it. Henry Cavill, Chuck Norris, Edris Alba, and LeBron James share a similar iconic experience in the realm of masculinity.

So, deep down, maybe it *is* okay if women want to be beautiful, desired, cherished, and connected. Maybe it *is* okay if men want to be strong, purposeful, assertive, and competitive, as long as they remain respectful.

Whether we consider this theory traditional or outdated, it clearly still has merit given the behavioral tendencies observed in each sex. It also paints an elegant picture of two people collectively harnessing the strengths and benefits of an entire spectrum of personality traits.

That picture does require a tactful balancing act, though.

The Masculine-Feminine Teeter-Totter

As we've covered, couples benefit from having both masculine and feminine elements because every trait is guaranteed to be beneficial at some point. What *doesn't* need to happen is for two people to over-load one trait. Two hotheads will burn the peace around them. Two partners hungry for control will starve each other of autonomy. Two soft souls will surrender when adversity looks their way.

This theory's wisdom lies in embracing each other's natural strengths when appropriate. This is an opportunity to think long and hard about what we truly want and who we aspire to be. Because if we're dealing with a balance-complement system, *knowing who we desire will tell us who we need to be, and knowing who we want to be can tell us who we need.*

For clarity's sake, let's look at a masculine-feminine teeter-totter. At the top, we have a male in the middle of the masculine domain, in touch with his feminine side. Complementing him is a female in the middle of the feminine domain, able to step into the masculine domain when she likes and when necessary.

They attract one another because they make each other feel balanced, recognize and appreciate what the other offers, and they have clear expectations about their roles in their relationship.

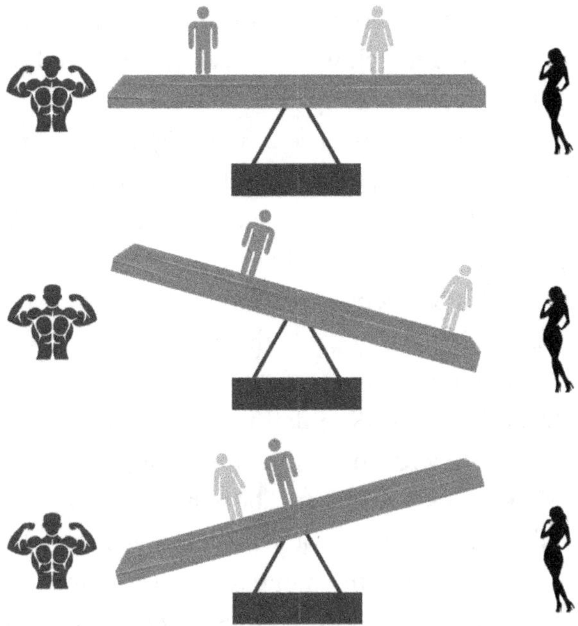

Figure 2: Balancing Masculine and Feminine Qualities

In the center, we have a male leaning slightly toward the feminine side, but still within his domain. He's easygoing, doesn't care for competition too much, and therefore doesn't have high aspirations, take initiative, or have a strong sense of independence.

Misaligned with him is a hardcore, feminine woman. She accentuates her beauty, takes joy in being desired, wants the man to handle the finances and work, and is very tender and compassionate. She fosters a seductive submissive nature because submissiveness invites dominance, and therefore amplifies power within her partner.

Unfortunately, they don't complement each other. Without an aggressive and competitive nature, the man won't achieve anything significant enough to provide for them both. Their sexual attraction and chemistry will lack because she wants an assertive, powerful, and testosterone-gorged man, which an unsuccessful male with weak aspirations is not.

If that man wants to be a match for a woman who's at the extreme of femininity, he'll have to move toward the extreme of masculinity. Or if she wants to be a match with him, she'll have to develop more masculine traits to make up for what he doesn't have.

Finally, at the bottom, we have a male right in the middle. He's noncompetitive, passive, malleable, and somewhat confused about his role. Misaligned with him is a woman with masculine qualities. She likes to be in control, dominates conversations, flaunts her success, and muzzles her gentleness and kindness to prove to others that she has thick skin to compete in the big leagues.

This last couple topples the teeter-totter. It breaks any semblance of balance. According to online dating results, most women prefer highly successful men with substantial resources, a healthy physique, and a strong sense of responsibility. Those men lean toward the more masculine end of the spectrum, and they either repel women with masculine qualities or usher them into feminine qualities.

Any woman settling far into the masculine domain, like in this last example, actually balances out with a noncompetitive man who won't put up a fight, speak up, be ambitious, or successful. Being a high performer herself, she'll despise him for his insignificant existence. She'll disrespect and walk all over him as she judgmentally challenges him to become more, against his nature and against the masculine-repelling force she embodies.

In all likelihood, a woman unwilling to relinquish an identity rooted in masculine traits will never truly be happy in a relationship. She's simply left with a broken teeter-totter she refuses to fix. Similarly, a man who refuses to pick up masculine traits will never be happy because he'll never be able to direct his own destiny and attract a good feminine woman who respects him.

No man wants to be yelled at, ordered around, nagged, or complained about by *anyone*, because these barrage-like forms of communication convey exhausting messages of inadequacy. But these messages may be especially draining, coming from a woman, as women typically function as men's primary source of energy, inspiration, and motivation.

Christians find this archetypal relationship in Genesis 2:18, which says God created a "helper suitable" for Adam. The translation of helper comes from the Hebrew word ezer. Other than that single instance, *ezer* refers only to God—the Creator of the universe, the giver of life, the all-sustaining force, the savior, and the source of love.

A better interpretation of that text would be to say that a woman is *just as absolutely vital for the life, existence, and well-being of man as God Himself*. She is *indispensable*; giver of life and vitality to man. To truly flourish in relationships, an equal on the opposite side of the teeter-totter is *absolutely necessary*.

Now that we understand the nature of the masculine-feminine teeter-totter, let's briefly analyze how we might navigate the traits of our respective domains to strike a complementary balance.

Leaning into a Lane

Order, control, and focus all go hand in hand, and chaos, freedom, and playfulness complement them. Masculine control doesn't take power for the sake of having power, but for the sake of well-kept responsibility and the relief of others' burdens. When a masculine individual exercises executive control, they do so with consideration for how others benefit.

If a man ever wants to tell a woman what to do, he must ensure it benefits her and communicates that power is in trustworthy hands. Something like, "Hey, let's sit down over there; those heels can't be comfortable after standing for so long!" Or "Go watch some *Gilmore Girls*, I'm going to make you dinner." Or maybe, "Honey, you should go get ready and put on some nice clothes! Dress the part—you're going to rock this exam!" I told my wife that this morning, right after making her a brain-healthy breakfast.

A man directing power responsibly allows a woman to lean into her femininity. Eventually, it enables him to ask for things without reactive resistance. Making a sandwich doesn't seem like such a big ask when you were told to go lie down and got an hour massage 2 hours ago. Proving power is well-placed builds a woman's confidence in her partner's decision-making ability and allows her to relax.

This isn't some ploy to make women servants in the end. Power is a privilege, not a right, and it carries a heavy cost. Those who decide a course of action *also* determine the consequences. It's only fair that the one creating a situation has to endure most of the consequences. For this reason, it's wise to unload any responsibility one is unprepared or unwilling to make others pay the price for.

My wife hates dealing with finances because it stresses her out, and she didn't grow up in a financially secure home. So, I handle it all. Even though I handle financial projections, cyclical bills, and general money management, I ensure she's aware of what's happening and has constant access to it. If anything were to happen to me, the consequences of my monopoly over all financial power would devastate her. I'm unwilling to let any hogging of power do her dirty like that.

If a couple delegates more power to one partner in an area, both partners should agree that the empowered party will bear the majority of the corresponding consequences. "If you get to choose what we eat and we get fat, it's your fault, and it'll be up to you to find us a way out... If you choose to get a pet when I don't want to, you assume all responsibility of its grooming, feeding, exercise, cleanup, etc." As Peter Parker's uncle Ben would say, "With great power comes great responsibility... and the absorption of consequences." I added that last part.

Another part of holding a couple's masculine power is speaking for their concerns. The other day, Abbey and I were staying with some friends, and one of our hosts got sick. Since the visit was on our way to visit our family, who had a baby, my wife was concerned we'd bring an illness with us if we stayed any longer.

Being closer friends with our hosts, I almost felt rude cutting our trip short. But the correct decision as the masculine representative was to absorb the reputation one might not want, even that of the party pooper, if it's for the sake of relieving reasonable concerns.

Despite most of the concern being with my wife, I was the one who spoke up and admitted it'd be best if we left. I *didn't* say, "My *wife* is concerned..." That'd be throwing her under the bus and using her as a shield against what they thought about me. Instead, the masculine serves as the unit's reputation shield, acting as its voice and absorbing the social consequences.

While we can imagine many benefits associated with power, we can also imagine many benefits associated with freedom, playfulness, and chaos. They hold the keys to novelty, adventure, and fun. These are *not* high-anxiety, stress-inducing, energy-intensive, body-breaking, or peace-disrupting matters. Rather, they're an *escape* from those very aspects of possessing power.

It's essentially impossible to recall a controlling, power-obsessed person who wasn't outrageously stressed and was having a good time. And while my wife isn't exactly that way, there's a reason I often take the wheel when we drive somewhere. I'm not only saving other people from piping-hot ESPN live commentary, but I'm setting a tone of peace and patience for everyone in the vehicle.

Relief from the burdens of power, control, and order offers freedom and opportunity for playfulness and serendipity. Abbey thrives as the one sparking tickle fights, blowing raspberries on my belly, breaking out in song, wanting to go on dates and travel, and experimenting with new recipes. She's the engine for novelty, playfulness, and new experiences in our relationship, and she's happiest when she's free and doesn't have to worry about due dates, bills, or the stressors of daily life.

Now, again, chaos doesn't represent spontaneously inviting stray garbage-wired raccoons into the house just to make life eventful. Chaos allows the orderly masculine to grow, change, unwind, move, dance, and escape the weight of all known things in the balance. It's the curiosity, fascination, and experimentation within the unknown that gives birth to creativity. Without encountering previously unknown or forgotten things, there's no awe or fire to life.

The most memorable part of any story is the unexpected turn: when a Western-attired armadillo riding on the back of a sombrero-wearing tortoise nods at the protagonist, causing them to crash into a stationary hot-dog-shaped van. Or when penguins smile and wave in a public place to flawlessly blend in. It's when things spin out of control, and there's a scramble to regain control.

If one wants a life partnership with fondly remembered moments, there needs to be a leader who leans into the unknown and the things beyond their control—a tester of boundaries and a playful spirit. There also needs to be a leader who consumes the chaos, dances with it, and eventually brings the dance to rest. Just as in Taoist philosophy, a couple must have one foot in order and one in chaos to create a fulfilling, meaningful long-term relationship.

Perhaps one way to enliven the chaotic, playful, and free feminine is to embrace one's inner child. It's something everyone wants but is usually afraid to do. I mean, the draw is obvious: life was so much simpler as a kid. It's a rude awakening to realize how exhausting it is simply to exist! Children don't have to worry about the costs of housing, internet, heating and cooling, insurance, food, gas, student loans, or taxes. Being a kid is an awesome deal!

Embracing one's inner child is an art that opportunistically resurrects innocence, purity, imagination, and wonder. One thing professional ICF coaches leverage for creativity and inspiration is inviting our clients to let go of judgment and let their imagination flow. We encourage letting go of the excuses we use to stay in our comfort zones and not pursue the things that make our hearts rejoice.

To embrace one's inner child, one must let go of the need to be serious, the smartest in the room, appear strong, and control what others think of them. They must release whatever prevents them from falling into wonder around them. One must ask questions, relish the unknown, grow sillier, and see a game in everything.

As far as I can tell, women who *tastefully* bring their inner child to life and embrace their femininity are the happiest. Their natural beauty flows, and they're beacons of light when they're not trying to force themselves to be serious all the time. Perhaps the reason women love a man with a sense of humor is that they settle them into the safe, disarmed, fun, playful, and joyful qualities of their natural feminine domain.

Maybe the reason women are drawn to men with ambition, drive, and a strong work ethic is that it means they don't have to carry as much pressure around success. Perhaps women love assertive and intentional men because they long to feel captivating and worthy of pursuit. Maybe all these things make them feel more themselves—a natural woman.

Here's my message to my fellow men concerning the qualities we've discussed so far: Embracing masculinity requires that we repeatedly analyze the justification for our actions and control, and *always* hold the suspicion that we could be out of line. *If we don't hold the fundamental belief that we could become a tyrant, we'll never guard ourselves from becoming one.*

We must defend and hold space for femininity as we would a delicate flower, which is our friend and brightens our lives. The ultimate gratitude we can show a feminine woman is cherishing her playfulness, admiring her spirit, honoring the faith and belief she has in our potential, accepting her invitations to freedom, fun, novelty, and play, and providing stability for her femininity to flourish.

Next, we have logic, intellect, intuition, and senses. Logic tells us someone is extraordinarily nice when they pay us a compliment and invite us to something. Intuition tells us they want to sell us something.

Obviously, women are extremely capable of logic and should use it. Honing and using intuition, however, is an indispensable skill because it's *completely frictionless* against logic. A woman not wanting to walk down a dark alley because of intuition overrides the statistical analysis a man might make about the likelihood of muggers waiting for two unsuspecting victims.

Intuition is subconscious pattern recognition, in contrast to conscious reasoning. One could fairly claim that the woman's intuitive suspicion about the dark alley came through her sense of smell. Smell is the one sense in which women have an advantage over men. On a perfectly still spring evening, Abbey's sniffer can smell a naked mole rat pitter-pattering 3.4 mph due southwest on Mongolian concrete. Okay, *not really.* But she *does* have a better sense of smell than I do. This is normal for women.

When given the sweaty shirts of men, ovulating women will rate the smell of physically fit men's shirts as more attractive. Being physically fit provides the optimal genes to pass on to offspring, and women actually smell and opt for the genetics that offer the highest fitness, health, and vitality for their offspring.[v] Talented sniffers indeed!

Women's superior sense of smell gets a heck of a lot more interesting when we consider that specific hormones correlate with specific emotional states. Emotional states closely correlate with intentions and actions. If we see someone angry, we might conclude they're looking for someone to smack. Pair this concept with women's higher activity in the mirror neuron system,[vi] and it's very reasonable to think they can genuinely possess a sort of subconscious genius.

If you're not familiar, the mirror neuron system essentially allows us to understand others' intentions, feelings, and actions. This class of brain cells is active when we perform an action and also when we see someone else doing the same or a similar action.

For example, the neurons will fire when we bury our faces in our hands. They'll *also* fire when we see someone *else* bury their face in their hands. We'll immediately resonate with their face-palming because we've done it ourselves, and we probably know how they feel. Watching their experience is like looking at ourselves in the mirror at a previous point in time.

When this neural system works well, it's the foundation for empathy and the social interaction that built civilization. When it works improperly, it's thought to be linked to disorders like autism, where social cues don't get picked up, and there's a misunderstanding of intentions, feelings, and social situations.[vii]

As for how a superior sensory intake and a more active mirror neuron system might create a subconscious superpower together: If women can better sense an emotional state via smelling hormones of aggression, stress, etc., and better gather others' facial expressions with their superior mirror-neuron system, then they can better resonate and empathize with others to project their most likely thoughts, intentions, and actions.

The unique aspect of this subconscious genius wouldn't manifest itself in logic's numerical probabilities, but rather in a gut feeling because they're empathizing with and experiencing the other party's intentions and emotions. *That*...is cool.

If this is really one of the ways intuition takes form, it's probably worth paying attention to. Experts estimate that the human gut has as many neurons as a cat's brain.[viii] So, if you believe a cat could want good things for you, consider the gut's pleas seriously. Hopefully, you have a cat that *doesn't* absolutely hate you, though...

While both men and women would be wise to lean into intuition, women seem better equipped with this emotional intelligence superpower. That's not to say men don't have their own mental strengths, however. Studies have concluded that men score 3-5 points higher than women on IQ tests, mainly because of a consistently larger gap in spatial intelligence.[ix]

Spatial intelligence is the precision with which one navigates space. A spatially intelligent individual excels at sports, driving, and video games—anything that requires approximating the location of physical objects relative to oneself. Both men and women bring unique brain advantages. If they respect, value, and leverage their differences, they'll be a happier and more effective team.

On to assertiveness and receptiveness. An assertive person dares to approach conflict, discomfort, challenges, and potential mates. Putting oneself on the line and risk-taking are second nature to men. That's why young men pay higher car insurance rates, are more likely to do backflips off cliffs to impress others, and roll Suburbans after going 55 mph on a suggested 20 mph turn in Boring, Oregon.

Assertiveness means recognizing that good things come to those who move. It's the realization that one catches more raindrops while running than standing still. It's knocking and seeing if a door opens —the curiosity and boldness to see what life will give. It's asking for a raise, owning up to our actions, being transparent about our intentions to see if they align with others', and sticking to our word— letting our yes be yes, and our no be no. It's recognizing that order, truth, and stability come from eliminating variables, and that the more we deal with things directly, the fewer variables there are.

Assuming marriage is a man's eventual goal, assertiveness is approaching a woman because he understands marriage is knocking at the same door for a lifetime. It's recognizing she could never begin to believe he will chase her forever if he never starts. It's taking the risk of knocking, knowing full well that 99% of the women answering the door won't be the one he commits his life to.

The complement of assertiveness is *receptivity:* the openness to experience. Someone leaning into receptivity would be curious about who's knocking on their door. It's the inspection of what's being offered, and an essential tool for weeding out individuals who aren't conducive to a strong, healthy, and productive partnership.

It therefore helps elevate the health of the dating pool. Without getting to know someone, there's little room to observe their short-comings and communicate the grounds for rejection. Detailed rejection forces people to reckon with the bar they know they need to meet to try again or secure a partner of equal desirability.

Finally, we have stable, competitive, and doing, which are complemented by flexible, nurturing, and being. The masculine is steady, unwavering, and working for something. In line with its intellectual tendency to process things in terms of cause-and-effect and black-and-white, masculine *fulfillment and meaning* are derived from *linear progress, turning chaos into order,* and *problem-solving.*

Hijacking this pathway to fulfillment are many deceptions. All of them imitate real-world progress or accomplishment. Video games, pornography, and gambling addictions are some prominent examples. If deceptions are accepted long enough, they essentially sedate the masculine sojourner, and time passes them by with no real-life experience.

To safeguard against sedation and the alienation of masculine fulfillment, one would be wise to choose an aspiration and work toward it, even if it's part-time. Lacking aspiration leaves no opportunity for focus. Without focus, consistency doesn't exist. Inconsistency means no meaningful progress. No progress results in no fulfillment of purpose.

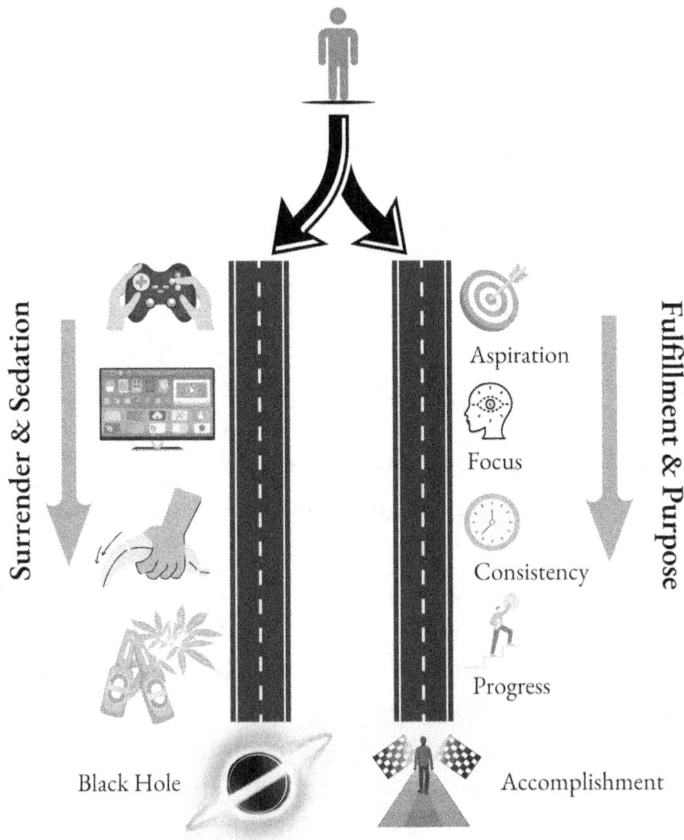

Figure 3: True and False Paths of Masculine Fulfillment and Purpose

Masculinity's path to fulfillment and purpose is the narrow, challenging road that only heroes take. The false path is easy to walk, but it leads to a black hole that drains our time on this planet, holds us captive, robs us of human experience, and leaves us feeling empty. True fulfillment is born through wholehearted devotion, not captivity. Peak purpose is found when our accomplishments benefit those we love.

As for flexible, nurturing, and being, feminine fulfillment and purpose don't depend on goal attainment. In connection with play-fulness, the feminine is wired to live in the present. The present is tangible and at hand, and therefore more malleable than the future, which is out of reach.

The primary masculine concern is to be great one day. The femi-nine concern is to bask in and explore the greatness of today. Femi-ninity's desire is to be cherished, loved, and thought of as beautiful and captivating *today*—to be safe, secure, and connected *today*.

In line with the tendency to be present, the feminine finds its purpose in being present *with* others. This doesn't mean necessarily *for* others. It doesn't involve being an exhausted servant, going unheard, being used or taken advantage of, or not being a person worthy of concern. Those being used aren't cherished. Serving without reciprocation highlights imbalance. And those without a voice will never be seen or known.

The mirror neuron system we discussed earlier is crucial to being present with others. Women, with more advanced mirroring systems, are, on average, naturally better equipped and inclined to empathize with others' experiences and step into their shoes. Feeling empathy for others is attuning to their emotions, and both their problems and celebrations become meaningfully shared. Empathetic wiring suggests it's not just *their* deal—it's *ours*.

Another way this living-for-more-than-one concept shows up is in the creation of new human life. Poetically, she takes another being into her body during sex. If she gets pregnant, she'll be eating for more than one, and throughout the child's life, her heart will beat for more than one. But a selfish woman, whose heart beats only for herself, inverts feminine nature and believes others live *for her*.

The *feminine truth,* then, is having community to connect with and belong to, building a family, and being present. The *feminine lie* is attention and worship. Instead of directing her playful, listening, receptive, and nurturing qualities toward others, she directs them from others toward herself.

This is her strongest temptation: to be adored, wanted, and pursued by many, and be the center of attention; to yearn for likes, comments, and followers on social media, and to attract others just for an ego boost. But the satisfaction never lasts. Feelings of emptiness and endless craving creep up just like with the masculine's lie.

The elements along the feminine path aren't necessarily sequential steps, but rather ingredients that make a sum greater than its parts. Play is where creative thoughtfulness, sweetness, purity, presence, and joy stem from. Empathy allows one to feel others' emotions and truly see and hold them dear.

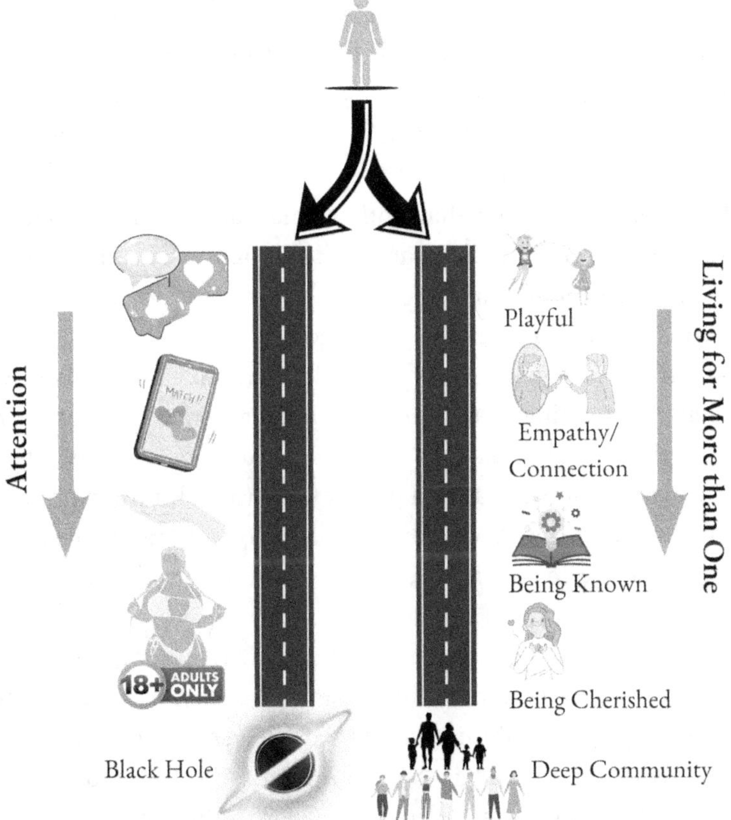

Figure 4: True and False Paths of Feminine Fulfillment and Purpose

Femininity's path to fulfillment is likely why women make up the bulk of human resource departments, nurses, teachers, childcare providers, and the like. They choose to nurture, listen, be playful, and give others the spotlight. And despite its astonishing demands, pains, and challenges, family building has long been the most direct path to feminine fulfillment.

Knowing these paths to fulfillment, we can observe whether potential partners will be assets that help us live rich and fulfilling lives or pose risks that lead us down a life-draining path.

Just as with the traits themselves, neither the masculine nor the feminine path is exclusive to either sex. *Both paths of meaning, purpose, and fulfillment apply to every human being.* On average, though, men are more likely to find greater fulfillment in pursuing goals and conventional success than are women, and women are more likely to be drawn to fully immerse themselves in family building and mean-ingful community. Though *everyone* wants success and a loving family, we all dedicate differing amounts of energy to each according to what fans the flame in us.

We should also note that both women and men have paths to fulfillment in which neither partner *is* the path itself. Ideal partners empower each other to pursue their desires and goals, and nurture their connections and sense of belonging.

The main takeaway of the masculine-feminine theory is *balance*. Balancing masculine and feminine characteristics in relationships requires that we ebb and flow together. It demands that we not be ruled by the stubbornness and pride of our ways, but that we eagerly deploy the *beauty of both* domains. Insisting on an unbalanced teeter-totter will be the reason it never teeters, and why we both eventually get off it.

Wrapping up, to get a general idea of where we might want to land on the scale of masculinity and femininity, it's helpful to be familiar with the distribution. Putting ourselves in the middle of our sex's respective domain gives us the greatest amount of potential complementary partners. Referring to *Figure 5,* that'd put us in SD 4-5 if we're male, and SD 6-7 if we're female.

Being in the middle means reasonably embodying one's native domain while also being attuned to the qualities of the other. This provides a couple with maximum flexibility to maintain balance, because wherever one partner is lacking, the other can step in effectively.

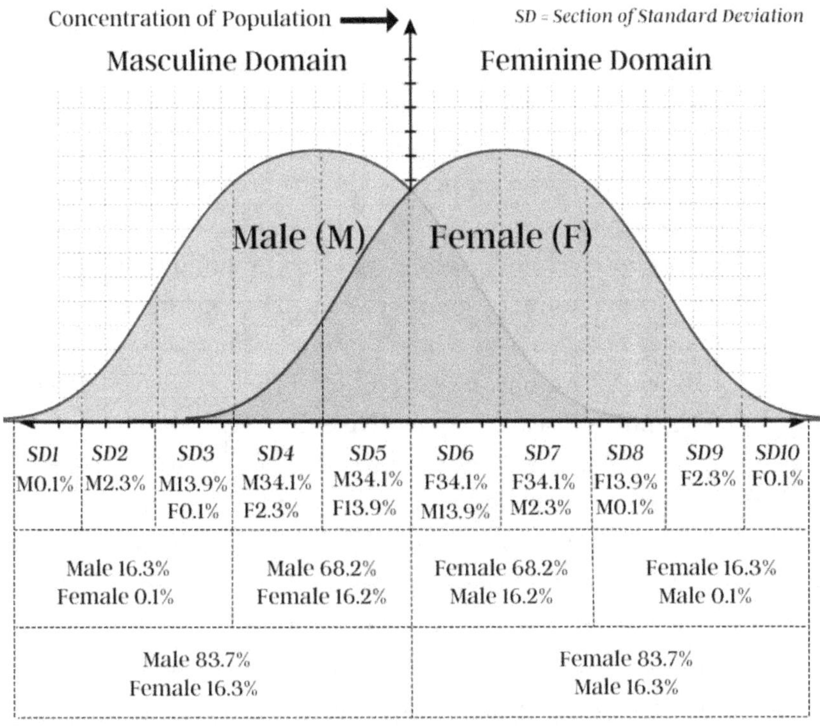

Figure 5: Theoretical Masculine-Feminine Distribution of Men and Women

If we choose to be at the extreme of either domain, we'll narrow our complementary options, making balance unlikely and challenging. Choosing to embody the opposite sex's domain slims our pickings even more, and may put us in danger of unhinging the teeter-totter.

But we'll leave the teeter-totter for now. Let's head to the market.

Sexual Economics Theory

I suppose you could say almost every theory possesses an element of transaction. Some theories, however, are *based* on transaction, and one of those is sexual economics. Sexual economics is the second of the two main old-world theories of mate selection, and it's the most stigmatized yet most instinctual of them all.

It's founded in evolutionary psychology, and is the origin of comments like, "*Men only care about one thing...*" and the grounds people use to objectify women—something not exclusively done by men. It represents a marketplace economy in which women are sellers and men are buyers.

By existing, women offer access to beauty, sex, and reproduction. Women can leverage their beauty and sexuality for far more than finding a mate. They can cause men to jump through hoops, fumble their words, buy ridiculous things, and offer their resources. Modeling, pornography, or sexual content like *OnlyFans* can be directly exchanged for money. They can even use their beauty to evade consequences such as speeding tickets.

Men essentially carry zero value by default. But with consistent hard work or inheritance, men can gain access to resources that they can offer in *exchange* for sexual access with women.

If a man wants to see some skin, perhaps some frisky shoulder, he might take her out to a fancy restaurant. Maybe if he wants a kiss, he'll have to be polite, open doors for her, and help her get seated. Or if he wants to be the only one with exclusive access to her in a relationship, he probably has to invest more emotionally and financially. Then, if he wants to have sex and make a baby with her, maybe he has to get her a special rock welded onto a circle of metal, put on an elaborate public ceremony, provide housing, food, and share anything else he has. Just an idea.

As buyers, men typically gain buying power with time. Their wealth and resources accumulate, and they acquire skills that increase their ability to collect resources. Hence, their mating marketplace value appreciates. It's like musical artist Russ writes: "I know I'm fine, but the money makes me handsomer... I'm 5'6", but the money make me 6'5"."

As males aim to accumulate resources, they leverage their birth-given advantages, such as strength or intelligence, to compete with one another for better access to resources. On rare occasions, this competition manifests as pride-filled, literal physical confrontation, with puffed-up chests, "You wanna go?!"s, and bar brawls.

Most of the time, it's more a matter of, "You want to get hired for this extremely physically demanding job? You need to be brawnier and taller than the average Joe. Want to get a raise? Increase your market value by getting a degree. Want to apply to a school to get a degree? Get good grades and score high on this standardized test. Want to get a specific job at this corporation after finishing your degree? You need to be at the top of your class." The list of examples goes on. We're all familiar with the competition for resources since it's not just men competing anymore.

Nevertheless, having more resources means better shelter, higher-quality food, greater autonomy over our schedules, more opportunities, access to superior healthcare, and better overall health. All those things represent a life of vitality, security, and safety. In those respects, the more extravagant a life a man can offer, the more women he'll be eligible to negotiate with. But given how difficult it is to accumulate resources, males may very well be invisible to females and not reach their prime mating negotiation years until they're 38-45 years old.

As for women, the sellers, their sexual marketplace value depreciates with time. Their beauty fades, they become less fertile with age, and new sellers enter the market. The prime years of their sexual-economic negotiation start when they reach complete biological sexual maturity, peak fertility, and bodily development, which is typically around 17-21 years old, and last until about 26-32.

It's somewhat subjective, and it depends on the woman, but for simplicity's sake, we'll say that from 17 to 32 years old, women have the most leverage to exchange their beauty for resources. Outside of that 15-year span, it's exceptionally unlikely that women will be in *high* mating demand because there'll be other women in their prime window for men to negotiate with.

Similar to men, women experience mating competition among themselves. The photos women take and publicize—their outfits and makeup—it's ultimately meant to attract and maintain men's resources. They don't prioritize beauty routines to impress other women in a friendly way. It's not "for the girls." No, women's subconscious motive for cosmetic enhancement is to compete with each other's desirability.

More beautiful women get more attention from men, and thus more access to men with greater resources. Competition in beauty is how women let each other know where they stand in the pecking order. No woman wants to be the most unattractive one in the room because that means she'll most likely be the poorest, most prone to bad health, most stressed out, most limited in life experience, and have the lowest chances of having a family.

At the same time, there's a limit to this competition. Women are subconsciously driven to slut-shame, gossip about, criticize, and alienate sexy women, mainly because they lower the marketplace value of their sex's primary negotiation power and leverage: *their beauty and sex appeal.*

When a woman dresses provocatively, that means other women will have to behave similarly to compete for men's attention, and then maybe men don't have to wine-and-dine them to see some frisky shoulder action. Or maybe they don't need to be kind or emotionally invested to see some titties—they just need a $12 subscription. Or perhaps, since some women have sex on the first date, other women might be worried they'll come across as selfish, prudish, or boring if they don't have sex. Hence, to keep each other in line and preserve leverage, women employ tactics such as shame, criticism, and exclusion.

Startlingly gorgeous women can be unfortunate victims of this female social behavior without even dressing sexily or revealing their bodies. They might even *try to opt out of the competition* with baggy sweatshirts and no makeup. Still, if they're attractive enough, other women put them down just to level out the disproportionate amount of attention they receive.[x]

In a nutshell, women must walk an *incredibly* fine line of indirectly competing in the desirability hierarchy by being beautiful but not *so* attractive as to give away negotiation power or alienate themselves from other women. While the life of a woman is complicated in many respects, it's especially challenging here.

This theory absolutely opposes any empowerment hypothesis of women sexualizing themselves because it actually *hands over* negotiation power to men. Men don't have to give as much to receive specific degrees of sexual access. If that other girl is empowering herself by having leisurely sex, asking for nothing in return, why should a man fulfill any prerequisite another woman has? If he can get sex for free somewhere else, why would he pay for it here?

Females handing out sex freely is significantly destructive for both men and women. It pressures other women in the marketplace to give more for less in return, and the hearts of all men deteriorate as they see poorly intentioned, exploitative men get rewarded. It makes *everyone* worse negotiators.

As one tries to incorporate this theory into their philosophy of romance and love, of course, not everything about mate selection hinges on age, beauty, and resources. Still, it's important to realize that these *are* instinctive human interests *everyone* considers to some extent.

There's a reason no one wants to be picked last on a team at recess, be the ugly duckling, or ride a rusty bike when everyone else is driving a nice shiny car. We simply understand what it means and what it's like to be desired or unwanted.

Is that fair? There's this story in the Bible about a widow named Ruth. Her husband, her sister-in-law's husband, and her mother-in-law's husband all died around the same time. *Sketchy.* But Ruth loved her mother-in-law, Naomi, so much that she swore to stay by her side and even serve her God, the God of the Hebrews. Since Naomi was also a widow, she couldn't provide for Ruth. So, she encouraged Ruth to capture the attention of a man named Boaz.

Boaz was a kind and generous man. Also, a *wealthy* man. Long story short, Ruth worked some of her ol'-reliable feminine magic and appeared at Boaz's feet in the dead of night while he was sleeping. After overcoming several obstacles, they eventually married and had children. They're actually ancestors of Jesus.

In the Christian community, Boaz is a baller. Women tell their jokes about wanting to find their Boaz but rejecting his terrible relatives: Broke-az, Dumb-az, Lazy-az, Short-az, Good-for-nothing-az, etc. Do men want to be rejected solely based on factors like their socioeconomic status or height? Probably not. Is it shallow? Maybe. Is it fair? Maybe not.

Do women want to be rejected solely because of their age and what they look like? Probably not. Is it shallow? Maybe. Is it fair? Maybe not. But almost everyone respects women's standards, and for good reason. Since women have traditionally taken a larger role in raising children, they have needed a supportive Has-himself-together-az—not an adult child who *adds* to their parental load. People have a harder time accepting men's preferences.

Regardless of which side of the sexual marketplace we're on, it's not productive for men and women to judge or look down on each other for what they instinctively desire. It's also unproductive for us to pout about the opposite sex not wanting to exchange with us when we're not trying to fulfill what they desire. And just because others think and want differently from us doesn't always mean they're wrong or that they should change. Sometimes, it just is what it is.

Can men resist the appeal of a young, beautiful woman? Sure. Can women detach themselves from wanting a tall, resourceful man? Maybe. These baseline desires aren't everything, and human attachment to them *isn't* all-enduring.

The roles can also be reversed because standards of desire aren't exclusive to either men or women. Women can have resources and attract men, and men can wield beauty to attract women. On *average*, though, men's social desirability and attractiveness largely depend on the resources and status they possess, while women's social desirability and attractiveness are primarily driven by their physical beauty.

The satisfaction of each sex's instinctual interests necessitates that partners entirely submit their negotiation power to one another. Giving up the power of resources is men's main submissive task, though they also give up their sexual appeal. Giving up the power of beauty is women's primary submissive task, though they also give up their resources.

Both submissions eliminate sexual economic participation and secure the enclosure of their relationship. Why look for a woman if you have no resources to offer? They were given to another. Why look for a man if you have no beauty to offer? It was given to another.

I imagine that part of the engineering behind the biblical covenant of marriage was to mitigate the risk involved in handing over sexual economic power. Instead of being exposed to the risk of someone stealing power they were given, they were *legally and personally* responsible for the power they inherited.

A woman couldn't just leave a man and take his resources. She'd also be terribly mistaken to splurge and waste her man's resources because those resources were now also hers. A man couldn't have sex outside of marriage and take advantage of a woman's beauty without putting all his power on the table. He was responsible for cherishing, caring for, and preserving the beauty that was now his. Talk about incentives to work and thrive together as a unit!

This theory urges us to be cautious in situations and relationships where power submission isn't mutual. Those who don't share or give power only take it. They'll be a leech on our well-being, tax our patience and sanity, and leave us drained rather than enrich our lives.

Perhaps this concept of mutual power submission is why we cast more shame, disgust, and neglect upon unsuccessful men. We view them as having squandered the potential and time they could've turned into valuable resources. This is especially relevant today because genetics no longer determines the bulk of productivity and economic potential.

A man who trades his time and energy for nothing is of little market value because he's already dedicated himself to something other than providing security for a woman. Maybe instead of gaining valuable skills, becoming more educated, and working more hours, he stares at a screen. He violates the most fundamental exchange of power between men and women.

Similarly, perhaps this concept is why we cast more shame and judgment on promiscuous women. We see women as having carelessly given away their highly valued power of beauty, thereby defacing an experience men find to be a most sacred privilege. A woman who gives her beauty to many men is an unreliable, temporary, and divided source of motivation, enjoyment, love, and energy. She violates the most fundamental exchange of power between men and women.

Cheating also violates this exchange. A cheating man relinquishes whatever security and resources he promised and gives them to another. He disrespects her beauty, integral to her identity, and tells her it's not worth the exchange. Likewise, a cheating woman robs a man of resources and gives the source of energy, purpose, and motivation to another. In both cases, cheating feels like the theft of life itself, making the severity and pain of disloyalty obvious.

To close, we'll outline what it means to be a good sexual-economic negotiator and how to gauge a good deal. Men who negotiate well accumulate skills and resources and manage them wisely. They recognize that the promiscuous, self-centered, and heavy-resource-needing woman is the path to ruin since she'll seek attention and resources long after any man gives her all of his. She'll constantly be looking for better deals.

A woman negotiating well looks like a reasonably modest woman. She requires significant personal and emotional investment before engaging in higher degrees of physical intimacy. The intelligent woman recognizes that men who impulsively offer or flaunt their resources to gain sexual access are reckless, have an expiration date on their interest and commitment, and are poor stewards of their resources.

The best negotiators know that *if the other party manages their assets poorly, they will manage and guard ours poorly as well*. So, gauging a good deal requires considering how our partners value us and how well they help us steward our assets. When a woman helps a man to be more than he is, supports his goals, respects him by not causing unnecessary stress, makes his life easier, and takes pleasure in satisfying his desires, that's a great deal.

While those are *also* good and applicable indicators for women, women should look for *generosity*. Generosity is giving *beyond* expectations, anticipating nothing in return. Giving without the need for compensation implies confidence, a life-giving nature, and a reassurance that there's plenty to offer. She knows she'll be safe and provided for.

Offering women compliments and not expecting reciprocated interest is generous. Telling a woman she doesn't have to go down on him, but he'd like to go down on her, is generous. Cleaning the home without mentioning it and putting her needs before his own is generous. Besides safety and resources, if she feels cherished and lovingly poured into, she'll know she got a great deal.

Overall, if both partners feel they received more than they bargained for, they negotiated a stellar deal.

Complementary Theory

There's an element of complementation in almost every mate-selection theory. Masculine-feminine theory would technically fall under this category if I didn't have so much to say about it. The complementary perspective essentially proposes that people's compatibility is determined by how their personalities fit together like puzzle pieces. By personality, I mean personality types as summarized in tests like the Myers-Briggs and the Big Five, as well as in astrology.

The Myers-Briggs measures four scales of how people (1) gain energy, (2) learn, (3) make decisions, and (4) organize life. Each scale has two traits.

Regarding the first scale, *extroverted* people get their energy from the outside world and other people. *Introverted* people recharge by being alone and in their heads. On the learning scale, *sensing* people process things in a linear, step-by-step manner. They use their logical senses to gather facts and derive their learning. *Intuitive* people pick up on the unspoken patterns of life, and their gut stores those lessons.

In decision-making, *thinking* people weigh the pros and cons. *Feeling* people decide by empathetically considering how others might be affected.

Lastly, *judging* individuals tend to use structures like lists and time-block schedules to organize their lives. They're planners who like to execute in advance. Then, we have *perceiving* people who highly value flexibility and freedom. They're spontaneous, take things as they come, decide impulsively, and can save to-do items for the last second.

Scales one and two suggest that *opposites,* or rather *complements,* are ideal for romantic compatibility. Introverts pair best with extroverts, and sensing individuals with intuitive ones. As for *similarities,* landing on the same area of the decision-making scale is beneficial. There seems to be no discernible pattern of compatibility for how we organize life—planning or spontaneous.

The Big Five personality test measures openness, conscientiousness, extroversion, agreeableness, and neuroticism, which conveniently form the acronym OCEAN. *Openness* encompasses an eagerness to learn, have new experiences, and be vividly creative and imaginative. People low in openness are non-spontaneous, poor problem-solvers, resistant to new experiences, and stubborn.

Conscientiousness entails being goal-oriented, responsible, and thoughtful of how one's own behavior affects others. People low in conscientiousness lack impulse control, disregard others' well-being, dislike schedules, procrastinate, and sometimes fail to complete tasks.

Extroversion, as we've already touched on, encompasses qualities such as outgoingness, emotional expressiveness, talkativeness, and a tendency to thrive in the spotlight. People low in extroversion are shy and prefer smaller groups or solitude.

Agreeableness involves being altruistic, trusting, affectionate, and kind. Agreeable people like to help, share, comfort, and empathize. People low in agreeableness are often socially unpleasant because they're typically conflict-prone and lack empathy and care for others.

Neuroticism is the inclination to sadness, emotional instability, anxiety, and moodiness, especially in response to perceived threats and stressors. Neurotic people experience mood swings, overthinking, irritability, and difficulty relaxing. People *low* in neuroticism are emotionally stable and resilient.

While men and women are more similar than they are different, women score higher on extroversion, agreeableness, and neuroticism. Men are more introverted, disagreeable, and less neurotic. They're more comfortable keeping to themselves, starting direct conflict, disregarding others' feelings, and being stoic.

For relationship compatibility, people should *match* their partner's *openness*. Conversation will flow more easily, interest in activities will better align, and worldviews will overlap more. Couples who are mismatched in openness experience one partner getting their way far more than the other, leaving one partner feeling held back or limited, which can lead to resentment.

Couples should also aim to *match* their partner's *conscientiousness*. Being a match supports smooth delegation of responsibilities and duties in a relationship. Mess and disorder will trouble couples equally. If they are too different in conscientiousness, they'll have difficulty understanding and accepting how the other delegates his or her time.

A *range of extroversion and introversion* can be helpful for couples. It helps them learn and grow from each other's approach to the world and enjoy their roles at social gatherings. However, having *too* wide a gap in this trait can be problematic because of differences in needs for socialization or isolation.

Significant mismatches in *agreeableness* lead partners to view each other as either too cold and harsh or too soft and naïve. *Fairly similar* scores allow couples to learn from each other's perspectives. Disagreeable partners can help their partners take better care of themselves and avoid being taken advantage of. Agreeable partners can help their partners establish rapport and be more understanding of others. A couple strategically leveraging each other's strengths will benefit their navigation toward their mutual goals.

Last, it's ideal for couples to *differ* slightly in *neuroticism*. Neurotic people are always on the lookout for threats, whereas less neurotic people stay calm. Both are beneficial in their own ways. Scoring too differently prevents partners from understanding each other. A low-scoring neurotic person views a high-scoring one as overly emotional and volatile. A high-scoring neurotic person views a low-scoring one as out of touch. That's the Big Five.

The last complementary theory we'll cover has recently experienced a surge in popularity. As of late, a whole 29%, nearly a third of Americans, believe in *astrology*.[xi] While different branches of astrology aim to explain various aspects of life, they're all based on the interpretation of celestial motion.

Natal astrology, the most well-known form of astrology, offers a blueprint for one's life purpose, strengths, and weaknesses based on their place and time of birth. Horary astrology functions as a future-predicting tool concerning specific questions and is home to tarot cards. Other branches reportedly predict world events and determine medical prognoses and treatments. We'll be reviewing *relationship astrology*, which is a subcategory of natal astrology.

Though it's foreign to some, finding meaning in the stars is an age-old human practice, and it's a fair one at that. We're just as much a part of the universe as the rest of the stars, and if there is discernible meaning here, why should the rest of it be excluded?

Human brains establish meaning by recognizing patterns. If I'm a kid at daycare and I keep smacking this other kid because he doesn't like *Pokémon,* and he keeps crying, that *probably* means he doesn't enjoy getting smacked. If Greg and Darnell both died from eating that purple berry, it *probably* means that the berry is poisonous and I shouldn't eat it. We're pattern recognition machines, and where there is pattern, we recognize meaning.

Therefore, it's only natural to interpret meaning from the patterns one sees in the mesmerizing night sky. Throughout history, many people and cultures have developed their own schools of astrology. The Greeks, Babylonians, Chinese, Hindus, Irish, Jews, Native Americans, Christians, and Muslims have all outlined their own versions.

With so many versions and schools of thought that originated at various times over thousands of years, one might be skeptical about whether one could know the correct version of astrology or if it adds up at all. Coming from a religious Christian worldview myself, I could also ask, how does one know which denomination of Christianity is correct? Or how does one know whose interpretation of the Bible or the Quran is accurate?

As for Christians, we all use the same book of truth for the most part, and yet we somehow emerge with significant tangible differences. So, just because not every subgroup shares the same interpretation of their guide of truth—in this case, the stars—doesn't mean they lack seeds of truth.

Now, I honestly don't know if all existing schools and practices of astrology overlap, but I'm summarizing relationship astrology under the assumption that they do. From square one, astrology prescribes meaning by interpreting patterns in (1) the constellations of stars within our Milky Way galaxy, (2) our solar system's planetary motion, (3) Earth's rotation, and (4) our moon's location.

While there are 88 constellations formally recognized by the International Astronomical Union, astrology uses the constellations marking out the path the sun takes throughout the year. Essentially, on the day people are born, Earth will have a specific constellation's plot across from it on the other side of the sun, which represents a person's sun sign. So, someone born on May 25 would have a Gemini sun sign, like in *Figure 6*.

Though there are technically *over* 12 constellations in the sun's path, the 12 zodiac signs of astrology each get a 30° plot of the 360° around the sun, 1/12th of the pie. This is regardless of the size of the constellations. It takes 38 days for the sun to pass through Taurus because it's so huge, but merely 5 days to pass through Scorpio. Each sign still gets a 30° plot and thus roughly a month out of the year.

The months of March and September host the two annual equinoxes. An equinox is when the Earth tilts enough for the sun's path in the sky to cross the Earth's equator, which separates the planet into two halves. As a result, the length of day and night everywhere in the world is about the same.

Equinoxes mark the beginning of the spring and fall seasons. Since spring represents renewal and revitalization with its blooming plant life and animal mating, the astrological calendar begins in March with Aries. Though equinox dates technically vary by a day or two each year, most astrology users typically use a static calendar for simplicity's sake.

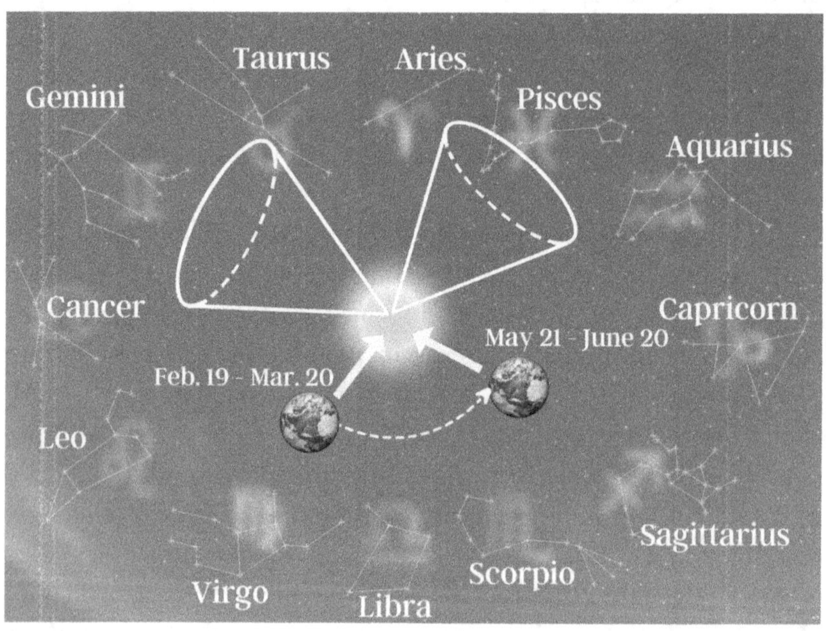

Figure 6: Sun Sign of Astrology

Sun signs help determine people's core identity and personality, but the rotation of the earth and the positions of the moon and planets at the time of birth also play a significant role. Hence, there are also moon, rising, and planetary signs.

Like the sun sign, whichever zodiac constellation is on the other side of the moon at the time of birth is the moon sign. Since it takes a month, or 30 days, for the moon to orbit the Earth and cycle through the 12 zodiacs, moon signs change about every 2.5 days.

Moon signs are supposed to determine how one deals with and expresses their emotions, longings, obsessions, and fears. They essentially describe the workings of one's inner world and how they bond with others.

Rising signs are a bit harder to describe astronomically, but they have a quick turnaround, changing every 2 hours, and are said to reveal how one projects oneself to the world and how others perceive them.

Planetary signs are equally as important to personality and behavior as are sun signs, but their details can pile up since there are so many of them, so I won't go into great detail. Astronomically, they work the same as sun and moon signs. They are located in a particular plot in the sky at one's time of birth and further diversify the zodiacs that affect and define them.

With the 11 components of (1) sun, (2) moon, (3) rising, (4) Mercury, (5) Venus, (6) Mars, (7) Jupiter, (8) Saturn, (9) Uranus, (10) Neptune, and (11) Pluto, all falling under the 12 zodiac signs, there are over 743,000,000,000 potential astrological combinations. In more advanced forms of astrology, that number can become exponentially larger.

Overall, sun, moon, rising, and planetary signs sum up the key aspects determining one's personality, character, and identity. Those aspects uniquely blend with those of others, which establishes the complementary system of relationship astrology.

As for how all this information came about and who assigned it to what zodiac plot, I haven't the foggiest. That's an inquiry for the ancients or people who've written entire books on it. The stars have told me nothing other than the fact that I will definitely, 100%

undoubtedly, for sure have a comeback hairline. That doesn't mean they haven't tried to tell me other things, I suppose.

Despite what doubt or skepticism one may have about this theory, I believe it's worth familiarizing oneself with. It can help us better understand others, step into their world, and meet them without judgment.

Zodiac Sign	Calendar Dates	Personality Description	Compatible With
Aries	*March 21 - April 19*	Independent, strong-willed, impulsive, argumentative, goal-driven, competitive, passionate, fearless, and energetic.	Leo, Sagittarius, Libra, Gemini, Aquarius
Taurus	*April 20 - May 20*	Grounded, hardworking, honest, laid-back, tenacious, loyal, persistent, sensual, patient, and stubborn.	Virgo, Capricorn, Cancer, Scorpio, Pisces
Gemini	*May 21 - June 20*	Social butterfly, witty, emotional, charming, curious, busy-minded, restless, excel in lauguage and communication, and carefree.	Aquarius, Libra, Aries, Leo, Sagittarius
Cancer	*June 21 - July 22*	Elite intuition, compassionate, sentimental, prioritize intimate relationships over other aspects in life, creative, giving, and nurturing.	Scorpio, Pisces, Virgo, Taurus, Capricorn
Leo	*July 23 - August 22*	Powerful presence, optimistic, intimidating, generous, inviting nature, action-taker, self-focused, high confidence, and charismatic.	Libra, Aries, Sagittarius, Leo, Gemini, Aquarius
Virgo	*August 23 - September 22*	Elegant, organized, poised, health-focused, analytical, value aesthetic, yearn for knowledge and intelligence, detail-focused, perfectionist.	Scorpio, Capricorn, Taurus, Cancer, Pisces
Libra	*September 23 - October 22*	Highly social, open-minded, romantic, easy to get along with, artistic, indecisive, good host, and prioritize intimate relationships.	Gemini, Aquarius, Leo, Sagittarius, Aries
Scorpio	*October 23 - November 21*	Value authenticity, spiritual, independent, power-seeker, guarded but soft to those who know them, mysterious, and fierce.	Cancer, Pisces, Taurus, Virgo, Capricorn
Sagittarius	*November 22 - December 21*	Brave, good leader, adventure seeker, free spirit, opt out of mainstream, unfiltered, philosopher, and entertainer.	Sagittarius, Aries, Leo, Gemini, Aquarius, Libra
Capricorn	*December 22 - January 19*	Independent, strong-willed, impulsive, argumentative, goal-driven, competitive, passionate, fearless, and energetic.	Capricorn, Virgo, Taurus, Cancer, Pisces, Scorpio
Aquarius	*January 20 - February 18*	Grounded, hardworking, honest, laid-back, tenacious, loyal, persistent, sensual, patient, and stubborn.	Aquarius, Gemini, Libra, Sagittarius, Aries, Leo
Pisces	*February 19 - March 20*	Social butterfly, witty, emotional, charming, curious, busy-minded, restless, excel in lauguage and communication, and carefree.	Cancer, Scorpio, Capricorn, Taurus, Virgo

Table 4: Natal Astrology Compatibility Chart

Astrology is only as cuckoo as its user wants it to be. Religions and their believers are no different. Astrologers who believe the future is written in the stars are no different from the Calvinists of Christianity, who believe everything is predetermined and that there's no free will. They merely use different books of truth to see the predetermined future and interpret the world.

Mainstream astrology users accept it as a framework that reveals people's nature while still allowing for nurture. The stars *do* have a say, but they don't determine everything because destiny is also influenced by choices and experiences.

To sunset this section, complementary theories lead romantic destinies to fit together like puzzle pieces. Some differences enhance couples' attraction, quality of life, and relationship longevity. Similarities also play a part in writing romantic destiny, however.

Let's see what story they tell.

Similarity Theory

Unlike the idea that people fit together like puzzle pieces and opposites attract, there's the idea that people overlap and attract those *similar* to them. Leading the charge here is the *mere exposure effect*. This phenomenon states that we develop a liking or disliking for things we're familiar with. So, as long as we don't grow to hate someone, this theory suggests that repeated exposure increases our likelihood of being attracted to them.

When we have to be around another person all the time, we'll subconsciously try to establish a peaceful atmosphere to get along and fit together because it's conducive to our well-being. Whereas bickering and stressful conflict wouldn't be. Hence, people who mesh and spend a lot of time together will eventually enjoy each other's company and can often develop some level of attraction.

We, humans, find deep comfort in what we're used to. If we have systems and they function okay and we're okay, it's a good idea not to mess with them. This is why, in psychology, it's widely acknowledged that the affection we received in our childhood can often be what we look for as adults. Even if the affection we received was twisted, restricted, or ultimately harmful, we *survived*.

Through this lens, the way our father ignored us is why we select someone whose attention is hard to get. Perhaps our nagging mother is why we ended up with a control freak. Or, on a positive note, a mother who hugged us all the time might attract us to an affectionate person. A father who always told us he was proud might endear us to those who compliment us.

A point of nuance, of course, is that psychology *also* recognizes that people have tendencies to pursue the *opposite* of their negative experiences to compensate for what they didn't have. Regardless, when we *do* look for partners with similar values, interests, worldviews, goals, and even appearances, we often seek to emulate the love from our childhood. *Similarities in mate selection are essentially pre-resolved conflicts and debates.*

Mate selection based on similarity is emphasized in those who highly value religion or other forms of tradition. One could think of religions and worldviews as stencils people use to trace their lives around. They come with preset values, goals, and life philosophies that people can base their decisions on. Hence, sharing the same worldview reduces the potential for conflict.

We don't need to be religious to benefit from similarity theory, though. Having similar interests will solve the problem of what to do when we spend time together. Shared goals will direct our focus and energy toward something we both care about. Similarities ensure *comfort* and *ease* in relationships because of the known nature they offer.

At the same time, we can also imagine *undesirable* things about similarity. Isolating ourselves in the known assures that we experience little novelty, adventure, challenge, and growth, which may trigger boredom and suffocate fulfillment. People who overly emphasize this theory can also end up with each other just because "it makes sense."

But true love is about a lot more than just "making sense." It comes through more than one theory and speaks more than one language. It may even speak five.

Love Languages

To summarize the reciprocal, affectionate, and altruistic ways humans interact and communicate with one another, Gary Chapman outlined five love languages. Those languages are: (1) words of affirmation, (2) quality time, (3) physical touch, (4) acts of service, and (5) receiving gifts. Knowing and speaking a partner's love languages is key to helping them feel valued, seen, appreciated, loved, and overall confident in their mate selection.

Words of affirmation look like positive verbal feedback, recognition, and assurance. Something like, "You look so beautiful, darling." Or maybe, "I'm not going anywhere. I'll be right here with you." And "You're doing better every day! I'm going to be amazed at what you'll be doing in a month!"

Affirmations stabilize and strengthen one's emotional state by altering one's reality for the better. If someone else thinks and says something positive about us, we either solidify the good we already see in ourselves or develop a more pleasant perspective of ourselves.

Those who speak this love language typically give great compliments, take time to recognize the good in others, offer helpful comments, and encourage those they share their words with. Since they speak the language, they find significant meaning in receiving words of affirmation themselves.

Quality time is the devotion of time and attention to others. It can be as low-key as watching a movie together or as energy-demanding as an intentional 5-hour conversation. As far as unintentional time goes, quality time could look like being in the same space doing different activities; one working on a project while wearing headphones and the other playing a game in the same room.

Mostly, though, sharing the *same line of focus* is the base ingredient in quality time. Hence, redirecting attention from the movie to one's phone, or staring off into the distance while they're talking, is unwelcome.

Individuals who speak this language enjoy doing activities together. The activity isn't as important as the time slot spent with the company. Since time is their currency of love, they feel neglectful when they're not able to give it to those they love. They also feel neglected, undervalued, and insignificant when they're not given time, since people typically make time for their priorities.

Physical touch is bodily contact. The small touches, like grazing a hand across your partner's back as you walk by, are essential to those with this language. Massages are like divinely written love letters to their bodies. Hugs are adrenaline shots to the soul. Cuddling is a comforting and recharging activity. Kisses are "I'm into you" reminders. Sex is the combination of all those things.

People with physical touch as their primary love language might give you a big ol' Southern hug as soon as they meet you. They communicate their presence through physical contact. Some people feel less alone when they're talked to or share space; physical touch people practice presence with others by holding their hand, rubbing their back, or placing a hand on their shoulder.

As you might assume, avoiding physical contact with these people makes them feel alone. So, if you want to speak love to a physical touch person, engaging in bodily contact will make them feel desired, important, comforted, and loved.

Acts of service are built upon the principle of giving away energy for the benefit of others. Every human activity and task in life requires energy. Laundry? Energy. Cooking? Energy. Home maintenance? Energy. Shopping? Energy. Sexual favors? Energy. It *all* requires energy.

Acts of service people aim to reduce the energy others have to spend, making their lives easier. They give energy, so others don't have to. People don't have to reorganize their closet, cook dinner, or vacuum their car if it's already done.

Energy is one of their highest values. So, when someone spends energy to make *their* life easier, they notice. They received a heap of energy they didn't have to expend themselves. Better yet is giving them energy they're not capable of delivering to themselves. They can't, for instance, give themselves a back rub. Giving energy is truly a service, and receiving it makes acts of service people feel loved, appreciated, and cared for.

Last, we have *receiving gifts*. Gifts physically embody the intentions, feelings, and love for and of others. Physical objects are tangible reminders of the love that was given to us. Hugs fade with memory, but objects stick around and take us back to the scenes where we received them.

Since those who speak this language feel loved, valued, and seen when they can hold and see a physical representation of someone's feelings for them, they will give gifts with the same purpose. They pack physical gifts full of meaning and sentimentality. That expensive rock is no longer just a rock. It's *obviously* a glimmering symbol of how you add stability, assurance, and beauty to their life and proclaims that they think you're a strong, responsible, and respectable individual. Pretty sweet rock, honestly.

Altogether, *love languages involve giving away our (1) words, (2) time, (3) space, (4) energy, and (5) objects.* Everyone speaks each language to a certain extent, but we usually have two or three primary ones. Thriving relationships understand each other's love languages and strive to speak them more thoroughly. Giving someone a rock while stiff-arming them when their primary love language is physical touch will devastate them. They'll feel unloved, and our intentions won't make it through.

Even if partners don't yet understand precisely what they're communicating, they do their best to adjust to their partner's needs and speak their languages. It may feel like speaking gibberish, but their partner will understand it as love. Partners meet each other where they're at by becoming aware of and learning their partner's native love languages.

The most effective negotiators in this theory are those who train themselves to speak *every* love language. This not only increases compatibility with more people but also empowers them to combine languages simultaneously.

A handmade piece of jewelry with a letter could be an example of combining love languages. It's a physical *gift* created through an *act of service*, paired with *physically* holding their hand as they spend *quality time* reading the letter full of *words of affirmation. All five languages, baby!*

In some ways, this theory is a hybrid of complements and similarities. For loving relationships to work, we must be able to communicate and receive love. That means sharing love languages in the long term. The differences, however, are also beneficial because they require us to grow our ability to love. As a result, we form a unit more effective at adding love, kindness, and light to the world.

We'll know we've found a winner when they're willing to learn our love languages and are patient and understanding of our differences. Those who are *unwilling* to grow in love languages reveal a lot about their potential as partners. They're prophecies of loveless relationships, adding nothing to the world.

Thank you, next!

Beauty-Personality Exchange

This mate-selection theory concerns the value exchange between beauty and personality in negotiation. These negotiations transpire almost entirely without our awareness—subconsciously. The two differing schools of thought giving rise to this subconscious theory are: (1) "There is *no* inverse relationship between beauty and personality," and (2) "There *is* an inverse relationship between beauty and personality." Let's explore these schools of thought and their influence on mating negotiation.

The first thought emerges from the union of the matching hypothesis and Berkson's paradox. The **matching hypothesis** states that *people of similar desirability and attractiveness tend to match together for long-term, healthy, and happy relationships.*[xii]

If there *is* a noticeable attractiveness gap, couples tend to be happier when the female is more attractive than the male.[xiii] Though that isn't to say women are into unattractive men. Rather, *slightly* less attractive men tend to compensate with "acts of kindness, sexual favors, or extra housework."[xiv] I mean, I'm not female, but I, too, get hot and bothered when I see housework get magically resolved.

Nevertheless, the fundamental reality is that even though we may gravitate toward people who are significantly more attractive than we are, we're far more likely to receive reciprocated interest and form a relationship with someone if they're closer to our level of attractiveness.[xv]

Berkson's paradox is a form of selection bias that leads to counterintuitive results. In dating, combining the matching hypothesis with Berkson's paradox creates the illusion that attractive people are crazier or more toxic, when research *counterintuitively* suggests the opposite: Beautiful people are *more* mentally stable and have *more* desirable personalities.[xvi] They may simply come across as more toxic in personal experience *because* of a mismatched degree of attractiveness with those who take romantic interest in them.

When there's a mismatch in beauty, the more attractive partner may not feel they need to put in as much effort to keep their partner. So, impressions of their personality may be poorer. Meanwhile, the less attractive partner compensates with personality and greater effort to match their partner's level of desirability.

This phenomenon makes it *seem* as if there's an inverse relationship between physical attractiveness and desirable personality traits. Meaning the more attractive someone is, the worse their personality will be. But in fact, if that more attractive partner broke up with their partner and dated someone even *more* beautiful than themselves, *they* would likely be the ones compensating with personality and effort while their partner put in less. So, there *is* evidence that the inverse relationship between beauty and good personality *doesn't* exist.

In this way, the matching hypothesis pulls two people of similar looks-based desirability together so that neither partner is significantly more attractive than the other, and neither is excessively compensating with personality or effort.

The second thought begs to differ. It claims there *is* an inverse relationship between beauty and personality. We'll call this perspective **Subconscious Social Desirability Engineering.**

When someone is beautiful, society automatically desires and glorifies them with little to no work on their part. The more beauty they have, the less they have to do to be socially desirable. The less beauty one has, well, something else that's desirable has to be offered. Fortunately, society also values personality traits such as intelligence, humor, brawn, bravery, cuteness, charisma, and kindness. These become a means to compete with physical beauty.

Requirements for social acceptance are written into our subconscious deeper than we realize. As kids, besides our parents teaching us social behavioral laws for acceptance, we subconsciously notice what people do and don't enjoy. Maybe we see that everyone wants to be around Geraldine Butler. It could be because she's the prettiest girl in school. Or perhaps, it's because she makes everyone laugh.

When we notice what people like and want—when we see what society demands—we subconsciously try to be the solution for that demand. Maybe we're not beautiful, but society *does* like funny people... so we crack jokes, refine them, provoke laughter, and accumulate reasons people might want us around.

Above all, those of us shaped by this perspective subconsciously know that if we want to be accepted and desired, we certainly cannot be unattractive *and* annoying. We must be enjoyable and desirable to *some* extent because being desired by society directly translates to how valued we are in the mating field and the quality and quantity of options we have.

This school of thought proposes that *society* engineers the characteristics and personalities we subconsciously develop, as social desirability depends on what we have to offer others. If it's not the gracefulness and arousing nature of beauty, it has to be something else that's in demand.

The lack of societal pressure on beautiful people and the incentive for non-beautiful people to develop personality give us room to imagine an inverse relationship between beauty and high-quality personality. Meaning, the more beautiful someone is, the less attractive their personality will be.

While these two schools of thought differ in semantics, they *both* fundamentally agree that personality *manifests* itself as a subconscious means of negotiating for beauty in a partner. And in their own ways, they describe how a diverse pool of mating candidates pair up and reach an equilibrium.

The reality is that beautiful people often have attractive personalities, and they frequently get together. Sometimes, conventionally unattractive people *really have* been forged by the flame and have the *best* personalities, allowing them to pair with people who seem totally out of their league. Other times, people have to intentionally compensate with effort to pair with a partner who is significantly more beautiful than they are. That attractiveness gap may not particularly incentivize their partner to behave and try their best, so they seem toxic.

All these scenarios and more exist, and there's no all-encompassing rule determining the exchange between beauty and personality. We can, however, confidently reiterate that *personality manifests as a subconscious means of negotiating for beauty.*

This theory's subconscious exchange of value is worth considering when seeking a partner who meets our personal standards of physical beauty and personality. If we're not able to attract a partner who meets the standards we want, it likely means we're not offering the level of desirable beauty or personality we *think* we have.

Since this theory operates almost entirely subconsciously, we may need to bring more awareness and intention to develop our personalities or improve our appearance to enhance the subconscious negotiation that occurs. Because when it comes to negotiating with the subconscious of other people and convincing them we have value, *there's a fine line between embodying confidence and appearing utterly delusional.*

As negotiators, if our persons of interest aren't subconsciously convinced we hold significant value as desirable mates, our first course of action *shouldn't* be to brand them as clueless or mistaken. Instead, our response should be to *fortify the things that do the subconscious convincing*. Meaning, if we want to match and stay with a highly desirable mate, we can increase our odds by putting *unyielding intentional effort* into both our appearance *and* personality.

Or we could let the odds ride as is, I suppose. Finding someone to be crazy about and love isn't everyone's greatest dream.

Independence Preference Spectrum

Oh, the dream of finding someone to spend the rest of our lives with. To cherish and to hold, to take on life together, to be lifelong best friends... not everyone has it. While finding a life partner is most people's desire, some yearn for relationships more than others. Some people are more independent, thrive on their own, and don't see themselves "settling down" until later in life, if at all.

The desire to be independent versus being in a relationship is a spectrum. At one end, one is entirely disinterested in being in a relationship and wants to spend most of their time free of emotional and relational ties. At the other end, one never wants to leave his or her partner's side. Both are extremes, and most healthy long-term relationships require a middle ground where partners can enjoyably spend most of their time together while also being comfortable and thriving in spaces and times without their partner.

That said, there's probably less than 0.5% of the population who prefer the extreme of being alone. Some people will be better off and live happier lives by remaining single for whatever reason. Their priorities and desires simply differ.

People are at different points on the spectrum, and it's important to recognize this because most partners won't be at the same point. One partner may prefer more independence, while the other aims to live more life together.

This theory says we've found a good match when we share similar desires for how to delegate our time together and apart. Let's look at yet another theory that tells us whether things add up.

Mathematical Theory

Humans have a 65-95-year window of time. Among those years are critical periods that hold the most power to determine the trajectory and outcome of one's entire life. Squander those years, and potential is lost forever.

Take, for example, a 22-year-old and a 27-year-old who start investing at the same time. They both invest $5,000 a year with a 10% annual return until they turn 60. When the 27-year-old turns 60, they'll have racked up $1.1 million. The 22-year-old, however, will have racked up $1.8 million by 60—a $700,000 difference. The potential life-transforming impact of $700,000 could be radical. However, once time is lost forever, we can never regain its usefulness.

This concept applies well to the finite time we have to form relationships. If we wait for the *perfect* relationship and refuse to settle or compromise, we could be single for decades. That's a grievous loss of time and potential. We could have built a meaningful life with someone, worked toward the alignment we initially wanted, and had companionship along the way.

But... what if a golden goose really *is* around the corner? Maybe we just need to keep looking, dating, waiting, or keep our options open! What if we're thinking about swapping our goose out with another goose we've been dreaming of?! How do we know what the right course of action is?

For those who believe in weighing decisions strategically and doing math for the best outcome, *the math has been done*. It's called *The Secretary Problem*. This calculation was first published in the *Scientific American* journal in 1960.

Picture this: You're the brand-new hiring manager for your organization, tasked with hiring a secretary. One hundred applicants are vying for the secretarial role, and you hope to find the best candidate possible. There are a few catches, however.

Once you interview and pass on a candidate, they're no longer invested in or hoping to work for your company, and they move on. Anyone you pass up, you cannot go back to recruit. And to state the obvious, once you hire someone, you don't interview the remaining applicants, so you'll never know if the best candidate was still down the line.

At what point do you stop interviewing candidates and hire someone? 20? 69? 80? The best candidate could very well have been applicant #14. They could just as well be applicant #89. So, how do you know when to stop interviewing, hire, and run the company as best as you can?

A couple of objectives lie in your path toward final hiring. Number one, you need to scope what's out there and learn what an excellent secretary is. You may *think* you know best, but there may be a secretary who'll set a whole new standard with their organization, welcoming presence, and professionalism. Without establishing that standard, you *can't* know whether you made a wise hiring decision.

Your second task is to hire at or above the standard. Mathematically, the second task should *start* with applicant #37. You've taken your time to see what's out there and have a good idea of what you should look for. The odds are you haven't come across the best candidate yet. If you only had 74 applicants, you'd be cutting it close, because you might have passed the best candidate in the first half. You might look back and wonder, *"What if?"*

However, starting your second task at #37 still leaves you with *most* of the candidates, meaning the likelihood of hiring at your standard is good. Chances are, you can find an equal or superior candidate in the following 37 applicants. For good measure, you leave 26 extra applicants as a safety net.

The prime years of dating and mating range from 18 to 40 years of age. This is the main window we humans can have children. It's when we feel our best, have the most energy to live life to the fullest, and have the beauty and hormones of our youth.

In this time frame, we're hiring a life partner and vetting candidates. We face the same tasks we did in the secretary problem. Our first task is to establish our standard for what it means to "hire" a stellar life partner, because we don't know exactly what we want or what's realistic without surveying the options. In dating, this first task is accomplished by having a set of *standards passed down* through *worldview, observation of others, personal dating experience,* or a combination of these.

When is it ideal to stop forming our standard? Taking the mathematical principle from the secretary problem, it'd be 37% through the "hiring" ages of 18-40, which is 26.1 years old. At 26, we have a good idea of what's out there and what's attainable for us. We know the kind of people who've applied to pair with us or entertained the idea. So, at that point, the logical course of action would be to pursue a life companionship with the *next or current* person who meets or exceeds our standards.

Given the odds of the situation and the finite time we have on this planet, passing them up is most likely just a waste of valuable years of increasingly fulfilling companionship. To make matters worse, people pair up over time, and there become fewer and fewer quality candidates to "interview." They enter relationships elsewhere.

So, there you have it, folks: a mathematical model of mate selection that calculates the ideal time to choose a partner. It models and explains how to identify who we want and can realistically partner with, and when it's wise to stop searching for someone better and commit to a relationship.

This theory is a practical way to silence what-ifs. The math shows that ideal relationships are made up of two people who exhaustively survey their options and choose to build something beautiful with their best possible pairing. They're also of the mindset that the sooner they start, the closer they'll get to that idealized soulmate status because lost time is lost potential. So, why not start at a mathematically ideal time?

Godspeed, and may the forces be with you.

External Forces

Some things will inevitably be beyond our control, which means there are varying degrees of credit to give external factors for their impact on our love stories.

The typical forces we credit are: (1) God's plan, (2) the law of attraction, (3) time itself, and (4) sheer chance. **God's plan** is precisely what it sounds like. It's when someone partially or fully credits a divine being for their romantic outcomes. The person may have a lot, some, or no power to affect how the divine plan unfolds.

Similarly, the **law of attraction's** magnitude of influence depends on who's using it. The fundamental philosophy of this law is that *positive thoughts manifest positive results* in one's life. Many practitioners of the theory use it in a positive psychology sense, in which positive thoughts lead to powerful, practical actions that move the party closer to the desired result.

Observe: "I'm going to marry a beautiful girl. Since I like beautiful girls, I think I'll become a photographer who helps models capture great photos for their portfolios... Wow! I just met this gorgeous model, and we get along really well! Thanks, law of attraction!"

More woo-woo users believe outcomes depend *solely* on cognitive belief, *regardless* of action. Want a billionaire husband? Easy. All you need to do is believe he wants you too, and he'll find you. You don't need to put yourself in places where you're more likely to meet a billionaire or exert any effort to attract and get him. If your desire doesn't come to fruition, however, it's simply because you didn't *believe* enough.

Next, we have **time itself.** In 2023, there was a TikTok trend in which women shared their grand awakenings to the reality that men get married when they're ready, *not* when they meet the right woman. It's not the woman; it's the *timing* that makes men commit to marriage.

While I was impressed by the sheer confidence required to reject any remote possibility that *they* could be the undesirable problem, there's certainly truth to their claim that timing is an essential detail.

Time holds all human experience. Experience shapes identity. People share identities during intimate conversations and interactions. Continuous intimacy depends on how well identities mesh together. This train of thought acknowledges that time is a significant factor in whether two people end up together.

If I had met my wife when I was 20, when I was fully ready and looking for a wife, she would've been 17—not only underage, but resistant to any intimacy or connection for another 6 years. I was also focused on finding a Seventh-day Adventist Christian woman at that time. Back-of-the-napkin math tells me we wouldn't have chosen each other. Time separates and brings people together. As for how much power it has, I suppose that's up for debate.

Finally, we have **sheer chance.** As a general rule of life, it's possible to do everything right and remain unrewarded because life offers no guarantees. We aren't promised a healthy, wealthy, and joyful life, and we're certainly not promised another day of it. *Murphey's law: Anything that can happen will happen*—best-case and worst-case scenarios included.

When sheer chance holds the power, the wisest course of action is to bend the probabilities in our favor and understand that's *all* we can do. Optimizing probabilities is one of this book's core tenets.

Whichever forces we believe in and to whatever degree we believe in them, it's crucial to consider how much power and influence we give them over the selection of our life partner. If commanding our own destiny is what we really want, we should reevaluate how much power and control we manually or voluntarily place in external forces.

Formulating Your Mate-Selection Strategy

The purpose of summarizing all these theories of mate selection is to highlight the various sets of rules we and others use to establish and maintain relationships. These sets of rules all exist and are active at the same time in the relationship world, even if we don't use, like, or believe in them. The rules of mating negotiation are up in the air, but we *can* track and make use of them.

This leads to an assortment of exchange dynamics, AKA partnership models, as all negotiators bring their own unique visions of what constitutes a meaningful, beneficial, and desirable romantic partnership.

What you're going to do now is something the life coaching industry calls an assessment wheel. But since this is my pony show, we're calling it an assessment pizza because, well, I like pizza. This pizza will expand your self-awareness by helping you visualize your unique mate-selection strategy. You use a unique combination of theories, and you see romance in a way that's certainly not shared by everyone. And while that's perfectly okay, understanding your personal strategy helps you identify those who speak your "languages" and direct your negotiation efforts accordingly.

On this pizza, you'll find that each slice represents a theory of mate selection. You're going to express how each theory resonates with you by shading in the slices on a scale of 1-10.

Where all the slice lines meet in the center, that's 1. The outside of the circle is 10. If a theory doesn't resonate with you at all, leave its slice blank. If a theory's principles perfectly align with how you think relationships and the world work, you'll fully shade that slice. If a theory resonates with how you feel and operate, but it's not a hill you'd die on or use as a primary compass in partnership, you'll shade it somewhere in between.

Feel free to copy the pizza onto a separate sheet of paper and shade it there for your personal convenience. Participating in this exercise is helpful because it captures and *illustrates* your philosophy of love. If you merely number the slices or imagine them in your head, the results will *remain abstract concepts*.

Upon finishing your assessment pizza, you'll find a mini coaching session with carefully curated questions. It's an opportunity for you to learn about yourself, identify areas of desired growth, and design specific actions to translate your learnings and desires into reality. In case it helps, I've provided summaries of each theory's philosophy. Shade away!

Mate-Selection Theory Summaries

- **Attachment Theory:** The quality, nature, and compatibility of the romantic attachments we form depend on the attachment styles we developed during childhood with our primary caregiver.
- **Masculine-Feminine Theory:** An archetypal theory that associates specific characteristics, traits, and "energies" with sexes based on behavioral tendencies and creation origin stories. Couples who strike a *collective* balance across all traits minimize conflict and promote a cohesive, effective partnership. Also provides a framework for what men and women can be.
- **Sexual Economics:** A marketplace dynamic based on evolutionary psychology where men provide resources and security to women in exchange for sexual access and reproduction. Results in men placing a higher preference on physical attractiveness and youthful fertility, while women place more emphasis on the resources men have and can preserve. Overall, the use of this theory is calibrated by how highly one values physical attractiveness and wealth.
- **Complementary Theory:** Differences can be beneficial and attractive, partners help each other grow, and ideal partnerships delegate roles and strengths to specific parties.
- **Similarity Theory:** Similarities are familiar and therefore comfortable, safe, endearing, and embody pre-solved conflicts.
- **Love Languages:** Partners seek those who can make them

feel seen, valued, and cherished by expressing love through words, time, space, energy, and tangible objects.

- **Beauty-Personality Exchange:** Desirable personality traits and relational effort manifest as subconscious means of negotiating for physical beauty.
- **Independence-Preference Spectrum:** A range of desiring to live life independent from a partner to sharing all of life's moments with a partner.
- **Mathematical Theory:** One can strategically utilize time and experience to optimize the probability of forming a high-quality relationship. At a critical point, lost time is lost potential for fulfillment and companionship.
- **External Forces:** Romantic relationships result from forces beyond our control.
- **Partner-Village Spectrum:** An honorable mention from *Chapter 1.* Family communities once divided various relational roles amongst themselves, i.e., sexual partner, sage, comedian, nurturer, protector, best friend, provider, etc. This spectrum ranges from outsourcing the majority of those roles among one's network to delegating all roles to a partner as "the whole package."

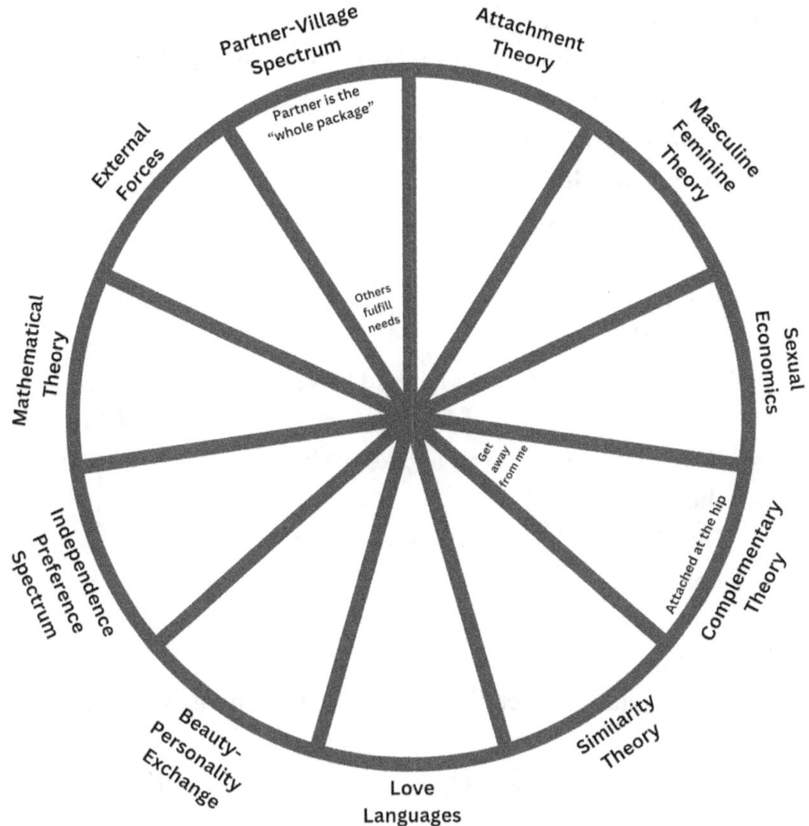

Figure 7: Personal Mate-Selection Strategy Assessment Pizza

MINI COACHING SESSION

Without rushing, thoughtfully pause after each question, and answer them in order. Forget about the drive to get through the sections and chapters of this book and focus on exploring your inner being. Let go of judgment and be curious!

- "What sort of themes or patterns do you notice in your pizza? Themes or patterns could be spiritual, intellectual, emotional, childhood-based, etc."
- "Which theory surprised you with how much it resonated with you? Why?"

- "Which theory do you think you're outgrowing?"
- "Which theories in your mate-selection strategy seem contradictory?"
- "What do you think the contradiction wants to teach you about yourself?"
- "What lesson do you think it wants to teach you about life?"
- "Which theory are you most proud of having in your personal strategy?"
- "Which theory do you wish had less power in your mind or strategy?"
- "Who do you need to be to take back that power and put it where you want?"
- "How is your chart inspiring you to grow? Phrase it as a goal."
- "If you could increase your belief in one theory, which would it be?"
- "How would you act differently if you increased it by one point?"
- "What resources can help you commit to acting that way?"

Now that we've finished identifying your unique mate-selection strategy, I'll unfold the fundamental philosophy that gives life to true love. Compatible mate-selection strategies help us achieve successful mating negotiations. They allow us to play by the same rules and form rewarding and fulfilling partnerships that help us build the lives we want. This philosophy allows us to take that success one step further and create true love.

Yes, dear reader, we're finally at the part where you can see the light radiating from the cracked lid of true love's treasure chest.

Time to look inside.

4

THE LOVE HERO'S NARRATIVE

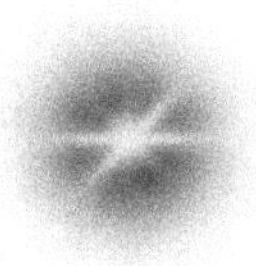

My dear, whatever one can have, I'll have with you,
However one can move, I'll move toward you,
Whatever one can be, I'll be for you,
However one can see, I'll see you,
Whatever one can give, I'll give you,
However one can live, I'll live with you,
Whatever one can believe, I'll believe in you,
Because, however one can love, my darling, I'll truly
    love you.

The most spectacular thing I'd ever seen was sitting just one table away from me in the university cafeteria. Crystal blue eyes, freckles sprinkled on her cheeks, the most adorable nose, and hair that looked like summer. I'd genuinely never seen such a beautiful woman before. Resisting double-takes took serious effort.

Long after laying eyes on her, her beauty stirred something mysterious in me. Girls had made my hormones run circles before, but this was *completely* different. Weeks went by and, for reasons I couldn't explain, she was making her way further into my heart;

making a home, warming it, setting up a few decorations—joy, happiness, fear, doubt, and hope, and settling in.

Every time I happened upon her in passing, I saw everything good in the world. I remember one day she passed me in a hallway after class. A phone pressed against her ear and something compelled her to let out a spurt of laughter. A delightfully surprised smile barged its way onto my face because that was the first time I'd ever heard laughter that sounded like music.

At a certain point, I became so lovesick and plagued with sleepless nights that I prayed not to run into her anymore. Feeling so deeply for someone I didn't even know seemed ridiculous to me. I didn't want the feelings I had for her.

Then, like an answer to prayer, days passed without seeing her, and eventually those days turned into months. Unbeknownst to me, she'd left the university. Yet despite her absence all that time, I failed to feel the relief I longed for. Instead, sadness and darkness followed me. In the midst of torturous feelings, apparently, she granted me illogical joy and inspiration that made all the heartache worthwhile.

That darkness lasted until a wave of awe crashed over me on a random winter day. I made my usual strides along the pavers that led to the cafeteria. Then, like seeing an angelic mirage through two sets of glass doors, she skipped down the stairs in slow motion—hair floating, fans blowing, studio lighting, and all.

In suppressed shock and disbelief, my hand reached for the door to open it for her. She could have been alone for all the attention I paid the world around her. Walking through the doorway, she said, "Thank you," and I responded with a broken, "Mhm." My voice might as well have cracked. Those were the first "words" we ever said to each other.

My spark came back, and the freefall into love with someone I didn't truly know resumed. It was the purest unconditional love I had ever known. Though she was gorgeously attractive, I had no desire to look at or think about her sexually. She was truly special in my mind, and somehow, someway, she made me look for and see the God of love and goodness everywhere. Perhaps that's what made her beauty captivating—*God*.

Regardless, my love had to remain unspoken and unrequited because of one unchanging obstacle: *a boyfriend*. If there was any way I was going to end up with her, only God Himself could make it happen. I not only could never imagine a man letting her go, but I felt undeserving of her—she felt too far out of reach. And since God seemed central to her life, He seemed like the only way to her heart. So, I chased this God and aspired to His character of love for her. Along the way, I fell in love with His character and with who He was shaping me into.

This girl stayed in my heart for over a year, and at some point, my miserable, love-bottled, and frustrated heart had to ask the only sensible question: "Why is it possible to be so 'in love' with someone I had only ever mumbled, 'Mhm' to?" And while I don't have the page count or the attention span to tell you the whole story of how the guy *didn't* get the girl, I *can* tell you the answer to that question. It made the whole heartache fiasco worth it.

The answer is that it introduced me to a narrative where I was always meant to become love in its entirety. Of course, since romance is one aspect of love, part of my destiny was to be in love with some-one, even if I didn't know her yet.

Skirting ever closer to embodying the epitome of love until the day we met was love expressed—*free* from a bottle. It was a statement that neither time nor space could separate me from loving her. My love story with her could begin by becoming a better man and growing my ability to love. I could love her by becoming love itself.

I suppose the only glaring question left to ask is, "What *is* love exactly?"

What Love Is Exactly

When we are 6, we might think of love as a fantastical, magical spell that consumes us. Not a bad take, honestly. At 17, we might think of love as whatever the drama compels us to do or whatever our bodies orchestrate within us. Living at an optimistic 24, we might think love is college-educated, aesthetically attractive, focused, and of a certain height. Reaching 30, we might think love is something responsible that won't divide our assets in half, but will make our lives easier, share the same life goals, and could raise wonderful children.

All the while, we can look back at previous chapters of our lives, shake our heads, laugh, and judge ourselves for our past naivety of love. But who's to say we're right? Who's to say *now* we know what love is? If it changed in the last 5 years, who's to say we won't know the "real" definition of love in another 5 years? Is love in its own time still love even though we grow up and change our definition? If so, does that mean all definitions of love can be true?

If an individual can have several definitions of love throughout their lifetime, it's certain there are plenty of definitions floating around in the space of romantic relationships. There's good reason for that: *They all hold a sense of truth*. To fully grasp what I'm getting at, let's look at two well-constructed theories of love.

The **triangular theory of love**, put forth by psychologist Robert Sternberg, builds all forms of love from three basic elements: intimacy, passion, and commitment. *Intimacy* represents feelings of closeness, connection, and deep bonding. *Passion* entails physical attraction and genetic chemistry, throttling sexual desire. *Commitment* is the decision to focus attention and energy on another party for an indefinite period of time.

Using unique combinations of the three basic elements, Sternberg distinguished seven types of love: (1) liking/friendship, (2) infatuation, (3) empty love, (4) fatuous or foolish love, (5) companionate love, (6) romantic love, and (7) consummate love.

Friendship needs scant explanation—it's feeling casually close to someone. It doesn't involve sexual attraction or lifelong commitment. Closest to friendship is *companionate love,* which is feeling close to someone and committing to them as a priority. It's the state of being a lifelong companion. Family would be an example of companionate love, as we feel close to them and don't typically cut off healthy ties.

Infatuation is a feeling of passion, attraction, or obsession towards someone without connection or commitment from either party. *Empty love* is going through the motions of a connection and commitment, but neither party feels close or passionate towards the other.

Fatuous love, also known as foolish love, is a matter of committing to someone and being passionate with them, but receiving *no* warm, intimate connection, as if to face a stone-cold wall. There's no long-term satisfaction, and it can make us feel alone even when we're around the other person.

Romantic love is the fiery drug we feel at the beginning of new sparks of romance. We feel close to them, fascinated by our rapidly developing feelings, and find them sexually desirable. It's possible to have both these things, however, *without* commitment.

Finally, *consummate love* is the union of all three elements. There's long-term, focused energy dedicated to one another, as well as sexual attraction, closeness, and the blossoming of well-being and overall satisfaction. Ideally, this is the type of love one would select if they were to invest themselves in a marriage or long-term relationship.

Types of Love	Intimacy	Passion	Commitment
Friendship	✓		
Infatuation		✓	
Empty			✓
Romantic	✓	✓	
Companionate	✓		✓
Fatuous		✓	✓
Consummate	✓	✓	✓

Table 5: Triangular Theory of Love

The second theory I'll share with you is the **color wheel theory of love** by psychologist John Alan Lee. Like colors, Lee proposes there are three primary elements. In color theory, the three primary colors are red, blue, and yellow. They mix to make secondary colors like purple, green, and orange, which then combine with other colors to create tertiary colors.

The three primary elements in this theory of love are eros, ludus, and storge. Mix them, and you can make secondary and tertiary types of love.

In Greek mythology, Eros, the god of love, was the son of Aphrodite, the goddess of beauty, fertility, and love. The Greek word *eros* embodies the powerful romantic element of love, in which lust, physical attraction, instinctual drive, and risk-taking arise.

Ludus is a Latin term that encompasses the elements of game, play, and sport. This type of love typically focuses on laughter and flirtation without attachment to a particular outcome and isn't necessarily in pursuit of long-term commitment.

Storge is the Greek term for the natural love shared between family. Highlighted themes are parent-child relationships, tender love, and cherishing one another.

When Lee combines eros and storge, the result is *agape*, a Greek term for benevolence and unconditional goodwill. Theoretically, you could keep on combining primary and secondary loves to make as many types of love as there are colors. But I won't go into further combinations for our attention spans' sake.

These two frameworks of love help us conceptualize how all definitions of love can coexist and hold some truth at the same time. **Love** is ultimately *the collection of all potential means for benevolent connection*. Each definition of love is a valid piece of the puzzle, even if incomplete on its own. Depending on which pieces we have, our puzzles will look different, and depending on which colors we mix, our color of love will vary.

Connecting this to *Chapter 3*, within each color or puzzle-piece combination, lie different theories of mate selection. For example, if lust and instinctual drive construct our definition of love, we'll prefer transactional theories like sexual economics or mathematical theory. Those theories clearly commodify and give tradable value to time, beauty, and sexuality—indulgence of eros.

If our primary definition of love is derived from the intimacy element of triangular theory, we'll opt for mate-selection theories such as complementary theory, similarity theory, and love languages. To be close, we'd want to recognize and deeply value what we both offer, enjoy each other's company, complement each other like puzzle pieces, and prioritize communicating love effectively.

Or perhaps our definition of love is mainly storge. We'd select mates using theories such as love languages, attachment theory, external forces, and masculine-feminine theory. Since we'd see love through a family-oriented lens, we'd search for the love languages we share with our families, work from the attachments we formed with them, highly value the external force that is our family's opinion on our relationship, and work to distribute the functional roles in our relationship.

Since mate-selection theories are at the mercy of definitions of love, definitions exert massive control over the form our lives take. If a man highly aligns with eros and therefore sexual economics, it alters his entire career disposition and personality development. He'll choose careers and personality traits that help him compete and succeed to earn more money because it's what he needs to attract his strongest desire: an attractive woman.

The significance of our definitions of love cannot be overstated. Which, of course, begs the question: "How *do* each of us get our definitions of love?"

How Definitions of Love Develop

Though it may not be particularly shocking, we develop our definitions of love through *experience.* Whatever love life itself shows us is what we'll believe love to be. Writing how we get our definitions as a simple rule: *We can only love to the degree to which we've been loved.* This is why we have sayings like "Hurt people hurt people." It means people who've received poor treatment treat others poorly. Love would also have its own rendition of this saying: "Loved people love people." One can only give what one has received.

Let's explore what learning love through experience looks like in the mysterious example of *parental love*. The love a parent has for their child is a love I'm looking forward to knowing just days before this book is published. Healthy parents say that they never could have imagined what it would be like to love their child. It's *always* beyond their prior comprehension. Only when one has a child can one understand a parent's love.

But who loved the parents so they could learn the love of a parent? Was it the newborn infant? Was it God? The universe? How about hereditary instinct? Who or what was it that found inexperienced people and called them worthy of receiving such a responsibility over an innocent and helpless living being? Who would love the parents so much that they would know they should die for their child without a second thought?

To receive a child is to be loved by the most sacred and encompassing power in existence—*whatever it is*. This act of love hands over the reins to life itself. That which gives and holds life in itself shares the responsibility to give and hold life. As the universe, with all its contents and time, shapes the child, so do the parents. Just as God has the child's destiny in His hands, so do the parents.

Parents are brought into the most sacred "Being" in existence, taken into the very identity of that which knows no greater thing, and fully experience what it means to be loved by and one with it. Let's decrypt that.

The Golden Rule is a concept Jesus taught. Matthew 7:12 contains the saying, "Do unto others as you would have them do unto you." Matthew 22:39 is home to, "Thou shalt love thy neighbor as thyself." I believe the latter is overlooked because it's usually understood in light of Matthew 7:12. People typically interpret it as "Love others as you love yourself."

But there is only *one* occurrence of the word "love." It's simply "... as yourself." I believe a more accurate interpretation is "Love others *as if they were you.*" Meaning others are an *extension* of us, *not* entirely separate beings. There's no them, there's only *we*. We're supposed to ask, "How would I love them if, when I looked into their eyes, *I saw myself?*"

The Greek word for love in this text is *agape*, which refers to selfless, unconditional love. So, while the English translation of Matthew 22:39 syntactically encourages the sharing of identity, the Greek word used for love *also* conveys a riddance of exclusive identity. Where there's less of a concept of self, there's room to share identity.

Parents receive this unconditional, selfless love from God or the universe; the creation of life, once a privilege reserved only for them, is now shared with the parents. The parents are now responsible for giving as much life, love, and well-being as they can. They now have the power to give and take away—to scar, judge, punish, protect, suffocate, nurture, imprison, and even the power to end life because it's so fragile. From a child's perspective, parents are effectively gods.

As healthy parents learn what it means to be "agaped" by and brought into sharing an identity with God or the universe—you pick —parents *also* learn to love like them. They learn the upper limits of selfless love in sharing identity. Parents often say, "Having kids is like having your heart running around outside your chest."

Indeed, the most sacred "Being" in existence loved those parents, and now they love just as they were loved—even if they didn't know where that love came from. The same goes for *any* love we know. If we know how to love a certain way— somehow, someway, maybe even vicariously—we've experienced receiving it.

The reason we may not know where a certain capacity to love comes from is that *seeing* and *conceptualizing* love, and all its definitions, is *not* the same as *experiencing* and *knowing it*. You can watch someone ride a bike, but when you sit on a bicycle and try to pedal for the first time, you realize you've learned and know, essentially, nothing.

That's because *conceptualizing application doesn't equal ability of application*. Through eyes and ears, we *conceptualize* love; by heart and spirit, we *know* it. When someone loves us heart to heart, they take us on a bike ride and hold us upright. We may have seen it with our eyes before, but *experiencing* it changes everything, and practice is still necessary if we want to love others as we have been loved.

And the bottom line remains: *We can only love to the degree we have been loved.*

Sources and Narratives

Considering that our definitions of love are formed by the love we receive, a bigger realization awaits on the horizon. Since *being* loved shapes our definitions, which in turn determine our mate-selection theories, there's a direct chain of causation going from our sources of love to the relationships or matches we negotiate to establish.

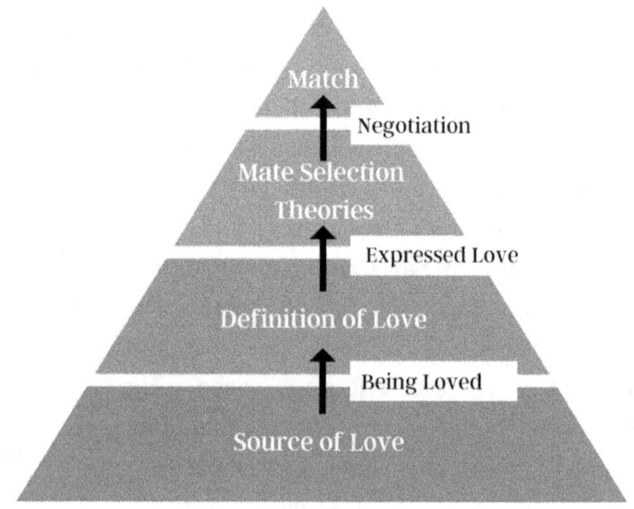

Figure 8: Love's Chain of Causation

Since we can't know or express love in ways we haven't been touched by, our *sources of love are ultimately responsible for the love we express.* Or in other words, sources of love serve as *reasons* to love, and being loved is one's *cause* to love.

Yet another way to frame *Love's Chain of Causation* is to call it a **narrative.** Since we can clearly outline how sources of love determine our matches, we can say that *sources narrate our love stories.* Every source of love has a corresponding romantic outcome and will continue to produce a specific love story until we select a new source and root cause.

For example, if our horny, downright randy biology is our primary source of love—our *reason* to love and seek relationships—love stories will burn out in a matter of months. The definition of love biology produces is based on feelings, emotions, and urges controlled by physical attraction. Those things alone aren't a reliable fuel source for relationship longevity or fulfillment.

The average honeymoon phase, when relationships run on the cocaine-like fuel of intoxicating attraction, partner-can-do-no-wrong vibes, and starry eyes, lasts 3 to 24 months. Having a feeling source of love dooms an individual to restart their love story every several months. The narrative of euphoric highs igniting and burning out periodically will repeat itself.

Or, instead of biology, perhaps our narrative centers on finding someone we're obsessed with, only to end up in heated fights. Maybe we keep finding someone to temporarily fill the emptiness or validate our worth. We could even repeatedly try to replicate the love we experienced in the past. All these narratives descend from particular sources of love, and when we don't change the story, the same plot keeps playing out with different people playing the same characters again and again. As of 2026, at least 15 actors have portrayed Superman, and 12 have portrayed Batman. Many people can come and go for the same role.

So, if we're tired of how our story is going—if we're tired of liars, Instagram idols, players, impostors, emotionally unavailable people, endless arguments and fights, unmet needs, or running relationships on willpower alone—it's time we change our narrative.

To do that, we need to change the source.

Adopting New Sources of Love

A narrative that produces extraordinary love requires an extraordinary source. Adopting that kind of source isn't necessarily easy or straightforward, however. The source not only has to *come to us,* initiate, and touch our hearts, but it also requires the *belief* and *acceptance* of its love. It can take years to accept profound love due to feeling unworthy, unready, or too comfortable with the status quo.

Some of us learn to believe we're not worthy of love because of the abuse, trauma, social rejection, neglect, or repeated personal mistakes we've experienced. When that's the case and a wildly contrarian love attempts to break into our lives, we're essentially asked to accept that most of our existence was how it *wasn't* supposed to be. We're just suddenly supposed to believe and accept that the entire narrative we've lived was a *lie* and that a life saturated with love was meant for us.

We're confronted with the choice to reject the world, its narratives, and our lived experience to believe we are who the new source of love *says* we are: *worthy of profound love.* And then live a narrative fitting of that identity. How is that "*easy*" to believe and embrace? To say it's bold is an understatement.

Identities and narratives are things we cling to dearly because they're our *tether to reality.* They provide a certain measure of security by outlining our place in the world, shaping our decisions, and charting our life trajectories. That's *a lot* of existential certainty to give up! Changing them requires an entire metamorphosis of being. Death and rebirth, frankly.

Since sources birth narratives and narratives hold characters, changing sources means characters change as well. Their entire identities transform. Their behavior, sense of purpose, desires, morality, friends, environment, family dynamics—*everything* changes. There's no way around this. *If identity doesn't change, one can trust that no new source has been adopted.*

My advice for those seeking an extraordinary source of love is to let your heart and spirit guide you. That internal guide is just as much a part of you as your intellect. Through eyes, ears, and intellect, we conceptualize love; by heart, spirit, and intuition, we *know* it. You know, the whole bike-riding thing.

A good starting point in attuning to that guide is to intentionally identify and name your feelings and emotions. "I feel angry. I feel frustrated. I feel sad. I feel joyful. I feel seen." This is *especially relevant to men,* as we typically *avoid* doing this. By increasing that awareness, we condition our hearts to become more aware and sensitive to the things that affect them. Or perhaps in other words, the more we attune ourselves to what we're experiencing, the more we recognize experiences overall.

That's important because when extraordinary sources reach out to us, they offer *experiences* and *feelings* of overwhelming love we can't fully understand or explain. We're simply left in awe and often moved to tears.

When the awe and tears start flowing, that's your sign that there's a deep well of love overflowing nearby. It just happens to overflow through the eyes, perhaps, because, ironically, you can't *see* the well. It's just something that's always been available inside of you as your birthright. And with that possibly cryptic thought, may the most profound source of love find you, wash over you, bless you, and keep you. That source will write the narrative of your romance and life as a whole.

Though I'm sure it's not the only extraordinary source, I'm going to walk through how the Christian source of love works so that everyone has access to one. It's the source I'm best able to conceptualize and communicate, and it has personally guided me through my profoundly meaningful love experience.

I encourage readers with other sources of love to be creative and, where possible, substitute language that aligns with their own sources.

The Christian Source of Love

Revisiting *Chapter 1's* summary of Christianity, the scene starts with a world fallen from perfect creation and an acknowledgment of humankind's brokenness. There's death, sadness, neglect, deception, chaos, suffering, disappointment, tragedy, betrayal, and decay—the symptoms of an imperfect world.

Over millennia, the Creator interacts with the humanity He created and eventually enters into a covenantal relationship with them through Israel. They become the starting point of a divine agreement and story arc: if humanity obeys God's commands, He will prosper them and redeem them to their original, perfect identity in His image of love.

Interestingly, the explicit set of commands He gives came in the form of what we could call an "image-of-love starter pack": Do not steal, do not murder, do not bear false witness, do not covet what your neighbor has, do not shag anyone else's spouse, etc. Essentially, they were instructed to be people others would want to be around and have a relationship with. By listening to His demands, they'd actually advance their prosperity and participate in their own return to perfection: the full embodiment of love.

In a roundabout way, the love He showed them in His promise of redemption and prosperity *caused* them to redeem themselves from imperfection by embodying the love starter pack and achieving prosperity. This God was the original *source of love* and the *reason* they knew, expressed, and embodied love the way they did.

From the time of Adam and Eve, the first humans, *the consequence of deviation from perfection was death*. To have a connection with the Source of Life and have everlasting life, one had to comply with the expectations of connection and oneness—love. Refusal to comply would decidedly cut off connection with the Source of Life, leading to decay and death. Aligning with the Creator and His image of love means choosing perfection and life; misaligning means choosing imperfection and death.

Israel understood this concept well because death and imperfection were, and of course still are, a fact of life. But if there was evidence of redemption in the short lifespan they had—that is, becoming a thriving society with prosperous and healthy lives—then perhaps it wasn't unrealistic to think there could be an escape from imperfection overall—maybe *even* from death itself.

One can actually see the cyclical effects of believing and embracing, and of disbelieving and abandoning this relational covenant in the Bible. The books *1 & 2 Kings* record kings and generations switching loyalty to the covenant on and off. One king leads Israel back to the covenant and brings prosperity through God, the next abandons it and brings ruin. Then one re-embraces the covenant, only to be followed by a covenant deserter.

Though this covenant proved reasonable to fully embrace solely for its practical benefits and prosperity, God apparently meant what He said. He would love humanity as He said He would, and indeed fully redeem them from imperfection—even to the point of conquering death. But how does one redeem others from death itself, you ask? Perhaps, in the same way God redeemed Israel's imperfections: *with love.*

Enter the Christian worldview's centerpiece: Jesus Christ of Nazareth. He's said to have come to Earth as God Himself, conceived in a virgin. While He was here, it's reported that He worked miracles of healing. On those healing escapades, He would tell people, "Your sins are forgiven," meaning, "your imperfection is removed, and your debt canceled." At that very moment, they were healed from their ailments, freed from their disabilities, and absolved of their demons.

Surely, as God's image-of-love starter pack brought Israel a transformative redemption from imperfection, Jesus carried on the covenant's story arc to the point of redemption from *physical and existential* imperfection—matters of life and death.

His only requirement for those in need of healing was that they have faith that redemption and healing were theirs for the taking. To heal their imperfections and gain wholeness, they merely needed to *accept* that love and wholeness were offered to them. That meant accepting a love and reality that contradicted their lived experience, and demanded a change in existential narrative and identity. Sound familiar? *Love's Chain of Causation.* Accepting love from a source *always precedes* its manifestation within oneself and in the world.

When Jesus forgave sins, it was about more than giving wrongdoings a pass; it was about redeeming all imperfections by introducing an extraordinary source of love and *charting a new narrative for humanity.* A narrative not of imperfection, absence of love, and death, but of perfection, love, and life.

Yet to fully chart a new narrative, the old must be finished. The cost of imperfection was still death, and that sentence remained unchanged. So, just as Jesus had the Source's authority and love to blot out overbearing imperfections of all kinds and set things right, He too would blot out death's sovereignty and absolve humanity's sentence.

He would absolve it not for a lack of consequences, not because anybody asked, and not because He had to—but because He loved humanity enough to *volunteer* to step into reality's courtroom, *share identity* with us, bear our sentence, and allow us to walk free from the old narrative as the gavel fell on Him.

One can only take on another's sentence when they're *not* also on the chopping block, though. Meaning, one would essentially need to be perfect and innocent, which is really only possible in an imperfect universe if one has an identity *above* reality itself. Perhaps someone with the power to heal, control the weather, walk on water, multiply food, or raise people from the dead. They'd have to be *the most sacred "Being"* in existence.

So, as Jesus would die, those reflecting His selfless, identity-sharing love would identify with Him to partake in His death. They'd have their old identities pass away, fulfilling the consequences of their imperfection. Liberated from the old narrative, humanity became free to choose a new one. And as perfect Jesus rose from the dead, He'd chart a new narrative where many more could receive life. *A source would be available to everyone.* All one would have to do to receive perfection and redemption from death is *believe* it was offered.

In this way, Jesus conquered death. Those ultimately believing and sharing His identity would partake of His resurrection, nullifying death's permanence. The snake's venom ran dry, a nightmare became a daydream, and a moment replaced where eternity once stood. So, though death still existed in the world, it lost its sting as resurrection and new life awaited at the end of the new narrative's story arc. There, on the day of Jesus' promised return, connection with God would be had in its entirety.

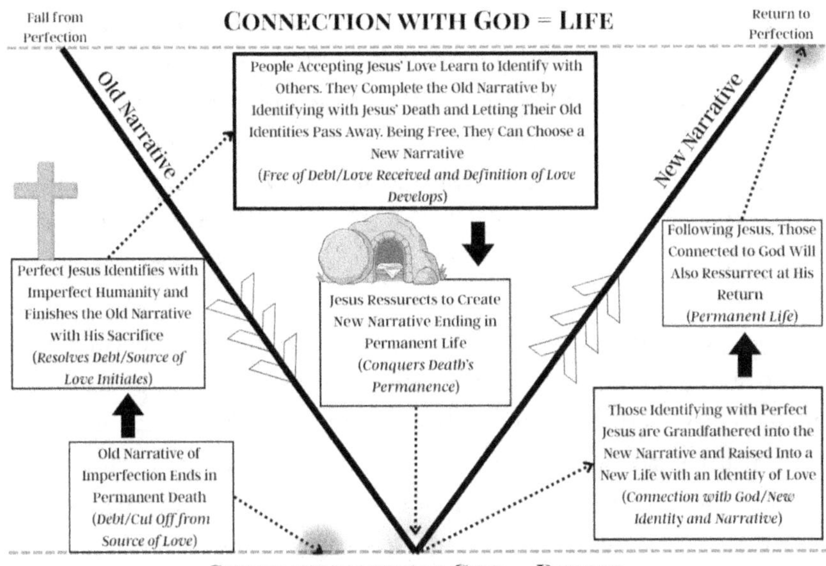

Figure 9: The Gospel

A significant part of this belief in the Christian message of human redemption inevitably involves *believing* that it's good for us. The word "gospel" literally means "good news." So, one cannot say they believe in the gospel if they don't believe it's good for them. If someone lives out a biblical spirituality that they believe robs them of life, rids them of joy, is ultimately bad for them—if it drains them and they dread it—then they don't have faith, they have indoctrination, brainwashing, and blackmail.

To accept the Christian source of love, one cannot feel slighted or forced. Accepting this source means believing God's character, law, and commandments accomplish *good*. This philosophy is *incompatible* with the mass-broadcast narrative where God blackmails humanity into obedience with an eternity in hell.

So, if the blackmail gospel is the obstacle between you and voluntarily accepting the Christian source of love, I urge you to reevaluate. Let a truth ring that there's a message of good news, not meant to harm you, but to give you hope and a future.

Because truly, what would it mean to believe someone did something *this* good for you? What would it mean if they loved you to the point of absorbing all the costs of imperfection and dying for you and remedying death itself? What would it do to you? What kind of person would you become? Who couldn't you *help* but become? What kind of love would you be capable of? This very conviction of identity shift is the cornerstone of the Christian redemption arc: *Being loved so much that Jesus gave His life for humanity, humanity channels that love to others.*

Here, Christians have a correct order of operations: Christians do not love to *be* loved; they love because they *are* loved to the absolute upper limits. They don't act perfectly to overturn imperfections; they act toward perfection because their imperfections *are deemed overturned*. They don't live a certain way to avoid judgment unto death; they live a certain way because they've *already conquered death*.

They don't change to be in compliance with God's law; they comply because they *are changed*. They don't build God's kingdom of love on Earth to be worthy as His sons and daughters; they're sons and daughters of God because a kingdom has *already been established*.

Any action outside of this order of operations is disingenuous Christianity. Or at the very least, it's Christianity that hasn't yet fully bloomed. It's how Christians get a bad rap. Eventually, a person's true identity emerges even amid polished, planned public actions because *motions of love* are not the same as having a loving *identity* rooted in Jesus.

When a Christian's manifestations of love don't line up with their claimed source, we know they've never actually known the source. If they lack all accounts of grace for other people, it's most likely because they've never experienced the grace of God themselves.

Those who've received grace show grace. The truly forgiven forgive. Those who understand, receive, and accept the full breadth of God's love give it in turn.

For just as the descendants of Adam and Eve leaned toward paths of imperfection, born in an identity fallen from love, now, through Jesus, the sons and daughters of God lean toward perfection, born into the redeemed form of humanity. Reborn in an extraordinary source of love, they become love itself.

The Love Hero's Narrative

Extraordinary sources of love that inspire overwhelming awe, waterworks, and inexplicable feelings are the bedrock of true love. Given that those sources provide experiences we can't fully explain, we're compelled to accept that true love's definition is *also* not fully concrete. Paradoxically, that's perfectly okay, and actually *contributes* to a trustworthy definition. **True love** is "the maximization of human flourishing and connection." Let's break that down.

The first prominent principle in this definition is that humans *connect to different degrees and in different ways*. So, for love to be maximized, it must use all available means to realize all potential for connection. True love is erotic, poetic, playful, fun, honest, vulnerable, selfless, mysterious, durable, empathetic, humble, kind, loyal, protective, exciting, joyful, hopeful, patient, forgiving, logical, intuitive—*everything* in the color wheel and triangular theories of love. Every type and way of loving falls under its wing. All of these foster flourishing and connection.

The second principle is that true love is very much a *human phenomenon*. True love in the context of this book isn't about distinguishing between love that is "real" or "not real," true or false. Nor is it purely about some transcendent or enlightened love that blissfully dissolves individuality. Any love we can imagine is only *part* of it. True love is a holistic, idealistic, and yet practical model of human romantic relationships.

We discussed various aspects of modern society and the landscape of relationships in *Chapter 1* because they're integral to being fully *human* and part of this world. Diet, pharmaceuticals, technology, culture, lifestyle, spirituality, socioeconomic and political developments—all these factors inevitably affect human flourishing and quality of life. Human beings have needs, and being healthy requires that those needs be met. Healthy people form healthy relationships, so human factors are an *inescapable* medium of true love.

The third principle rests on the definition of the word "maximization." *Maximization* is the process of making something as great as possible. This means true love is not a static thing or fixed threshold —it's a *conceptually infinite process*. There is no "we created true love." There is only "we are *creating* true love." True love is a living, breathing thing that can pass away, akin to a garden. If it isn't growing and bearing fruit, *it's not alive. If there's no quality of novel growth in one's ability to love and experience in love, it is, by definition, not true love.*

This aspect of growth makes true love rare because it's not something we stumble upon. It's something we have to *create*. Though by "create," I'm essentially referring to the intentional willpower directing our actions. Love streams from a source, so we don't really create it. We simply have the creative ability to *channel* love from a source or to muffle and ignore it when it beckons our hearts. We either refuse or choose to be our source's real-world representation— infusing its love into every aspect of human life, sustaining and enriching connection.

Deliberately channeling love from an infinite source for the sake of embodying infinite love is what we'll call the "**Love Hero's Narrative.**" *True love is created via the fusion of two people,* **Love Heroes***, living the Love Hero's Narrative.* That fusion is the only key to an otherwise unobtainable treasure. As long as each person draws from a source that produces this narrative, they can create true love.

The Christian source uses the human redemption arc toward the image of God to arrive at the Love Hero's Narrative. When Christians talk about embodying the image of a God who supposedly created the fabric of the universe and everything we see by speaking it into existence, we're talking about an *infinitely* powerful being.

Psalm 147:5 says God is mighty in power and His understanding is without measure—*unquantifiable.* Psalm 139 talks about God's presence *everywhere.* 1 Timothy 1 speaks of God's *immortality.* A standout theme of God's image is an infinite nature: infinitely powerful, knowing, and present in space and time.

Since the Bible also claims that God is love, we're drawn to conclude that love is *also* of an infinite nature. Therefore, *the goal of becoming love itself inevitably becomes an endless pursuit.* Christians never reach a point where we've "made it."

The analogy of a garden is elegant for both a personal undertaking of the Love Hero's Narrative *and* for true-love relationships. Both require tender care and growth. The narrative is a *private* garden that cultivates one's ability and *potential* to extend love, eagerly sharing it with others when appropriate. It's a *personal* decision and journey.

True love, the pinnacle of human romantic love, is a *joint* garden where two souls *fully harvest,* share, and further cultivate the love they've nurtured and grown in their own gardens and narratives. It's a *mutual* endeavor that amplifies love, maximizes connection, and leads to highly successful relationships.

Scientific literature actually links growth traits directly to high performance and success. A 1998 study tested the effects of different types of praise on 5th graders. After an exam, students would either receive praise for their intelligence and ability or for their hard work and effort. Intelligence-based praise would be something like, "You got this score! You're so smart!" Effort-based praise would be, "You must've worked really hard to solve that problem!"

After multiple rounds of testing and praise, a few valuable findings emerged. First, children receiving intelligence-based praise were more likely to invest in performance goals where they might find the same validation of their intelligence. That's instead of learning goals, where they might not know what they're doing, and high performance is less likely.

Second, upon experiencing failure, students praised for intelligence showed less persistence, lower task enjoyment, and worse task performance than students praised for effort. Their resilience was low. This is most likely because, third, those praised for intelligence were more likely to interpret intelligence as a fixed trait. Meanwhile, children praised for effort and hard work believed it to be open to improvement—*a growth trait.*[i]

There's no such thing as a relationship without challenges. Everyone encounters conflict at some point, and conflict demands that we communicate, adapt, and problem-solve. A Love Hero's orientation toward infinite growth in love leads them to consistently improve their functioning. As a result, they conquer challenges more easily and elect growth goals of love rather than static ones, which are potent forces for human flourishing.

Finding a fantastic life partner or finding "the one" are decent goals. A *better* goal is to increase the likelihood we'll pair with our life partner. Finding "the one" is a lofty goal with a fixed mindset. Through a fixed mindset, breakups become *failures*. Time without our partners becomes miserable and meaningless. Daters who aren't them become a waste of time. Experiences without them could always be brighter, and we're never living to our fullest. It's very cut and dry. While there's a bright burning light in that lens, it's all the way at the end of a tediously long tunnel with easily fading motivation and inspiration.

Increasing the likelihood of pairing with our life partners is a growth-based goal. Breakups become learning opportunities for what we want and what we don't want—for what works and what doesn't. Time without our partner becomes time for us to more fully come into our own, grow our own garden, and be a truly unique and beautiful individual who's intentionally prepared for them.

Daters who aren't them become practice for charisma, direct communication, vulnerability, open-mindedness, and overall personal growth. Experiences without them become stories that define who we are, stories our partners will hear and, one day, poetically align with their own.

Likewise, a decent goal for marriage is staying together. It aims at eye level. It focuses on maintenance and relies on determination. A *better* goal is to increase the likelihood that we stay together. It aims *higher,* provides goals and motivation, and stimulates daily creativity. Maybe we can increase the likelihood by getting them a gift they didn't even know they wanted, cooking up 5-star meals regularly, or granting them sexual fantasies. Growth and learning goals will always bring more life to the love in our relationships than fixed goals.

These progress-oriented aspects of true love call us to both humble ourselves and continually grow in our ability to negotiate. Regarding humility, a growth mindset takes pressure off being right or wrong. Being wrong becomes a learning moment and an opportunity to perform better in the future—not a failure. We should welcome guidance that draws us closer to the infinite goal in our narrative.

As for growth in negotiation ability, the Love Hero's Narrative automatically increases negotiating power because we continually build new wisdom, skills, virtues, and bodies. Those assets are a fountain of health, joy, success, pleasure, and peace, and typically represent a phenomenal deal in mating negotiations. Since everyone likes a good deal, Love Heroes will be in demand.

Still, we haven't fully grasped what it means to live this narrative. While it's responsible for many benefits and the creation of true love, it doesn't come without challenges and sacrifices. One principle makes this abundantly clear: It's not enough to simply pursue the infinite goal—the infinite goal must be a Love Hero's *highest priority.*

In Christianity, this principle has a very specific title.

The First Commandment

We'll begin our understanding of this principle by considering a passage of Jesus' wisdom on adultery in Matthew 5. In verses 29-30, he says:

> "If your right eye causes you to stumble, gouge it out and throw it
> away. It is better for you to lose one part of your body than for your

whole body to be thrown into hell. And if your right hand causes you to stumble, cut it off and throw it away. It is better for you to lose one part of your body than for your whole body to go into hell."

Talk about the sacrifice of priorities. Let's apply this concept to a hypothetical situation of a man's relationship with social media. What happens when a woman catches a man's eye on social media? He might go to her profile and look at more photos. What happens when he looks at more photos? He progressively uncovers her in his mind. What happens when he uncovers her? He expresses his desire for her. What happens to the average man who desires her?

He'll wish for a woman like her, might message her, and she'll probably ignore him. What happens to the man who covets and is denied his desires? He becomes upset, obsessed, infuriated, and stuck. Because of one little thing, his mind becomes trapped and tortured. His spirit turns bitter, and he loses sight of the important things in his life.

What would he lose if he threw social media out of his life? He might not have access to memes or see updates about his friends' lives, which he no doubt compares himself to and might also covet. What does he lose if he keeps social media? He loses his personal sanity by enduring a hell of obsession, unquenchable desire, bitterness, infuriation, lack of focus, and depression.

Cutting off social media would cut him off from the memes he enjoys, but it would also cut off his entire being from jumping into a living hell repeatedly. "It is better for you to lose one part of your body than for your whole body to go into hell." What Jesus is teaching in this context is to get rid of whatever tempts us to do wrong to ourselves. Because while we may be satisfying a desire, it'll cause much more harm than it's worth.

In technical habit formation language, that might be something like, "Eliminate the trigger to the bad habit because the bad habit will destroy you." For example, stop buying candy if seeing candy in the house triggers us to want to eat it, which leads to weight gain and health issues.

In Love Hero language, the message is this: "If we're carrying something that actively derails us from the path we want to be on, we should stop carrying it." Which, as we'll understand shortly, is an expansion of the Bible's first commandment: "You shall have no other gods before me."

Before I continue, I'd like to pause and remind us all that this book is about true love. While there's relationship advice in here, we don't have to listen to all of it if we're okay with a functional relationship with two flat tires and an engine spewing out smoke. Only if we want a relationship of legendary love do we have to consider these concepts nonnegotiable.

This commandment shouldn't come across as an order. It's a philosophical truth to live by if we want true love. It's not a rule. *It's an opportunity.* If we want a garden, this is how it's made. If we don't mind an overgrown and neglected backyard with raccoons and gophers making turf war, then we do our own thing. I digress.

Resuming the First Commandment, Love Heroes can have absolutely no other god before love. But what is a god? Well, as poetic as it is, a god is what shapes us. A *god* is where we place our self-value, get our sense of identity and aspirations, and it's what we sacrifice for. Gods are pretty easy to spot.

Let's consider someone who works in programming, takes pride in it, and dedicates all their free time to learning new programming skills. They set programming as their god. It holds their aspirations, identity, and free time, and they sacrifice for it.

If they went out on a date, they'd share that they're a programmer. When asked about their hobbies, they'd say they enjoy programming. If someone asked what makes them confident, they'd say programming. If someone asked about their biggest fear, they might say, "being fired" or "AI making human programmers obsolete."

And if we asked them what it takes to be a programmer like them, they might say, "You can't spare any time for family, other hobbies, or exercise." They sacrifice other areas of life for it. Sometimes they sacrifice their close relationships.

That was a very cut-and-dry case. Still, the criteria remain for those of us with foggier gods. Whenever I need to calculate what my god is, it consistently reveals itself as my #1 evidence-based value. Values are priorities set in our hearts. They're what we hold in high regard and will sacrifice for. They're subjective principles that guide the direction of our lives by determining our habits, thoughts, and actions.

Values can be subjects, traits, or activities. Subjects might be family, money, power, success, balance, efficiency, etc. Examples of traits would be honesty, beauty, kindness, cleanliness, bravery, etc. Activities could be reading, exercising, making music, spending time with family, traveling, etc.

An evidence-based value proves to be at the top of our list of values in reality, in contrast to ideal values, which are what we'd ideally like our values to be on paper. Ideal values and evidence-based values can often differ, creating dissonance within our being. To determine our evidence-based values and, ultimately, our gods, we're going to do an exercise I've designed to raise awareness of value dissonance.

To prepare for listing your values, I'd like you to briefly ponder these questions:

- What's something that really irks you? What does that tell you about what you value?
- What's the most meaningful thing you own?
- What would your parents or best friends say you care about most?
- What brings you the greatest joy?
- What do you admire about the person you admire most?
- What's your greatest mission in life?
- What motivates you like nothing else?

LIST YOUR CURRENT TOP 5 VALUES IN LIFE:

1.

2.

3.

4.

5.

BEFORE THE NEXT STEP, do any refining you can. If your top value in life is your job, is work what you really value, or is it a deeper value of providing for your family? Or perhaps, to manage what others think of you? If it's reading, is it actually entertainment or fun? Or perhaps, knowledge and wisdom? Or maybe even the comfort of escaping this reality? Get as deep as you can. Next, list your values in order of how you've been prioritizing them through your actions.

TOP 5 EVIDENCE-BASED VALUES:

1.

2.

3.

4.

5.

OUR FIRST EVIDENCE-BASED value is our god. It's what we sacrifice for, and where we've put most of our spare money, time, and energy. Everything else bends around it like water flowing around a boulder in a river. It's the centerpiece that controls and influences our actions and emotions.

As I was first designing this exercise, I listed my ideal values as: (1) God and marriage, (2) writing, (3) social connection, (4) business building, and (5) entertainment. When I looked at the evidence, it was basically: (1) video games, (2) research and YouTube, (3) God and marriage, (4) writing, and (5) social connection. *Quite* disordered.

Looking back, though I wanted to say writing was my second priority, I'd write for about 5 hours per week and play 10-20 hours of video games. Per the evidence, it was easy to say video games were my priority.

The evidence-based analysis of video games over marriage is tricky. I'd get off the game if my wife asked me to, and I'd still make time for her. That might classify her as a higher priority. But other criteria were at play. For one, I'd get really frustrated and feel like a loser if I wasn't doing well and lost a lot of games. Not progressing in my goals on top of feeling like a loser affected my testosterone, made me more irritable, and disrupted my daily routines.

So, not only did it affect self-esteem, but it also affected important things like my behavior, relationship dynamics, cooking decisions, and our household's sleep patterns. It also consumed most of my free time, motivation, and concentration. My schedule flowed around it, and I sacrificed my ideal priorities for it.

To make matters worse, even *if* I found success in video games, it would truly amount to nothing in the real world. I'd know this calculation, yet I'd carry on. The only time it didn't feel like a burden was when I cut it off completely.

If gods were elected by evidence-based votes, video games were my god. I've gone through that cycle multiple times in my lifetime. It's a hard decision every time, but I never regret cutting out a foreign, non-infinite-love god. It makes me more considerate, helpful, kind, productive, generous, romantic, and family-oriented, among other things. I speak love like it's my first nature.

Looking at your lists, I implore you to identify the centerpiece of your life. What does your self-worth revolve around? Social media? Video games? What do you sacrifice for? Streaming services? Alcohol? What influences your behavior and actions? Weed? Pornography? **Gods** can be many things, but they *always prescribe identity, self-worth, aspirations, and they always demand submission, sacrifice, particular behaviors and decisions, and almost all our thoughts.*

If we want to create true love, we can have no other god higher than the epitome of love, and no higher priority than becoming love itself. We must cut off any other #1 evidence-based desire, and let the other gods go. Temptation will abound because gods often offer elements of comfort, safety, purpose, success, status, community, and connection. They often satisfy the false paths of masculine and feminine fulfillment. The chains connecting us to them don't seem to be all that bad.

Regardless, Love Heroes choose to be chain-breakers. They know love conquers all other gods. They know it is the King of kings and Ruler among rulers, as their eyes see the quality-of-life differences unfold. Infinite sources of love kneel before no one and are second to none.

Love Heroes give whatever it takes to become love itself and become beautiful creations that are benevolent to all. That, however, brings its own unique challenges in mating negotiations. Since they have a lot to offer, some would exploit and play games with them, ultimately sabotaging the creation of true love.

So let's talk about how Love Heroes live this narrative and manage themselves wisely to avoid sabotage and establish a true-love garden. Let's talk about what it means to negotiate like a Love Hero.

The Negotiation Game

The negotiation game occurs on *Love's Chain of Causation* between *Mate-Selection Theories* and *Match*. In this game analogy of mating negotiations, **cards** represent assets that attract partners and contribute to relationship success. These include wealth, beauty, intelligence, athleticism, and a range of skills and traits, such as good listening, tasty cooking, patience, honesty, selflessness, and humor.

Having few cards to play is synonymous with immaturity, poor relationship skills, limited practical life experience, toxic character traits, low proficiency in mate-selection theories, and being overall unfit for mating negotiations.

This game involves: (1) flirting, (2) tactfully exchanging our cards for cards we need and desire, and (3) narrative alignment. **Flirting** sparks romantic interest and gets negotiators to take their seats at the negotiation table to exchange cards. When someone excels at flirting, we say they "have game." If someone has game and exchanges cards *without* any intention of aligning narratives for long-term mating negotiations, that's when we say they're "playing games." Think of situationships, attention addicts, friends with benefits, commitment-averse or indecisive relationship prospects, etc.

Negotiations end in *deals*. Narrative alignment ensures that those exchanging cards pursue the same deal because specific narratives yield specific outcomes. If two people keep playing the game *well knowing* they're not seeking the same deal—that a deal isn't on the table, and that nobody's going to win—they're playing a meaningless game.

To win the negotiation game and form a match, both negotiators must engage in *all three*. They must (1) express interest and initiate mating negotiations, (2) both see and like what the other person offers, and (3) agree on the negotiation's objective. Expressing interest is the *easy* part. Narratives and their accompanying objectives make or break negotiations with or without our permission. That means the bulk of this game is how we play our cards. If we're superb negotiators, we'll have plenty of cards to play with and practice elegant strategy.

One-trick ponies who feel the need to show off their assets are examples of bad negotiators with poor gameplay. People find show-offs off-putting for fair reasons. Arrogantly calling attention to oneself by putting all our chips on the table is neither elegant nor classy and often reflects desperation, insecurity, and a need for vali-dation. Without tact, they're trying to make a quick sale by being flashy, which raises suspicions about a lack of substance.

Hence, we can safely assume one or all these things about people who lack strategy: (1) they don't have a lot of cards to play with, (2) they don't play well, or (3) there's not much, if anything, beyond their cards' face value.

Once upon a time, I worked at a summer camp with this cute girl we'll call Doris. Doris had dietary restrictions, and the gluten-free options at the time weren't what they are now. They had terrible texture and certainly didn't taste very good.

On days when bread, waffles, pizza, or other gluten-containing products were served, she had few options. But I never heard her complain. We playfully flirted every now and then, but she did that with a lot of guys, so I didn't feel encouraged to express my romantic interest—engage in direct mating negotiation. If she was offering the same level of interest to plenty of other guys, she didn't seem like a good person to share my cards with.

Regardless, my heart yearned to care for her. So, every day off, I'd drive to Bend, Oregon, and buy bottles of Odwalla smoothie blends to give her daily access to a healthy, nutritious treat. I even coordinated a secret distribution plan with the head chef. I'd be her Odwalla Santa, covertly sponsoring her supplemental smoothies and sneaking into the walk-in fridge at night to leave more bottles.

My caution about whether she was a good person to show more cards to lasted for maybe a year. Sometimes I'd show an exclusive card or two to see if she would narrow her focus and engage in direct negotiation. One of those instances was a memory of us crossing the Walla Walla University campus on a 3° F winter night to a friend's house. Once inside, her arms and hands shook uncontrollably, and fear flooded her face as she couldn't feel her fingers. Being a musician, that could be a problem.

As she took a seat to gather herself, several people gathered around her in concern. I navigated to the kitchen, filled a bowl with lukewarm water, and got down to her level to hold it while she dipped her fingers in and brought them to room temperature. If quick, thoughtful, and safety-ensuring acts didn't communicate that I'd be an excellent person to engage in mating negotiations with, not much else was going to get her attention.

Month after month passed as I waited for her to show that she was a suitable person to reveal my cards to, but I was never convinced she felt uniquely interested in me compared to others. She never got to know me deeply because of it. I kept getting the impression that her flirting with many men was just part of who she was, and that was enough to make me believe negotiating with her long-term wasn't a smart idea. So, I folded and kept my cards secret for someone else to discover. To this day, she doesn't know who Odwalla Santa was.

I tell this story to introduce some standout elements of elegant negotiation. *Elite mating negotiators reserve their cards for strategic opportunities to control how much interest they stimulate from others.* They don't recklessly flash their cards. Rather, they may play it like that classic *Hallmark* undercover royalty who's gone to America but didn't want to attract "small-city person from the local shop" for the wrong reasons.

They recognize that human beings have finite energy and that cards require energy. That demands strategic and sustainable card play. Some cards are shown only to select individuals in specific situations, and they're played for high impact without misrepresenting what they can commit to giving long-term. Exceptional gameplay essentially means one ultimately has the skills to play the lifelong, energy-exchanging game of mating consistency well and be invaluable life allies. Because a big part of life is navigating and negotiating with *the rest of the world.*

This strategic and intentional gameplay has three crucial effects: (1) it paints an enchanting picture of us, (2) it protects other people, and (3) it protects us.

First, foreshadowing cards or surprising people with them gives us an aura of confidence and mystery. That attracts others' interest. When Abbey and I first started dating, we were taking things slow. I didn't kiss her until the fourth date— three weeks in. The entire time, she was curious whether I actually wanted to kiss her or if I just kissed like a chimpanzee under the influence and wanted to hide it. It built mystery, stimulated curiosity, and generated riveting tension.

Abbey also reserved her cards and played them strategically. Amid taking it slow, she acknowledged my restraint by not rushing into physical intimacy. Although there was a potent attraction between us, I wanted to delay the physical aspect of the relationship so we could focus on showing other cards. I wanted to make it clear that I wasn't in the relationship solely for physical gain.

While making those physical boundaries, I commented she was beautiful, and I flirtatiously suggested I was pretty sure she had nice boobs, but didn't need to rush to find out. Suddenly, a proud smirk landed on her face. Her back straightened, and she giggled, saying, *"You have no idea."*

What? My eyes widened, and I inhaled through a jaw-dropped smile as my hands clung for dear life on top of my head. To say I picked up on a sense of confidence and that she piqued my interest would be a *vast* understatement. With strategy, she let me know she had a legendary sexual economics mate-selection card, but didn't fully dangle it in front of me.

Second, strategically reserving cards protects others in several ways. It prevents us from arousing interest in people we're not interested in and spares them from rejection. Regarding the girl with frozen hands, if it were any other girl I had *no* interest in, I might have asked the group, "Should we put her hands in a bowl of lukewarm water to warm them up?" With that course of action, the homeowner would've provided the necessary materials, and I still would've contributed to the girl's well-being, maintained my loving identity, and prevented what could've otherwise been a misleading initiation in mating negotiation.

Reserving cards also protects people in situations where *we* are curious about exploring mating negotiation with them, but have a sneaking suspicion our interest won't last. It protects them from becoming too emotionally invested in us only for us to eventually become disinterested and reject them.

As a personal rule, I cautiously hesitated to show my cards to women who weren't particularly attractive to me. If I were merely fond of the energy they carried, I'd only dip my toes into negotiation. It's well known that people become more physically attractive to us when we find their personality and spirit attractive. So, I'd give the kindling ample time and multiple opportunities to spark. If no spark came, I wouldn't force anything without the assurance that there'd be a sustainable physical-attraction flame. It may not have been very pleasant for some women to negotiate with me lightly, only for it to fizzle out. To me, however, it was a hell of a lot better than seeing all my cards, becoming deeply attached, and having their hearts broken.

I *also* had a rule to hesitate showing my cards to attractive women, as they may be more prone to narcissism. Which leads us to our longest and arguably most important point for our relationship sanity. Hone in if your mind is wandering. This could save you a lot of pain and heartache. Point *three* is that strategic negotiation filters out and *protects us* from members of the Dark Triad: narcissists, Machiavellians, and psychopaths—those who'd take advantage of us.

Narcissists seek attention, manipulate others, have a large, loud, and proud personality, yet have low self-esteem, and are vain and charismatic. **Machiavellians** are cold, long-term manipulators, immoral thinkers, and have such an intense craving for pleasure, success, money, and power that they'll stop at nothing to get them. That includes stepping all over us. They'd see us as a practical means to get what they want. Finally, **psychopaths** are thrill-seekers who are manipulative, impulsive, and display antisocial behavior.

Despite how unattractive and undesirable the Dark Triad is, narcissists and psychopaths actually correlate with *high* levels of success in short-term dating.[ii] This is probably for several reasons, but I'd bet the biggest is that they're *manipulative.*

Andrew Bustamante, a former CIA spy, has publicly shared the CIA's account of manipulation and its gravity on outcomes. According to the CIA, *manipulation and motivation are two sides of the same coin.* This coin carries the acronym **RICE:** *Reward, Ideology, Coercion, and Ego.*

Reward, the third strongest of these, leverages people's desires. If we want to motivate someone to complete their task faster, we might offer them a reward they want, like ice cream or a concert ticket. If we want to manipulate someone, we might offer a reward they want in exchange for completing a task we want them to do.

Manipulative examples might be, "Oh, I don't even want to know what unholy things I'd do to the person who bought me tickets to

Coachella..." or "I will buy you this car... or give you this ring... If you have sex with me 5 times a week."

The line between motivation and manipulation can seem murky. The biggest difference, however, is that with motivation, the task in focus is something the motivated person *already wanted* or was already doing on their own. With manipulation, the task in question aligns with the manipulator's desires.

Ideology is a system of beliefs, ideas, and principles one holds dear. This is the strongest component of the RICE coin. People will often die for their beliefs sooner than they'll die for rewards, threats, and even their egos.

Here's how we might motivate someone using ideology. If they're a Christian, we might tell them, "God will help you through every challenge you face, and He'll love you whether you complete this task or not."

If we want to manipulate them so we can avoid guilt or accountability, we might say, "I *thought* Christians were *supposed* to be accepting and loving." Or if we want something from them, we might say, "I *thought* Christians were *supposed* to be selfless and generous."

Coercion is the weakest of the RICE coin's tactics, and its currency leverages negative things like shame, guilt, and blackmail. I suppose I can't think of any examples of motivation for this one other than someone being driven by their own guilt to make amends and atone. But if we wanted to manipulate someone with coercion, we'd guilt-trip them, or blackmail them by threatening to leak explicit photos of them on a crime-ridden private island or something.

Finally, we have **ego**, the second strongest core motivator. The *ego* is the image of oneself. People like to see themselves a certain way, and they want others to see them that way too. The ego motivator is concerned with preserving both self and public image.

If we wanted to motivate someone through ego, we might ask them a coaching question like, "What strengths do you need to draw on to accomplish this task?" We're essentially asking them to search the image they have of themselves, bring the helpful traits to the surface, and use them as resources to accomplish their goal.

Then, if we wanted to manipulate someone, we might use social pressure. "Wow, you're not going to jump? I knew you were a scaredy-cat." Or maybe, "You're not going to have sex with me? Jeez, such a prude." Both comments aim to get under the skin, tempting the ego to engage in image preservation. If the person doesn't want to be seen as how the manipulator portrays them, they'll do what the manipulator wants.

Overall, it makes sense that Dark Triad members would be more successful than others in dating and short-term relationships because they freely use *both* sides of the RICE coin. They use more tactics to get what they want from others. There are no second thoughts about exploiting the gullible honeymoon stagers who don't want the party to stop.

Manipulators naturally excel at bending reality to the point where they fool others and delude themselves. *Love bombing* is a typical manipulation tactic in which one exaggerates and flashes cards they don't normally have or play. They also have no desire or plan to use them in the future.

For example, say a couple got in a fight, and the girl is actively ending their romance by leaving the apartment for a few days. Then suddenly, as if to get jump-hyped by Jesus in a private pep rally, receiving a medal, entrance applause, and a splash of Holy Water, the man changes his tune. He begs her to come back, starts buying flowers, sponsors shopping sprees, listens when she talks, and is super charismatic, kind, and thoughtful. *He's really changed this time!*

Sure enough, she comes back, and they both eventually forget he doesn't *actually* desire to hold those cards in his hand. The cards fly away with the wind soon after, and the cycle starts over with another conflict, causing her to leave.

Manipulators regularly tease the idea that they have plenty of cards when they're really just *renting* them. They don't actually own those cards. It's for this reason that narcissists have a false sense of confidence accompanied by low self-esteem. Machiavellians and psychopaths are *so* deluded that they believe their renting of cards is the same as owning them. Therefore, they have full confidence.

They may also appear confident, charming, and charismatic because people are so simple to them. They're just stepping stones to get what they want. So, they'll take out whatever loans of deception they need to rent cards, and they'll wave those babies around like free candy. They'll present whatever card they need to because they're only concerned about getting *something,* not about being with *someone.* That's very low stakes, and it's not nearly as nerve-racking. People are complex! *Objects* are not.

Flashing cards makes them seem like they'd be quite the catch. But this flashy strategy is only meant to lure us into revealing our entire hand so they can see what they can get from us. In the long term, they'll prove they never really held those cards and that they're bad mating negotiators through and through. Though if they wanted to prolong the manipulation, they may show us a shiny card now and then to keep us in their back pocket.

When we think of manipulators, we should picture those who are *hot one minute and cold the next,* and overall inconsistent. They show convincing interest sporadically but don't commit. They seem genuine in some moments, then suddenly seem like they're hiding something. To stay in the shadows and keep us guessing, they give us thrilling attention, cut it off, and then resume a week or more later. Being the subject of this manipulation is actually quite addictive because receiving sporadic attention mimics the dopamine effect of gambling, where random, unpredictable wins give us highs. By and large, if we feel like our hearts are being played with, it's probably because we're being played with.

Just knowing these things about Dark Triad members is enough to meaningfully protect ourselves and avoid trouble and wasted time. Fundamentally, we know that *they don't negotiate well.* On top of that, though, they also have to overcome the natural protective elements of narratives.

If people can't tell us exactly what they're looking for, then they lack a destination. And if they don't have a solid sense of identity within a bigger picture, then they lack direction and a starting point.

Identities, starting points, destinations, and direction are all required for a narrative.

Assuming they *do* have a narrative, it still has to align with our Love Hero's Narrative. If it doesn't, their actions will quickly prove it. They'll avoid accountability, correction, growth, communication, vulnerability, honesty, and personal sacrifice, and regularly cause trouble. Dark Triad members are far too impulsive and impatient to be considerate and accommodate anyone else's agenda for long. They'd rather lash out, break character, and seek someone more susceptible to manipulation. Meaning those whose stories don't align with ours naturally get filtered out.

As a bonus, narratives make our own relationships and hearts *more durable*. Because if relationships are our final destination and we reach it, we might naturally ask, *"Okay... What now? I have a spouse. Do I just...water it?"*

Those who think relationships are the final destination will be more easily disheartened when it's less rosy than they once envisioned. If marriage is the 100% completion point, and it's less enjoyable than the 74% mark, then we're more likely to want to go *backward* and get out rather than continue.

But when relationships *aren't* the ultimate destination of our narrative, we place purpose *outside* the relationship itself. A meaningful, fascinating, and inspirational destination is never where we *already are* or even a variation of it. So the person we're *currently* with can *never* be our final stop.

Wise people have their world revolve around a solid narrative, *not around characters they can't control;* they view love lives as *stories, not* individual people. So, if we're dating, our task is to grow into who we aspire to be and be curious about who the universe will cast for the character roles of our narrative.

People have tried to be the co-lead in our narrative, and more will continue to try. We may have tried out for co-lead roles to no avail, but we'll keep auditioning. Instead of viewing not landing a co-lead part as rejection of our innermost being, we can view it as the universe not yet casting our partner and co-lead. We can stop freaking out about forcing crossovers with someone else's narrative because it'll fit when it fits. In the meantime, we try to make our narrative as attractive and appealing as possible.

Overall, if we want the passion and purpose necessary to make our relationships endure, the narrative of growing into the likeness of infinite love is a wise choice. It operates before and during lifelong partnership, making our search, relationships, and hearts more durable. In principle, after successfully negotiating, those living the Love Hero's Narrative create true love and walk together in a harmonious, *endless story.*

A harmonic perk of this journey's infinite aspect is that it helps us *resist* the urge to keep score in our relationships. Because when both parties have the main aspiration to do and be more, comparisons with others aren't the focus. This *doesn't* mean we won't notice when we're the only ones trying or that we can't express our needs. It simply means our focus is less on what our partners are doing and more on living the Love Hero's Narrative.

Scorekeeping also faces resistance because it's essentially impossible for partners to be in identical places on an *infinite* journey. There are too many places to land, considering as many mate-selection theories and expressions of love as there are.

As long as growth is happening, one person will always have more capacity to love. *The score will always be uneven.* It may be close and intangible. It may even flip in the other direction. But it will never be equal. If it's obvious that effort and capacity for love are far from matched, one might benefit from seeking a partner closer to their capacity. Partners on this journey should be teammates, not mentors and mentees.

Through a Christian lens, again, we're not aloof about whether we're the only ones trying. Nevertheless, the mission we inherit from God is to bountifully love the world. A Christian's job as a significant other is to imagine how God would love our partners through us if He were essentially a little alien running an elaborate command center in our brains. What actions would He direct? Based on how He sees our partners, how would He love them? If He is forgiving, how would He react? If He is supportive, what would He say? Or perhaps will we let them go on living without knowing how much God loves, sees, and cares for them?

In a sentence, our task is to *translate and relay the love we know God has for our partners*. We should act as if we were the only middlemen assigned to deliver His message of love to them.

Every time my wife tells me I'm such a great man, I don't really get an ego-kick out of it. That's because I believe she's truly complimenting the source of love I elected. In my mind, the only reason I'm "great" is because I'm an effective translator. I see her through the eyes of my God and do my best to leave it to Him to do the whole alien-control-room-in-the-brain thing.

I can't take pride in the incredible cards I have and show because they're ultimately God's. He gave me His cards because He took me as His son. So, while I own those cards through inheritance, taking pride in them would be like working on a group project, letting someone else put in all their genius, and then taking all the credit. I'm not a renter of cards, but what I own was given to me.

Another way I'd describe being a translator for God's love is listening to my heart's first instinct. This is an art I practiced for years before I met Abbey. I first heard the idea in a sermon where the pastor put a twist on the 10-second rule.

Rather than being about eating chili-cheese-fry hot dogs fresh off the floor, it was about listening to our conscience and its calls to do good. He said that whenever we feel the urge to do something kind for others, we should do it within 10 seconds. Don't stand around contemplating how it would come across, whether we have enough energy, how we're going to engage in the kindness, or whether we might regret it—no. *Just do it*.

It's a habit for me now. Even if I don't want to do something—say, make extra food in the middle of my heavy workday while Abbey's vegging out on the couch—I ask her if she wants some. I may feel like she should be the one making food since she's not working, but I put out the kindness anyway.

From where I'm standing, it wasn't me who offered her that favor.

It was ultimately the Source of Love flowing through me. I just allowed its love to reach her. I'm an instrument, not the engine. Whatever "score" I have was given to me. It's a good reason to be confident, but it bears no weight for an inflated ego.

Love Heroes are simply outstanding translators and messengers for their sources of love.

Chapter's End

The legendary treasure of true love demands nothing less than a hero. *Thus far*, we know that Love Heroes aren't incentivized to exist and that they deny the natural order of an imperfect world. They're aware of and overcome the obstacles of the modern relationship landscape, and choose true paths of fulfillment and a peaceful heart in a world at war.

They accept an extraordinary love that's often counterintuitive to their lived experience and increasingly strive to embody the nature of its source. This infinite aspiration of love's embodiment cannot be anything but their greatest priority. And for the obstacles they overcome, the good they do, or any awesomeness they possess, they resist prideful and glorified egos because they're merely messengers.

Since Love Heroes are an exception to the rule, they make up a vast minority of the population and, therefore, of relationships and marriages. If people didn't settle for anything less than true love, I imagine there wouldn't be many relationships. Like I've said, though, everyone has different appetites for love and romance, so not everyone cares about it. There's also never really been a tangible blueprint for true love before, so not everyone even *knows* about it or believes in it.

The whole reason I'm writing this book is that, if true love is what someone wholeheartedly desires or even cares to explore, there should be a map that leads them to it. It's my deepest desire that more Love Heroes rise so that other Love Heroes can pair with them. Everything in this book is the same blueprint that led me to my miracle and the creation of true love.

I found my wife at my absolute breaking point—completely void of the hope that I'd find a Love Hero. They say, "You find your life partner when you least expect it." I've heard that saying so many times... and I still *hate it* with a burning passion to this day. It always made me want to invent a time machine just so I could escort those words back into people's mouths. It doesn't always have something to do with us—and *certainly* not our expectations.

Finding a Love Hero match to create true love with is simply beyond our total control. For a match to be made, we not only need to *choose* to live the Love Hero's Narrative, but someone *else* must choose the same. *Then* we have to run into them *and* negotiate *successfully*. We can control the first, none of the second, and only influence the last two. "Expectation" has *very little* to do with it.

With the wisdom I've gained over the years, I can say I was truly ready to match with a Love Hero since the age of 20. Yet I found her after 6 years of being an intentional Love Hero. Nothing changed over those years other than growing my capacity to love and becoming more open to matching with non-Christian Love Heroes. At any point, someone else who was right for me could've come along and successfully negotiated with me. I didn't need to "least expect it." I just needed the right Love Hero to exist and bump into me.

A large reason I believe and advocate that there's more than one way to align with the Love Hero's Narrative is that my wife wasn't necessarily a Christian when we met. She wasn't even Christian when we got married, at least not in any conventional sense.

I went through 4 years of Christian high school, 4.33 years of Christian university, 3 years of Christian graduate school, and consistently attended church throughout those years. Of the women I met, not many seemed like Love Heroes. After considering mutual attraction, age range, and initial negotiations, I perceived zero viable options.

In the central hubs of Christianity, I couldn't find *a single* woman to negotiate with successfully or accompany toward the infinite essence of love. But on a dating app date with a girl who *avoided* calling herself a Christian, I'd never had so much of God's love access me. Never had I seen such a miracle or met such a Love Hero.

Her mother raised her with various religious influences, mainly Christianity, Buddhism, and Hinduism. Ironically, my mother-in-law often calls God "Source." I share this to encourage everyone to choose their own generous sources of love.

IN REVIEW, as long as our source is infinite, it'll serve as a wonderful educator of love. It'll provide us with *experiences* of profound love, shape our *definition* of love, and serve as our very *reason* to love. Life, friends, and family inevitably influence how we love and live. But infinite sources of love are the sole origins of the Love Hero's Narrative.

This narrative holds the exclusive and inspiring mandate to compose our identities as **Love Heroes**—those *who pursue the embodiment of an infinite epitome of love and grow to excel across all mate-selection theories and expressions of love.*

The term Love Hero derives its meaning from overcoming the natural order of an imperfect world and becoming love itself, no matter the cost. Love Heroes go down a path few are on, and since so few dedicate themselves to creating a true love story, they also bear the daunting possibility of being alone. Still, they live by the fundamental philosophy that enables the creation of true love—an ever-growing, all-encompassing garden that maximizes human connection and flourishing.

Altogether, *the Love Hero narrative optimizes for highly successful, healthy, long-term relationships. It does so by offering confidence, growth goals, desirable cards and traits, humility in conflict, unnecessary heartbreak prevention, a filter for toxic mating candidates, a mysterious aura, resistance to scorekeeping, an increasingly sharp mating-negotiation strategy, and a mission to love all humanity, expanding one's capacity for love.*

It's also worth noting that, essentially, all the principles we've discussed apply equally to *friendships*. Poor friendships can pave one-way streets where we put in all the emotional energy, show up for them without reciprocation, and respect their standards and boundaries, only for them to care less for ours. Love Heroes have a natural filter that protects against this kind of exploitation.

This doesn't mean we can't give unless we get something in return. It just means we need to be aware of our limits when it comes to giving to relationships and people who drain us, leaving us feeling burned out. Love Heroes aren't perfect, infinite sources of love, no matter how hard we try to channel their love. As humans, we still have limits and finite energy. Anything beyond those limits can only be satisfied by infinite sources themselves. Overall, sustainable, fulfilling friendships come through *mutual* channeling of love.

Finally, now that we know more about strategic negotiations and can conceptually take successful negotiations one step further to create true love, we're going to get more specific and stack our hand with cards people actually want. These cards will aid us in initial and lifelong negotiations. It's our calling to spend every breath becoming a miracle for our miracle and a gift for a gift we could never truly deserve.

Yet we're not just doing this to find or keep a match. We're doing it because, as Love Heroes, our task is to deliver a message of profound love from our source. Whether someone else answers the call and delivers the same message to us or not, we're going to love others appropriately by becoming love itself.

So, as we dive deeper into creating true love's magic, pick a card. *Every card.*

5

WHAT TO NEGOTIATE WITH

Any leftover clothing tightly laced her figure, leaving little to the imagination. Moisture glazed both our skin as my shirt was already off. Of course, we were at the beach in Warren Dunes in Michigan.

Summer-heated asphalt guided my friends and me there to escape the worries of our education. That's when she showed up; this beautiful girl walking in the sun's spotlight, accompanied by a Chihuahua. Being a curious little fellow, he trotted up to meet me as she set their stuff up next to us. We'll call him Theodore. After this distinguished gentleman introduced himself, I returned the gesture to the girl and struck up a conversation.

Our exchange eventually waded its way into the water. With each passing minute, pieces of our hearts we hadn't planned on sharing made their way out loud. Tears actually began to streak down her cheeks, adding to the waist-deep water. Even things like her childhood and her deceased father glided across the water between us. Everything flowed like an unexpected dream. That is, until a beach patrol abruptly brought us back to reality because they saw Theodore off-leash. The well-behaved gentleman, they did not see—only a blatant criminal trying to outrun the law.

Without a warning, and in front of a beach full of people, they immediately instructed her to leave. Embarrassment and sadness covered her face while her hands gathered her things one by one. The mall-cop-like patrol squad lingered and watched the whole time. Our time was cut short, and my heart wasn't thrilled about it. Her arms juggled a panic-packed bag overflowing with items as her eyes made their way to mine. Rather than make eye contact, she peered straight into my soul and said, "I'm really glad I met you, Andrew." And that was goodbye.

Months later, the absence of her phone number haunted me. That translated to sleepless nights. But without her last name, there was no trace of her on social media. My only leads were a 3-month-old memory of what she looked like, her first name, that she was sort of a Seventh-day Adventist Christian, that she worked at Chipotle, and that she was from a general part of Chicago. A city of *2.7 million people.*

One Saturday morning, sheer determination put me in a suit and behind a driving wheel on its way to Chicago. Churches seemed like my best odds to see her again. Not everyone attends church, though. Four destinations awaited the recital of my situation and the question of whether anyone knew her. But aside from church members advertising some of their own single family members, she was nowhere to be found.

So, like blindly throwing a Hail Mary dart at the board, my GPS and appetite led me to a Chipotle. While in line, my lifeline courage inquired about a blonde girl with green eyes named... Regina George. First employee, nothing. Second, nope. But the third... still no. It was actually an eavesdropping coworker in the back who overheard and approached, saying she knew a girl by the name and description who worked at another Chipotle about 10 minutes away.

Could I seriously have found her? Like a vacuum with a vengeance, I inhaled my food and grabbed one napkin for my face and another for my pen. Their doors had probably never been so violently burst open after that. With a new destination and a few zoomies and left and right turns, I stood before her restaurant's manager. However, instead of asking him for a job, I replayed the story of how I met Regina one more time and placed a napkin in his hand, which read:

Warren Dunes, we met in the summer. Theodore and I were homies. I should've asked for your number. Date sometime? 1-800-420-6769. Andrew Barcenas.

I did everything I could to honor the mutual interest and connection we formed on that beach. The rest was in the hands of a manager and her response. So many variables in this experience should've made the venture fail, but later that evening, she called me, and we set up a date. And though it's an abrupt ending, that date concluded with a walk after dinner, and her telling me she didn't do relationships. I believed her, respected our differences, and we went our separate ways.

My search for her began because of the unyielding love I've witnessed my God have for humanity. Although He doesn't force His way into our lives, He cares amid millions to search for our hearts and deliver His love to us. Regardless of how it turned out, I channeled love the way my source taught me and played the cards I'd been given. Namely, the card of "Going to the Ends of the Earth for Love."

We'll spend this chapter understanding how the Love Hero's Narrative reaches into every part of our identity and lives, making each part a desirable card. Though every card presents its own unique challenges, they ultimately make us more attractive because they're fundamentally aimed at enriching others' lives. That increases our negotiation power and the likelihood that we create true love.

Let's deal.

The Card of Being Interesting

If you've ever met someone who's boring, odds are they came across that way because there was nothing original about them—they never *produced* anything. They didn't pursue a unique dream, have a mission on their heart, go on their own adventures, or have a strong sense of identity.

Instead, they were content to sit around, work to live, watch movies and TV, read story after story, order takeout, play video game after video game, buy trendy item after trendy item, scroll on their phones, and care less to write a story of their own. Maybe they even consumed themselves by recording everything they did and posting it on social media.

And while we aren't here for other people's entertainment, Love Heroes are naturally interesting and captivating because we're more producers than consumers. The heroic purpose of channeling endless love brings beautiful things into the world that wouldn't be here without us. We leave love in our wake, and the waves we make sway other people's stories. Producing positive effects on others becomes a central theme in our stories, and it prompts people to ask, "Why did they make me feel the way I feel? What's different about them?"

Curiosity lies at the heart of what's different. As Love Heroes, we dedicate ourselves to channeling goodness into the world, regardless of how it may receive us. That means there's a degree of mystery about how life unfolds when we follow our hearts. We're curious what life returns when we give it our hearts.

The same goes for our new acquaintances. New acquaintances are possible companions. Friendship companions, mentor companions, mentee companions, romantic companions, or you name it. So, as we give our hearts, we're always curious about what role people will play in our narrative—main character or otherwise.

Having genuine curiosity and interest in others is kind, flattering, and encouraging of others' stories because we assume there is more to people than meets the eye—*we value them*. If someone saw us that way, maybe we'd believe it too. They'd make us feel like more than we think we are. This curiosity is intoxicating, *especially* when it remains detached from outcome.

Most people use curiosity to fish for something they want or to vet *if* people fit into their story. Love Heroes explore *how* people fit. They could fit as a beautiful stranger passing in line, an enlightening sage, or an opportunity for compassion we'll never see again. Whichever way, our curiosity leads us to see them as having value and belonging in our stories.

Paired with confidence, true heart-led curiosity carries "with or without you" energy because it explores people without *needing* anything particular from them. When people don't need anything from us, their presence lifts a weight off our shoulders, energizing and giving us life. People seek those who give life. *They're attractive.* People pity and avoid needy individuals because they tend to make life more complicated and heavy—they drain life of its energy. They're *un*attractive.

When we lean into our curiosity, set aside any agenda, and carry a warm energy of hope, goodwill, and kindness toward others, we reveal ourselves as life-giving people who have something bigger at work within us. People who follow their hearts and have direction in a grander narrative are mysterious and fascinating.

Following convictions of the heart is at the core of every captivating story. For starters, when we sense there's a plot, we're intrigued and want to find out what happens next. Better yet, we're interested in how the plot applies to *our* lives. Best yet, when we sense an available, meaningful, and adventurous role in a riveting plot, it's exhilarating to think we might fill it.

Listening to the heart also makes us fascinating because it *keeps us scarce*. One does not simply dip their toes into passions, beliefs, and convictions of the heart. When one sees a way to live life to the fullest, *they slam the accelerator.* As the saying goes, "People want what they can't have." It's the rule of supply and demand—one of the most basic principles in economics. This rule applies to many things in life, including relationships.

Say, 1,000 people want an Ultimate Collector's Series (UCS) Harambe Silverback Gorilla Lego set, but only 100 exist right now. That means there's more demand than supply. Lego could price-gouge its products and charge 400% of its usual prices. That inflated price, of course, will discourage people from buying, and demand will drop to something like 100 buyers. Now, after selling those initial 100 sets, no one will be willing to buy at that outrageously inflated price.

So, when the next 100 UCS Harambes come out, there will be more supply than demand. To correct this, they'll lower the inflated price to 200% of what they'd typically charge, since they know people still want it, just not at the crazy 400% price increase. People become interested again, and now 200 buyers are willing to place orders. Demand again exceeds supply because product availability is insufficient to meet the number of willing buyers.

In short, the scarcer something is, the more demand and value it typically fetches. This concept helps explain why diamonds and gold are worth so much. They're rare, and people want them for their precious beauty.

Being a person who's in short supply isn't about seeing a text and not responding right away to seem like we're busy. It's about *actually* being busy with things our hearts are called to do and enjoy. It's about having options to fill our time with the things we love.

If we play the game of supply and demand in relationships by acting scarce when we're really not, *we're lying*. The truth will eventually come out. When they fall for our deception, we'll eventually be together in our home, and they'll notice most of our time is spent laughing to ourselves, scrolling on Instagram, or watching Netflix while eating pizza.

What then? They'll discover the truth that we're not in demand because we're never actually busy outside of our jobs, if we even have one, and their interest in us will decrease or disappear. We not only lied to them but also probably wasted their time. They want to live an interesting story, not another common charade. In the end, *those who play the supply-and-demand game in relationships are destined to lose, while those who ignore the game by focusing on their narrative and convictions will win.*

It's also worth noting that demand and value are always contextual to the market they're in. We could date a 9/10 hot person, and they might always be in demand because everyone slides into their inbox. Obviously, the people sliding into a non-single person's inbox don't really value relationships because they're actively trying to compromise one. Therefore, they're expressing *sex market* demand, *not* necessarily *life-partnership market* demand.

Because of all this attention, the hot partner could get an inflated ego from their sexual marketplace demand and misinterpret their sex appeal value for their relationship value. Loving couples build marriages on relationship value. Therefore, to Love Heroes, whose demand is for true love, a 9/10 attractive person carries negligible weight if they don't possess values that juxtapose their sex-appeal value.

The point being, we're to follow our hearts to be interesting and find things we love doing. It could be a hobby, or multiple hobbies. But if there's zero passion for the journey we're taking, there's little convincing others to join us. If we have no purpose outside of a romantic partner, we'll get old and boring to people after a few weeks. Again, a character cannot *be* a narrative. Characters play *parts* in stories.

Pick up pickleball, basketball, crocheting, knitting, sewing, cooking, volunteering, dance classes, an instrument, board games, writing, informative reading, run club, anything! We must produce something within ourselves and in the world.

Creating a love story requires that we *produce*. We cannot simply consume media and spectate other stories. Spectators watch stories happen—they *don't* take part in them. Producers fund, write, cast, and perform their own narratives.

So, go. Be interesting!

The Card of Holistic Education

When we picture ourselves becoming well-rounded individuals in love, choosing to become someone like Jesus would be a solid choice. As far as I can tell, Jesus was a perfectly well-rounded individual.

He didn't explicitly come across as an introvert or an extrovert. He was empathetic unto tears, intelligent unto playing 4D chess with his antagonists, physically skilled unto carpentry and fishing, understanding beyond life and death, generous unto giving his own life, and loving unto children, politicians, thieves, prostitutes, murderers, foreigners, plague carriers, and men and women of all ethnicities alike. That's a *long* road of personal depth to travel.

I love viewing Jesus as an aspiration-worthy example because He assigns everyone the same task to strive toward, regardless of where they stand. Any personality works well in pursuing His example of love. An introvert should strive to be a bit more social and pull themselves out of their mind. An extrovert should challenge themselves to spend more time in solitude to meditate.

The empathetic and the emotional should learn to hold their intuition's conclusions longer to give reason and stoicism a say. The intelligent should leave some calculations to their gut, intuition, and emotions. All traits have a time to shine and a time to shade, and we would do well to grow into all of them.

Growing into all of them allows us to express strength and contribute to every situation. Whatever empowers us to contribute to the lives of others is a part of the Love Hero's Narrative. With time, we could eventually become everything one could ever want or need. A listener, talker, leader, supporter, empath, you name it.

The art of becoming everything one could ever need carries a couple of benefits. First, it widens our field of compatible partners and makes mate selection easier. If we know how to be anything, we can step back in the areas where our partners naturally shine. Then, we can step up in the areas where there's shade and a need for contribution.

Second, Love Heroes become virtually self-sufficient. Of course, we're social beings, and we'll always need people in our lives. There *are* things we can't provide for ourselves. But Love Heroes aren't exhausting to be around because we're as low-maintenance and need-free as they come. That grants a sacred freedom to love and operate out of *want rather than need.*

Let's observe "want versus need" practically. As any great story starts, imagine you're alone on an island, starving to death with a volleyball named Wilson. You haven't eaten in fourteen days, and the hallucinations are beginning to set in. The palm trees look like corn on the cob, and the genie lamp you found four days ago looks like a mango covered in aggressive, overly attached mud.

You rush to grab the mango and start rubbing and clawing off the mud, and suddenly, your wildest hallucination fabulously announces himself as your one-wish genie. Though you don't fully believe the situation is real, you decide you're fully on board and willing to comply with your hallucination. So, you wish for an unimaginably large banquet. In the blink of an eye, a banquet appears before you, only its layout is quite odd.

The plates taunt you about your dire situation by being on the sand and at different distances from you. One is at your feet, one is twenty meters away, another is twenty meters past that one, and so on, twenty meters apart.

As if desperate to crush your primal debut on the National Geographic channel, you approach the nearest plate and begin militantly shoveling the expired, cooked Kraft Mac n' Cheese into your mouth. You were so hungry that instinctual needs took over.

Because of its magical nature, the plate only runs out of food when you've had your fill. You roll onto your back so you don't have to dig a hole in the sand for your stomach, and bask in relief. You've fulfilled your needs.

After some time, out of curiosity, you go to see what lies on the other plates. The plate twenty meters away is a pizza with your favorite topping, and you think to yourself, "Oh... that might've... been nice, actually..."

You then visit the next plate and find a tail end of Steelhead with asparagus and mashed potatoes. That seems a little more balanced and satisfying. Scratching your head in borderline regret, you move forward and find an organic Wagyu steak cooked to perfection, with caramelized onions and garlic adding to its glaze. Naturally, it comes with an organic salad, organic roasted Brussels sprouts, and a cool glass of your favorite beverage.

Tragically, enough time has passed that the beautiful meals you feasted your eyes on have mostly gone bad and succumbed to the scavengers of the island. As your blood pressure rises, your muscles tighten up, and your face turns red, you refuse to go any further because it would only cause you more fury and pain.

The point of this story is to say that if we blindly act out of desperation and satisfy our needs with the nearest relief, we ignore the compass of desire. Chances are, our immediate needs never live up to our truest desires, which will eventually lead us to contempt. Therefore, if we want to love someone as unconditionally as a human can, we should aspire to free ourselves of need. Not out of a spirit of hyper-independence and not needing anybody, but to put as little pressure on our partners as possible and ensure *both* our needs and desires are met.

This intentional well-roundedness goes beyond personality. It extends to many other proficiencies: laundry, cooking, woodworking, gardening, housekeeping, medical knowledge, philosophical wisdom, emotional intelligence, community building, financial literacy, physical health, humor, artistic talent, conflict resolution—literally anything that could be useful to a potential partner or make our unified lives easier.

Overall, personal and holistic growth increases our negotiation power, expanding our options for finding and keeping a high-quality match. The more well-rounded we are, the freer we are to satisfy our own needs and build relationships out of genuine desire.

The Card of Prioritizing Sleep Health

Believe it or not, sleep has a monumental impact on our dating and relationships. For starters, it makes us more physically attractive. In a 2017 study, participants rated photographs of people based on five metrics: (1) how much they'd like to interact with them, (2) attractiveness, (3) health, (4) sleepiness, and (5) trustworthiness.

People consistently perceived photographs of sleep-deprived individuals as *less socially desirable, less attractive, less healthy, and sleepier.*

There was no difference in trustworthiness. The findings suggest people "avoid contact with sleep-deprived, or sleepy-looking individuals, as a strategy to reduce health risk and poor interactions."[i]

Reflection likely leads one to conclude the researchers are correct. Tired people rarely bring any energy to social interactions. They won't be carrying any parties on their backs or raising any roofs. Rather, their tiredness would likely be a bore or a social repellent.

Continuing the reflection, we've all dealt with a sleepy parent, sibling, friend, or partner before. Their grumpiness isn't a force any logical person would want to reckon with. Recognizing that pattern, we might avoid someone who looks tired because they're likely to be in a bad mood and have poor social interactions. We've all learned the ancient proverb: *To avoid a sleepyhead is to let a grumpy pants get to bed.*

There could also be subconscious instincts passed down through human history informing us that looking sleepy is a sign of poor health. There's a buffet of academic literature concluding that sleep deprivation weakens the immune system. For example, after a single night of 4 hours of sleep, immune cells vital to eliminating cancerous and virus-infected cells reduce their activity by about 30%.[ii] So, the chances of sleepy-looking people losing an immune battle are significant. They might just be a plague factory, and being around them could get us sick. That's not exactly attractive.

As far as we know, sleep deprivation is associated with cancer, dementia, Alzheimer's disease, poor blood sugar regulation, diabetes, cardiovascular disease, heart attack, insatiable appetite, poor microbiome health, weight gain, obesity, infertility, sexual dysfunction, chronic pain, injury, strokes, lower productivity, depression, anxiety, and even suicide.

It also worsens decision-making, learning, memory, and creativity. Being *awake for 19 straight hours* leaves us with a cognitive impairment equal to being legally drunk,[iii] slows our reaction speeds by about 50%, and significantly reduces our accuracy in mental calculation.[iv] As for learning and memory, sleep is when our brains review events from the day and organize information into either solidified or to-be-forgotten information.[v] Remembering an anniversary or a small, meaningful detail requires rest.

Then, concerning creativity, dreams brought about the invention and creation of the periodic table of elements, the sewing machine, Google, DNA's structure, Einstein's Theory of Relativity, *The Terminator*, the *Twilight* series, and a plethora of musical pieces. The Beatles, Michael Jackson, Jimi Hendrix, Queen, The Police, Florence and the Machine, Billy Joel, Johnny Cash, and The Killers have all recorded music based on tunes encountered in their sleep.

Creativity is key to success and romance. So, if we want to write our love stories and life accomplishments as best as we can, sleep is *nonnegotiable*. Here are a few tips to improve our sleep, because the *number* of hours isn't everything. Adults need 7-9 hours of *restful* sleep.

First, we should *limit sound stimuli*. Meaning, there shouldn't be background noise. If we have a fan going or live in a busy city like New York, we might benefit from some earplugs. We shouldn't be listening to music or watching TV shows, as these media keep our brains partially active while we sleep, leaving us feeling unrested upon waking. I sometimes use silicone earplugs because they're very gentle on the ears. Just keep good earplug hygiene if you choose to go that route.

Next, we should keep a consistent sleep schedule. This means going to bed at the same time every night and waking up on schedule. The best way to optimize our sleep schedule is to *experiment* for a few weeks and cut off media and other stimuli by around 8:00 PM or earlier, and let our bodies tell us when we're getting tired and should go to bed. If we naturally stay awake until 3:00 AM for a few weeks, so be it—we're night owls.

Night owls are one of the few different sleeper types. They actually get more energy later in the night and benefit from sleeping in, and make up about 30% of people.[vi] The other 70% of people roughly match their sleep schedules to the rise and fall of the sun because our bodies cyclically flush out and produce a sleepiness hormone called melatonin. That said, making our *sleeping areas* as *dark* as possible would help us sleep better.

Next, *exercise* functions as a prescription for insomniacs—those with trouble sleeping.[vii] Exercise fatigues our bodies and helps us to fall asleep. Our brains naturally need rest because we use them all day. But our bodies don't always move a ton, and having a restless body can prevent quality sleep. If we follow this tip, we should make sure our exercise routine ends at least 2 hours before bed so our bodies have time to settle down.

Eating right and on time will also aid our sleep endeavors. We should avoid foods that cause bloating, stomachaches, or pain. That food is obviously not doing us any good and might actually damage our guts, which could be catastrophic for our overall health. If we don't sacrifice the food that harms us and our sleep, the food will sacrifice our well-being.

We should aim to finish eating at least 3 hours before bedtime. If we go to bed at 11:10 PM, we'll want to take our last bite at about 8:10 PM. Snackies before bed aren't ideal because digestion takes energy and, like watching TV, requires some brainpower, which disrupts sleep's restfulness. This is a struggle because, listen—I know how divine a 10:00 PM Taco Bell run is.

When we cover sobriety, we'll see how being sober from marijuana and alcohol benefits our sleep. For now, our final tip will be to sleep in a cool room around 65° Fahrenheit (18.33° Celsius). This temperature is the sweet spot for our bodies. Our bodies like to drop their temperature by 1-2° F as our metabolic processes slow down, and 65° isn't warm enough to keep our bodies hot like they're running on all cylinders. Bodies also don't want to spend a ton of energy struggling to stay warm, so it's just warm enough to let the body's heating mechanism take a rest.

In sum, Love Heroes get good sleep to remember important details, look attractive to their partners, optimize their health, maintain a pleasant attitude, and have energy to give as much as they can.

The Card of Dietary Habits

We've talked some about diet in this book already, and I don't want to write a book about nutrition, so we'll mainly reemphasize the principle of whole foods and talk about eating less sugar.

Whole foods are unprocessed foods that come directly from trees, bushes, herbaceous plants, the soil, and animals. Clif Bars are not a whole food. They're closer than gummy worms, but they're not classified as whole foods. Hot dogs, chicken nuggets, pizza, French fries, and juice are all examples of processed foods, *not* whole foods. Whole foods have undergone no processing other than cutting or washing and have been combined with no oils or other additives.

A healthy aspiration would be to eat 80% whole foods and leave room for some mildly processed foods. This task distances us from cereal boxes, chip bags, frozen pizzas, candy, cakes, protein bars, ice cream, noodle cups, etc., but still allows us to enjoy life. That may seem overwhelming, and that's fine. We have a growth mindset! If we're starting a dietary health journey from square one, the ultimate answer to how healthy we should eat is simply: "healthier than we're eating now."

One place to start is by cutting down on the most commonly available highly processed food: *refined sugar*. Refined sugar is terrible for a few reasons. If you'll remember from *Chapter 1*, when we consume food, our bodies spend energy breaking it down and absorbing nutrients. Whole foods require plenty of energy to break down, whereas processed foods require very little. Therefore, our overall calorie intake from processed foods is typically greater than from whole foods.

Processed foods are a wonderful solution for solving the problem of starvation. Served as a main dietary staple, though, they lead to poor metabolic health and obesity. *Metabolic health* essentially defines human health at the cellular level rather than by appearance, symptoms, or body composition. The human body is so accustomed to breaking down whole foods and deriving nutrients from them that our cells don't handle the altered nature of processed foods well.

Then, of course, regarding obesity, absorbing more calories from processed foods eventually causes us to gain weight from the excess calories we store. Whatever energy we don't use will go straight to our hips or our body's favorite fat storehouse.

If that weren't disastrous enough, processed foods also dilute nutrient density, meaning fewer nutrients per unit of weight. Nutrient density helps us feel full because we eat food for more than just energy. Our bodies need things like vitamins, minerals, and electrolytes. We even have a hormone notifying us we've gotten what we need and can stop eating. It's called leptin, and it squawks at our brains until it's satisfied with the nutrients we've gotten.

Most processed foods are whole foods broken down to their basics. White rice and brown rice are actually the same plant—only white rice is processed, removing the bran and germ, which contain fiber and several vitamins and minerals. Once broken down, certain nutrients are lost, and depending on the food, manufacturers may add fillers.

Filler content gives processed foods more volume while adding virtually no nutritional value. Typical fillers are low-cost, readily available ingredients such as corn, wheat, soy, vegetable glycerin, and plant hulls. They're commonly found in cereals, low-cost cheeses, crackers, and some fast-food meat products. The result is a dilution of nutrient density. So, even if we're having a bloating competition with the nearest hot-air balloon, we still won't feel full. Leptin won't have signaled that we've satisfied our needed nutrient threshold. Ultimately, processed foods are low in nutrients, which leads us to overeat and absorb more calories.

This applies to all processed foods, but *especially* sugar. Sugar is the most processed food on the planet with *zero* nutritional value. Yes, *zero*. It's also incredibly addictive and can make our energy levels plummet, which isn't ideal for being good company or writing our best love stories.

The plummet I'm referring to is the spike in blood-glucose levels —glucose spikes. You might know it as a "sugar crash." Glucose spikes overwhelm the mitochondria in our cells. As you may remember from 6th grade, mitochondria are the "powerhouse of the cell," and they use glucose molecules as their fuel. When glucose spikes and over-saturates the blood, our powerhouses go into over-drive and eventually get overwhelmed because there's only so much energy processing they can do at once.

After being pelted with innumerable glucose molecules, the mito-chondria form a workers' union, write an open letter of complaint, put on some shades, flip off the boss, go on strike, and walk away in slow motion after lighting a dumpster fire in the middle of a busy roadway. Which is why they say, "If ya glucose spike, ya mitochondria strike."

Okay, no one *really* says that. But that's the principle. When our powerhouses shut down, we feel lethargic. Diabetes is an illness characterized by glucose spikes, and its dangerous nature is simply that the body completely shuts down because of the glucose overload on the cells. As we get older, our bodies become less resilient to glucose spikes. They hit us harder, and we can more easily develop type 2 diabetes.

While we can avoid spikes by reducing or eliminating our refined sugar intake, there are other hacks as well. First, we can make sure we *eat fiber before we consume sugar*. Plants contain fiber, which gives them structure. Bones are to animals as fiber is to plants. Fiber is fascinating because it gets all up in the sugar absorption process, slowing its entry into the bloodstream and decreasing glucose spikes.[viii] Saving dessert for last is actually a smart idea after all!

Other helpful strategies include drinking more water, exercising, getting enough sleep, drinking less alcohol, adding apple cider vinegar to our diet, maintaining a healthy weight, and eating fewer processed carbohydrates. Toning down the candy bars, ice cream, and soda pop would be a smart move.

Overall, our diet influences our energy levels, mental health, physical health, and attractiveness. Having plenty of energy and being mentally healthy make us a joy to be around. Physical health makes us attractive because eventually our bodies are supposed to mend with theirs. Maintaining a healthy diet benefits our partners, making it a sacred thing and an avenue of love.

It's actually quite amazing what whole foods can do for us. Turmeric, broccoli, flaxseed, and garlic are all very effective at helping us fight cancer.[ix] Eating ginger before and during menstruation reduces blood loss and can reduce pain intensity.[x] Pistachios can increase blood flow to the penis and enhance erections.[xi] Nature's Candy ❌. Nature's Viagra ✅.

So, here's your invitation to research how food can transform your relationships and quality of life. With enough dedication, you'll eventually excel at cooking, which is not only great for you but also for your partner's mental health, physical health, and attractiveness. Which, I suppose, is really also a benefit to you.

The Card of Exercise

Exercise is a very dynamic card. It's easy to get started, staves off diseases like dementia, can be enjoyable, helps keep us at a healthy weight, makes us physically appealing, and improves our mood, memory, emotional regulation, and learning.

People frequently claim that exercise is difficult to commit to. This is most likely because it's easy to get discouraged by intimidating standards, such as the CDC's recommendation for 2 days of muscle-strengthening per week and 150 minutes of moderate-intensity exercise. Moderate intensity exercise is sweat-inducing and works our hearts at 64-76% of their capacity. According to the CDC, only 28% of Americans are meeting this recommendation.[xii] It's a big ask if we're starting from 0 minutes and 0 days of exercise, so plenty of us tune out.

It doesn't have to be overwhelming, though. Although that threshold is recommended, *it's not the threshold with the greatest benefit*. Wild benefits start from simply not sitting as much. Sitting down for 10 hours a day increases our likelihood of developing dementia by 8%. The kicker, though? Sitting down for 12 hours a day increases that likelihood to 63%![xiii]

Just sitting for 2 hours less a day can dramatically decrease our likelihood of developing a tragic illness that's aggressively on the rise. We're not even talking about exercise yet. We're just talking about the benefits of somewhat passive non-sitting activities, like standing during an office break, getting groceries, going for a walk, taking the stairs, or cooking.

The benefits of exercise taper off as we become more active. Though I don't have any hard evidence for you, there's probably more benefit in going from 0 to 50 minutes of exercise per week than there is in going from 50 to 150 minutes. *Getting started is the most valuable part of the entire process.*

So, ignoring the sigh-inducing goal of 150 minutes, we should simply get started. Because when we ask ourselves, "How much exercise should I be doing?" the answer is almost surely this: *"More than we're doing now."* One push-up would be better than doing none. One squat to drop it low to our favorite song would be better than being a potato while the vibes are absolutely churning.

Activities we enjoy are a fantastic starting point for exercise. If it's choreographing our own dance routine to the latest Nickelback album, we'll do what must be done. We don't have to start a gym membership. I enjoy playing basketball, spikeball, pickleball, and walking my dog. Maybe your cup of tea is cycling outside, mountain biking, swimming, or obstacle courses. Whatever's enjoyable to us should be easy to start.

Over time, physical activity will build our bodies. Our bodies work in such a way that when a demand is placed on them, they adapt so the next time the demand is made, it's less stressful. Whatever body parts we use, they'll strengthen and develop. But if particular body parts don't get used, the body lets them wither away. Muscles take energy to maintain, and if they're not being used, there's no use in having them. They'd just be taking up precious resources. This is good for us to realize for a couple of reasons.

For one, if we want a capable, sexy bod, we know we need to stay active. Otherwise, our muscles will shrink. Two, it teaches us that muscles are valuable assets not only for their looks and use but for what they do passively to keep us in shape. They consume energy and resources.

This passive energy consumption occurs throughout the body. Moving and being active require energy, but we also spend energy just staying alive and keeping the lights on. Breathing, seeing, hearing, smelling, detoxifying the body, and defending against illness all require energy. These passive activities are the basic processes subsidizing our existence, and they're summarized as the basal metabolic rate (BMR).

The BMR burns 60-70% of the calories we eat. Digestion burns another 10%, and physical activity burns 10-30%. So, we *burn about 80% of our calories passively*. Developing muscles is the best way to increase BMR because having muscles requires the body to sustain them with nutrients and energy. That energy can come from fat. We'd be wise to weight train, eat plenty of protein, and get plenty of sleep to grow muscles. Those habits won't only make us look and feel better, but also raise our BMR to burn calories passively.

Building a strong body is a valuable card in negotiations because it allows us to offer and partake in adventurous stories. It also typically means we're sexually attractive. Revisiting the lesson from the sleep section, looking healthy is attractive because social interactions are more likely to be positive, and we won't seem like an illness factory.

Finally, an exercise card is valuable because it improves our mood, emotional regulation, memory, and learning. A highly underrated personal quality is *mental stability*. Consistently being in bad moods and having little control over our emotions doesn't exactly make us likable people. No one wants to walk on eggshells or have to constantly stabilize or appease someone else. It's high-maintenance and exhausting.

If we want a long-term romance, we should do everything in our power to be pleasant, stable, and likable. Exercise is one of the things in our power because it directly affects the endocannabinoid system (ECS). The ECS participates in the formation of new neural pathways (neuroplasticity), learning and memory, neuron production, inflammation, appetite regulation, digestion, energy balance, and the regulation of stress and emotions.[xiv]

The ECS is what tetrahydrocannabinol (THC), the psychoactive compound in marijuana, interacts with. Marijuana's interaction with the ECS stunts our learning and memory capacity,[xv] has an anti-inflammatory effect, gives us the munchies, slows our digestion, relaxes us into a low-energy state, and soothes our stress and emotional intensity.

You can take your pick of what's good and bad from that list, but exercise actually affects *all* those things positively. It increases neuroplasticity[xvi] and enhances learning and memory by increasing blood flow and generating more neurons in the hippocampus. The hippocampus is the part of the brain responsible for emotional regulation, learning, and memory.[xvii]

Exercise also has anti-inflammatory effects, helps relieve pain by producing endorphins, promotes healthy digestion, improves overall energy, helps regulate stress and emotions, and even treats depression and anxiety *as effectively* as medication and therapy.[xviii]

In conclusion, exercise is a massive card with other cards hidden in it because it lowers our emotional maintenance requirements, helps us feel good, and creates a nice, healthy body that our partners get to call home.

As we regard ourselves as homes, it's a loving thing to care for them as sacred places we're preparing for true love to dwell in. Should it be dirty? Should it be difficult to find rest in? Do we want the architecture to look dated? Do we want it to be a sad space? Of course not! Our partners deserve the best.

We must also consider the Golden Rule of "do unto others as you'd have them do unto you." If we're not willing to give a beautiful, carefully nurtured, and sculpted body to our partner, then we don't have the right to ask it from them. And we *want* hot, healthy bods. Let's earn the privilege to ask for one!

The Card of Sobriety

As I begin this section, I want to explicitly state this isn't some judgment on those using recreational drugs. I know recreational drugs are considered normal. This section is simply a true love calculation, which aspires beyond normalcy to create something exceptional.

Drugs have a long history with humanity. Some 4,000 years ago, opium came onto the scene, and humans have been experimenting with drugs and altering their conscious experiences ever since. We do this for a couple of reasons.

The first reason is that life is extremely difficult. Yet despite how challenging life may seem right now, modern living is far more comfortable than in ancient times. The other day on Instagram, I saw a friend post a picture of a red, shockingly swollen ankle after an allergic reaction to a mosquito bite that *wasn't* diseased. It went on to get infected, needing antibiotics. That would've been a death sentence or a lost leg 200 years ago. Maybe both.

Though life can be cruel, it certainly hasn't always been as kind as it is now. As a species, we've been swallowed by earthquake fissures, crushed by boulders, burnt to ash by volcanoes, starved to death by famine, drowned by flash floods, and rotted by plague. Today, at least, we have warnings for most of these things. And that's just nature. When it comes to things we've done to each other, we've also had family slaughtered before our eyes, been brutally sexually assaulted, publicly tortured, and enslaved under tyranny. We have quite a different picture today, even if some of these elements are still present.

Point being: The human condition has always carried some level of trauma, and where there's trauma, there's a need for escape. Which is where drugs are helpful. We take recreational drugs to feel a certain way, or rather, we take them to *not* feel a certain way. Depending on what drug we take, the panic that worries us won't be center-stage. The pain we want to numb won't be screaming throughout our bodies. Or the sadness we feel imprisoned by will seem to melt away.

Our emotions and state of mind are brain broadcasts that tell us what's happening in our environment and alert us to anything that needs changing. The excitement of meeting someone new at a party is a broadcast urging us to romantically transform our lives with them. Sadness from loneliness is a broadcast telling us we need company. Stress and anxiety are broadcasts telling us to respond to, neutralize, or flee from our sources of worry. Grief is a broadcast telling us that a part of us and our model of the world has been erased, and any attempt to establish a new reality does not compute. So for a time, crisis abounds, no matter what we do.

There are different coping skills and strategies helpful in addressing broadcasts calling for change, but drugs are a hack to temporarily bypass those needs. They basically serve to muffle or silence the alerts in our brains. In some respects, regular drug usage is a retreat from the truth and an active retreat from a reality that feels unbearable. Occasional use is fun; daily use is an attempt to *terraform* one's world without addressing the fundamental need.

I won't pretend to understand everyone's retreat from reality, nor can I imagine all the circumstances driving them to retreat. Yet, despite how difficult life is and how justifiable a retreat from reality may seem, true love and its growth nature are *inaccessible* in false realities with silenced broadcasts for change.

Today's most common terraforming drugs are alcohol, marijuana, pornography, and certain video games. Alcohol is an addictive substance that slows information processing in the brain and delays communication between the brain and the body. Under its influence, we have less control over emotions and impulses. This can manifest as personality changes, such as the abnormal display of courage, spontaneity, extreme friendliness, edgy humor, blissful happiness, unwarranted anger, unashamed physical touch, pure honesty, and sheer unbothered peace.

While we can see these as desirable changes, they may ultimately prevent and delay us from actively becoming who we want to be. Instead of actually *being* courageous and approaching a woman, we might take some liquid courage and go strike up a conversation.

Instead of *being* fun people, we might drink so that no walls stand in the way of our spontaneity and silliness. With a slower nervous system, we're less likely to pick up subtle social cues, guard against embarrassment, and consciously adjust our behavior.

It can also act as a mind-numbing strategy to avoid responsibility, grief, heartbreak, and disappointment, all of which need processing. When we don't process what we need to, we smother the truth, avoid vulnerability and connection with our partners, and deny their support.

Alcohol can also affect how we love by causing potent damage to our sleep quality. As we've covered, sleep quality is vital for interacting well with our partners. A study on young adults found that consuming alcohol at least 1 hour before bed reduced melatonin production by up to 19%.[xix] Again, melatonin is the hormone that puts us into deep, restful sleep. Lower melatonin levels are linked to poorer sleep,[xx] which contributes to hangover symptoms, including headaches, general fatigue, increased anxiety, and poor moods.[xxi]

Another factor contributing to those symptoms is alcohol's drastic effect on heart rate variability (HRV). HRV measures the consistency of our heartbeats. Heartbeat-rhythm irregularities increase when we're ill, stressed, physically active, overworked, experiencing powerful emotions, or reacting to external stimuli. Compared to one's baseline, more irregularities indicate that the body *isn't* truly resting, recovering, or stress-free. Fewer irregularities are linked to better physical health and sleep.

One study measured the baseline HRV of over 4,000 individuals and tracked it across three levels of alcohol consumption: 0.25, 0.5, and 0.75 grams per kilogram of body weight or more. For a 150-lb (68 kg) person, the low intake category for their body weight would be 0.57 oz of alcohol—about 1 glass of wine. The moderate category drank about 2 glasses, and the high-intake category drank 3 or more.

Although participants didn't include the timing of their alcohol consumption, the results were a concerning omen. The groups' irregularities increased by 9.3%, 24.0%, and 39.2%. Meaning, their sleep quality and daily bodily recovery plummeted by up to 40%.[xxii]

Knowing what we know about sleep, it's also safe to say it elevated their bodily discomfort, irritability, and drowsiness. I don't wake my wife up one second earlier than her natural sleep cycle does because I prefer to live. I know a well-rested Abbey is an Abbey who's able to love to the best of her ability.

Yet another caveat of alcohol is its cost. According to the most recent data, the average American spends $583 on alcohol every year.[xxiii] While that may seem insignificant to some, if we took that money every year and invested it in a general stock index like the S&P 500, after 30 years, we'd have around $106,073.[xxiv] Since finance is one of the most significant sources of stress and conflict, putting money to work rather than drinking it would benefit any couple.

We should also consider the cost savings we encounter by avoiding alcohol-caused diseases. According to the World Health Organization (WHO), alcohol is a Group 1 carcinogen, which is the highest-risk class of cancer-causing substances. In this group, alcohol has the unfortunate company of asbestos, radiation, and tobacco. We know alcohol causes at least seven types of cancer, with breast cancer and colon cancer being the most common. The WHO acknowledges there's *no safe amount of alcohol.*[xxv]

In sum, alcohol can serve as an obstacle to true love by hindering personal development, financial excellence, and a healthy body by harming our sleep quality and elevating our risk for disease and organ damage.

Transitioning to frequent marijuana use, we'll remember from the exercise section that it beneficially relaxes us into a low-energy state, lowers our emotional intensity, soothes our stress, and has an anti-inflammatory effect. On the negative end, it stunts our learning and memory capacity, prevents necessary confrontation, impairs judgment and cognitive ability, delays development of healthy coping mechanisms, increases the risk of developing chronic psychoses like schizophrenia, and dampens aspiration, motivation, achievement, and life satisfaction.[xxvi]

Marijuana's effect on learning and memory is especially potent in youth and young adults because their brains are still developing until about 25 years old. This is particularly notable because adolescence and young adulthood are the prime years in which humans should prepare to negotiate a life partnership through personal development. That growth requires *massive* learning and information retention. Alongside personal development and remembering important dates and events, memory also serves love by storing minor details. The simple Taco Bell order of a girl I fell for years ago is still ingrained in my mind: two bean burritos, no onions.

For both our sakes, I won't run through all of marijuana's negative applications to love. We can imagine just fine how impaired judgment and thinking ability would affect the way we treat, consider, and cater to a partner. It's easy to see why increasing the odds of developing psychoses like schizophrenia wouldn't benefit our partner. We can see how delaying healthy coping strategies for our anxieties would burden them.

What I will talk about, though, are marijuana's effects on confrontation and ambition. While we rarely think of confrontation as a good thing, it addresses issues that need to be remedied. If we continually shift into an unbothered, go-with-the-flow emotional state, we'll never address the important issues that eventually turn into reasons we don't like the other person. Confrontation and resolution *increase* the likelihood that we'll grow and like each other.

As for ambition, it inherently possesses a sense of urgency and progress. Stress and anxiety are messages that circumstances need to change. Without those emotions, motivation is damp, urgency turns into "it *could* get done," and progress turns into procrastination. Without the fight-or-flight response of stress and anxiety, there's no fight.

Love Heroes fight to get where they are. They sacrifice comfort, embrace growing pains, build resiliency, overwrite parts of themselves, practice when they don't want to, rise to unfair occasions, get rejected, and experience heartbreak. Embodying the epitome of love is a lofty ambition, and collecting obstacles isn't part of that journey.

Just for fun, let's do the same financial exercise we did with alcohol. According to LendEDU, in states where marijuana is legal, the average marijuana consumer spends $111.05 per month on weed products. Per year, that's $1,333. After investing that money for 30 years, we'd have $242,531.[xxvii] Cigarettes are *much* worse. American cigarette smokers with a pack-a-day habit spend around $3,800 a year. Their hypothetical 30-year investment comes to $691,385. Of course, it also comes with many health risks.

Finally, let's briefly address the "risk-free drugs" of video games and pornography. Both play on the dopamine reward system, the bedrock for most addictions we talked about in *Chapter 1*. Video games can simulate the satisfaction of almost any desire or need, and porn allows us sexual indulgence without connection, resistance, or risk of contracting sexually transmitted illnesses (STIs).

Both delude us into a low-risk, high-reward reality. We don't have to risk anything other than maybe a computer virus to look up porn and do our lustful business to achieve blissful orgasms. Nor do we have to risk our lives to pursue virtual accomplishments and experience euphoria. This contradicts reality, where *high rewards demand high risk.*

The reality is, we have to risk *a lot* to approach someone we find attractive, build a genuine connection, negotiate, establish a relationship, have sex, and build a life together. There are *so many places* where that plan can fall apart. Every ounce of motivation, energy, and focus counts to keep it together.

Sexual energy is one of the most powerful motivators for development and progress. There's a reason online dopamine-detox movements like No-Fap and No-Nut-November exist. If we're *already* being sexually satisfied in a way, there's little need to aspire to be someone who could attract a mate to meet that need.

The same principle can apply to virtual and real-world progress and accomplishment. If we're already getting a kick out of virtual progress and accomplishments, we won't feel the extra desperation or enthusiasm necessary for significant success in the real world. And while I'm not trying to say video games are evil, they become obstacles when they steal vital motivation and time from building a better life and loving our partners better.

To conclude, we can do what we want recreationally. Fun is a part of life, and using drugs for entertainment every now and then probably won't take over our lives or derail our ability to love. Issues only arise when we use them to silence alarms for change, terraform our worlds, or make them gods.

Life is hard, no doubt. But Love Heroes view any and all "negative" feelings as calls to develop coping skills, stand their ground, overcome challenges, and make the changes they need to create the life they want.

Sobriety is a card that ensures our motivation and energy stay where they belong for a Love Hero: in becoming more whole, growing in love, and creating a loving relationship.

The Card of Social Influences

"Tell me who your friends are, and I will tell you who you are." It's a Spanish saying that's been around for centuries.

"You're the average of the five people you spend the most time with." Wise words spoken by Jim Rohn.

"When the character of a man is not clear to you, look at his friends." A Japanese proverb.

"Show me who your friends are, and I will show you your future." Anonymous.

"Tell me your sources of love, and I'll tell you how you love." That's me.

Humans are beings of momentum. We can imagine ourselves as independent, righteous, and strong-willed individuals, but in the end, we all mold to our environment to a significant degree. The company we keep inevitably shapes who we become. Psychology calls this the *social proximity effect.* It's alive and well in purchase habits, decisions of right and wrong, optimistic vs pessimistic views, relationship decisions, language use, politics, and more.

For those wanting specifics, hanging around people who smoke and drink makes us more likely to adopt those habits.[xxviii] We are more likely to buy things that those close to us buy, and their values bleed into ours.[xxix] One study found that if a friend of a friend gets divorced, we're 33% more likely to get a divorce ourselves. If a close friend or family member gets divorced, the likelihood jumps to 75%. Then if two or more close connections get divorced, we're 147% more likely![xxx]

The authors of *Crucial Accountability* conducted a line-cutting social experiment. A local mall served as their playground. The initial question: "Would you stand up and speak up to a line cutter?" With pride, essentially, everyone said yes. Later, however, when the researchers sent their agents to cut in line at the movie theater, no one *said a word.*

A university library would serve as their next experiment. Only in this context did the troublemakers make a ruckus, basically throwing a party in the silent environment. Again, no one spoke up. To up the ante, they infiltrated the university cafeteria, sat next to some students, and sampled their pie and fries *without* permission. As one would hope, some spoke up. The majority, however, stayed silent.

The point is, even to strangers, we prefer to blend in. This phenomenon crosses generations and age categories. We adapt to new environments, even when they conflict with our current values and beliefs.

When I'm around swearing sailors, I swear more often. I'll often try the TV shows, music, sports, and books my friends enjoy. Sometimes I use the language I see in memes. And if the boys start knitting, you can bet your bottom dollar that tomorrow I'll pull up with a tricked-out needle set and a premium yarn blend of Chilean Vicuña and Tibetan Cashmere.

When it comes to who we're going to be, we must choose influences wisely. Inputs of productivity, sobriety, ambition, fun, intelligence, kindness, wealth, and respect will make us all those things. It's not that we'd try to extract things from these sorts of people, but rather we'd want the presence of their positive habits, values, thoughts, and decisions to carry some momentum into our lives. Every friend I have has something I'd like to bring to life or improve within myself. I deeply respect them all, and my heart adores them in special ways.

As much as the social proximity effect advises us who to include in our lives, it also warns us who to *exclude*. This doesn't necessarily mean we avoid befriending and extending kindness to people with momentum we don't want to be like. It just means we need to be *extremely* self-aware to guard the habits and values we want to keep. If we notice ourselves slipping into choices, values, and habits we don't like, it's best to avoid their influences altogether.

However, if we feel confident in standing our ground, our behaviors and choices can positively influence others. We don't need to try to change anyone, though. Exemplifying goodness is enough to invite others to embrace positive momentum.

The basic principles behind these social decisions are: (1) we should prioritize influences that carry positive momentum into our lives, (2) we should be cautious of influences carrying momentum we don't want, (3) we should be generous to others and want to enhance their life without judgment, and (4) we can't force people to change—they must want to change.

In sum, social circles determine one's growth trajectory and identity outcomes. When we surround ourselves with people we admire, we'll unconsciously carry some of their being into our being. These people are called friends, and they help us become who we want to become.

Friends enhance healthy momentum and discourage unhealthy momentum. True friends care about how our lives are going and will answer truthfully when we ask them an honest question. Try asking these:

- "What would you find most difficult about being in a relationship with me?"
- "What's something objectively unattractive about me I can change?"
- "Is the person I'm dating the one for me? Why?"
- "How is being with my current significant other changing me for the worse and for the better?"
- "In what ways am I too hard on my significant other?"
- "In what ways am I the problem?"

Friends are a resource for growth and success, and they're a grossly underestimated asset and card. We must choose them wisely, because they either make us or break us.

The Card of Romance

We shuffled down the porch steps of my house and trampled over some grass to get to the curb. My hand reached ahead to prop open the uphill-facing passenger-side door, allowing her to easily step in and strap in. I walked around to join her, turned the ignition key, paused, and placed a blindfold on her lap. Wide eyes and a curious smile sprang on her face, and after a brief inquiry, the blindfold did the same, tying a knot at the back of her head.

Music roared as I drove around the neighborhood, back and forth and in circles for about 10 minutes. We ended up about a block away from where we started. "We're here, but keep the blindfold on," I instructed. Grabbing my supplies, I exited the car and gave her my guiding hand, leading her to casually commit a misdemeanor: trespassing.

To avoid any unnecessary attention, we parked away from streetlights and wandered through dirt mounds and construction areas on the route to our destination. It wasn't long until we climbed onto an unfinished porch and meandered through where double doors were yet to be built. The center of the room called to me, and I instructed her to wait still as anticipation built with her and the room.

In my supply bag, lay a Bluetooth speaker and a set of battery-powered candles. In haste, candles sprouted throughout the room one by one, and the speaker rested a to-be fireplace. "Connected to 'Device, welcome, Master Andrew, '" the Bluetooth speaker announced. The voices of Bon Iver, Novo Amor, Canyon City, and others began to fill the room and spill out where windows should be. Like a magnet, my body closed the space between us. I gave her the okay to remove her blindfold, and her face bloomed as she met a bare-bones house under construction.

Spellbound, seeing her in wonder, I drew closer and reached for her hands. Our eyes met, I took the first step, and we began to dance. Her wavy brown hair pressed against my chest, and we orbited each other as serenades guided us through ebb and flow. Beams of moonlight streaked their way through the several unfinished skylight windows in the ceiling like a comedically small disco ball.

After etching that moment into memory, we wandered the house, pointing out what goes where, and settled on a windowsill overlooking a street. Other unfinished homes peered back. As our bodies sat on the house's edge, my fingers dove into my pocket and pulled out a garnet necklace. That's when the question at the edge of its seat stood up, and asked her to be my girlfriend. With a resounding "Yes!" she brushed her hair to the side, donned the necklace with my help, and we designed another moment with our lips.

Retracing my steps in this memory and others, I believe there's a formula for romance; an equation, if you will. This card, more than others, is one I aim to teach you.

Being romantic isn't just about expressing love. Picturesque romance is more about leaving the current world behind and creating perfect moments. These artistic moments have *anticipation, risk, vulnerability, connection, beauty, play, poetry, and surprise.* And they're all co-dependent.

Anticipation is tension built within a narrative. Sequences of events that kindle curiosity and tease expectations generate narratives. Those in the dark are told something is coming, but they'll have to tag along to find out what it is. The simple question, "What's going to come next in this sequence of events?" lies at the heart and paves the way for a grand reveal.

Vulnerability is the exposé of the heart. It's when we remove our filters, bury our pride, mute our sense of self-preservation, tell the truth, risk injury, and show sides of ourselves others rarely see.

Expressing vulnerability toward a romantic interest leaves them with two possible responses. One, they can see us without our armor and reject us. Or two, they can take off their own armor and reveal their heart in a shared sacred space where lies, charades, and games pass away.

If what we seek is a reward as valuable and remarkable as a genuine intimate connection, we have to be vulnerable and risk what's valuable to us. To receive the reward of a heart, we must put our hearts at stake. High risk, high reward.

Once upon a time, Bob Goff's book, *Love Does*, inspired me to dream big about love regardless of the odds. Midway through my reading, a gorgeous professional female soccer player appeared in my social media feed. I was instantly smitten. As a buddy of mine and I exchanged messages, she came up in conversation, and the bluff that I was going to ask her out escaped my mouth.

Perhaps he just wanted to see if I would do it or if I was all talk, but on one of our calls, he said, "I'm coming out there with you, and we'll get you to ask her out!" A credit card launched his cross-country flight from California, and eventually landed him on an 800-mile road trip with me starting in Chicago.

Our journey held lake campouts, sneaking into campgrounds late and leaving early to avoid fines, touring national parks, janky motels, and trunk-cooked meals. At its end, in Cary, North Carolina, awaited a romantic stunt in front of thousands of people.

The traffic outside the stadium parking lot stood still as the moment of truth approached. A sense of peace intruded on my nerves with the turn of a key. The engine and I shared a sigh of relief. Pulling the door latch, my body wandered to the roadside, where a bush full of flowers welcomed fans on their way in. My hand grazed the shrubs as my eyes browsed for the brightest blossom. One spoke to me, and I planted it inside my breast pocket as part of my wooing plan.

Back at the steering wheel, little by little, the line moved along until our car found a grass parking space. There, my backseat snazzification routine commenced, and I brushed up as much as one could on a road trip. The sign I drew up at home to ask out my crush fit snug under my arm, and we printed footsteps toward the stadium entrance.

At the entrance, security checked our tickets and asked to see my sign, which had a lightweight jacket draped over it. The first strangers to witness my heart on public display were going to be a couple of security guards. Was I about to get my sign trashed in front of a bunch of people and get barred from entry? Blood began rushing to my face, and it suddenly got hotter.

Their eyes surveyed my masterpiece for a brief moment and disinterestedly gestured for me to pass through. "Must be a common occurrence..." I thought. Maybe they were just looking for profanity, not to smother some poor fool's dreams.

In the clear, past them, I re-concealed the sign under the jacket and made a beeline for our field-side seats. After a few announcements and some patriotic traditions, the match commenced. Even though the letters on my sign were large, they probably weren't big enough for those sitting on the opposite side of the field to read, which is where the team benches were.

Unfortunately, my crush wasn't a starter either, so I couldn't even be sure she was on the other side of the field. *Do bench players show up at all the games? What if she had a sick day?* Whatever the case, now and then, like a prairie dog, I'd pop up my sign, hoping it'd find her eyes, and bashfully duck it back into hiding.

As is customary at most live sporting events, there's a cameraman who walks around getting footage of fans and putting their cheers or crazy outfits on screen. He had already passed by us once. The pressure of the camera and big screen grew with every step he took. It started to get hot again, and my hands decided they didn't need blood. Was I going to pass out? Throw up? *Whose stupid idea was this?!*

When his presence lingered behind me, I couldn't speak. Maybe we came all this way for nothing. The sound of internal defeat was deafening, and only the sound of my man Pabby's voice snapped me out of it. With the boldness of the ultimate wingman, he harnessed the cameraman's attention. "Hey, man! Can we get a shot of this?" The footage specialist curiously glanced at the sign. "Oh-ho-ho, yeah! We've gotta get that, hold on, buddy!"

In my mind, my hands were cradling my head because of what was about to happen; in reality, my hands stayed on my lap because I was about to be on camera in front of thousands of people. As the prophecy foretold, Pabby would get me to ask this girl out. He was my strength when I was weak, my voice when I couldn't speak, and the best there was in me. He lifted me up when I couldn't reach and gave me faith because he believed. As Celine Dion might put it. Truly, this wouldn't be happening without him.

My moment had finally come, and the cameraman took his stance, aiming his lens directly at me. So, I flashed my titties—no, I'm kidding—I flashed a smile filled with emotions like WHYYY, embarrassment, excitement, and hope, and cheered my sign above my head. It took all my focus to stay sane in this vulnerable moment. All I knew was that this was going to be the best chance she saw my sign.

Pabby was even camera-ready when I got on screen. Not a pit stain in sight, baby! The front of the sign read, "How many signs does it take to get a date with #27?" As a gesture of showmanship, when I flipped it, it said, "Hopefully not Morgan one," since her name was Morgan.

After what seemed like 23 seconds, my moment of vulnerable fame was finally over. Would I get the date? Would I be rejected? Honestly, I was just relieved it was over. I crossed the country to ask out a girl, and the rest didn't even matter. The stunt had spent all my mental energy, and I felt a tremendous sense of accomplishment. What seemed impossible just moments ago was now written in history.

It was only after the game, when she and her team did their gratuitous lap around the field for their fans, that I realized she was actually there. Upon finishing their lap, they were free to walk around, and she paused on the other side of the field, blushing, looking at me and my sign.

Showing Some Courage

Mental calculations seemed to be flowing through her mind as a couple of teammates huddled around her like a posse of elementary school girls, gossiping, teasing, and poking her to answer all their curiosities. "Who's that silly boy over there who likes you? Do you think he's cute?"

Waving my sign around is all I could do. My brain was so spent, I even forgot to pull out the letter I wrote and the flower I picked. In the end, she turned her back, and I never got to say a word to her.

Would things have been different if I had pulled out the letter and flower? Maybe. But things turned out the way they were supposed to. I didn't know it at the time, but she was at least in the talking stage with an NBA player. Though he was the most notorious dirty player in the NCAA during his college basketball career, the minimum salary for an NBA player was about $900,000. So, I can't really blame her for her conclusion in mental math.

Not only would he have great genes and a handsome salary, but entertaining a sweet romantic public gesture would mess with something that's not broken. It'd be unnecessarily insulting to him.

Regardless, the point of this story is vulnerability. Putting ourselves out there, free to be rejected, is vulnerable because it can cause us tangible damage. The crowd could've booed me; the security guard could've ripped up my sign and told me to go home; the cameraman could've slapped me and told me that's his girlfriend; or my crush could've told me no, which she did.

Despite the venture's failure, there was something I didn't expect. I didn't expect to feel like a *triumphant hero*. It takes an armored soldier to willingly step into war and into harm's way. But it takes a hero to take off their armor, risk it all, and bravely go forward alone to connect with those on the other side. The most astoundingly perfect moments of love aren't created by calculated, guarded steps, but by vulnerable and wonderful moments of courage.

When we risk something of ourselves in vulnerability, we tell a truth that can come from no one else. The thing is, if the other party understands what we're communicating and sticks around, that means whatever we showed them resonates with them. If they're not bolting in the opposite direction, they're somehow seeing a way for our unique truth to fit into their narrative. That's called connection.

Connection is the mutual attachment to sacred truth. By sacred truth, I mean what really controls our stories: our dearest beliefs, values, desires, and pillars of identity. If two people share sacred truths, they're automatically attached to a piece of each other. They just might also co-create a beautiful and enriching lifelong narrative together.

The sacred truth I revealed to Morgan was a belief that love is worth risking everything for. It was worth the cross-country trip, the energy it takes to write a letter, the potential humiliation, and the small thought of picking a flower. To me, love is worth taking a shot that's longer than the long shot.

From her perspective, the uncertainty surrounding me seemed unreasonable. Certainly not reasonable enough to risk her relationship with an NBA player. It was unreasonable because either she had already found a connection or our beliefs were simply contradictory. Hence, presenting my sacred truth proved fruitless, and our narratives didn't align. We didn't connect.

Vulnerability is a prerequisite for the principal component that all romance revolves around: the **recognition of beauty**. There are 3 types of romantic gestures acknowledging beauty. Those are acts recognizing and acknowledging (1) that the partner is beautiful, (2) how *we* see the world as beautiful, or (3) how *they* see the world as beautiful.

The first is the most flattering, but it's typically short-lived because partners can't really co-create the romantic experience with us. It's hopefully uncomfortable for them to engage and sit in their own self-adoration. These recognitions of beauty include writing songs about them, giving them thoughtful gifts, adoring their bodies with massage, and offering compliments. Type 1 gestures are pretty much things people can't do for themselves.

Type 2 takes our appreciation of the beauty we see in the world and invites our partners to see it, too. These recognitions require vulnerability because we're allowing them to step into our being and see the world as we do. They could find our view uninteresting and cause us subtle sadness by not seeing it the way we do. *Or* they could see the beauty in it and scoot their being evermore in line with our own.

These beauty acknowledgments could inspire themed playlists for how we feel about them, convince us to take them to our favorite hiking spot, prompt us to revisit places that hold precious memories, or push us to share one of our hobbies with them. They're pretty much invitations to step into our innermost world, past, present, and future. It's an invitation to step into a narrative once exclusive to us and create original memories we prefer to co-author with them.

Last, type 3 is recognizing the beauty our partners see in the world by deepening our exposure to it and finding beauty in it ourselves. This recognition communicates that we *see* our partners' innermost world. Seeing this inner world demands profound listening and attention to detail. It requires us to take the time and effort to see the world through their eyes, accompany their emotions, and tenderly whisper that we adore the way they see it.

Type 3 is essentially the inverse of type 2. Instead of sharing our favorite spot, concert artist, precious memory, or hobby, we're stepping into their favorites. These acknowledge that we pay attention to what they adore, and that we truly see them as sacred. They express how interested, proud, and overjoyed we are in witnessing the story they're writing in the world. So much, in fact, that we propose to be honored as co-authors of the beauty they see in their narrative.

As magnificent as types 2 and 3 are, their caveat is that they can *also* be grounds for extinguishing a romantic spark. One reason is that we can be mistaken for desperate. We can avoid appearing desperate by having *no expectations* and giving all our recognitions as *genuinely free* gifts. The other reason is that if a person isn't ready to be seen with, exposed to, or invited to so much vulnerability, it can scare them off. Placing their hearts into someone else's hands or holding someone else's heart just might not be a risk they're willing to take yet.

Nevertheless, I don't believe recognitions of beauty are ever regrettable. If they reveal they aren't ready for the vulnerability required for true love, it's never our job to make them ready for it. That's a daring leap they have to make on their own. They just cut to the chase that they can't give what we're looking for.

In some cases, people might react by putting themselves at a distance because they're not *used to* vulnerability due to a guarded family, culture, or society. They might also need to take things at a snail's pace because they still have some healing to do. In these situations, we face the difficult decision of whether to stick around. We could take the chance that with time, effort, vulnerability, and connection, they'll take the leap and commit. Or, we could spend time and effort only to reach a dead end.

My experience with this decision is that I never stuck around long. As I've witnessed with the Christian God, one can give love in a moment, but it may not resonate and be accepted for decades. I was always happy to love vulnerably and selflessly as my source of love instructed me to. But I was never so confident as to expect that my love would suddenly transform someone else to be ready for vulnerability and connection. That certainly wasn't the case for that girl from Chicago.

So, over time, if we channel love without expectation and they don't reciprocate interest, it would be wise to continue our search elsewhere. We can't live forever on a one-way love street, and we also can't force someone to be somewhere they're not. They have to choose it in their own time.

With this course of action, they can realize love's wonder when it's gone and witness how beautiful and transformative it is. With this understanding, they can come back around to us as an evolution takes place in their hearts. Just as beautiful, if that evolution takes place and they don't come back to us, we'll have blessed them by introducing them to a wonderful love. Somewhere in the distant future, that seed of love we planted may allow them to find someone they're able to love the way they couldn't love us. I'll leave it there.

The next components in the romance equation are **play** and **poetry. Play** is the release from attachment to social boundaries and to how reality really is. It's kind of a combination between knowing zero social cues and psychosis. It's characteristic of not knowing social cues in the way that it disregards what's normally socially acceptable. Play skirts the boundaries and tests the limits of "stepping over the line."

As for the psychosis bit, well, children play in different worlds all the time by letting go of reality and creating alternative ones. They understand not everyone lives in their world, but they don't care—they're going to say, see, and do what they want, regardless of what society deems acceptable.

It's only when they get older that they actually start caring about what people think of them. But in their age of innocence, they role-play as heroes, monsters, animals, and fairies. The really cool ones are undercover time-traveling secret-agent dinosaurs. Yet, we don't refer to these tiny humans as psychedelic crackheads or delusional schizophrenics. We simply find them to be in an endearing phase of childhood.

The truth is, everyone participates in play. Though for adults, some forms of play are more socially acceptable than others. Acceptable and even idolized forms of adult play are acting, reading, sports, video games, and various other hobbies. People take on unique and fantastical identities in film, and no one bats an eye.

Even by watching, listening, and becoming immersed in stories, we take part in play. Every time we go to the theater, stream a TV show, play a video game campaign, or read a book, we're escaping our reality and are briefly living in a made-up story in a fictional universe. We all briefly "believe" that the dragons, spells, people, and technologies in fictional stories exist.

But if we're the only adults on the playground dressed up as a turtle wizard pretending to run from monsters with the other children and our pet weasel, *we're* suddenly the weird ones. Parents will cautiously transplant their children to a park free of wackos. Possibly call the police. There's certainly a line with adult play, but we all still do play.

A beautiful piece of wisdom I learned from *Tuesdays with Morrie* is that we are every age up to our own. We *know* how to be toddlers who will believe anything they're told. We *know* how to be an innocent, sweet, and imaginative seven-year-old. We *know* how to be snobby and disrespectful teenagers.

Equally in line with this wisdom is a quote attributed to Charles Bukowski: *"The problem is, we look for someone to grow old together, while the secret is to find someone to stay a child with."* If we can *fractionally* reproduce the playfulness of a child, we'll be able to invent powerful and perfect romantic moments.

Thankfully, in a past lifetime, we were all children. We all played unashamedly, knew how to be anything we wanted to be, and thought it perfectly acceptable to escape and create our own worlds. Romance requires us to resurrect that playful ability. It demands we face, embrace, and team up with our inner child to skirt around boundaries.

Poetry is the act of complementing and adding meaning. It's the dance of complementary ideas: spring and fall, life and death, blossoming love and heartbreak, victory and defeat. Adding meaning is like telling someone a song reminds us of them or creating a piece of jewelry inspired by their eyes.

Finally, we have the latter half of anticipation: surprise. **Surprise** is the climax of all the tension built up in a narrative. It's the relief after holding one's breath and the taste of a sweet kiss after hovering on the brink of their lips. It's the reception of a gift one never expected and the answer to the question, "What's going to happen?"

Of course, there's also a fair amount of surprise for the romancer. Are the partners going to trust us? Are they going to go with the flow? How well are they going to co-author and play with us? Will they be vulnerable? How do they respond to challenges and the unknown? What risks will they take?

If we condense all these elements of romance, we can write them into the equation shown in *Figure 10*.

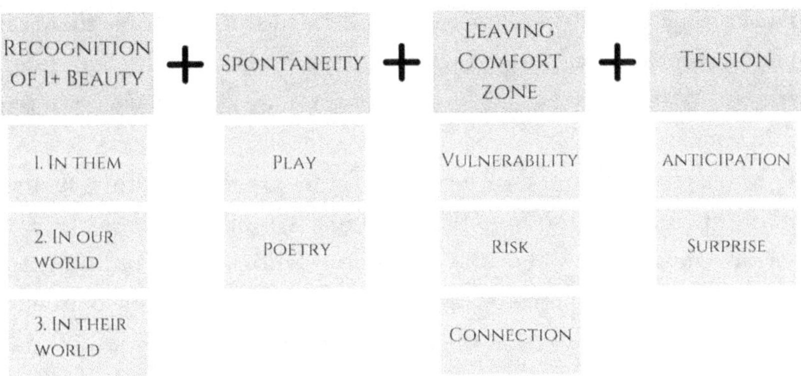

Figure 10: The Romance Equation

To better understand this equation and bring it to life, let's put it to the test by analyzing a couple of my stories. First, we have Regina George. I didn't ask her out until 3 months after our interaction. We simply saw each other at the beach, connected in conversation, and paused for a cliffhanger.

Most likely, we both reflected on that day, wondering "What if…?" We felt a sense of anticipation that would probably never be answered. Then, in going to find her, I risked embarrassment, wasted time, hope, and my ego because she could always reject me.

Going to the lengths I did was clearly a surprise, and leaving my napkin note clearly communicated my interest in her. No one goes to those lengths unless they obviously deem it worth the risk. That's a tremendous compliment and recognition of something desirable about her—some sort of beauty. Type I, to be precise.

On that napkin, I also called back to our moment on the beach and bantered that Theodore and I were homies. That adds an element of playfulness, as if she would go on a date with me just because her dog loved me. The opportunity also provided a poetic opportunity. After all these months, she could add meaning to my gesture and answer the song of romance by making a phone call and going on a date. By meeting up, she also stepped into risk and vulnerability.

Toward the end of our date, we sat in her car, building more anticipation. In a pocket of silence, I asked her to play a song that was meaningful to her and asked why it carried meaning. She chose *Last Letter* by Witt Lowry because her dad passed away from cancer a few years back.

And even though it took a miracle for us to see each other again, I intentionally killed the romance equation by not capitalizing on any tension. She clearly stated she didn't do relationships. Continuing to fan the flame of romance by kissing her would be a means to an end. I could see the brick wall at the end of the tunnel as clear as day. As I said, if people aren't ready, we can't make them be. But, there we have it: acknowledgment of beauty, spontaneity, leaving the comfort zone, and tension were all there.

In the next analysis, my under-construction-house scene had anticipation in the blindfold and the simulation-like drive around the neighborhood. The surprise was in the location and the reveal of what we were there to do. With the serenades, dancing, and relationship proposition, I created tension, invited her to play spontaneously, and was vulnerable. When someone can say no, there's always vulnerability.

To up the stakes, I combined it with an element of risk we haven't really talked about yet: *literal danger*. Although the risk was extremely low and lighthearted, trespassing is still a risk with possible legal ramifications or even violent defense by landowners.

This literal risk of trespassing may or may not be something I've done more than once. But if I *had* done it more than once, there would've been essentially no chance of running into anybody, and I always would've been respectful to property owners with zero harm, zero waste, zero privacy violations, and zero trace.

Now, this isn't a recommendation to harmlessly break the law just to generate a romantic moment. Legitimate risks have real consequences. But theoretically, if one could find a reasonably safe way to add an element of actual risk, it would enhance romantic experience. Being in places we're not supposed to be or haven't been, and doing things we're not supposed to do, adds layers of stimulation, memorability, and adventure.

This is because the mysterious unknown naturally generates adrenaline, amplifies tension, forces us to leave the comfort zone within reason, and demands that we spar with unforeseen variables.

The appetite for danger and risk basically runs in human DNA. It's why archetypes like Beauty and the Beast exist. This archetype presents how women crave danger in romance. A beauty meets a brawny, aggressive, ambitious, and daring beast-like man. Then, this uncontrollable beast suddenly becomes utterly captivated by the beauty and narrows all of its intense lust and focus onto her.

A powerful fascination, fantasy, and sense of awe awaken in the woman. "*They want me? I* can bend the beast to *my* will?" No doubt, being chosen makes everyone feel special. But a beauty taming a beast that not even other beasts can tame is an ego boost on a whole other level.

Experiencing the euphoric praise-like attention given to her, she wants it to remain there. She loves the challenge of taming him and the power at her fingertips. Additionally, ambitious and powerful men are more successful and useful. Taming the beast and keeping it for herself will secure her and her offspring a fruitful and secure future. But here, the beauty faces a complicated dilemma. Her fascination and interest stem from the taming, the challenge, and the special attention.

If she successfully tames the beast, the beast will no longer be a beast. Because how do you tame a beast? You remove the risk it poses. You domesticate it entirely. Then it becomes livestock. And what livestock is at the top of the food chain? What livestock is useful in protecting against threats or manages and wrestles chaos well? That's a job for a shepherd or guardian. *Or a beast.*

The beauty's dilemma is that if she exterminates the risk and completely domesticates the beast, she loses the root of her interest and a significant usefulness in the beast. His aggression, strength, and risk-taking all forecast the security and success she wanted. At the same time, if she allows the beast to remain a beast, perhaps, with his passionate sexual appetite, he'll become interested in indulging in another beauty and leave her.

So, what's she to do? Extinguish the flame in her own heart or wait and see if the beast might extinguish it? The solution is to find a *man.* Which is why the beast turns into a human in the Beauty and the Beast story. The beast doesn't suddenly change personality and turn into a boy. No, he softens a little, becoming a man, but doesn't revert all the way to the harmlessness of a child. He maintains some sense of his beast-like nature and personality.

Unfortunately, men are a rare breed. Men have mastery over themselves. Their aggression and sexual appetite are under control and focused, and their ambition stays steady. They take calculated risks, and their strength is both thriving and reserved.

The beauty finds her fun in "taming" him, but it's all a ruse because he tames himself. If she has power over him, it's only because he voluntarily gives it to her. He stands his ground and doesn't always bend to the woman's wishes as if she were his master. Men are beasts with self-control.

The Beauty and the Beast archetype is what's behind women's love for bad boys and best-selling novels like *50 Shades of Grey* and *Twilight*. This theme also shows up in females' pornographic preferences. A book written by curious Google engineers, called *A Billion Wicked Thoughts,* found that women preferred porn and romance novels revolving around characters like doctors, cowboys, bosses, princes, kings, surgeons, billionaires, knights, and the like. These keywords are at the top of their respective "food chains" with plenty of risk and power composing their lifestyles. Beauty and the Beast is one of the most prominent female fantasies.

As for the inverse male fantasy, that archetype might look something like a man meeting a youthful, innocent, and beautiful virgin and transforming her into a sex-obsessed woman who won't stop begging him for more.

Regardless, this tangent points out that risk is deeply woven into the main female fantasy. Leaving the comfort zone and taking on risk is core to maintaining a woman's passion, and both men and women would be wise to recognize this. Women need to know how not to extinguish their own flame of passion. Men need to know how to fan the flame of passion without letting it get out of control. They need to possess and control an element of danger.

But back to analyzing my trespassing story, the last variables in the romance equation were beauty and poetry. Months before this event, she shared how she enjoyed the peace of walking around under-construction houses and imagining what each home would become.

Well, I stored that information and transformed it into a Hallmark moment. I combined all recognitions of beauty. She found empty houses beautiful. I found nighttime, dancing, and privacy beautiful. And finally, I highlighted her beauty by requesting an exclusive relationship and adorning her neck with a necklace. In all of those things, I added complementary meaning to information previously held by her and me. *Poetry*.

Though that's the end of our analysis, let's run through a hypothetical thought process of planning something romantic. Since beauty is the centerpiece of all romantic experiences, that's our starting point. After we think of the centerpiece, we should add poetry—we should add meaning.

That could be as simple as making two recognitions of beauty complement each other. She loved empty houses. I loved nighttime. I found a way for them to connect and fit each other: dance in an empty house at night. Beauty and poetry, check.

Since leaving the comfort zone often accompanies play, planning any play would be a natural next move. To plan play, we need to identify which boundaries to skirt. Is it the boundary of a private property? Is it the social boundary of speaking in a silly voice, simulating what the dog in front of us is saying?

Perhaps we could benefit from channeling our inner child since we are every age up to our own. What kind of play would a 6, 10, or 14-year-old us be capable of planning? Looking for images in clouds? Painting on each other?Pretending to host a cooking show? Imagining the floor is lava? Spontaneous tickling? Coming up with random names for species of plants on the hike? Smooching off the ice cream we wiped on their faces? What's the play?

Next, even though play is lighthearted, we should always plant sacred truths in our shared experiences. When we smooch something off their face, it should be because we adore their face. When we make up a funny name for a plant, it's because we want to hear them laugh. Defining and expressing these deeper adorations and sacred truths expresses vulnerability and our feelings toward them.

We can easily communicate vulnerability through love languages. Words of affirmation, especially. "I can't help but tickle you because I absolutely treasure your laugh." Or maybe, "I wanted to make a mock cooking show with you because I love spending time and creating with you. I wish we could spend more time together." Both statements bear a piece of the naked heart.

Second to last in our creation of a romantic moment, we need to add tension. The day Abbey became my girlfriend, we were on an afternoon electric bike ride in Minto-Brown Island Park in Salem, Oregon. Trees swayed over and danced in front of us as we rested on a bench. Her shoulders nestled in my right arm, and I worked up the courage to ask her to be my girlfriend. We'd only been dating for 16 days. Delighted, she accepted me as her first boyfriend.

Our eyes met, we gazed at each other's lips, and I said, "I want to kiss you, but now seems like too obvious a time to do it. I'd like it to be special." The tension in the open space was shot and given a second life. If I hadn't called it out and hadn't kissed her, it would've just been awkward. But now, she *anticipated* a kiss. She just didn't know when.

We got back on our bikes and, just a few minutes later, I spotted a trail opening into the forest. My brake pads hugged the wheels, and I led the way, turning into a shaded forest. Row after row of evergreens breezed past us, and sunlight sparsely beamed through the trees. Deep in the forest, we came upon a break in the trees, with only a few sapling bushes occupying the small open space.

A flood of passion unleashed throughout my entire body and carried me off my bike. "This is the place," I thought. All alone, with only the trees, shrubs, and squirrels to watch, our helmets unclipped and fell off. Our eyes locked. Any words would've interrupted where both our minds were going. I steadily approached her, compressing the tension in the air, stood with my face hovering over hers, placed my hand on her lower back, tilted my head, and said, "I'll take that kiss now." My arms pressed her body against mine, and a few seconds were savored before our lips touched. There was magic, and there were fireworks.

Without tension, there's no vibrant romance. When we design a romantic experience, we create narrative tension by veiling what comes next. This veil of *mystery* can be either literal or unspoken. **Literal** veils are like blindfolds, having them close their eyes, a wrapped gift, or hidden contents in a backpack. It's literal because something is *actively* being hidden from their sight and reach.

I often default to bringing a backpack because anything can fit in it. Temperature-preserved liquids, food, cameras, blankets, a sweet Jumbo Jenga set for two, whatever, really. Our partners may know something is up, but they don't get to see beyond the literal veil until the moment of surprise.

The **unspoken** veil of mystery involves never bringing awareness to tension and having its anticipation hide in the shadow of *other* anticipation. For example, when going on a hike, we anticipate a pleasant view at the top. That's literal tension because we know it's coming, but it's hidden beyond what we can see.

Unspoken tension piggybacks on that anticipation and whips out a whopping proposal with a fatty, shimmering rock to put on their finger at the top. There was never any awareness or anticipation brought to that aspect of the event. Most likely. Maybe the photography team and flower bearers following in the distance gave us away.

For Christmas 2023, I bought gold strips, wire for a gemstone setting, and a large topaz, the color of my wife's honey brown eyes. As a surprise, I crafted a custom piece of jewelry by hand. Mind you, I'd done nothing remotely close to that in my life.

As a rule, my wife and I agree that lying is acceptable only for pleasant surprises. That's the only delayed truth in our relationship. As I would go work on the piece at her friend's house, I'd tell her I was going to hang out with a buddy of mine or go to the gym and would be gone for hours at a time.

Whenever she'd ask how it went, I'd be sure to be doing something else to avoid eye contact. I'd also give vague responses because I'm a *terrible* liar. By delaying the truth, I exercised the unspoken version of mystery. She didn't know I was hiding anything. Yet, unrelated to what I was hiding, she had some baseline anticipation because of the upcoming holiday.

Eventually, after one of my outings, she asked about how hanging out with my friend was, and the terrible liar in me couldn't have been worse. I couldn't avoid eye contact, so accepting defeat, a huge grin exploded on my face, and I squealed out the cognitive equivalent of:

"Hehehe! What?! Nothing! Leave me alone! Don't ask me anything! Hehehe!"

At that point, the unspoken veiled mystery became literal because she now knew something was happening. Her eyes rolled gracefully with a smirk, and she diverted her attention to something else. This is the skeletal structure of narrative tension. It's simply about what comes next in a sequence of events.

Creating sexual tension in a romantic experience is essentially one layer deeper than narrative tension because it requires leaving the comfort zone by teasing the natural risks and dangers of physical contact.

Although we seldom think of it this way, sexuality is inherently dangerous. When sexual contact is unwelcome, it can inflict horrific trauma. But even when it *is* welcome, we can still contract STIs, get our hearts broken, and endure accidental physical injury. Sex can hold numbing bliss and beautiful connection, but also great destruction. It's home to both. Hence, anything with a sexual nature inherently possesses an element of danger.

It's even possible to stimulate sexual tension *without* physical touch. A gaze or a phrase that forecasts physical touch can trigger it. Reacting to her tight dress with narrow eyes and a smolder elevates sexual tension. Biting her bottom lip when she sees him in a tux makes both of them want to get in their birthday suits. Gestures and gazes like these are either off-putting *or* invigorating precisely *because* they forecast physical contact. It just depends on what's welcome and what's not.

The experimentation of what's a welcome advance and what's not is essentially the invaluable art of **flirting**. We can consider flirting the earliest stage of romance because it's where we explicitly communicate what type of interest we have in another person. A *lack* of effective flirting will ensure romantic interest goes unnoticed.

To really bring this to life, let's say we want a relationship that's composed of a total of 200% expressed interest—100% from them, 100% from us. If neither of us expresses interest at all, that means there's 0% expressed interest in that relationship. 0% is much farther from 200% than 100% is. Failing to express direct interest fails to guarantee the relationship is even halfway to where it needs to be to become real. Expressing interest through flirting is *vital*.

Since women are the more effective communicators of the two sexes, they're typically the ones to initiate flirting. Though none of these flirting strategies are exclusive to women, women use prolonged eye contact, touch their hair and face, orient their bodies toward the person they're interested in, maintain an open body posture, initiate touch, mirror, use compliments, engage in banter, and use laughter. Let's analyze each of these.

Prolonged eye contact obviously uses the eyes. We use our eyes to gather information. If we prolong looking at something, we're trying to collect as much information as possible. So, when we make eye contact, we're attempting to extract information about what kind of information others are trying to extract from us. Avoiding eye contact means we *don't* want to know what kind of information other parties are seeking.

Prolonging eye contact communicates that we're interested in learning more about someone, *especially* about how interested they are in us. Breaking eye contact too quickly can communicate a lack of confidence or disinterest. If we were confident, we'd have plenty of valuable information for them to find in our eyes. And if we *were* interested, we would seek more information from them.

Next, touching the hair and face brings attention to certain features. Putting on lipstick, biting the bottom lip, or sipping from a straw all draw attention to the lips. Resting a cheek on her hand might highlight the clarity or softness of her skin. Playing with hair draws attention to stereotypical femininity in long, flowy hair. In short, touching on particular features is, more or less, a way of saying, "Welcome to the smoke show! This is what I got."

Body orientation is basically the direction of where one's belly button is pointing. If we want to flirt with body orientation, we need to point our belly button at them like there's a spotlight coming out of it. When two belly buttons face each other, getting closer would be comfortable, and people could fit together into a nice, snug hug. It communicates an interest in how they might fit together.

If the person's belly button is perpendicular to us, like a T, getting closer won't fit very well. Our face will stare at the side of their head, and our belly button will face one of their hips. It's communicating incompatibility and a sincere plea to abort the mission.

An open body posture means arms and legs aren't crossed, and shoulders are neither raised nor shrugged forward. A closed body posture represents protective behavior, implying that vulnerability isn't on the table.

In closed postures, we might clench our fists when we feel unsafe and stressed because we might have to defend ourselves. We might cross our arms to protect our hearts or other vital organs. Women might orient their bodies away from attention and cross their legs while standing to communicate, "You have no business between these legs, and you never will."

Breaking the **physical touch** barrier is a potent form of flirting best initiated by women. Since physical touch has an inherent danger and males are the denser sex, male initiation of touch can be threatening and uncomfortable, especially if the female hasn't already expressed interest through other flirting methods.

When men introduce physical touch, they should frame it in a positive light. For example, imagine him putting a hand on her shoulder to help someone else squeeze by, or lightly placing a hand on her mid-back to invite her to take a seat somewhere. If she had already broken the touch barrier, the man might be more direct and slowly touch her hand by lifting it to ask her a question about a particular ring or bracelet.

A female breaking the touch barrier might look like briefly placing her hand on the top of his hand or knee after he shares something vulnerable. It could look like a playful slap on his arm or a light push on his chest after he teased her or said something funny. She could also fix his button-up shirt's collar or tuck in the tag on his t-shirt. Breaking the touch barrier communicates a desire to be close and a comfort level with vulnerability.

Mirroring is the repetition of others' actions and words, like a game of Copycat. Though it's almost always subconscious when used, common mirroring would include laughing after someone says something and repeating what they said, like "Oh my goodness, told him, 'the bread is supposed to be on the *outside* of sandwiches!'" By repeating what others say, we not only prove we're listening but that we're in sync with them.

To mirror actions, we'll mirror emotion-filled facial expressions and body posture. If their face carries a deeply pensive look or seems surprised, we carry the same energy. If they have an arm resting on the counter, holding a drink, or leaning against a wall, so are we.

The flirtatious purpose of mirroring is to establish common ground. People who are on common ground often make good allies and partners. Their shared qualities make them compatible. The subconscious persuasion happening here is essentially: "We use the same words, think the same things, make the same facial expressions, and find joy in the same things. Oh, em gee, are we the same person?? Probably soulmates, right??"

Compliments are a form of mirroring because they highlight the fact that our values complement theirs. Telling someone we like their outfit means we have similar tastes in style. People with a similar style look good in the same picture. Perhaps it's a sign of compatibility!

Great compliments are meaningful and specific. "You have such a beautiful smile—I can tell it's loaded with joy," or "I absolutely love the way you styled your hair, it frames your face so well!" Ineffective and generic examples would be like "You're pretty," "Hey, good-lookin'!" or "How you doin'?"

The best compliments are gateways to conversation because they're basically pickup lines. For example, say we made strong eye contact for 5 hot seconds. The conversation that could follow might look something like this:

Hi. You have some insane confidence in your eyes, and I need to know what that's about. I'm Liam. What's your name?

Hi, Liam, I'm Elenore.

Beautiful. So, why are you so confident, Elenore?

I... have a few tricks up my sleeve. But I don't show tricks just for free.

A hustler... I see. Well, let me buy you dinner sometime.

Ahh, tempting. You're cute, but I don't go out with strangers.

For you, I'm an open book. What do you want to know?

What should I know?

Well, I'm a gentleman, can make some mean banana bread, I have a dog named Moose, and I'm very into you.

Oooo, a charmer. I suppose the open book is a good read so far.

Does that mean you're open to booking a dinner date?

Clever. How about you guess a number between 1 and 10? If you get the right number, you get my number.

Easy, 10.

That was literally the worst number you could have picked! It was 1. Lucky for you, it has a 1 in it, and I like your vibe!

I'll take it!

PEOPLE KNOW this kind of full and direct flirtation as banter. **Banter** is a mini-mating negotiation session framed as a fast-paced, playful laying down of cards, challenging the other person to counter our cards. Challenges serve as doses of anticipation, gradually building tension that needs to be resolved at some point.

Let's analyze the conversation above. "I don't show tricks just for free." This communicates that Elenore confirms she has plenty of cards, reasons to be confident, and that she requires something to make her cough up any information. Liam is thus required to rise to her challenge—he must surpass "free" by buying dinner. Simultaneously, he challenges her to quality time where she'll get the chance to showcase the "tricks up her sleeve."

She replies with, "You're cute," communicating her interest and encouraging him to keep elevating the tension. Furthermore, she challenges his challenge by demanding information about him because she doesn't "date strangers." He responds with *another* challenge. If she truly wanted to know something about him, she would know what to ask. Again, Elenore answers his challenge with another challenge requiring him to give up some golden eggs, with, "What *should* I know?" What valuable cards do you have to play?

You get how this goes. Their challenges go back and forth until the rising anticipation gets out of control, with an almost impossible challenge where he has a 10% chance of getting her number. By embracing her challenge with full confidence, immediately saying, "Easy," he challenges her challenging game as if it were easy.

If he gets the number right, he looks like a rock star. There's a sweet release of tension when he gets her number, and then they plan a dinner date. If he gets the number wrong, his confidence proves to be completely unwarranted, and his humorous humiliation challenges her to save him from embarrassment by giving him a consolation prize: her number.

By offering a challenge in response to an impossible challenge, *both* the success and failure of her challenge are likely to provide a favorable release of tension.

Aside from being a mini-mating negotiation session where we

discover some of each other's cards, the purpose and benefit of banter is in determining how well the other party deals with the challenges of life. If they can banter and play well, they're more likely to meet the stresses and challenges of life with the same resiliency, strength, optimism, and confidence. That's it for compliments and banter.

Finally, we have **laughter**, which is a sort of affirmation. It communicates that we follow their train of thought, take joy in what they're saying, and support it. If we don't support what people say, we cringe, clench our teeth, argue, or shift our attention. Laughter shows that we *like* it when our attention is on them because it benefits those around them. It says, we want *our* attention on them.

In sum, I'd compare flirting to the previews, teasers, and trailers advertising an upcoming movie. These things build excitement and curiosity about what's coming. Flirting is the advertisement that builds excitement for the first touch, first kiss, or whatever physical contact is to come.

One of the most disappointing phenomena in movie advertising is when a preview *looks* great, but the movie itself is an absolute belly flop when we finally see it. Giving people great previews to trick them into experiencing a flop is a fantastic way to disappoint and never hear from them again. Nobody appreciates being misled. Therefore, it's not only important to build sexual tension effectively when we flirt, but the sexual tension *also* needs to be released and resolved pleasantly.

Whatever seductive image we're curating about ourselves through our flirting, we need to back it up with evidence. We can't be a bunch of phonies. This evidence has to be fortified through proactive research and education that inform intentional self-development and our appearance and health.

Say we're building sexual tension up to a kiss, for example. The appearance of our lips tells many tales about us and our health. Having crusty lips can disclose that we don't drink enough water, only breathe through our mouths, or have poor hygiene. It could also give the impression that we don't even care about our appearance, which isn't sexy. Either way, crusty lips will clear out the kissing booth line in no time.

If we want to keep the line coming back for more, we might do our research find that we should stay hydrated, regularly brush our teeth, floss, tongue-scrape, use chapstick, and avoid harmful substances to our bodies and breath. These oral health practices keep lips smooch-worthy and prevent stinky bacteria from multiplying in our mouths and digestive tracts. According to the Oral Health Foundation, bad breath is the *number one reason* people don't get a second date.[xxxi]

Zooming out from flirtation back to sexual tension, it seems there are a couple of influences increasing the frequency of forecasting and initiating unwelcome physical touch. This, of course, makes for uncomfortable and unwanted sexual tension.

One influence is that a bulk of social activity has shifted from in-person to digital, leading to lower social intelligence. Real-world personal interactions are where we learn social norms and micro-expressive cues that communicate boundaries. Without those learnings, we're more likely to violate boundaries and social norms.

The second influence is pornography's extreme nature and its heavy cultural acceptance. Pornography is simply extreme because it's *entertainment,* not a reflection of natural inclination. To be more specific about its cultural acceptance, bondage and discipline, dominance and submission, and sadomasochism (BDSM) are becoming more prevalent and normalized. While this topic isn't in here to kink shame, interests like BDSM and their impact on the relationship world are a meaningful conversation.

BDSM makes both men and women the subjects of acts like choking, whipping, hitting, tying up, gagging, and other dominating acts that can be painful and harmful. I suppose the motivation driving BDSM is the thrill of danger. Though Louise Perry dubs it a disguised outlet for men to beat women.

Nevertheless, if people aren't of the same mind, you can see how forecasting physical touch or the creation of sexual tension could be troubling. One minute, they're grazing their fingers on your back like you're Claude Monet's first blank canvas, and the next, they're trying to choke the living daylights out of you for what, a life insurance payout?

This is your clear call to action to *not* be the fool who assumes everyone sees sexuality the same. Not everyone receives the same sexual indoctrination or education—especially with porn in the mix. I, for example, before looking up BDSM's meaning or being exposed to media clips, had *zero* thoughts or instinct to choke out a woman during sex. I have no natural inclination to suspend anyone from the ceiling in a trendy yoga position with an apple in their mouth.

But porn regularly influences people to test the upper limits of danger in sexual tension. In fact, 40% of American women and 69% of American men view porn annually.[xxxii] Websites with pornographic content make up about 12% of all websites on the internet.[xxxiii] That's a lot of influence.

To whatever degree we decide to use danger to stimulate sexual tension, *we must read the room*. It's our job to know what our partners find electrifying or unsafe. We want to stimulate sexual tension, not traumatize anyone.

In the end, sexual tension exists because danger and uncertainty pave the way for novelty. Sexual tension is in a spontaneous kiss after we tell them to keep their eyes closed and thoughtfully caress their face until we lay one on them; it's alive in unprotected sex and when we use blindfolds. Will we survive the danger presented to us?

If we do, how does that affect our intimate trust? What does that mean for what we can overcome together? Is my heart and life safe in this person's hands when threats come around? These are the kinds of subconscious anticipatory questions we answer when we play with sexual tension. It's about what comes next beyond the veil.

To conclude the topic of tension, I've visually mapped its components in *Figure 11*. Creating narrative tension requires we build anticipation by presenting a mystery that resolves in the grand reveal. We show them what's in the backpack, remove the blindfold, give them the gift, and so on.

Preferably, though, we want to go as deep as *sexual* tension. This requires us to combine narrative tension with the risk of physical touch. If we exclude the physical touch aspect of risk in *leaving the comfort zone*, we won't create sexual tension, and there's a possibility our intentions may get misconstrued. By that, I mean they may not pick up on the fact we were trying to romance them, and they instead interpret our actions as platonic—purely friendly.

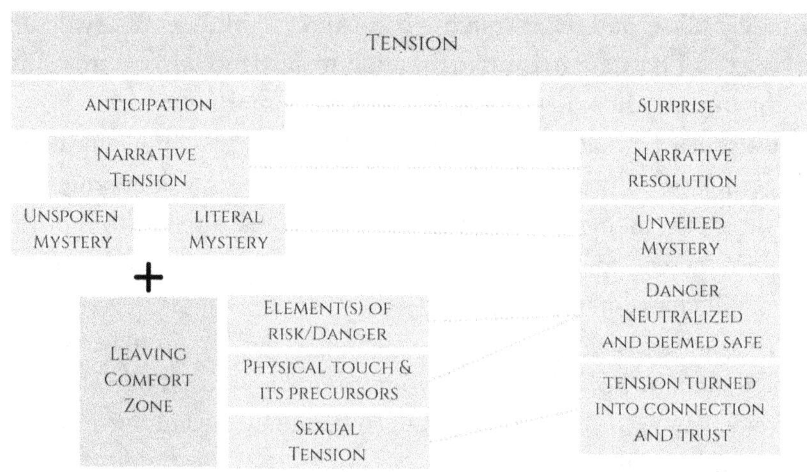

Figure 11: Anatomy of Tension

Leaving our comfort zone always involves risk because dealing with the unknown means there's no prior experience to help us predict outcomes with full confidence. Unknowns mean anything can happen.

Any risk and danger would suffice as an amplifier of tension, but only the danger of physical touch creates sexual tension. This includes precursors to physical touch, like facial expressions and seductive language. Where there's no physical touch or any of its precursors, there's no sexual tension.

When we go as deep as sexual tension, the goal is to resolve the danger of physical touch by proving ourselves safe and our touch exciting. So, whatever all the sexual tension was building up to, we want to ensure it's a positive and pleasant experience. Proving ourselves to be safe people to be vulnerable with establishes connection and trust, which both open the door to confronting riskier experiences together. Naturally, this builds more sexual tension to explore and resolve in the future.

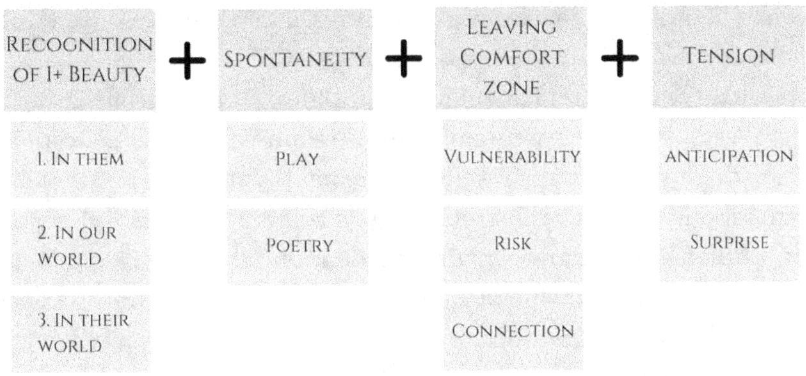

Figure 12: Romance Equation for Summary Purposes

That concludes the thought process and equation we might go through when planning a romantic encounter. Every element is connected, mutually relies on, and enriches each other.

We can't really go wrong trying to create a romantic experience. As long as we remain in a playful state, don't get carried away with the concept of danger, bullrush vulnerability, or traumatize anyone, romantic gestures that land smoothly will be charming. By crashing and burning, our romantic gestures may be humorous and pathetic, but they'll admire our effort and vulnerability. Therefore, our gestures will still be charming.

Honestly, I'd say the most romantic moments happen when there's a bit of crashing and burning. When we're not on script, that's when the most spontaneous and genuine play happens. That's when we truly leave our known worlds behind and dance together to create perfect moments.

Cards of Life: Financial Well-Being

Financial well-being means we've established security, are building wealth, and are progressively increasing our freedom to create true love. It allows us to go on more adventures, attain the things we value most, and live without the stress of scarcity.

Finances are a fundamental pillar of life, but aside from Europe, the West's school curriculum doesn't require financial education. Since there are so many resources already saying what needs to be said, I'll only do three things to help you achieve financial well-being for a fuller life and more mating negotiation power: (1) recommend resources for financial literacy, (2) set expectations about the financial state of the Western world, and (3) suggest some ways one might navigate that world.

The first point should be your main takeaway. Financial intelligence and literacy resources already exist outside this book, and they're things you must learn on your own time. The other two points are simply my words to the wise. Point one is a list of book resources I think are valuable:

1. *The Psychology of Money* by Morgan Housel
2. *Atomic Habits* by James Clear
3. *Total Money Makeover* by Dave Ramsey
4. *The Intelligent Investor* by James Graham
5. *Rich Dad Poor Dad* by Robert T. Kiyosaki
6. *I Will Teach You to Be Rich* by Ramit Sethi
7. *Your Money or Your Life* by Vicki Robin and Joe Dominguez
8. *The Millionaire Next Door* by Thomas J. Stanley and William D. Danko
9. *Deep Work* by Cal Newport
10. *The Personal MBA* by Josh Kaufman

Not all these books are strictly about finances. Some focus on business basics, while others present philosophy and develop skills fundamental to financial literacy, such as discipline and persistence.

If you can't make time to read or listen to audiobook versions of them, feel free to look up video summaries of each book's principles and wisdom. I believe reading for the full experience would be best, but wisdom is the most important takeaway.

Second, to prevent my presentation of economic expectations from becoming too depressing, I'm going to remain very vague. I know you don't know much about what I know, and I know it requires a lot of trust, but all I need you to understand is that *the financial climate is going to get much worse, and life will continue to get harder.* Not to drop an anxiety bomb on your foreseeable future.

Everything will keep getting more expensive, wars will continue, and the money we earn will cover fewer and fewer expenses. Automation and AI will continue to destroy jobs, and economic instability and inequality will keep rising. Government policy won't move fast enough to require companies to adequately share the profits of innovation with the broader public.

This reality will be a downhill process over the next decade or two, which isn't long. The economic rules also won't be the same as those of previous generations because our financial system is unsustainable, poorly managed, and nearing the end of its life cycle. If you explore the history of world superpowers, like in Ray Dalio's book *The Changing World Order,* you'll find that our world transforms over and over again. Nations and powers wrestle for dominance, and shifts in power reset economic rules across the known world. Only this time, the new cycle's transformation includes artificial intelligence and nuclear weapons, further complicating things.

This is just where we land on the timeline. Almost *every* generation in human history has felt like it's been handed world-ending harsh conditions. If they didn't get a changing world order, they got famine, plague, war, nuclear threats, oppression, or natural disasters. Historically, experiencing peace and prosperity has been the *exception* rather than the rule.

My task here is to help you *anticipate the rule* and urge you not to pout, waste time, or be unprepared as an era of exception comes to an end. The worst-case scenario for me in presenting this view is that I'm wrong, everything is fine, you heed my caution, and you become more financially secure. You'll take your time learning financial literacy and its principles, including government policy, loan types, interest rates, retirement accounts, world economic structure, social trends, business practices, assets and liabilities, expenses and income streams, budgets, tax law, tax strategy, investment strategies, good debt and bad debt, and you'll become more economically prosperous. I hope that's the case. Erring on the side of caution and resilience never really hurt anyone.

With those economic expectations set, we can move to our third point: navigating this world. Your own financial literacy will help you avoid unnecessary risk and navigate the economic climate, so I'm only going to sparsely cover *unconventional* navigation.

Presently, unconventional risk management means being particularly cautious with our financial decisions if we don't *perfectly* understand our future livelihood. Now is *not* the time to get a brand-new car we can barely afford or take out crushing student loan debt if the careers we have or want may not even be around in 5 years. This is a time to minimize financial obligations and risks, and reduce nagging debt.

From my understanding of AI, the only safe careers are those that highly value human connection, such as healthcare and education. Any other sector—legal, transportation, coding, engineering, writing, digital design, retail, food service, marketing, film, hospitality, construction, law enforcement—all can and will likely experience significant job displacement by AI over the next 10-20 years.

Whatever technological innovations and automations have amazed you in the past few years are just the beginning. Those advancements will only accelerate. Technology develops *exponentially*, not linearly. ARK research estimates that modern technological innovation will be at least *1,000 times more* disruptive and transformative to human life than the industrial age.[xxxiv] That age saw the dawn of electricity, automobiles, and the telephone. So, again, I reiterate, *now is not the time to overload on risk.* The income we plan to use may not even be available in a few years. Maybe even months.

That's enough of cautionary tales, though. I'll share *one* main practical way to develop a financial well-being card, and then several ideas you can explore on your own.

Once we've educated ourselves in financial literacy and reduced any excessive risk appetite, if we can't find a good wealth-generating line of work, the next best thing for us to do is *acquire valuable life skills.*

Life skills are *by far* the most underrated financial asset. Fixing a broken-down car is expensive. If we learned auto mechanics from YouTube, we might save over 50% on repair costs. I was once quoted $1,700 to replace my brake pads and rotors. After buying all the parts *and* necessary tools, I still saved about $900. Changing my own oil has also saved me a lot of money over the years.

I've cut my own hair since 2015. In Portland, Oregon, haircuts cost men about $25 at the lowest. At a non-chain barber shop, think $35-50 on average. Since I cut my hair about once a month, I've saved $3,000-$6,000 over the past 10 years.

To really emphasize this point, I've plugged a scenario into multiple LLMs like ChatGPT, Gemini, and Grok. If we're in a relationship and we cook 85% of our meals when we eat two meals a day, cut our own hair, make both our coffees, and give our partners an hour massage once a week, we'd generate around $20,440 in value per year. If we have a *single* child and take care of them, bump that to $30,000-$40,000 in value.

Maybe our income doesn't earn $75,000 per year. But with the right skill sets, a $55,000 salary can mimic the economic prowess and lifestyle of someone who earns $20,000 more, assuming they don't share the same skill sets.

So, my advice to those who can't find well-paying jobs in a job-dwindling era is to focus on finding work that equips them with practical, value-producing skills. Think construction, tire shops, restaurants, cafés, communications, etc. Once we have thoroughly developed the skills we want, we can move on to the next job and continue building skill sets that reduce our expenses and increase our power in mating negotiation. The rarer the skill, the greater the value it can produce.

Other unconventional ideas to increase financial well-being include:

1. Switch to more sustainable hobbies (hiking, bird-watching, volunteering, etc.).
2. Study consumer psychology to manage expenses (e.g., letting go of the need to care about how others perceive our socioeconomic status, understanding marketing, and avoiding pointless name brands).
3. Ditch expensive drug habits and coping strategies that don't lead to true healing.
4. Build friendships/connections where we can exchange value and support each other.
5. Build multiple income streams (like creating a small business, running a side hustle, or doing freelance work).
6. Re-embrace a village mentality—leverage family and close-knit assets for support (like moving in with family, borrowing tools, or sharing childcare responsibilities).
7. Protect personal health and assets with good health insurance, diet, and exercise.

Ultimately, financial well-being frees us from the exhausting stress of financial insecurity, equips us with attractive skills, and therefore helps us live fuller lives and write beautiful love stories. *Now is not the time to stew in frustration* at the state of the world. If we don't focus, gain skills, learn financial literacy, and bolster our financial well-being now, life will only get harder later.

This is your call to action and the fire under your butt. No one is coming to save you. So, if you haven't started yet, don't panic, but *get moving.*

Chapter's End

All the cards we've covered somehow benefit our partners. Whether it's through looking sexy, living longer, emotional stability, or creating romance, each card enriches the narrative our partners live. That's attractive, and people generously negotiate for high-quality cards if they want a truly beautiful and fulfilling life story.

One cannot attain these cards passively, however. They're directly inherited through the Love Hero's Narrative and the identity of infinite love it bestows. Love Heroes intentionally benefit others and consistently practice love with anyone and everyone, even when nothing is given in return. Like the sun affects and warms everything within its orbit, so do Love Heroes. We practice love with our neighbors, the old lady crossing the street, the cat or dog on the sidewalk, our enemies, the homeless guy, our family, and so on.

When we're focusing on developing a specific card, there's no easier, lower-stakes practice than on those we don't want or need anything from. So, if we need to practice flirting, compliment the cashier at the checkout and make their day, or challenge ourselves to maintain eye contact when we're saying something meaningful. If we need to practice our banter, hit our boys or girl friends with playful challenges, cheeky teases, or roasts.

If we only ever flash cards of love when we want something from someone, our actions revolve around our desires, making *our desires* our priority rather than our Love Hero identity. This is the trap self-proclaimed "nice guys" fall into. They flash around all these sweet and charismatic cards, but they have underlying motives.

When they get rejected, they completely flip, get angry, and start berating and despising women. These nice guys merely rent cards. Doing a nice thing for a pretty girl for something in return doesn't make one a nice guy or a good person. It just makes them a guy who acted out a nice thing. Being a nice person means doing nice things for *everyone,* no matter the outcome.

I believe the Love Hero's Narrative and these cards are so crucial that I advise anyone who's considering scrapping their marriage to try scrapping the cards they're holding *first*. Before one gives in to their misery, they should try scrapping and remaking their diets, sleep patterns, exercise routines, financial habits, romance practices, hobbies, interests, etc. Many psychological virtues depend on these cards.

Holding these cards anew won't only help each partner think straighter, be more resilient and flexible, and function out of desire instead of need, but they'll also be more attracted to one another. Because in the end, what people really want for long-term relationships are Love Heroes. They want purpose, valorous ideals that fashion a beautiful world, and a fulfilling journey. Love Heroes serve all these means.

As for honorable-mention cards, I'd definitely recommend *personal hygiene, fashion*, and *humor*. We cover the cards of communication and emotional intelligence throughout this book, so we don't need dedicated sections for those, per se.

And now that we've taken care of our end of the deal by sweetening negotiations with valuable cards, thus manifesting a Love Hero identity, we can outline what we should negotiate *for*.

We've chosen to be a miracle. Now, we can ask for one.

6

WHAT TO NEGOTIATE FOR

I'd just walked into a new week-long program designed to help Hispanic students enter the medical field. My plan at the time was to become a physical therapist. We attendees got to know one another, and one girl immediately caught my attention—a Latina with a face like Angelina Jolie and green eyes.

Most of the experience is a haze, but looking back, I do cringe at how teen-romance some of it was. My original piano and guitar pieces made their way across keys and frets for her. Our hands drew together like they'd missed each other their whole lives and exchanged massages, all in front of other people. Any time we could spend one-on-one, we took it—during breaks and late nights on the phone under the stars. I still remember the crisp smell of the Southern California night air. It was a hormonal romantic fling, to say the least.

I also remember getting indirectly publicly addressed because of how distracting and disruptive we were. After coming back from a break in the presentation, the presenters addressed "the cohort" by saying, "We just want to reiterate why you're all here. Let's keep our hands to ourselves and respect the space we're sharing."

There were only *two* people with their hands all over each other. I was one of them. Well, maybe there were more, but I would've never known because I had no peripheral vision when I was around her. Textbook hormone-driven 17-year-old boy.

On the last day I saw her, we went into a random building, found a lounge area, and relaxed on a couch, cuddling as we split a pair of wired headphones and listened to music. It was *almost as if* we had little to talk about. That only lasted about half an hour until she needed to meet her family to get picked up. I decided to accompany her across the university campus to her rendezvous point. As we were about to round the corner to where her family was picking her up, we found ourselves in a courtyard facing each other. Her green eyes gazed up at me, alternating focus between my eyes and my lips. Then, something in my gut told me this wasn't the time.

I held strong eye contact and said, "I get the feeling you want me to kiss you, but this doesn't feel like the right time." As if to understand, her gaze softened, and she nodded, seeming to agree. So, we rounded the corner into her parents' line of sight and said our final goodbyes. She walked into the distance, and after a suspicious glare from her father and a closed car door, she was gone.

Hours later, I took my flight home and called her maybe one more time before I reconnected with Pabby, the friend I later went to North Carolina with. He called me to tell me one of the strangest things I'd ever heard: "Yeah, dude, we were talking about you and how things were going, and she said it was all a bet. Like, she made a bet that she could get a guy just within the week she was here. I just wanted to give you a heads-up."

Indeed, what sane person makes a bet they can get someone's heart and invests a ton of time and energy when they know it's going to blow up in their face? Was she re-enacting *How to Lose a Guy in 10 Days*? I'll admit, I was surprised. But mostly, I was just weirded out and deeply bothered that she would do that. No part of me wanted to be with someone like that.

So, almost immediately after I got off the phone with Pabby, I told her the long distance wouldn't work out. My standards and boundaries had been violated. Namely, the obvious unspoken boundary of

"I'm not going to be someone's bet" and the standard of "I won't allow lying." She simply didn't live up to the expectations I had for a partner.

Standards and Boundaries

Standards are the parameters we set that people need to fall *inside* of. Boundaries are the parameters we set that people need not cross and stay *outside* of. Together, they *navigate the specifics of our mate-selection theories* and form a picture of what we want in a relationship, which is another way of saying that they form our expectations. Allow me to demonstrate.

Standards are the things others need to be or do:

- "They tell me the truth."
- "They put effort into their health."
- "They're not addicted to drugs."
- "They're not a cheater."

Boundaries are the things others need to stay out of or refrain from:

- "I'm not okay with my organized space being messed up."
- "I'm not okay with others talking over or interrupting me."
- "I'm not okay with others making me the butt of their jokes in public."
- "I'm not okay with others watching me go to the bathroom."

Expectations are the combination of what others need to do *and* refrain from:

- "I expect them not to gossip about me just for the sake of complaining and making themselves look better." The *standard* is that they shouldn't be selfish, and the

boundary is that others shouldn't taint their name
unnecessarily.

- "I expect them not to shut me out." The *standard* is that
they should communicate their feelings, and the *boundary*
is not having an immature partner.
- "I expect them not to yell curse words at me." The *standard*
is that they should be respectful, and the *boundary* is not
to be seen as less than. Yelling curse words or derogatory
nicknames exhibits a belief of superiority.

As we can see, expectations can possess *both* standards and
boundaries. To make true love flourish, we need to intentionally set
our standards and boundaries. We need to have appropriate expectations because true love is a garden after all. Gardens need boundaries
to keep out unwanted trampling, pests, and to prevent the invasion of
weeds. They also have specific needs and standards to flourish, such
as nutrient-rich soil, good plant neighbors, fertilizer, sunshine, and
water.

Standards are what we want to say yes to and negotiate for. If we
don't know what we want to say yes to, we lack the benchmarks to
determine whether we have our desires. It doesn't matter the quality
of the person we're in a relationship with. *If we have no expectations or
aspirations for the relationship, it will never satisfy us.* Satisfaction
requires the fulfillment of an aspiration.

Boundaries *protect* our every yes. They are the sea of no's we
refuse to put up with, and they're the guidelines protecting a garden's
ability to flourish.

Standards and boundaries are fundamental to how all relationships function, including non-romantic ones. They instruct and lay
out the rules for how to behave, interact, support, and communicate.
When we meet someone's standards, we demonstrate competency
and fulfill their desires. When we adhere to boundaries, we show
respect.

Respect is the *regard for the traditions, feelings, rights, or wishes of
others.* Since our standards and boundaries represent our self-

proclaimed rights, wishes, and expectations, we can define **disrespect** as the *disregard of standards or the violation of boundaries.*

If we can say, "I *don't* aspire to be someone who disrespects my partner," then we should *stop* violating boundaries and put *heavy* effort into meeting standards. If someone regularly proves the mantra, "I'm happy and comfortable disrespecting my partner and couldn't be bothered to change my behavior," they're not someone we want to be with.

Disrespecting someone isn't the same as losing respect for someone. Respect is lost when there are no consequences for disrespect. While disrespect requires the bad acting of one party, *loss* of respect requires the bad acting of one party *and* the permission of the disrespected. When there are no consequences for disrespect, we're giving it permission to occur. Giving others permission to disrespect us reinforces the idea that we aren't worthy of respect, thereby promoting a loss of respect for ourselves.

Being disrespected doesn't always warrant getting hot and bothered, though. For one, others might not be aware of our standards and boundaries until they've trampled on them. To us, it might scream disrespect. To them, it could just be another Tuesday that they're trying their darned best.

Second, people make mistakes when they get caught up in emotions. Making mistakes makes us human. Acknowledging, accepting, and wanting to redeem our actions makes us *responsible adults.* We should be happy to give our partners opportunities to improve and treat us better. If we choose correctly, they're a Love Hero eager to grow and love better.

Third, it's completely normal for people to poke around and see where standards and boundaries are. It's more or less the reason why we have the social concept of play. All animals with social relationships play.

When puppies grow up with their litter, they play to discover standards and boundaries. As they wrestle, they'll break out their tiny teeth and test how hard they can bite. If the other puppy yelps, maybe biting that hard is off limits. Or maybe... it was just the place they bit. So, why not try biting just as hard somewhere else to see what the pattern is and find the boundary? Whatever combination of actions they try—if the other dog's tail is wagging, they're sneezing, and not yelping—then they're all still in play mode, learning what they can and can't do. All is well.

Children also play to learn standards and boundaries. If they make another kid cry, whatever they did is a no-no because they know whatever causes crying isn't enjoyable. They'll also test their parents' boundaries. "Is this boundary they told me not to cross *actually* a boundary?" If a consequence follows, it's *definitely* a boundary. With no consequences, it's simply a dummy electric fence Mommy and Daddy set up. The child now understands that violating their parents' word is acceptable. Without consequences, parents give permission for disrespect.

As a result, the child *loses* respect for their parents and comes to understand that obeying them is optional. *Unless*, of course, someone reactivates the electric fence and enforces real consequences. If they're cruel parents, they'll repeatedly flick the electric fence on and off to confuse the child about what's expected of them.

The absence of standards and boundaries for children not only fosters disrespect but also chaos in their lives. Entering the world as a child is akin to being given a board game that everyone else also has. We can either play the game blindly and make up our own rules, or we can be taught and embrace the rules most other people use. If we get to make up our own rules, who's going to want to play with us? We certainly won't want to play together. "My checker only gets to move one space, but yours can move five? I don't want to play with you, buster!"

We enter this world socially blind. Social standards and boundaries are the walls that tell us where others walk and how they behave. If there are no walls, our blindness leads us to meander in the wilderness where we'll be lucky to graze someone else's fingertips. So, if we have or plan to have kids, we must take note. Providing our children with a solid set of standards and boundaries will teach them to respect and play well with others, ultimately foreshadowing successful adult relationships.

As for ourselves, since we grew up in different homes and cultures and have our own personal preferences, we'll all inevitably have a few standards and boundaries that differ. We all walk into dating and relationships a *little* blind. Naturally, just like we learned when we were kids, we'll poke and prod around in our new relationships to see what boundaries people have. We'll see what we can get away with and what standards we need to meet. We'll even try some poking and prodding to see if the walls can move at all.

As the newness of relationships fades, walls naturally change throughout different life stages. Meaning, *continual* standard and boundary negotiation is a *must*. Sure, we met the standards and boundaries in the college student environment, but the game rules change slightly when we move in together, and both have jobs. The standards and boundaries will need to adjust to the context of the new world we're both partially walking into blindly.

They'll change again when we get a dog, go on vacation, have one kid, and again when we have another kid. They'll change regularly as the kids get older, when they move out, and again when we're grandparents. Then they'll change when we both retire.

When negotiations end for a given stage, and things are running smoothly, *most* poking and prodding is done by women. By "most," I mean that while men are *not* excluded, I'll primarily write from the perspective that women are the pokers and prodders since they do it more. *You may reverse the roles whenever you wish.*

I suspect there are a few reasons for women's pokey predisposition. For one, the feminine is the domain of the characteristic of play. By its very nature, play skirts boundaries to clarify them and is, of course, prone to stirring up drama. Second, poking and prodding serve a more intelligent and strategic purpose for women. They use play as both a conscious and subconscious *testing tool* to measure a man's *competency, love, and commitment.*

This testing of men comes in two different forms: (1) respectful and (2) disrespectful. The response of men also comes in two forms:

(1) reassurance and (2) distress. **Reassurance** confirms he is strong, stable, reliable, and trustworthy, and that he can build a flourishing home environment for a family and a fulfilling life. **Distress** exposes his weaknesses, his incompetence as a mate, and his inability to establish and maintain a healthy, safe, and secure relationship and home environment.

A **respectful test** *doesn't* violate any boundaries and merely measures a man's resolve. Can he stand his ground? Does he have control over his emotions? Is he open-minded and resilient? Most of the time, respectful tests are eloquently crafted, elite complex questions like "Would you still love me if I were a worm?"

Other times, it's "Would you still love me if I were 300 lbs?" Or "Do you still think I'm pretty?" More boldly, she could directly ask, "Do you watch porn?" If he's addicted to seeing *other* women naked, he's not exceptionally secure relationship material. It's a fair question. Or it could be every guy's favorite question: "Do you think I'm prettier than her?"

Men might ask questions like this, but far less often. Mostly, especially in the dating stage, men just want to know if a woman is an emotional ticking time bomb. If she explodes at the slightest disagreement or respectful testing question, she's going to saturate his life with stress and make him feel like he's always walking on eggshells. If she's *not* easily offended and doesn't carry the baseline temperament of a cornered, feral raccoon, she'll sing him a song of peace, making her sacred and worthy of preservation and protection.

When it's not a question that's testing a man, it might be an action testing an unspoken boundary. For example, she could mess with his organized stuff when she mentally deduces he likes organization but hasn't *explicitly* told her not to mess with his orderly space. If he level-headedly clarifies a boundary not to mess with his stuff, she knows he's not a weak man and has self-control and self-respect. If he says nothing, she'll begin to believe he's weak because he didn't stand up for himself.

A **disrespectful test** *intentionally* violates boundaries. Both men and women will naturally perform this test at least once or twice just to observe each other's emotional stability, strength, and confidence. If a party doesn't tolerate disrespect and imposes consequences for boundary violations, they're reassuring the other party that they're strong, confident, and emotionally invested.

By consequences, I do <u>not</u> mean physical or emotional abuse like physical violence and derogatory labeling. I mean *communicating* and clarifying a boundary, highlighting its gravity, sincerely warning the other person not to do it again, taking time to cool off, or even legitimately warning that the relationship will end if they cannot respect the boundary. Or any combination of those.

Chances are, they won't disrespectfully test each other very often if they know breakups are on the table. If they do, they increase the odds of a distressful response and a breakup.

Disrespectful tests are meant to elicit strong emotional responses. If a man has a significant emotional reaction, positive or negative— again, not an abusive one—it communicates he cares about the woman and that he's invested. He's essentially asking, "*Why?* Why would you put this stress on our relationship when things were going well? Why would you disturb the peace?"

Men who express emotional investment show they're reliable and trustworthy because investing their heart in the relationship means they have a stake in it. They're not going to flip a negotiation table haphazardly when it has their beating heart sitting on it.

If the man is indifferent toward the disrespect, it means he's emotionally uninvested or a pushover. *Both* warrant concern. If he's uninvested, he couldn't care less if the relationship or connection survives. That means he's providing no stability, security, or safety. If he's a pushover and anyone can walk over him, he's a weak man who won't be able to provide a stable and secure environment. He fails the test, and as a result, she loses respect for him. She won't be against being friends with him, but she'll never fawn over him or consider him a viable mate. She can't rely on him to have a backbone or carry masculine energy.

Outside of one or two disrespectful tests, the motivation for repeatedly performing these tests is typically when a woman finds reason to doubt a man's commitment. Instead of reassuring after a recent test, he responded in a distressed manner. This repeated testing is sometimes called insecurity. *It is not.* It's simply a man failing the competent, reliable, strong partner litmus test, which casts doubt on whether he'll be a suitable partner. So, she must test him again.

Maybe their relationship has always been a little toxic, and she caught him flirting with other women. Or maybe he didn't keep a promise. Those are definitely cracks in his reliable reputation. To gauge his emotional investment, she might flirt with another man in his presence. Though it certainly wouldn't be the best way to communicate, the disrespect could very well provoke an emotional response and open the floor to discuss what she finds distressing.

It could lead to the establishment of clear new boundaries or serve as a reminder of nonnegotiable standards. This testing doesn't make her crazy. *It makes her smart and concerned about her future.* That man is the original instigator of this chaos, and if he calls her crazy, he actually might be a psychopath manipulating her.

The other motivation for repeatedly performing disrespectful tests *is* actual insecurity. **Insecurity** is the *refusal to accept reassurance from a partner.* Those who repeatedly perform disrespectful tests despite receiving reassurance are the ones we label as insecure, toxic, or "crazy."

They're the ones who regularly check their partner's phone without reason, blatantly topple reality and lie to their partners and friends and family, hide their misbehavior from others, take zero accountability, constantly place their partner in "it's them or me" scenarios, and regularly communicate in unacceptable manners like overly exaggerating emotions, yelling, screaming, etc. None of those things increases the likelihood that we like each other.

The reason they're labeled as crazy is that they choose to believe in a reality contrary to the evidence. For example, when a man *proves* himself to be a competent, strong, and reliable partner, flagging him and testing him as anything other than what the evidence points to *is crazy*. Someone who tells you that a pink, fluffy dinosaur is in front of you when you can plainly see there's not *is delusional*.

Perhaps the reason the most beautiful women are stereotyped as "crazy" is that their most significant attractive quality—their physical appearance—fades over time. The thing many men want most from them is going to disappear from their very eyes. That may reasonably cause them more concern for the durability of a man's interest. Hence, a source of insecurity and a need for repeated testing.

Again, it's completely *normal* for women to periodically seek out disagreements to butt heads with men to test their stability, competence, and commitment. With the right reassurance, she can relax knowing those needs are met.

What's *not* normal is repeated testing in the midst of reassuring answers. Unfortunately, this off-putting practice and energy in women has become more saturated in Western culture. Feminism, in combination with all its great good, promotes masculine qualities among women. Traits such as aggression and disagreeableness empower them to compete with men for economic success and independence, and be "boss babes" who never back down. This independence provides a safety net against all the historical failures, abuses, and downfalls of male power.

The trade-off, however, is that it's now normalized in Western culture for women to be headstrong, refuse to accept defeat, and keep fighting. That's a problem because women *also use disagreements as tests* to determine if men are reliable and strong.

So, women are now using the *same hose for two different purposes: competition and compatibility testing*. The hose typically used for testing men is now often spraying abrasive conflict down their throats whenever casual disagreements arise. Consequently, women with abrasive masculine qualities often portray an insufferable persona, appearing to test men endlessly.

Instead of casually coming across disagreements, having a civil conversation, and understanding each other's differences, it's as if women with those masculine qualities walk around with a megaphone screaming, "Who wants a piece of this?! Huh?! You, buddy?! I'm strong and independent! I WILL END YOU."

Even when men display competency, and it would be beneficial to rely on them, these types of women and their relentless need for conflict and victory label themselves as "crazy." Because when men pass the competency test and it's *still* not enough to invite a woman to a masculine-feminine balance, women who engage in to-the-death disagreements appear to act just like the "hot-crazy" stereotype women. They perform endless unwarranted tests, no matter how much reassurance they have.

I can recall several women I thought were cute whose attractiveness immediately evaporated at the first sight of their heated aggression on an everyday topic. I would simply smile and wave with the boys, and scurry away ASAP. Because what did I sense? *An insatiable distress response.* If she's willing to test abrasively in a trivial conversation with someone who's not even fighting her, she will dig in her heels and be abrasive to any end. We could be on the same team, and she'd probably still fight me, elevating stress and destroying peace.

A man will only put up with a woman's craziness for as long as he's motivated by her beauty or as long as he believes there's hope he can reassure her. When a man finally accepts that she can't be reassured, he gives up on her insecurity and leaves her. Her constant tests for validation with no relief in sight will just become too high-maintenance. It's not a question of *if,* but a question of *when* insecurity will destroy a relationship. *This goes for both men and women.*

From a man's perspective, here's my heads-up to the Western "strong and independent women" with unmovable masculine qualities produced over the last 50 years: *Since mate-competency testing and female expression of abrasive masculine qualities use the same hose of conflict, "toxic, crazy" women and women with masculine qualities are essentially indistinguishable to us.* It's just another one of those trade-offs that's no one's fault.

Even with exceptional attractiveness, the chances of maintaining a good man's interest and love are slim to none because good men don't tolerate toxicity. *We extinguish it.* If attractiveness has any effect at all, it's that it only delays the inevitable, where we certainly won't commit to marriage.

Relentless testing robs us of time and energy. If a woman doesn't get the message that their life and environment are in good hands, we won't repeat it indefinitely. We have a world to better and the next generation to raise. We won't spend our time fighting to appease a grown-ass woman's insatiable appetite for distrust, competition, and drama. I'm *absolutely positive* that good women have a similar message for insecure, emotionally immature, unreliable, and crazy men.

To conclude all this poking and prodding, testing and responding, we find a cautionary tale. When a woman tests, or even disagrees and fights too much, she comes across as annoying, insecure, high-maintenance, or crazy to men. When she doesn't prod at all, both parties may very well find themselves out of touch with the standards and boundaries of their relationship.

Maybe the man needed a wake-up call. Without her maintenance checks, both are more likely to become callous, disinterested, and disconnected. Nothing and no one is calling them to renew their assurances in the relationship and spark growth. It's an intelligent and vital practice requiring a strategic balance and a delicate touch.

If any female readers are offended by all of this and object, saying, "I do not and would not do that!" I'd recommend a perspective shift. Smart women are proactive about their security. They routinely check whether the beams holding up their house are rotting and about to collapse in on them. *Smart women test men.* Because straying, dishonest, unreliable, and uninvested men bring the very ruin nightmares themselves fear.

Personally, I do my very best to be an exceptionally proactive husband by performing these tests for my wife. We have a very secure relationship. She observes no suspicious behavior because I never actually have anything to hide from her. I constantly remind her that I'm obsessed with her and that I'm uninterested in other women.

Regardless, now and then, maybe it's just coming across social media videos that make her curious, but I'll still get a "If I magically turned 70 right now, would you still love me?" She's fantastic.

Summing it all up:

- **Respectful** tests don't violate any standards or boundaries.
- **Disrespectful** tests intentionally violate standards and boundaries.
- **Reassuring** responses confirm the man's investment and reliability.
- **Distressing** responses expose a man's unreliability or disinterest.

TEST

	RESPECTFUL	DISRESPECTFUL
REASSURANCE	Mild emotional pushback Man stands his ground but maintains his interest Man reconfirms his commitment Man **can be trusted** and can therefore build a safe environment for a family	Intense emotional pushback reveal his emotional investment Man doesn't tolerate disrespect and either offers or threatens consequences (*EXCLUDING ABUSE*) Consequences show he's not a pushover Men who are not pushovers are strong and **can be trusted** provide safe and secure environments
DISTRESS	No emotional pushback Man always agrees with her and appeases her demands Man appears weak but committed Man **cannot be trusted** to be the backbone of a partnership because he's a pushover ("simps" and "radical male feminists" embrace this corner)	Total emotional rejection realizes her insecurities OR man allows disrespect Emotional rejection implies man can't be trusted to provide security Man allowing disrespect causes woman to lose respect for him, meaning he **cannot be trusted** to provide a secure and safe environment

Table 5: Testing and Responding Matrix

Where to Set the Bar

Now that we've defined what standards and boundaries are and how to use them to find a reliable and compatible partner, let's recommend some specific traits to look for. While there's obviously no exhaustive description of the perfect partner because everyone's preferences vary with their own mate-selection strategy, we can still establish a healthy foundation.

This foundation is based on both my experience and research into traits highly predictive of relationship success. Naturally, this list includes the aspirational traits we discussed in *Chapter 5*.

1. Interesting—Having goals, aspirations, or ambitions not dependent on a relationship, like hobbies or business ideas. Being purpose-filled produces an aura of mystery.
2. Holistically Growing—Having an appetite for new knowledge and for becoming a better and more capable person.
3. Sleep-Prioritized—Getting the proper amount of sleep to stabilize emotions, boost mental energy, attractiveness, and bodily fitness.
4. Healthy Diet—Mainly eating whole foods to strengthen and preserve mental health, mood, and the number of years we have good health, known as healthspan.
5. Exercise-Participating—Partaking in exercise to boost mental performance, stay in shape, be sexy, extend healthspan, and offer good epigenetics to offspring.
6. Positive Social Circle—Surrounding ourselves with individuals who exhibit beneficial behavior. Friends who help each other aim high, contribute to each other's success, and make each other better.
7. Romantic—Stimulating sexual tension, and inviting partners to create new experiences, become closer, and be vulnerable.

8. Emotional Stability—Being highly resilient to negative emotions like anxiety, fear, anger, sadness, and irritability. Good impulse control, realistically optimistic, and having effective coping strategies. *Not emotionless.*

9. Excellent Listening Skills—Not talking over each other, being able to paraphrase each other, and being genuinely curious to learn and hear more about one's partner.

10. Superb Communication Skills—Can methodically and reasonably verbalize what they want and need.

11. Generous—Being eager to give energy, time, effort, gifts, submission, sexual favors, goodwill, etc.

12. Reasonably Physically Attractive—Having facial features pleasant to the eyes and a healthy body, tempting for sex.

13. Partnership-Focused—The partnership is equally important as the individual.

14. Open-minded—Being open to being wrong and to learning new things. One's goal is to search for what's right.

15. Humility—Seeing others as equally deserving of respect.

16. Orderly—Capable and willing to be organized and cooperate in delegating energy to the greatest priorities when necessary.

17. Positively Biased—Predisposed to assuming everything we do or say is done with good intentions. For example, "I know they meant well... I know they aren't trying to insult my intelligence by helping... I know they're not trying to be mean... I'm going to believe in and treat them as the best version of themselves..." This quality's importance cannot be overstated.

18. Attention-content—Not having an insatiable appetite for attention. Reject sources of attention and any flirtatious advances as they're not beneficial for the relationship's health.

19. Reliability—Sticking to one's word, contributing to a

stable reality unpolluted by casual lies, telling the truth,
and exhibiting consistent behavior.

20. Healthy Self-Esteem—Having an optimistic, not
hypercritical, view of themselves.

21. Good God—Whatever centerpiece their life revolves
around, it puts them on a growth-oriented path to become
a better person and gives them a sense of purpose and
narrative.

AT FIRST GLANCE, this list might seem like I'm trying to describe a hot Mother Teresa or sexy Gandhi—a too good to be true, unrealistically wonderful person we're supposedly attracted to. I'm actually just describing a healthy person who's ready to create true love because they've done the work and built evidence for their identity of love.

Essentially, this entire list can be practiced and lived *outside* of romantic relationships. Building and fine-tuning this healthy foundation within ourselves before we get into relationships is like our future selves traveling back in time to prevent damaging, relationship-threatening disagreements. We waste years in singledom *only if we don't resolve disagreements in advance.*

And just because someone doesn't fulfill this entire list doesn't mean we should instantly disqualify them as a potential mate. There will always be differences in people's standards and boundaries. For Love Heroes, trajectory is what's important. This list gives us a strong sense of direction.

This dichotomy between "instantly disqualifying a candidate because of our differences" and "openness to the potential trajectory with a candidate despite our differences" is the battle between the modern terms relation-shopping and relation-shipping.

Relation-shopping is when we require partners to fulfill a shopping list to meet our exact needs and wants. From the relation-shopping frame of mind, if we were to go to a store, the store must have our entire checklist of items lest we take our business elsewhere.

Maybe Walmart has all but one item on our shopping list. However, since they don't have it *all*, we walk out empty-handed and take our business to Target. If Target didn't have it all, then onto TJ Maxx. If not TJ's, onto the next.

Little did we realize there were phenomenal deals at Walmart, Target, and TJ's. It's pretty ridiculous to expect one store to have absolutely everything on the list at the best prices we dream of, isn't it? It's also pretty ridiculous not to consider giving our business to stores with good prices when almost everything on our list is there, isn't it? Maybe they'll carry the item(s) we want later down the line—we never know!

We often do the same thing with relationships. We demand that people have our entire checklist, without a single thing we don't like or a sore-thumb difference in expectations. Even though they may have most of the noble qualities or items we want, and even though they may shine brighter than we wished for in some respects—if they don't have it all—we disqualify those candidates.

Relation-shoppers are sometimes called "maximizers" because they don't settle for anything less than the best possible deal, and they're unfit for true love. Their sky-high resistance to even the smallest differences is a recurring distress response to tests and compatibility filters. People with overactive distress responses will break down the stability of any relationship. Hence, they're unfit for the vibrancy of true love.

Relation-shipping is the act of building a garden-like relationship with a human being, not a "Build-a-Partner" mannequin at an assembly line. Relation-shippers don't throw candidates away at the sight of minor differences. They understand that much of life's beauty lies in the fact that nobody's perfect and everyone's evolving. The people we're in relationships with today differ from the people they'll be in a year. And the relationship we have now differs from the relationship we'll have in a year. Trajectory is what's important.

Love Heroes are relation-shippers who've done the hard work of building a healthy foundation and are ready to *duke it out* at the relationship negotiation table. We have plenty of cards to lay down and have a clear picture of who we are and where we're going. All we're looking for is someone who shares a similar foundation, keeps pace with our card play and negotiation, and is interested in fusing trajectories.

Put 'em up!

Disagreements

Disagreements occur regularly in any relationship. Navigating them properly helps both partners in a relationship get what they want. **Disagreements** are differences or incompatibilities in standards, boundaries, and expectations. Though they can be used as tests to measure resolve, as we just discussed, they also arise naturally and thus serve as *passive compatibility filters*.

Disagreements can be as simple as where to eat. They might want fast food, but maybe our standard today is fine dining. Values are a significant source of disagreement. They might think lying sometimes is okay, but maybe we have a boundary never to lie, no matter what. Or they might have a standard that humans shouldn't kill and eat other animals, but our standard is that there's a circle of life on this planet, and it's okay to be a part of it.

Disagreements can take many forms, but two things are certain: (1) they're inevitable in relationships and (2) they're key to personal growth. Concerning growth, they help us see the world more holistically. We usually only have our own perspective to see through to understand the world.

Encountering different perspectives, even those incompatible with ours, means we have more data with which to interpret the world. More data results in a more accurate picture. Being open-minded and listening to those who disagree with us is critical if we actually care about what's right.

Otherwise, it's pretty arrogant to think that out of 8,300,000,000 perspectives on this planet, we *just happen* to have the correct one. Think about it this way: the chances of winning the lottery are about 1 in 300,000,000. That means we are almost *28 times more likely to win the lottery than we are to have the sharpest perspective on the planet.*

A terribly common habit we have today is mistaking disagreements for disrespect. This is a consequence of needing to *be* right instead of pursuing *what is* right. When we seek to *be* right, we see others as opponents in a narcissistic tug-of-war, where we all step on each other and feel disrespected. When we pursue what *is* right, we see others as fellow travelers on the path to the truth, and we collaborate on where to go together.

Another way of saying it is that ego and self-centeredness are the key ingredients to turn disagreements into disrespect. The solution or antidote is to have an underlying goal or destination. Piece of cake for a Love Hero! Let's paint a picture of why this is.

The world isn't a stagnant place. Everyone has their own perspectives and goals, and they're all driving toward them. When we seek to be right, we dig our heels into the road to stay exactly where we are and defend that position. If the world isn't staying still, however, we're placing ourselves in the middle of highway traffic, where we get offended and shocked as different perspectives bulldoze over us. If we kept moving towards a destination, however, there might be no one to run us over at all.

In this sense, the disrespect we feel is less about others violating our boundaries and more about us setting boundaries where they don't belong. Every time we dig in our heels, we willingly place ourselves in harm's way, where we claim to be on the best path—elevating ourselves above others. By being self-centered and refusing to listen, we essentially recruit others to help us feel offended, disrespected, and attacked, and produce painful conflict.

Here's an example for clarity. Take a couple with different dreams—different standards. One dreams of living in Australia, while the other dreams of living in the United States of America. They find themselves in disagreement. Whose dream is the right dream?

Well, if the man shamelessly digs in his heels and boldly claims the obvious best choice for both of them is to embrace his dream, he clearly puts himself and his dream above his partner. It's pretty self-centered to say, "Your dream doesn't matter as much as mine."

In fact, that's pretty dang disrespectful, isn't it? But how did we get here? Wasn't it just a disagreement? Wasn't it just a difference in standards? We got here by bringing ego into the mix. We got here by someone setting their standards and boundaries *over* the other's, saying, "Your standards and boundaries aren't as good or important as mine." We got here by tearing down their standards and boundaries with the need to *be* right.

Truthfully, in scenarios like this, no one can rightfully say whose standards and dreams are more important than the other's, and that's okay. Negotiations naturally have a limit because not all disagreements can be resolved objectively. Sometimes "right" isn't even in the equation. Disagreeing about what color to paint the wall is almost never of any objective consequence.

According to Gottman Research, *69% of all relationship problems are unsolvable.*[i] There will never be such a thing as having zero disagreements in a relationship, much less solving them all. What is certainly *doable*, however, is not to turn disagreements into disrespect. It just requires that we not place our standards and boundaries above another's. On the left side of *Figure 13*, we visualize that disagreements stem from incompatible standards and boundaries—the circles don't overlap. Disrespect is on the right, where we place our standards and boundaries over theirs.

This might *seem* obvious, but we disrespect people like this all the time. We regularly disagree and deem our values higher than others'. Carnivores do it, vegans do it—pro-abortionists, anti-abortionists, sober, non-sober, conservative, liberal, religious, non-religious, pro-vax, anti-vax—we *all* do it. We all flex our moral superiority and disrespect others by calling them and their standards and boundaries naïve or stupid. Then they feel disrespected and return the favor.

This isn't to say there's no such thing as right and wrong. We should certainly always advocate for what we believe is right, but we don't need to flail about dramatically and preach to be right. It's completely unnecessary to elevate ourselves above others to advocate for what's right. We can simply treat others as allies on the way to what's right and *ask them questions* about how they know they're going in the right direction. With the right approach and a peaceful heart, many are more open-minded than we give them credit for.

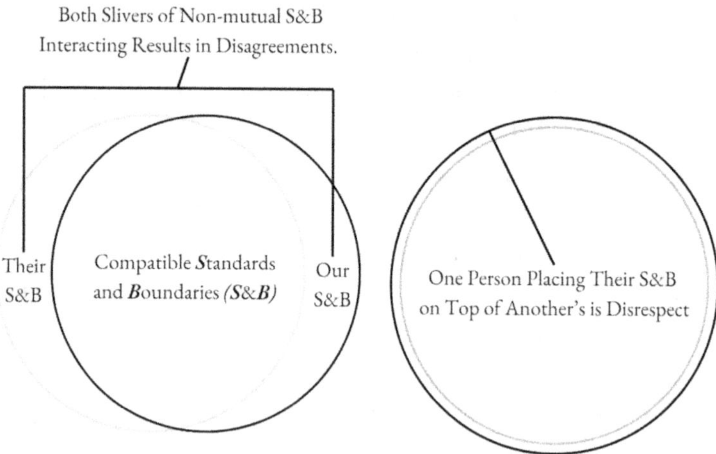

Figure 13: Visualizing Disagreements and Disrespect

Concerning disagreements where objectivity is possible, *what's right is whatever increases the likelihood that our relationship flourishes.* Of course, as we've discussed, prioritizing what's right requires that we set aside *who's* right—ego. By definition, setting aside ego means we approach disagreements with humility, even critically analyzing ourselves voluntarily.

So, welcome to the uncomfortable heavyweight pursuit of situational awareness, self-awareness, and self-reflection. Here, if we want to convince someone else that submitting to our standards and boundaries is the right thing to do, we have to know the ins and outs of why we believe those expectations are right. We can't just say, "I need you to be clean because I enjoy cleanliness." That's the same as, "My standards and boundaries are more important than yours."

To continue using cleanliness as an example, if we want a clean space, our standards and boundaries of cleanliness need to leverage something conducive to the success of the relationship. So, instead of our preferences being right just because we enjoy being clean, perhaps now it's right because doing small tasks of cleanliness fosters a productive momentum and culture of success.

What do I mean? Have you ever had a really unproductive morning, maybe by staying in bed too long or scrolling on social media? Then, since a sizable portion of the day had already passed with nothing done, you gave up on making it a productive day and continued goofing off? Well, that's the principle of momentum manifesting destructively. There was a failure at the start of the day, and it kept snowballing into other losses, making the entire day a loss with no sustenance for success.

There are two sides to this coin, however. Positive momentum *also* snowballs and supports success. If we woke up, made our beds, exercised, and made breakfast, we'd have successfully completed three tasks and had three wins for the day. Since our day would already be filled with wins, it's much more natural to create even more wins.

Psychologically, when we complete minor tasks, our brains interpret them as small wins, which snowball. Small wins increase confidence and motivation to complete larger, more ambitious tasks. Overcoming large and difficult tasks is where we find great success. Greater success typically leads to greater resources.

Having greater resources means less stress and scarcity, so we can do and get the things we like. That makes us more likely to be happy. Being happier means we're more likely to treat each other better. Treating each other better increases the likelihood we'll stay together and have a successful relationship.

That is what I mean by heavyweight situational awareness, self-awareness, and self-reflection. We must search the depths of our hearts to understand why our standards and boundaries exist. The deeper we know our why, the less ego is involved in the battle for greater self-importance, and the better we resolve our disagreements. This specific "what's right" was at least 7 layers deep.

Since all Love Heroes aspire to higher and higher standards, those who have the deepest non-ego-based standards and boundaries are the closest to what's right. Disagreeing with what's right could very well imply one partner acknowledges they don't want to contribute to the relationship's success. Lack of trying after agreeing would also make that acknowledgment.

Together, subjectivity and the deeper why represent the upper limits of resolving disagreements. Deeper whys can get us to a tangible answer about what's right in disagreements, while subjectivity allows contradictory perspectives to be equally deserving of getting their way—the color of the walls, for example.

So, what do we do with all this information about disagreements? First, we can take a chill pill, stop being hostile to everyone who disagrees with us, and remind ourselves to view others as allies and to understand that many disagreements involve several equally valid opinions.

Second, we can acknowledge that anyone who consistently places his or her standards and boundaries above those of others doesn't respect others. *We don't want to be those people.* Third, we can understand how disagreements serve as a passive mating compatibility filter.

Intentionally exhibiting edgy behavior to provoke disagreement and observe their resolve and sanity is a compatibility *test*. We've already covered that. *Happening upon* disagreements and observing how the differences get along serves as a compatibility *filter*. Anyone who gets exceedingly upset or hostile over disagreements is likely to cause problems, frequent fights, and additional stress, all of which are undesirable outcomes. If everyone remains respectful and maintains reasonable emotional stability, they pass as potential mates.

There's a natural breaking point to everyone's level-headedness, however. No matter how much we fortify our emotional stability and humility, and pursue what's right, with the right size disagreement, *egos will eventually kick in*. We'll begin to feel a sense of self-preservation, and both parties will enter a distress response, questioning the relationship's viability.

This is the reality of big disagreements. They're typically instant-breakup issues, such as heavy drug addiction, domestic abuse, conflicting desires for kids, differing preferences for monogamy, cheating, unshared attraction, conflicting religions, immediate family opposed to our partners, or conflicting philosophies of money. They could also be things like differing lifelong travel goals, incompatible life missions, different fitness aspirations, or mismatched forever-home/lifestyle dreams.

Big disagreements are born of the standards and boundaries stitched directly into our hearts—so close to our identities that rupturing them causes existential crises. If anyone tries to undo or violate any of those stitches, they'll 100% come face-to-face with our ego, and blatant disrespect will be directly or indirectly exchanged. By definition, the ego disregards others. Disregarding others is disrespectful.

To highlight the gravity of big disagreements, I'd argue that most quarter-, mid-, and late-life crises result from big disagreements people have *within themselves*. They either (1) never properly set up their standards and boundaries for themselves and are at a loss for where they should go in life, (2) don't currently honor and meet the standards and boundaries they have for themselves, or (3) have failed to adjust and renegotiate their standards and boundaries as they transitioned through different stages of life.

The hard part about these crises is that since we obviously can't break up with ourselves, we're stuck in a silent room, face-to-face with the origin of our big disagreements: *ourselves*. We find ourselves doomed to stew in feelings of failure because we haven't met our own standards, or feel unworthy of respect for violating our own boundaries.

The only escape options from the torture of life crises are to (1) set up and clarify new standards and boundaries, or (2) meet our current standards and boundaries by doing some super-duper serious life rearrangement.

In relationships, however, we *can* break up with the origin of our big disagreements. There are even two ways to do it! We can either (1) break up with our standards and boundaries, which are pieces of us, *or* (2) we can break up with our partners. Both are heart-wrenching surgical procedures, but a *breakup occurs either way.* We either sacrifice a piece of ourselves or we sacrifice someone else.

The darkest period of my life led me to take option 1. To be honest with you, it took me to a point where I really didn't care if I lived or died. And in short, the sacrifice didn't even work in the end. The good parts of myself I tried to smother and bury rolled away a stone and resurrected anew. So, frankly, I'm not entirely sure how viable option 1 is. It's probably best to cut someone else off than to cut off a standard or boundary we absolutely cherish.

If we really want kids and they don't, breaking up solves the problem. Staying with them forces us to drown our dreams of having and loving children and all the beautiful memories of a future passed. Sacrificing standards and boundaries like that will most likely lead to *more* pain and resentment than breaking up would.

It's my sincere belief that not breaking up with a partner over a big disagreement early on is the *single greatest cause* of relational devastation down the road. Big disagreements simply call for abandoning negotiations.

They set egos loose. Someone is *forced* to sacrifice their core standards and boundaries for the other person, which means disrespect occurs. That's *Figure 13.* If they stay together after the disrespect of one's core being, there'll be a loss of respect because consequences weren't enforced.

Loss of respect will eventually activate a life crisis in the one who had to sacrifice their core standards and boundaries. To resolve their life crisis, they'll have to reevaluate their expectations. That will almost certainly result in reclaiming the standards and boundaries they once sacrificed, thereby reestablishing the big disagreement. Only this time, self won't be the sacrifice—it'll be the partner.

Big disagreements inevitably lead to the eventual crumbling of a relationship. This math doesn't lie. It just depends on how much time and energy a person is willing to spend on a relationship that will never foster true love.

Toning down to **medium-sized disagreements**—they're distanced enough from the heart and ego to test each other's emotional stability but not enough to dismantle mating negotiations or cause breakups. Medium-sized disagreements don't cause anyone to lash out in self-preservation. Though medium-sized disagreements may provoke disrespect, they're only disrespectful enough to trigger an emotional defense and start a standards-and-boundaries negotiation session.

At this level of disagreement, we find a negotiation currency we'll call "goodwill." In these negotiation sessions, one or both parties need to embrace the other's standards and boundaries. By both, I mean either the parties agree to disagree, or they compromise to partially get what they want.

Though these issues may be ever-recurring, they're not hills anyone in the relationship will die on because they accept and understand their differences and compromises. This is where the "69% of problems in relationships are unsolvable" statistic from the Gottman Institute really comes from.

Submission is when one party adjusts to the other's standards and boundary preferences. It's the grace of giving up what we want to give our partners what they want. When people give us what we want, it makes us want to give them what they want.

It's a you scratch my back, I'll scratch yours kind of energy. Hence, there's a subconscious currency exchanged when we submit during disagreements. **Goodwill** is the currency that makes us want to give our partners the things that make them happy and the things they desire.

If one party is doing all or most of the submitting, that means one partner is trying to control their environment and partner too much. When we resolve almost every disagreement in our favor, we're not seeing our partners as teammates; we're seeing them as obstacles to make our world the way we want it. Relationships are about creating a world *both* partners want. That requires us to give up things we want, submit, and build goodwill.

So, here's an omen to all the control-freaks out there: if we never submit and let our partner prevail in disagreements, we won't have a partner—*we'll have a slave made in our own image.*

If they actually do everything we say, we'll face a mirror showing us our flaws, and any shortcomings we hate in the relationship will ultimately be our own. The imperfect image in the mirror's frame will disgust us because there's no one to blame but ourselves. And we will thrash and weep as we cast the puppet-mastered portrait of ourselves, our enslaved partner, into the abyss of breakups time and time again. We must loosen our grip and balance submissions in both medium-sized and small disagreements. It's vital to true love.

Some examples of medium-sized disagreements might be disclosing a private detail about one's sex life to a close friend, saying something hurtful, violating a previously established boundary around a small disagreement, and really anything that pushes just the right buttons, testing one's patience. Ultimately, these disagreements are big enough to cause discomfort, trigger communication, and demand a change.

One of my marriage's not-so-distant medium-sized problems was that when Abbey would make a suggestion, I'd almost always ignore it. If I were trying to accomplish a task, she'd recommend what to do, and I just wouldn't try it her way for whatever reason. I'm pretty sure this was often the case, even if I *asked* her for suggestions. How annoying!

She eventually bared her heart on the issue: "I've noticed when I suggest something, you don't listen to me. It doesn't feel good to be ignored and not to have my suggestions considered." I will never forget what she said next. With deep sadness and a shrinking face on the brink of tears, she said, "I have good ideas too..."

That made me want to cry. Was I communicating that I thought she was stupid? Was I seeing her as competition in that if she was right about something, *I* would be the stupid one? What happened to the "we" in "wedded team"? I want an intelligent wife. Why would I *not* nurture and support that?

Maybe it was a pride thing, an effort to hold on to individuality, or an effort to show I was smart. I honestly don't know how to pinpoint it. Maybe it was a mix of all the above. But I listen to her suggestions now. And I tell her she's smart.

Even if I'm already about to do what she recommends, as often as I can, I try to stay away from saying, "I know," and proceed as if I didn't know. In those situations, we both came up with the same idea at the same time. And if I want to be seen as intelligent, she deserves to be seen as intelligent too.

"I know," says, "I don't need your help." It says, "I don't want you to think I'm incompetent." These are things we worry about and say when we're facing *competition*. Partners are teammates who nurture each other's strengths and trade goodwill on disagreements because maybe their own ideas aren't always the best, and there's learning in store for them.

In the end, medium-sized disagreements lead to a stronger foundation of ever more clearly understood, reinforced, and aligned standards and boundaries. Though these disagreements might hurt, it's important and reassuring to know they don't necessarily threaten the relationship. In fact, they offer growth. One might even say that medium-sized disagreements *strengthen* relationships and are where we find the gold of personal growth.

If the same a medium-sized disagreement ever came up again, it wouldn't be a medium-sized problem. It would be a big problem, since a party deliberately disregarded the clearly set boundaries and ignored the communication. Now, the problem is not the problem. The problem is the disrespect and careless valuation of the other person and their standards and boundaries. That's breakup stuff.

Then, of course, we have **small disagreements**. These are like the direction the toilet paper unrolls, leaving the toilet seat up, leaving dishes in the sink one at a time, chewing with their mouth open, breathing through their mouth, collecting Legos, not putting their clothes in the hamper, leaving makeup products everywhere, etc. If I could relate them to a modern term, these disagreements would be "icks." They're the things that don't disrespect us in any meaningful, personal way, yet they bring out a sense of disgust or annoyance within us.

My wife and I have developed healthy submission habits for small disagreements. If she wants me to hang up my coat instead of leaving it on a chair or on the couch, that's easy. Am I willing to fight for my right to leave it on the couch? Certainly not. That's unnecessary conflict, and it's also not where my coat belongs. Plus, submitting to her in that small disagreement builds goodwill for when I have something I want her to submit to me about.

She used to leave her towel everywhere after she showered, even on the floor sometimes. She doesn't anymore—not as often. I don't leave my shoes in the middle of the hallway now. We don't interrupt each other when we're busy working on a task. We change the music genre when the other isn't feeling it.

These disagreements are small enough that they aren't hills we're willing to die on. We submit to each other in these situations and store up goodwill to be exchanged for a reciprocal submission in the future.

There's a concerning omen in small disagreements, however. Since medium-sized disagreements are always big enough to garner attention and address, there's *always* submission from one or both parties. With small disagreements, however, it's common for a party *not* to submit because (1) the issue didn't seem significant enough to submit for, or because (2) the other party didn't communicate that it was an issue at all. In either scenario, issues go unresolved and burrow themselves under our skin.

Small disagreements are the only extremely threatening disagreements we need to worry about. They're silent killers of relationships, hiding in plain sight. Big disagreements inevitably end relationships when they come up, so they don't warrant worry. Worry is warranted only when uncertainty is in the air.

Medium-sized disagreements are always big enough to communicate about, so even though they cause pain, they're always addressed. But when small things go unaddressed, they keep building until they either become multiple medium-sized problems or a big problem that results in a breakup.

This is why couples on relationship panels will say, "The key to a successful marriage is communication, communication, communication, baby..." as they smile into each other's eyes and nod in agreement, thinking they really nailed it. While they're telling the truth, it's also one of the most absolutely *useless* pieces of relationship advice one could ever receive because *there's zero context. Communication about what?*

What they're referring to is communication about different-sized disagreements regarding standards and boundaries. Somehow, one of the biggest kept secrets for successful relationships is *liking each other.* To like each other, we need to feel that our standards are being met and that our boundaries are being respected.

Failure to satisfy this "secret" of liking each other is where we find the root cause of contempt. **Contempt** is the feeling of despising one's partner. The opposite of liking is despising. That means if something isn't causing our partner to like us, chances are, it's making them despise us. We, humans, don't enjoy being around people we despise.

We create distance between them and us. When the person we despise is our partner, we distance our hearts from theirs and begin to disconnect from them. That's why contempt is *the #1 relationship killer.* We don't mind moving on from people we don't feel connected to.

When we don't communicate about the small disagreements that bother us, we plant seeds of contempt—we actively help our partners become less likable to us. The purpose of "communication, communication, communication..." is to empower our partners to be more likable to us and vice versa.

Figure 14 represents the blueprint of how all the key terms in disagreements fit together: (1) various disagreement sizes, (2) submission, (3) goodwill, (4) contempt, and (5) compromise. As we can see, communication is the centerpiece, or key, that holds relationships together and empowers them to flourish and grow. So, given its critical nature, we're going to rock a quick overview.

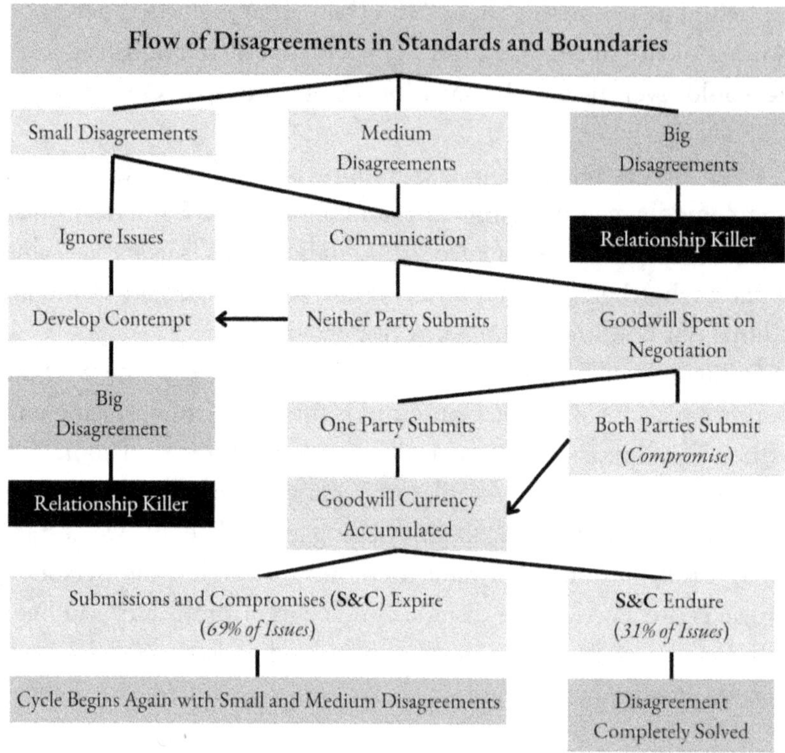

Figure 14: Anatomy of Disagreements

Communication: The Golden Centerpiece Nurturing True Love

A Love Hero's goal of communication is to *increase the likelihood that we like one another.* Searching for what's right instead of who's right is a sound principle to live by, but it's not enough to solve every disagreement. Most often, *there are no perfectly right answers in an imperfect world.* Because of this reality, we must eliminate seeds of contempt through communication and exchange goodwill toward one another through reciprocal submission.

Given this goal of liking one another, the underlying **message** in effective communication is: (T) **This** makes me like you less. (I) **I** want to like you. And (P) **Please,** change this behavior. **TIP.** Obviously, that's abrasive if we come out swinging *only* with those words.

A realistic example of that structure might be: "(T) I really don't like it when you casually talk to people of the opposite sex in public. (I) It makes me uncomfortable and makes me feel a way towards you I don't want to feel. (P) Please don't casually talk to other people of the opposite sex in public anymore."

One of the beautiful things about setting what's right instead of who's right as a priority is that it makes us curious and prompts us to ask questions about the submission being asked of us. There's no blind surrender.

So, continuing with our example, as curious people, we might ask ourselves, "Why should I *not* be the one to submit in this disagreement? What am I making room for when I submit? Goodwill? By granting their request and showing compassion for their discomfort, am I increasing the likelihood that the relationship will endure? Or am I simply allowing myself to be shaped by their insecurities and coddling the porcelain fragility of our relationship? And if I am coddling it, am I somehow *harming* the relationship?"

Chances are, we might *actually* do the relationship a disservice if we bend to their will and submit in this case. Since growth and increased alignment are the ultimate goals in true love relationships, a wise response would be a compromise. This compromise could have multiple components and look different, but we'll go with three for now.

First, we can state our disagreement by saying we genuinely don't see how the request at hand is healthy or beneficial to the likelihood of our relationship's success.

Second, we can partially submit and agree to be shorter in our conversations with people of the opposite sex temporarily, *solely* for the sake of their relief. Third, in exchange, we can request that they submit to us by engaging in introspection with a therapist to explore whether their standards and boundaries need to change, rather than our behavior.

Assuming both parties agreed to those terms, both expressed

what they needed, were willing to sacrifice and submit to one another, and contributed to the bank of goodwill. In the end, both partners learned they're willing to work together and are likely to grow stronger together.

Stepping deeper into the fray of communication, past the underlying message, we can further tune the precision of our communication as we escalate levels of disagreement. For this venture, we'll be adapting the communication method laid out by the authors of *Crucial Accountability*. The acronym for their method is CPR. It's extremely useful for establishing or reminding others of our standards and boundaries, and keeping them accountable.

In the first stage of CPR communication, we outline the issue's *content* and its consequences. Let's imagine that both our partners and we work full-time jobs and have busy schedules. We take the time to cook a meal while our partner relaxes on the couch. They say "thank you" after the meal, and they don't intend to clean the kitchen because we usually take care of it. We can bring up the content of our friction with them by requesting a behavior we want to see them *start,* rather than asking them to *stop* a specific behavior.

The **Content** of the message: "I'm really glad you enjoyed dinner. (T) I know we've both had a long day, but it would really mean a lot to me if you could help clean the kitchen. (I) I've been wanting to read but haven't had time to relax. You taking initiative in kitchen work would really make me feel like you want me to have opportunities to relax and do things I love, too. (P) Could we please regularly split up the kitchen duties, with me doing the cooking and you doing the cleaning?"

Assuming they're compatible with us and not completely unreasonable, they should submit and agree to implement the new behavioral standard of helping with the kitchen workload. In establishing these new standards, we've reached a compromise.

We clearly outlined the problem's content: we do all or most of the kitchen work at home. Then we communicated how it affected us and how it made us feel. If we're super fancy, we let them know how much we appreciate them every time they fulfill the new standard. "I really love it when you help me in handling the kitchen. It relieves me of so much stress and helps me unwind! Thank you so much. I love you!" You know, positively affirm the behavior we like.

If the issue persists even after communicating and establishing a new standard or boundary, we escalate the communication and move on to **Patterns**. Here, we directly highlight our concern that a pattern is forming around the issue. We're concerned they're not able to respect the expectations we established with them.

"Hey, honey, there are dirty dishes in the sink from yesterday, and I need to use some of them. We're also going to add some more today. (T) If this becomes a pattern, it's not sustainable for me. As we agreed, I can't be the only one contributing energy in the kitchen. (I) It's too much for me, and I need your help to be my best self. (P) So, please, from now on, whenever we're done eating, clean the dishes so we can close the kitchen, and I can have the dishes I need to cook ready to go tomorrow. Can we agree on that?"

"'Yeah, sorry, I just forgot...'"

"Thank you!"

Of course, at this point in our minds, we're bummed, and they're bummed. It was uncomfortable for us to say and for them to hear, and they're probably either grumpy at us or disappointed in themselves. The problem is, we're also unconsciously or consciously thinking that those who can't keep *small* commitments are genuinely a risk for large commitments and the submissions they require.

So, it's necessary that we help them become aware and resilient in resolving disagreements and keeping commitments. Because if they can't, we really shouldn't trust them with the enormous commitment of a relationship. We're not at that point yet, though. It's not quite at the level of big disagreement. However, if a pattern forms, we're certainly on our way to one. Hopefully, they hear us and understand our concern about the developing pattern.

Kicking it up a notch with the next violation, we communicate how deep the problem could run by bringing up the **Relationship**. In this episode of communication, we express our concern about what this issue could do to the relationship, and that it's a *big* problem. We tell them we've attempted to resolve the issue multiple times, have been clear about our standards and boundaries, and yet the problem persists.

Again, nobody likes people who repeatedly violate their boundaries and actively run away from their standards. It's disrespectful, and we don't have the time or energy to tolerate disrespect. It's a waste of *everyone's* time. So, if the behavior continues, it's going to change the relationship *with or without our consent.*

We reserve our romantic relationships for people we like and who like us. If we keep nagging, we won't like them, and they won't like us. This is serious town now. If they won't take responsibility and be serious about the small commitments, like keeping their word, we'll relieve them of their significant responsibility of being in a *relationship* with us.

"Craig, I need you to sit down with me. We've talked about this dish-cleaning issue before, and it's still a problem. I've let you know it's not something I'm willing to do, and yet you're still not willing to contribute without me repeatedly asking. I don't want to be nagging you all the time, and I'm sure you don't enjoy hearing me ask time and time again. It's exhausting! Now, this issue about dishes isn't even about dishes anymore—it's something bigger."

"(T) It's causing us not to like each other. You get grumpy when I ask; I'm grumpy that I have to ask; and I can feel contempt growing inside me. Worse, when you don't show up for me in the little ways, especially when you say you will, it suffocates my faith that you'll show up for me in the big ways—when times and tasks are *actually* really hard. (I) Now, this issue is no longer about my need for help and clean dishes. This is about my need for a reliable, stick-to-their-word, and team-minded partner.

(P) If that's not something you're interested in being, we'll have to reconsider whether this relationship works because what's going on is unsustainable, and it's not what I'm looking for. Let's take some time to think, and when you're ready, let me know where you're at."

That *Relationship* message took a lot of disrespect and refusal of submission to get to. It's a very reasonable, kind, clear, methodical, and loving way to communicate to get what we want: the fulfillment of our standards and respect for our boundaries.

In closing, the deepest motivation of communication in true love is to increase the likelihood that we'll like each other. Because being fond of each other is the principal theme, we're communicating the things that threaten to make us dislike each other (T). By putting effort into communication, we're telling them we care about how we relate to one another—we *want* to like them (I). Last, we're communicating exactly what we need from them to genuinely like them (P).

While TIP is the core message in all communication aimed at resolving disagreements, CPR communication addresses different intensities of disagreements. As the first venture in communication, *content* addresses small and medium-sized disagreements.

Medium-sized disagreements typically involve a certain level of attachment to differences, so it's understandable if the other party stumbles in perfectly upholding the newly established standards and boundaries. Similarly, small disagreements can often be perceived as unimportant, so we should be patient with how our partners adjust.

If an issue persists despite emphasizing the content several times, highlighting *patterns* helps us draw acute attention to the fact that we're noticing their attachment to a behavior that's *opposite* to what we need. Addressing patterns is uncomfortable for everyone, but it can ultimately lead to meaningful growth and proof that we work well as a couple.

Last, addressing the state of the *relationship* communicates that we're on the verge of a big disagreement. We're attempting to determine whether the relationship is salvageable. Depending on their response, we'll either have a submission or a relationship-ending disagreement on our hands.

Let's wrap this up!

Chapter's End

Standards and boundaries set the expectations for the qualities, traits, and behaviors we want in a partner and relationship. They're the fine details of the mate-selection theories we use in mating negotiation. Defining those details before we get into relationships is important because, without expectations, we'll never be satisfied. Satisfaction requires the fulfillment of a demand.

Disagreements are differences in standards and boundaries. Depending on the severity of our differences, disagreements serve as compatibility filters. They shut down mating negotiations and fuel breakups with those we're too different from.

Those who make it through each other's compatibility filters manage small- to medium-sized disagreements through communication, submission, goodwill, and compromise. Careful management of disagreements, paired with a growth philosophy, allows us to flourish in relationships with those who don't meet our every standard.

Though solutions to issues in disagreements are often subjective, cyclical, and unsolvable, we should seek what's objectively right whenever possible. This practice inevitably leads us to grow together and increases the likelihood we'll reach our mutual goals and desires in life.

The earlier we adopt this life practice, the sooner we establish healthy foundations and are better prepared to manage disagreements effectively. Like I said at the beginning of this chapter, developing a healthy foundation is like our future selves traveling back in time to prevent damaging disagreements from ever happening.

So, let's have a chat with our future selves, shall we?

Future-Self Exercise Prep

We're about to embark on a meditative exercise meant to expand self-awareness to better nurture a true-love garden.

I encourage you to find a comfortable posture and let go of any judgment. It's okay to dream optimistically because anything is possible in the future, and it's healthy to have things to look forward to. Let go of the obstacles you see before you. We're about to jump 10 years into the future. A lot can happen in 10 years.

When it's time to read the questions, read one at a time, close your eyes, and imagine your future self's response to fully immerse yourself in the conversation and simulation. Be patient with the answers, and if something doesn't come to you right away, just sit with it and wait for some inspiration.

Once you're satisfied with an answer, you can open your eyes and read the next question. When you're ready, jump in.

Future-Self Relationship Coaching Exercise

Your butt is uncomfortable sitting on one of the many large boulders lining the rocky beach. It's hard to really care, though, because you haven't felt this much peace for who knows how long. A brisk breeze runs its fingers through and plays with your obviously present, glorious locks. The sun is massaging your skin, and the crashing ocean waves are pushing and pulling your spirit like a cat kneading a blanket.

Seagulls and other birds are doing their hunting and playing tag. You could stay here for a while. You close your eyes, breathe deeply through your nose, hold that breath, and exhale. As you expel air from your lungs, you open your eyes and look to your left.

The line of people outside the white-and-red lighthouse has completely disappeared. Curious, your legs push you upright and escort you over to explore the nostalgia and memories etched into the frame of the almost archaic building. Your hand latches onto the entrance door handle, and you pause, looking up at the sheer height of the odd cylinder-shaped construction.

Giving a smirk of mild impression, you crack open the heavy rusty door on its rickety hinges. There are no lights inside. You survey your surroundings and, to your surprise, there aren't any caution signs or warnings. Also, nobody else seems to mind. So you slip inside to proceed on your tour, gradually shutting the door behind you until it gently nuzzles up against your back. The light making its way in from the tiptop of the lighthouse is the only thing staving off perfect darkness.

You carefully begin navigating your way toward the spiral stairs by feeling the cold, rough walls until you take your first steps onto the metal-grate stairs. This lighthouse must be at least 8 stories high— should be wonderful exercise. The higher you go, the more your eyes seem to adjust.

Around the second story, however, you notice an odd, faint, and slow pulsation of light rising from the base of the lighthouse and heading toward its peak. Almost like lights framing the runway for planes to take off. But it's every square inch of the walls closing you in.

On about the third story, you notice colors in the pulsating light patterns. Faint, pastel blue, red, and green. This isn't weird at all! On the fourth story, you notice a gentle upward breeze, and you realize the higher you go, the brighter the lights get, and the pulsation accelerates. Reaching floor six, you question whether this is some government brainwashing or hypnotism experiment, but your curiosity really hopes it's something more magical.

So, you press on, and by the time you get to the seventh story, the lights are so bright, and the pulsations so fast, they could trigger an epileptic episode, and the breeze could easily mess up anyone's good hair day. Just when you think it couldn't get more intense and you're struggling to place your steps, you reach the top of the lighthouse. Still standing on the steps, you eagerly peek your head to view what lies at the bottom edge of the windows. You're shocked to see...grass —land level with the top of the lighthouse.

You summit the metal-grated stairs to see the entire view, but the beach and rocks you saw earlier aren't down below anymore. *There is no below.* You look behind you into the lighthouse only to discover the pulsations and wind have ceased. The walls of the lighthouse are a pure, lucid white, and it's completely silent. All you see is the spiral metal-grated staircase and the creaky door at the bottom.

Redirecting your attention to the world at the top of the lighthouse, you approach a glass gate separating the metal-grate flooring from the luscious green grass. You pensively place your hands on it, pause, and push it open, causing the glass to sing a pleasant note. You cautiously stick your foot out to test the ground. "It's solid," you reassure yourself.

Amazed, you put more weight on your leg, and the ground is so trustworthy, you bring out your other leg. You can stand and walk around! *This is real.* Wide-eyed, you laugh and almost frolic in this questionable environment, but pause when you see a home.

Deep in your intuition, you sense something familiar. You sense that it's *your* home. But you don't remember living there. You don't know how, you don't know why, but you know this is your home. With a sincere reverence, you near its face. *What does the home look like? What landscape surrounds it? What color paints the front door?*

As you get closer, you see yourself walking inside through a window. You look older... but fantastic. *What clothes are you wearing?*

You build up some courage to quench your curiosity and walk right up to the front door. Raising your arm, you wind up your knuckles and knock. After a brief moment and some audible approaching footsteps, your future self opens the door. As they meet your eyes, they're ecstatic to see you, but not surprised. Eagerly and jubilantly, they say, "Please, come in!" They invite you to sit down and ask how you're doing—how you're *really* doing. Go ahead and tell them.

After you share, you both pause, as if to acknowledge, in the silence, that you have questions for your future self. They could obviously imagine that if they were sitting across from their future self, they would have some questions too. Smiling and gently nodding in approval, they say, "Go ahead." As you bear your questions, you intently wait and listen to their every word before asking the next.

You can ask,

- "What's something I really need to learn right now?"
- "What is the biggest challenge I'm going to have to face?"
- "What am I doing well right now?"
- "What truth do you think I'm running from?"
- "What are the most beautiful ways in which I will grow?"
- "What are your top values?"

- "What are the things you cherish and love most about your partner?"
- "What things does your partner cherish and love most about you?"
- "What are the most unexpected ways you express love to your partner?"
- "What kindness do they show you that still surprises you?"
- "What is admirable about the way you handle disagreements with your partner?"
- "Who do I need to be to experience the love you have?"
- "What's a nickname I can call you?"
- Now, ask them any question you want.

Somehow, time works differently here, and it's already dark. You hear your future spouse calling from another room, "Honey, are you coming to bed?" Your future self shrugs, smirks, stands up, and says, "Duty calls." You mirror their standing because it's time to leave, and your future self says, "Oh, wait! I have something for you. Hold on, I'll go get it!"

They take off to another room and leave you to wander the living room. You scope out the house's atmosphere and notice some of the picture frames on the furniture. *What do the pictures in the frames tell you about your future self's relationship?*

Your future self returns after a short hiatus and is happy to hand you a piece of notepaper. Written on it is a heartfelt message that you needed to hear. *What does the message say?*

Looking back up from their note, you see your future self closing the gap between the two of you to give you a hug. You open your arms and receive a hug that embraces your very soul. It lasts longer than you expect. Letting you go, but with their hands still on your shoulders, they lovingly peer into your eyes, thank you for the visit, and invite you back anytime you want.

They walk with you back to the door, open it, and you pass through the doorway as you both gesture a fond goodbye. After watching you take several steps into the distance, they close the door behind you.

You make your way back to the lighthouse and see it's still white inside and silent. In deep thought, you walk all the way to the bottom and sit down on the metal-grate steps. Once more, you're unconcerned with your bum's discomfort. Surrounded by the white abyss, you close your eyes on those steps, feel a chilled breeze returning, and feel your soul move back to now. Feel wherever your feet are touching. Feel how you're sitting—your posture. Notice your breath.

Now, take a few minutes to take some notes.

7

UNFIT AND FAILED NEGOTIATIONS

It was my last year of undergrad, and I was head over heels for one of my family friends from my hometown. She was younger, though—a college freshman. And my super-senior year was about to commence, since I had spent most of an academic year abroad. I didn't get held back, okay?

A couple of things stopped me from asking her out. First, I wanted to give her the opportunity I had in my freshman year: to decide who she wanted to be and to establish a relationship with God. The only other thing was, well, she was *sort of,* kind of, almost like, you could say... the little sister of my most recent ex. I hadn't even kissed her sister, though, so I still saw a chance.

Throughout the school year, my support and encouragement accompanied her as she had flings, made new friends, found a deeper relationship with God, made her own decisions, and grew into who she wanted to be. All the while, my heart's captivation never faded.

In its beautiful prison cell, it eventually put my love's confession into a song, as I couldn't yet confess it to her. I *could* vaguely confess it to everyone else, though. And the university coffee shop's open-mic nights were the perfect place to do it. So, I signed up and invited her.

Though when that night came, my performance came and went,

and my search through the sea of faces failed to find hers. I do earnestly wonder if I finished that song of hope with defeat written all over my face. By the time she showed up, my fingers were well away from my guitar strings.

She shared her disappointment at missing my performance after everyone had mostly left the building. That's when the thought of replaying it for her jolted me. A more perfect opportunity couldn't have been planned. She cheerfully obliged. So, my guitar nestled in my arms once more, and my fingers began to waltz over the fretboard. Our heads leaned close together, and a hushed one-on-one performance was had instead.

Periodically, my eyes and smile would find hers. But most of all, I was just trying to keep my sheep together. Never could I have imagined serenading her one-on-one. Yet her presence sat still, blissfully taking in the words of a love song she didn't even know was about her. The lyrics of *It Makes No Sense to Me* filled her heart and ears:

> *You're paralyzing me, making me want to dance at the*
> > *same time.*
> *You're energizing me like a plant soaking up the sunshine.*
> *The way you laugh, you giggle, purifies my soul.*
> *The way you sing has got joy jolting through my bones.*
> *It makes no sense to me...*
> *...You are my everything, yet we're nothing as of right now.*
> *You're the girl from another world, but we live in the same*
> > *town.*
> *What I'd give to truly hold your heart.*
> *I just know this: you are truly set apart.*
> *It makes no sense to me...*
> *...You're hypnotizing me as I stare at you twirl in the*
> > *moonlight.*
> *You're burglarizing me as you steal my heart in a free fight.*
> *I've given up trying to figure you out.*
> *Because in love, it's the mystery that's profound.*
> *It makes no sense to me.*

Starry eyes and a melty, admiring look dawned on her face when I finished, and she jumped to hug me tight. "I love it!" Everything I dreamed of feeling flooded over me in that moment. Somehow, my guitar didn't drop to the floor.

Not much dampened my spirit of loving her from afar that year. As long as I was a good man who stayed in her life, bringing her the most consistency, laughter, support, and joy, I knew every other man would be measured against me. I was steep competition, even if she didn't know I was competing for her heart. Even in her family's eyes, I was a first-round draft pick.

Perhaps one of the few speed bumps, albeit possibly rather a very firm brick wall, was what she said to me on a Saturday morning at church. Dressed to the nines, I was due to speak up front that day. From across the room, she galloped up to me with bright eyes, gave me a hug, and said, "You look so handsome!" Her genuine words were very welcome. Her next words, however, were not.

I actually don't even remember exactly what she said because I tried to erase it from my memory. It was something along the lines of, "You're like a brother to me." My face turned surprised with a crooked smile, and I briefly nodded to acknowledge her good intentions before saying, "Oh, alright." Then, my attention quickly diverted to my imminent tasks as a means to dodge the comment. There was no thank you or "I feel the same," or any impression that I was explicitly open to the position of brother.

Despite that setback, I remained undeterred. When sufficient time had passed since I dated her sister, say about a year, I'd tell her how I felt. Until then, I'd support and encourage her as she developed into who she wanted to be. I encouraged her to work at a summer camp where I used to work, since it's where some of my deepest personal and faith development took place. Some of my best friendships in life also came from there. I hoped she'd find the same blessings.

As it'd turn out, she got hired. And that's when I decided to plan on working there after the normal camp weeks with the sole purpose of confessing my love. Serendipitously, my work overlapped with the typical staff retreat, and I was invited to attend. *Perfect!* Go on a retreat with the girl I love? *Say less, I'm in!* I could already imagine riding happily ever after into the sunset.

It only took about half a day to realize she'd started a summer camp fling and that it *wasn't* going to be perfect. A conflict brewed in my mind, "*I don't pursue taken women. So, what now? Well, they're not officially dating, just publicly interested, I suppose. Summer camp flings usually don't even last. Who am I kidding? I came to confess my love after months, almost a year of patience, and that's exactly what I'm going to do.*"

So, I went on that Oregon beach retreat, mentally facepalming and faking my best positive spirit. Everyone gathered and socialized around the beach bonfire on the first evening of the trip. Instead of watching them fling their fling around, I stuck in my headphones, channeling a mix of hopeful and depressing music, and wandered into the distant darkness alone. Part of me wished she'd see me wandering off and come looking for me. My heartache was the only thing following me, though.

Pools of water the ocean left behind scattered the beach, and I walked beside them. Fixing my eyes on the cliffs in the distance, I noticed faint flashes around me. My feet stopped in their tracks. "Is... someone taking pictures of me? Or is my phone's light blinking because of a message?" My phone was sitting in my pocket, though, and couldn't go through my jeans. Curious, I scanned my surroundings to find a culprit. But no one was around. No flashlights, nothing. "Weird. Press on, I suppose."

Glimmers of light returned only a few steps later. Yet again, there was no one and nothing around. It felt like a Looney Tunes character was perfectly mirroring my every move with a dim spotlight. I took a few more steps, now looking at the sand beneath my feet, and, to my amazement, witnessed a rippling glow around my feet. As if to orchestrate a stadium cheer, vibrant blue bioluminescent plankton celebrated every step I planted on the damp sand with shockwaves of light. A little tap dance came over me until another light went off.

Straightening my face, I thought, "Holy freaking sheep. Sheila!" That's for sure her real name. Immediately, my head turned back toward the bonfire, and my body followed. A romantic moment was engineered in my mind as I bolted to pull her into a supernatural moment. The cloak of darkness fell off as I neared the fire. After a brief scan, I found her sitting next to *fling* boy, and I literally gave zero sheeps. I did *not* care.

Careless of the conclusions others might draw, I placed my hand on her shoulder and gave her a light push while finding my breath. Sincerity and excitement filled my voice as I said, "Come with me!" Sparked with curiosity, she didn't miss a beat, and I gestured for her to jog along with me. "*Bye-bye, fling boy!*"

We trotted down the beach until I could tell we were at the edge of the plankton's favorite watering hole. At a standstill, my arm comedically propped open for her to latch onto. "Hold on to my arm and don't open your eyes!" I playfully demanded. "Okay, okay, I promise!" Linking her arm into mine, step after step, we entered the playground of plankton celebrations. If we could walk on water in the dark, perhaps this is what it would look like.

At the most intense spot, I told her to stand still, and then I paced about 20 feet out in front of her. "I'm going to ask you a question," I cast my voice to her. Her lips formed a smirk. I waited a couple of seconds to build up tension. "Have you ever walked on the stars?"

"*What?*" she replied, with a playful, puzzled grin. "Open your eyes and walk straight toward me slowly." Her eyelids parted, beheld me in front of her, and she took a few unhurried steps with her focus on me. After those first few steps, I said, "Now look at your feet." Shocked to see glowing pulsations radiating from her feet, she began skipping as her spirit floated around in euphoria.

Only two factors prevented me from asking her to dance on those stars. One, it would've been a bit too bold, given that she was just hanging out with another guy 5 minutes before. Or she could get super uncomfortable and avoid me for the rest of the summer. I had two weeks. There was no rush.

Second, she hadn't shown me enough of her cards for it to make sense that I make my intentions explicitly obvious—more than they already were at least. I wanted a moment like that to be shared with someone who *also* loved me. Instead, I settled for watching her delightfully dance with the stars twirling around her. My heart could've burst.

Overwhelmed by the rare supernatural experience, she flew to me and wrapped her arms around me, saying, "Thank you so much for showing me!" No instruction was needed: she held onto my arm with a smile the whole walk back. I returned her to her seat next to him and disappeared into the darkness with my headphones once again. Only this time, with a spirit so high that not even jealousy or bitterness could reach me. Operation *Mr. Steal Yo Girl* was now proceeding at maximum velocity. "*Sorry, lover boy. The only reason I came here was to confess my love. I came to absolutely send it. And that's exactly what I'm going to do.*"

Lover boy left after the retreat ended, and Sheila and I were among the staff working the rest of the summer. Any aching heart, tears, or void left by her friends after they went home would be met with my support and a long, snug, possibly spinning hug. *Ya boy wasn't playing no games now.* Every opportunity I had to create tension and plant seeds of the obvious, I used. If anyone wanted to gossip and spill their suspicions about my "secret," it'd be that much less talking for me to do.

Many days were spent bantering and laughing, but moments of sincerity periodically appeared. Inspired by one of our conversations, I wrote her a song for one of her life questions. It was called *The Plan*. It empathized with and addressed her concerns about God's calling or plan for her life. The key message was this: *Instead of being concerned with where we think God wants us, we should be concerned with taking God with us wherever we choose to go.*

That same day, we found ourselves alone in the staff lounge, and I witnessed more of her sadness over missing her friends and, probably, fling boy. Feeling for her and not wanting to pry, but only to give, I eventually offered a kind smile, gestured to the floor, and said, "Come lie down." My hands met her to massage the body around her aching heart, as we were accustomed to doing, but for over an hour.

When my hands finally lifted, I gently kissed her on the top of the head to no response. Sheila was out *cold*.

So, I left her to nap, went to some programming, did my bedtime routine, and paced up to the dust-landscaped softball field to talk to a friend eager for an update. Just me, the stars, and a phone to my face, I chatted about important mission milestones and the amazing opportunities I'd come across. But amidst the play-by-play review, Sheila and her department partner approached on a large all-terrain vehicle called a ranger.

For anonymity's sake, we'll just humbly refer to her partner as the *"Friggin' GOAT."* I recognized that they were coming to put away some equipment in the sports shed. So, under the guise of the ranger's roaring engine, I blurted out, *"She's here, gotta go!"* and left my poor chap on a cliffhanger.

They were surprised to see me in the distance as I came near, and asked me what I was doing up there all alone. In the dark. By myself. With no one else. I told them I was on a phone call. Since that response from a guy *not* on the phone, standing alone in the dark in the middle of nowhere wasn't suspicious *at all*, they invited me to get inside the vehicle with them.

Just as I took my seat, I looked the Friggin' GOAT straight in the eyes and asked him, "Friggin' GOAT, can we please go for a joy ride around camp?" His eyes narrowed, and his smirk said, "Say less." He proceeded to exit the camp premises, evading its strict speed limit. Sheila donned one of my jackets to escape the frosty night as we rolled up to the security shack at the camp's entrance/exit. Our stellar driver yelled out to the security guard on duty, "Hey, Kingsley, we, uh, dropped something, uh, out on the road earlier, and we need to go find it!"

Despite the terrible persuasion and laughable excuse, we revved our way down the long dirt entry road. Once out of the shack's sight, the Friggin' GOAT throttled it like we were in *Fast and Furious 27*, and Sheila grabbed my hand, interlocking her fingers. The thrill of breaking the rules, the wind rushing past our faces, and the challenge of staying stable were enough to make it difficult to manage my breath. Holding her hand left me gasping for air.

It was such an innocent and unplanned miracle. To me, it signified that, no matter what happened next or what she chose, God answered my prayers by surprising me with opportunities. Details as small as a friend reaching out on the phone made this specific miracle possible. Regardless of how many events came together over those weeks, I believed my God showed up for me, and it was truly an honor.

And though I'd head back to my bed on a high, I wouldn't be getting much sleep that night. Because the next day I'd be handing her the letter confessing my long-requited love as we drove to our hometown. *Another opportunity.* Fast-forward to then, we settled into the seats carrying us home, where I surprised her with coffee cake and a cinnamon roll. A modest tummy led her to offer to share and feed me while driving. The car speakers performed a concert of our favorite songs as we alternated DJs and sang our hearts out. It was a blast, as always.

When it was my turn, I put on the playlist I had planned as background music for her while she read my love letter. As the key song approached to cue me to hand her my letter, though, I began losing blood in my hands. They became totally numb from nervousness.

That's not *great* when you're driving at country-highway speeds. Chris Martin struck his notes, but I just couldn't bring myself to follow through. I was a deer in the headlights... Until serendipity stepped in once more. The music's brawn caused her to eventually announce, "Yeah... I really can't hear anything..." Which was absolutely my cue to turn down the music, look at her, and say, "Sheila..."

Her face turned to me, and in a calm, easy voice, she inquired, "Yeah?" My lungs sucked in a breath, hoping courage was one of air's elements. "The word of the day is peace." I exhaled. She smiled gently and redirected a pensive stare out the front windshield. "Take some deep breaths with me on the count of three." Immediately, I started huffing only to cut myself off, bursting into laughter because I forgot to count.

Escaping the laughter breaking my anxiety's ice, I regrouped and said, "Okay, okay, shoot, let's try that again! One... two... three." We both inhaled deeply and exhaled together five times. With the final exhale, I released the latch that held the center console shut. "I have a farewell letter for you." It was farewell because a cross-country move to Michigan to get my master's degree awaited me shortly. I extended my arm and handed her a few sheets of paper folded together.

Her hands cradled the letter like it could break. After a brief pause, she asked if she could read it right there. The playlist I designed for emotional reminiscence accompanied her as she read. Laughter and tears filled the space here and there. Meanwhile, I quietly sang along, mostly trying to soothe myself. Her eyes traced each page as I had hoped she would: *utterly glued.*

I ended up taking the perfect number of wrong turns to give her time to finish it before we got to her house. Pulling onto her street, she lifted her eyes from the magnetic pages and peered at me, smiling with tears in her eyes. It was a mix of emotions I'd never seen in anyone before. It kind of looked like she wanted to slap me while also crying tears of "*How could I not know you loved me like this?*" Not even *You'll Be in My Heart* by Phil Collins, which brought her to laughter, could break us out of the sentimental space.

Our chariot's tires halted in her driveway. I extended my hand and asked if I could pray with her. She grabbed my hand, interlocked her fingers tightly, and placed her other hand on top. As soon as I said, "Amen," we opened our eyes to see her best friend in front of the car running out to her. Sheila threw my hand away like it was the plague and plowed the door open to give her bestie the biggest hug of all time.

One final matter remained. I went inside to briefly visit with her family and found a moment to give Sheila her favorite candy bars and a flash drive with a couple of playlists I made for her. Also on that device was a recorded version of the song I wrote and sang for her in that coffee shop in college. I'd spent hours recording it before I left for camp. That was the last thing I absolutely needed to do for my own peace. After that, I'd know I did absolutely everything within my power to breathe every breath of love into a love story between us. I hugged everyone else and embraced Sheila for the last time.

It wasn't the goodbye I was hoping for, as we didn't get to discuss anything. But I had also had so many prayers answered on my mission that I couldn't have asked for anything more. I went home, packed, and left at 3:00 AM the next morning to move from Oregon to Michigan.

On the drive out, I cried for 2.5 hours. We're talking like gasping-for-breath-as-quietly-as-you-possibly-can-because-your-dad-is-sitting-right-next-to-you-sleeping-for-the-next-30-hours crying.

It didn't take long until I just let the tears fall and quit wiping them away. I could've cried for how my mom wept in my arms before I left, telling me how much she was going to miss me. I could've cried that I was moving far, far away from home. I even could've cried that only about 1 in 1,000-10,000 sea turtle hatchlings survive to adulthood. And that freaking *sucks*, dude.

Instead, I cried because I felt like I was leaving behind the love of my life. I mourned not knowing the next time I'd hear her laugh, sing at the top of her lungs, or feel her head rest against my chest during a hug. And despite how deeply it pierced my soul, I let the memories seared into my mind play on a loop. Then, I thanked my God for the privilege of loving so deeply.

And that's how my time with Sheila ended. In tears, experiencing the beauty of all emotions at once. *It was utterly magnificent.*

Sometimes, no matter how much we love or want someone—no matter how many things have gone right and fallen into place—no matter how many beautiful memories we've made with someone—no matter how much love we've poured out... it just doesn't work out. Sometimes, no matter how much it seems meant to be, it isn't always meant to last.

As for Sheila and the other guy, I'm happy to say they eventually got their happily-ever-after! He was no fling boy after all. He was the *real deal*. If Sheila or he is reading this, I hope the details in my story serve as an encouragement to you two.

Regardless of how this story comes across, the other man was *chosen*. It takes *one heck* of a love story to trump all the effort I went through, so I want you to know what you have is real. I hope you keep on nurturing what you have. I'm sure it's beautiful.

The Love Hero's Journey

"Is true love possible without first experiencing heartbreak?" That question piqued my curiosity and led me to conduct a poll among my peers about true love. As unexplained and subjective as I left its definition, I asked, "To those of you who think you've undoubtedly found true love, did you experience a devastating heartbreak beforehand?" *A whopping 75% of them said yes.*

Mind you, this is a decently well-educated, principled, financially secure, and healthy young adult demographic I polled. This type of demographic faces fewer obstacles and, in theory, should have a less painful path to creating healthy relationships. Yet, even though not every poll participant said they endured devastating heartbreak before finding true love, 75% is still the vast majority.

My suspicion, after adding the conditions we're about to, is that it's probably closer to 100%. The first condition is embracing the same definition of true love presented in this book. Second, we define "devastating heartbreak" as broadly as being crushed by a first love, ending a deeply intertwined long-term relationship, enduring a quarter-life or mid-life crisis, losing a cherished loved one, getting divorced, or even remaining in a dead marriage/relationship that our hearts are drowning in. So, we're not even limiting heartbreak to relationship contexts as one might assume.

These scenarios are identity-quaking trials that carve chasms of grief into our souls. On one side of the chasm stands the person we were before; on the other, we stand—fragments of who we once were. We don't know exactly how the pieces fit together, but we do know they can never go back to how they were. The version of us that existed before heartbreak doesn't exist anymore. Our life's garden has been burnt to ashes and must be completely reborn, little by little.

Poetically, this is a common event in a narratology archetype called the hero's journey. Its structure fell into place by studying a great share of the most prized myths and legends throughout history. The hero's journey is essentially the skeletal structure of a hero's storyline—though not all its elements always fall in the same order. In short, a hero goes on an adventure, overcomes a crisis, and returns home transformed. We find this archetype engraved within the narratives of *The Lord of the Rings, Star Wars, The Hunger Games,* and more.

Let's adapt Christopher Vogler's 12-step version of this journey into a true-love context.

ONE — THE ORDINARY WORLD

A hero exists in normalcy and lives in a humble setting. They appear to be exactly like an ordinary individual with nothing particularly special about them. In relationships, this is the purity of early childhood. When we're young children, we're essentially oblivious to and disinterested in pursuing romantic endeavors.

TWO — THE CALL TO ADVENTURE

Amidst the safe and ordinary routine, the hero-to-be encounters a problem, a challenge, and a beckoning to the unknown. In typical hero mythology, The Call typically manifests as a distant forest, a hidden kingdom, a secret treasure, or a latent power.

The Call happens when we begin to form a subconscious *romantic ideal for ourselves.* This call can take place at different times for everyone. For me, it probably occurred around age 8. My wife started developing crushes at age 4.

As children, we can tell partnership is what's "supposed to happen" because it's built into society at every corner. Even if we don't totally understand it just yet, we know that whatever people in relationships have is probably in our future too. So, we play with the concept of an ideal partner being out there and dream of how fantastic our lives would be with the people we crush on.

THREE — REFUSAL OF THE CALL

When a future hero receives a call, they refuse it at first and stay put. It might be because they have other obligations, or because they feel afraid or inadequate.

In relationships, the Refusal of the Call is a general state of unreadiness. Unreadiness can mean many things, including a fear of vulnerability and commitment, a need for healing, or a lack of confidence, maturity, or knowledge of what we want. For kids, it could simply mean they haven't hit puberty yet. As for true love, however, it's more specific. It's the refusal to pursue the embodiment of an infinite definition of love. It's staying attached to the way we are, being overly prideful, and resisting change.

FOUR — MEETING THE MENTOR

There eventually comes a moment when the hero says, "To hell with it," and they accept the call. When this happens, a mentor or magical guide bursts onto the scene. Typically, they give the hero advice, guidance, an artifact, or a healing potion that will aid them in a dire situation down the quest's timeline.

When a heart is ready to experience love, it searches relentlessly and uses whatever help it can find. Throughout the past century or two, that help probably looked like people in healthy relationships we looked up to—people who could give us advice—mentors. Nowadays, Meeting the Mentor probably looks more like dating apps, books, podcasts, therapists, coaches, influencers, and the occasional pair of parents.

Dating apps and books function like magical potions or artifacts because they lay out a supernatural buffet of candidates and novel strategies to accompany heroes in their quest to create true love. Advice and guidance from one's chosen mentor will help when the hero finds themselves at a crossroads in their relationships or dating.

Five — Crossing the First Threshold

Here, the adventurer fully commits to stepping into the unknown —the new world. In the context of true-love relationships, we fully commit ourselves to discovering what true love means and dealing with whatever obstacles come our way.

We don't know exactly what true love is, but we want something more than the relationships that have become commonplace around us. We find them so disenchanting that we're willing to venture into uncharted waters in hopes of finding a remedy, cure, or miracle that enables us to write an extraordinary love story.

Bonus — The Meeting with the Goddess

I included this stage from a different version of the hero's journey because I think it's especially relevant to a Love Hero. This is the moment in the story when the hero meets the other half of their internal being. For men, the goddess embodies the epitome of feminine ideals and perfect beauty. For women, they encounter a heavenly husband, representative of masculine ideals, who brings peace to their desires.

You may recognize my Meeting with the Goddess in the story I shared at the start of *Chapter 4*. It was a meeting or observation of someone who embodied feminine ideals, humbling beauty, and someone who even beckoned me unto divinity—to pursue the epitome of love I saw in God.

In relationships, this stage is pretty self-explanatory. We encounter divine representations of our other halves. They seem out of reach as we put them on a pedestal. We're infatuated and see them as a perfect human being, so we feel humbled by feelings of unworthiness and awe. Though they're most certainly *not* perfect, they inspire us to strive to be worthy of them in the future. They motivate us to press forward on our quest to become a Love Hero and to create true love.

Six — Tests, Allies, and Enemies

As the hero learns to navigate the choppy landscape of the unknown world, they encounter new characters and a series of tests and challenges testing their resolve. All the duress they undergo in this stage grants them the first significant signs of character development.

Tests and challenges are openings for setbacks, failure, and derailment of their journey. Temptation is a prominent example of these trials. They typically take the form of pleasure or the easing of pain in exchange for the hero's sacrifice of their values.

It's common for storytellers to portray the temptation of pain relief as heroes seeing hallucinations or visions of loved ones and being invited to join them. The hero must then decide whether to stay in the temptation's comfortable illusion or recognize that the temptation isn't real and pull away.

Another common temptation is to join the more powerful opposing side, such as Darth Vader inviting Luke to overthrow the emperor and take power for themselves in *Star Wars*. Or like Frodo in *The Lord of the Rings,* being tempted to keep the ring instead of destroying it.

As I'm sure you can guess, pleasure temptations are lustful, seductive temptresses or womanizers sedating and sidetracking heroes from their values and journey. Tests and challenges leave heroes bruised from failure, humbled from being knocked down, and weighing the validity of their values as they're forced to reflect.

Also in the unknown lie allies and enemies—those traveling a similar journey and those seeking to oppose the hero's progress. *Allies* are friends with similar goals who hope to uplift one another and support each other through challenges and failures. *Enemies* are antagonists who leech off a hero's strength, exploit their weaknesses for personal gain, poison their values, and stall their progress.

Translating this to the relationship world, we regularly encounter tests and challenges because the dating world is about as orderly as the Wild West. While there are common rules and themes we recognize from media, culture, or past relationships, not everyone shares the same rules or communicates effectively or in the same way.

Hence, our dating profiles get created, we swipe away, and maybe we didn't get the memo that selfies weren't okay. Maybe the people we take a liking to at the bar receive our flirtatious advances only to get offended and walk away. We expect our dating prospects to treat us a certain way, and they do the utterly unexpected. We inevitably make mistakes, get misinterpreted, and receive rejections.

In the end, the challenges we face lead to failed mating negotiations and emotional slumps. Every time, we have to absorb the shock of failure, get back up, and try again.

Sometimes we face temptations that test the stability of our values, standards, boundaries, and identity. Some things we thought were nonnegotiable suddenly become negotiable with a certain person or for a certain amount of time as we lower our standards and boundaries. Maybe we consider indulging in pleasure to cover the pain of rejection and failure. We could ease pain and numb the heartache of being alone by returning to an ex. Even the temptation to avoid rejection's heartache by not initiating requires us to muffle our aspiration for true love.

In these scenarios, "big-ticket items" seduce, bribe, and sedate us into overlooking things we definitely shouldn't. Identity and values become juggled beakers in an alchemist's frantic attempt to concoct a potion remedying their unquenched desire for true love. Only that potion will never work.

Despite the temptations, tests, and trials, this war zone of dating and love—this place where we juggle beakers—*is also where we grow to realize what we want and what we don't.* The unknown in the environment and within ourselves begins to become known and solidified. We begin growing in the way we perceive the world, other people, and ourselves. We realize that some change is good and actually necessary for growth.

The enemies we encounter are simply those we learn we don't want to be around and connect with. Allies are living the same life stage: going on the same adventure for true love, supporting our growth and journey, and connecting with us along the way. Some of these companions, we'll keep forever as friends.

SEVEN — APPROACH TO THE INNERMOST CAVE

The approach to the innermost cave symbolizes the edge of the most dangerous place in the unknown world. Once the hero crosses the threshold of the cave, there's no going back from the grievous potential damage it poses. Therefore, a hero often braces themselves to face the monumental challenge that lies in wait.

In true love's context, this brace is the realization that something isn't working. We question whether what we thought was love is, in fact, love at all. The dates are dead ends, the expectations aren't met, the relationships we form aren't thriving, and our dreams fail to come alive.

Here, with a deep exhale, we let go of the shopping list of cards we were told to flash for others and the shopping list we were told to get out of others. Much of who we were at the time of The Call also appears to have faded as we come to peace with letting much of our individuality go.

The nice-guy routine, bad-boy routine, bubbly-girl routine—the people-pleaser, the perfectionist, the constantly manicured feminine, the highly individualized definition of ourselves—they all fade. Any remnants of our attachment to the way we are pass away. Only bare hearts fully open to pursuing the infinite essence of love remain.

We become open to being wrong, not having it all together, not hiding our flaws, and letting people see us for all we authentically are. Then, we come to peace with being remade. We take courage in letting go of rigid control. We're willing to try new strategies, listen to what others really want, look for the flaws within ourselves, see ourselves in others, and grow in ways we've always resisted and never imagined. The foundation for actively rebuilding ourselves in the image of an infinite definition of love is laid.

EIGHT — THE SUPREME ORDEAL

The apex of the journey is where a hero must face their greatest fear and make peace with that which has the greatest power over their life. This great power could be a friend group, community, addiction, political party, spouse or partner, parent or guardian, belief system, or religion—anything that holds the greatest sway over how one's life unfolds.

For all intents and purposes, it's coming face-to-face and wrestling with one's god. We battle against the order that upholds the structure of our world. It's about more than standing at the cave entrance, being open-minded, and growing at our own pace. It's about being sucked into the cave, being forced to face death and life-shattering circumstances, and being made into something new.

For illustration, we'll look at the beloved *Star Wars* saga. Luke Skywalker, the main protagonist of the *Star Wars Episode IV-VI* trilogy, faces his supreme ordeal when he encounters his father, Darth Vader. His father, formerly known as Anakin Skywalker, is an overshadowing power in Luke's life in a couple of ways. First, he's the most feared embodiment of raw power on the antagonistic side of the galactic empire. Second, he's Luke's father and one of his only two living family members.

In Luke's supreme ordeal, he's caught in a lightsaber duel with his father in *Episode VI - Return of the Jedi*. He wrestles with the greatest power in his world and is forced to continuously weigh whether he should (1) forgive his father for spearheading the oppression of the galaxy or (2) feed his hatred for his father because of his evil insistence. As the duel builds in suspense, Vader says he'd try to turn Leia, Luke's sister, to the dark side to serve the Empire.

At that point, Luke gives in to his anger and starts beating down daddy dearest. His green lightsaber clobbers his father's red. He doesn't want to see his sister become a victim or slave to evil. With a flurry of attacks, Luke bests Vader and cuts off the same right hand his father took from him earlier in the saga, and finds himself at a crossroads.

This is rock bottom. He's cut off his father's hand, and he's about to execute him. His entire identity of "doing good" weighs in the balance. He's lost himself. The audience watches in suspense as to whether he can come back.

The violent, contemptuous path is being encouraged by the evil emperor standing over his shoulder. "*Do it*. Now, fulfill your destiny, and take your father's place at my side," he hears. To do this would be to make peace with Vader in a way that sees him succumb to and align with his ideology of evil, hatred, and darkness. Furthermore, if Luke killed his father, he might even attempt to murder the emperor, leaving him changed and lost forever.

If he succeeded, in all likelihood, this new identity committing double-homicide could *not* reconcile with his former "good" identity. So, he might take the empire for himself and run it in a way that mixed the empire's oppressive nature with the rebel philosophy he'd developed along the way. This path would define Luke as a tragic hero—one who never completes the Hero's Journey.

Instead, Luke refuses to execute his father and throws away his lightsaber, symbolizing his forgiveness of his father and the death of an identity in hatred. In his forgiveness, he chooses to gracefully see and accept his father in a beneficent light. In this light, his father is the man Anakin Skywalker: truly good and meant to one day bring balance to the Force rather than siding with the oppressors.

Despising Luke's decision, the evil emperor begins electrocuting Luke to death with force lightning. However, because of Luke's forgiveness and mercy, Vader experiences an internal dilemma. He glances back and forth between his tortured son and the emperor inflicting his cruelty.

The weight of the love Luke showed him awakens the goodness in Vader—*Anakin*. As the emperor electrocutes his son, Anakin picks up the emperor like Padmé on their wedding night, and WWE-launches his sparky ass over some railing to free-fall down an explosive reactor shaft. The emperor dies, and Anakin finally achieves his destiny as the one who brings balance to the Force and lasting peace. At least until *Disney* needed to turn the money printer back on... Regardless, it was all made possible through a certain death and Luke's atonement with his father, the greatest power in his life.

Campbell's version of this stage is called "Atonement with the Father," where the father represents the greatest power in one's life. Fundamentally, this stage is about adding to the strength of a hero. Whatever power overshadows them, it's better used as an ally and for growth rather than made into an enemy. One who can stand up to the greatest power in his or her life and make it an ally will always become stronger in the end.

Of course, standing against the power of a father doesn't come without friction. A hero must maintain much of what they know and believe in, and *mix* it with the good they see in the power overshadowing them. It's this partial *denial and acceptance* of the great power that demands atonement. It's the "I love you, Dad, and I'll always love you. I want you in my life, but I need to walk my own path and be my own person. I hope you'll understand and be there for me even through choices you don't agree with."

To take this step, the hero must be ready to let go and forgive the father if he refuses to accept them. Either way, they've made peace with the powers that be. The father may not be at peace with them, but the hero harbors no hatred or contempt. In fact, they incorporate and regard the father as an ally in their life before the father even reciprocates.

Eventually, just as Luke's forgiveness, love, and acceptance of his father's come-what-may decision awakened Anakin, the hero stirs a reciprocated acceptance and peace from their greatest power, realizing a new ally and a new ideology. An ideology made of the best of the hero and the best of the father.

Atonement with the Father and the Supreme Ordeal are key developments for the hero. Standing up to the greatest power in their life prepares them to reckon with the unseen pinnacle of gargantuan obstacles that lie ahead. It's this rock bottom that represents a death and rebirth. And it's this death that makes them so formidable as heroes. Only those who have already died understand what it truly means to sacrifice.

For Love Heroes, this stage means battling with heartbreak and returning stronger. We atone with the greatest power by partially denying it, accepting it, and using it to align with infinite love. Most often, this plays out by letting the gates of our souls open, being vulnerable, placing our beating hearts in the hands of another, and having it shatter on the ground, leaving us with the pieces—heartbroken.

Heartbreak, as I stated at the beginning of this chapter, is not solely reserved for romantic heartbreak. It could be a loved one dying, a midlife crisis, a monumental failure of sorts, or battling belief systems. Whichever it is, *it's rock bottom.*

As we hold the pieces of our hearts like sand sifting through our fingertips, we've died in a way. Our identity is in tatters. It once largely rested with someone or something else, but now, those things are gone. We don't exactly know who we are anymore. We don't know where we fit in this unraveled world. The very will to live seems fleeting.

It's in this heartbreak that we realize a sacred truth: we aren't individualistic at all. As the ancient religions have repeated for millennia, our very beings are connected to the beings around us. The soul speaks: *"I know you are there, death and void of non-existence. I sit, relieved, in non-existence with you, being no one. But I also still stand before you. Therefore, I shall be myself and no one. I shall be everyone."* And while we walk through this valley of shadows and death, the heartbreak that shows us this sacred truth becomes the very seed for new life to sprout up.

As it sprouts, light breaks into our depressive cave. We begin to notice how important the small interactions are. We see ourselves in others, treat them differently, and synchronize with the joys and sorrows in their eyes. The wind, streams, waves, trees, and animals begin to speak in ways we understand. Spawning within us: a reverence for the other life teeming around us and the ground beneath our feet.

Then, the sprout becomes a sapling. Its roots grow deeper, and new foundations begin to solidify. Newly connected with the world and other beings around us, we become something new—capable of growing a breathtaking, life-bursting garden. This sacred interconnectedness is born only from true heartbrokenness. It cannot be taught through words.

From a more scientific perspective, The Supreme Ordeal is home to monumental milestones in theories of human psychology. Among other theories, it's the beginnings of the *Self-Actualization* stage in Abraham Maslow's *Hierarchy of Needs*, the *Post-Conventional* stage in Lawrence Kohlberg's *Stages of Moral Development*, the *Post-Formal Operational Thinking* stage in Jean Piaget's *Cognitive Development Theory*, and the *Individuative-Reflective* stage in James Fowler's *Stages of Faith*.

Cumulatively, these stages are characterized by:

1. Worldview fragmentation, shattering spiritual experiences, or crises that render a belief system invalid, allowing for an existential death and rebirth.
2. Beliefs shifting their origin from external authorities, such as communities or family, to internal personal conviction, responsibility, and discernment.
3. Understanding that truth is not absolute and that laws are not always correct, leading one to critically question life assumptions.
4. Synthesizing and embracing paradoxical and contradictory viewpoints.
5. Integrating emotion with logic, embracing the fullness of humanity.
6. Prioritizing universal good and well-being over personal risk and desire. While we're individuals with needs, there's a mission and purpose to bless the world we're ultimately one with.

According to the creators of these theories, the vast majority of adults never reach these milestones. The fact of the matter is, a dreadful void stands before the dawn of a wonderful creation, and heartbreak is the terrible gatekeeper of true love. Few overcome it.

Nine — Reward

The hero receives a reward once they overcome the lofty odds stacked against them. In mythology, it's a treasure of some sort: a physical object, sacred knowledge, or freedom from the greatest power in their life.

Following recovery from heartbreak, as I essentially just stated in stage 8, Love Heroes gain the reward of the ability to love profoundly. They've already been to the most frightening abyss of heartbreak, and despite what remaining fear they may have about returning to it, they're free to love bravely and fiercely. They're also more connected and in touch than ever, and they see connections waiting around every corner. Their reward is a fertile soil with which to grow a garden of true love.

Ten — The Road Back

Not everything gets settled from the Supreme Ordeal. If there are any stones left unturned, they may come after the hero and attempt to prevent them from returning home with their reward.

Parents, friends, or exes might have a second opinion or rebuttal. The great power may change its mind or wish to spar again. The antagonist might stand bloodied in the distance, demanding a rematch. Thus, the hero must decide whether to return to the ordinary world or remain and fight only for the sake of conquering challenges. This delay can happen even though there's nothing to be gained since the hero already holds the reward.

For Love Heroes, the temptation of the *Road Back* is the continual test of our commitment to our new identities. Has it *truly* set in, and do we believe we've received our reward? Have we *really* conquered the greatest power in our lives? What happens when a parent dies on a hill instead of accepting us? Or what happens when an ex reaches out to us again? What about old toxic or sedative habits trying to sneak their way back into our lives and cause us to relapse? How will we react when negative influences try to reenter our lives? Will we leave the challenges we've conquered behind or stay and battle their ghosts? Will we continue to fight pointless battles or choose peace and go build a beautiful garden?

Love heroes accept the resolution they've received, make peace with the past, and trust their new identity holds the greatest reward. There's nothing to win on the *Road Back*, and there's nothing to learn in what *used to* be the unknown. We've taken all the lessons and become stronger. Turning back would only replay a storyline we've already lived and waste our valuable time.

Eleven — Resurrection

A hero faces their second life-or-death moment in an ultimate test. This is the final showdown between the villain and the hero, where the stakes couldn't be higher. The hero needs everything they've learned and received on their journey to be victorious over the antagonist. In the end, the hero fully completes the transformation they started in the Supreme Ordeal. They're now the absolute definition of a lionhearted hero. A sapling no longer.

Love heroes go through Resurrection when they fully open themselves back up to heartbreak. They've received the sacred truth of interconnectedness as their reward, and now, to plant a *joint* garden, they must again approach the void of heartbreak to be reborn once more with their partner. For only by the willingness to be utterly destroyed can one be completely recreated.

At the climax of this journey, they cease to be and live solely as individuals. As if under a trance, their beings blissfully mesh together, and the two heroes become one. One garden. One flesh. Ceremony or not. And at long last, they create true love.

Twelve — Return with the Elixir

The hero returns to the ordinary world from the unknown world. Upon their return, there's a celebration. For they've endured hardship, conquered extraordinary challenges, and risked it all. The hero has changed for the better, and it's clear that they bring new skills, knowledge, or items back with them. The elixir is often used to better the lives of those in the ordinary world whom the hero originally left behind.

Returning with the Elixir is no doubt Love Heroes having their true love amplify the love and good in the world. Being fused together as one, they begin passing down their wisdom, raising the next generation, strengthening each other's passion to change the world for the better, and continuing to grow in the essence of infinite love.

~

And that's the Love Hero's Journey! I share this to highlight that heartbreak, existential devastation, and a rebirth of identity are just inevitable parts of how Love Heroes and their creation of true love come to be.

Only those who've been burned can fully understand what it means to have reverence for fire. Only those who've witnessed their garden scorch to ashes will have the vigor and passion to preserve and nurture a garden to ensure its full bloom. And only those whose individualistic identity has died understand true interconnectedness and self-sacrifice.

Though it can be any of the heartbreaks we've mentioned, most of us in the pursuit of true love will either experience or dispense heartbreak in the form of romantic rejection. At multiple points in our lives, we'll probably either bear our bare hearts and be destroyed, or hold someone else's heart and drop it into a black hole as shadows seem to cover our faces and horror music plays in the background.

The hard truth about creating true love is that it doesn't always bloom even if we want it to. Heartbreak through rejection is typically just part of the process. Therefore, it's important to understand *what* breakups are, how to absorb the devastation of their heartbreak, and why and how we should ever break someone's heart.

Breakup Types

The depth of connection people have determines what type of breakup they'll have. The first type of breakup is ending *committed relationships* cleanly due to big disagreements and incompatibilities. Regardless of what time or energy we put in, big disagreements don't allow relationships to thrive. Breakups become necessary.

When a garden can't be healthy or bear fruit, we shouldn't force it to exist. We must tear it down and neither nurture it nor dedicate time and energy to it. That means we stop talking to exes, stop trying to keep a connection, and invest our time and energy into new connections. This allows new gardens to form with new people. Clean break.

The second type is when we're merely *getting to know people* in the dating process, and cut it off because we can already foresee big disagreements. We can already see infertile ground where a garden of true love won't grow. The passive incompatibility filters are at work. These are the easiest breakups and rejections because the stakes are very low. There isn't much emotional attachment yet. We shouldn't, however, underestimate the importance of practicing these types of breakups.

Many young adults today engage in *ghosting*—cutting off communication without providing closure or answers. This practice of avoiding hard conversations will ultimately harm them and their future partner. When hard issues come up, those who don't practice uncomfortable conversations won't *magically* know how to have them when they inevitably come. If their practice is normally to disappear when hard times come, then that's going to be their instinct.

The third and last type of breakup is probably the most strenuous type because it's not a true breakup. This garden collapse requires *both* partners to excruciatingly suppress and alter the foundations of their being just to stay together amid their big disagreements—perhaps out of obligation.

They both desperately need to be reborn, but they naturally prevent each other from doing so. The remnants of the identity they try to leave behind keep getting pulled back by their partner. No matter how much they prune the conflicting plants, they always grow back because much of the soil—the partner they're stuck with—remains the same. Disrespect becomes the air they breathe, and contempt takes the place of peace in their silence.

Married couples are the only ones for whom this type of "breakup" *could* be appropriate or feasible. Even then, comeback stories are painfully rare. A crumbling marriage yearning to create true love would have to buy into the Love Hero's Journey. They'd both have to go on a journey where they're both seriously trying to leave their war-torn marriage behind for a more harmonious one with the *same person*. Inherently, they'd have to look for and endure synchronous heartbreak.

Then, they'd have to rise, being born from the ashes to build a new relationship brick by brick—all the while being called to old wars on the Road Back. They'd remember the knives stuck in their backs by this person, but also look to them for hope. They'd remember all the times they withheld grace from them, but have to offer forgiveness and patience freely.

Their partner is an aggregate of their greatest power in the Supreme Ordeal, the face of the overarching villain, the source of their agony and suffering, their greatest ally, and an embodiment of the source of their redemption, peace, and salvation. It only sounds overwhelmingly challenging and miserable because it is. I'd say it's a bit like trying to completely rebuild a boat while it's on the water. Painfully limited wiggle room. People spend *years* in couples therapy trying to rebuild their foundations. If I had a choice, I would *never select this option*.

The horror of this type of breakup highlights the importance of the first two. Those who muzzle big disagreements and build relationships on top of them do themselves a disservice and *will* ultimately regret it. Furthermore, the consequences of big disagreements only grow more complex over time. We'd save ourselves so much pain if we simply planted a new garden. If you're unmarried or haven't already financially and residentially tied yourself to another person, consider yourself warned.

Now, let's spend some time really solidifying why we should break up.

The Why of Breakups

The why of breakups is due to big disagreements, as we just covered. We'll recall that these disagreements are either born from cascading small disagreements or the outright inability to mutually respect the core boundaries and standards of each other's mating negotiation strategies. They're often over things like religion, values, long-distance, life goals, unshared attraction, or families being at each other's throats.

Since we know the big disagreements screaming in our faces are our why, our next task will be to make these whys *clear*. Meaning, we'll myth-bust the most common excuses for not breaking up. Let's go!

THE PROS AND CONS LIST

Pros and cons lists don't really work. If the life is being sucked out of us, making us question our relationship, no pro-leaning list is going to save our relationship. Life being sucked out of us usually means we have a big disagreement ready to explode, and coming up with a pros and cons list is like covering a pallet of explosives with a baby blanket. Big disagreements are *sheer incompatibilities*, not something we get over. They explode and cause harm no matter what and are nonnegotiable.

Big disagreements drain our energy because they require us to drown and deny core parts of our being. When we do this, we aren't authentic or fully present. If we aren't fully present, we cannot give or receive vulnerable company. In the end, staying in the relationship will probably make us feel more alone than we do on our own.

The ratio on a pros and cons list simply *doesn't matter*. If someone gives us a 20-oz glass of water with 0.05 oz of deadly poison in it and they tell us 0.01 oz can kill someone, are we going to drink it? Why not? The ratio of water to poison isn't *that* bad—it's 400 to 1. We choose not to because *it's still enough to kill us*. In the same way, big disagreements are deadly poison no matter what. They'll kill a relationship eventually, and the longer the relationship fights the poison, the more agonizing the journey will be.

"I DON'T WANT TO HURT THEM."

It's sweet that we don't want to hurt anyone. Unfortunately, as we continue through this myth-busting, it'll become abundantly clear that hurting others in the romance space is *unavoidable*. This sentiment of "not wanting to hurt them" involves a constant juggle of staying in relationships, waiting to see whether something miraculously changes or something disastrous happens, leaving us with no other option but to break up and shatter their heart into a gazillion pieces.

This no-harm dilemma is like answering one of those ethical dilemmas. Like the *Trolley Problem*: "There are two train tracks. One track has one person tied to it, and the other has a hundred people tied down to it. The train is heading toward the hundred. Do you change the track and intentionally kill the one to save the hundred?"

It literally doesn't matter which we choose. *They're all shitty options,* and the solution won't be perfect regardless of which we choose. We either intentionally kill someone or stand by and watch a hundred be slain. It's traumatic, and there's no way around it. But that's the imperfect universe we live in. Unfortunately, we aren't powerful enough to change its nature. We must accept that suffering is an inevitable component of reality.

If we're juggling whether to break up with our partners, we're *already* actively harming everyone involved. We're hurting them because our heart isn't fully in it. It's painful to look into someone's eyes and know their heart doesn't fully belong to you. We're hurting ourselves by forcing an *act* of being fully invested in the relationship. So, if we're asking whether forcing ourselves to be inauthentic is healthy, the answer is *no*—it's hurtful. That's why this excuse is invalid. *Pain comes either way.*

This excuse to stall breakups gets even more complex when there's a quake to the relationship's foundation, and someone sticks in phrases like "I have no reason to live without you..." If we recall back to *Chapter 4*, we'll actually recognize phrases like these to be *extremely manipulative.*

Intentional or not, these phrases employ at least 2 out of the 4 manipulative strategies: coercion and ego. Coercion involves guilt, blackmail, or bullying someone into performing a desired behavior. As a clear-cut example, one could instigate a big fight with overreaction, do some yelling and name-calling, reach a resolution, and then, in the aftermath, for the sake of unconscious security, say something like "I literally could not live without you..."

Instead of setting things right with an apology and lasting behavioral change, the coercer places guilt on the other person if they choose to leave their toxic presence. It makes breaking up more difficult because one's ego is now involved. The underlying question thrown in the face of the manipulated is this: *"I'm not someone who would cut off their ability or reason to live, am I?"*

Breaking up would harm their own ego and the other person's feelings. This manipulation could be completely unconscious to the manipulative party. Or they could also genuinely be manipulating themselves into believing the other person is a monster if they decide to break up with them. In that case, not breaking up with that person is giving in to their delusion and entertaining their manipulation.

On the bright side, those who know what manipulation is can recognize it. If one recognizes they're being manipulated into staying in a relationship, it can instantly provoke a sense of disgust and prompt them to collapse the garden in the blink of an eye. Others manipulating us hurts us, and in that case, someone is still getting hurt.

Sunk Cost Fallacy

The sunk cost fallacy occurs when someone is reluctant to abandon their cause because of how much they've invested in it. For example, if a gambler has spent $500 on 92 slot machine attempts, and the chance of winning is 1 in 100, they might say, "Oh, the win has got to come soon, surely within the next 8! I've put in 92/100 tries so far!"

In reality, the chances of winning are still 1 in 100 with every try. They just try to convince themselves otherwise because they've already lost $500 and "can't" turn back now.

The same is true for education and jobs. "I've studied this for so many years, I have to use the degree I got! Otherwise, I wasted all that time." That person doesn't *have* to do anything. I have a Bachelor of Health Science and a Master of Divinity, and I worked at Costco for a significant portion of my time as an aspiring author. Putting in time and energy doesn't mean we *have* to do anything.

The same is true for relationships. "We have so much history together... we've put in so much time and effort into our relation-ship... our lives are so intertwined!" My guess is this is the *number one excuse for resisting breakups.* It's not only painful to break up but also *inconvenient.*

Painful in the way we'd watch the garden we worked on so hard collapse and burn; inconvenient because we'd have to untangle and split up the friend groups we formed, the objects we co-owned, the pets we shared, or the space we collectively paid for. Yet we mar the picture of true love when our greatest inspirations for staying together are the *fear of pain* and the *inconvenience* of splitting up.

The sunk cost fallacy is a phenomenon driven by fear, as people don't want to see time, energy, or money go to waste. This fallacy doesn't hold up in general, but it especially doesn't hold up in rela-tionships. We don't leave relationships empty-handed. A significant portion of the progress we make in relationships sticks with us as personal development and vital relationship skills.

An important thing to understand is that *we* are the soil that grows the garden of relationships. If we become better at nurturing love, we lay a healthy, fertile foundation for future relationships to stand on and grow beautifully.

In short, past relationships are never a waste. We learn and grow, and others do too. The sunk cost fallacy doesn't hold up in relationships.

"MAYBE IT'S UNREALISTIC TO EXPECT ANYTHING MORE."

We've all probably entered a space where we question our expectations. We beckon ourselves to be "realistic" because, perhaps, we're asking for too much. Maybe we don't deserve to be treated and loved the way we're dreaming of.

So much of what we believe true love looks like is shaped by fairy tales, movies, propaganda telling us we deserve everything no matter what, and the plethora of content we see on the internet. Adding all these influences together requires us to define the line between truth and fable. Locating the line incorrectly can paint a picture that's too unrealistically glamorous, with laughable disappointment awaiting us. It can also paint a picture too humble, with expectations of receiving a bag of rusty nickels when we really should be getting gold.

The simple remedy for this mental gymnastics routine is to measure our own ability to love and seek out someone with a similar capacity. Regardless of how much of a Love Hero we are, or whatever degree we can love, cherish, and sacrifice for others, we know we're not being unrealistic in finding an "equal," since we're the living proof that type of love exists.

The short of it is that Love Heroes manifest themselves as miracles in this world, and a match requires two of a kind. It's not about keeping score. It's about having two parties who are equally invested in tending to a garden.

"**Being in a subpar relationship is better than being single.**"

Better is certainly relative in this context because there is a list of questions we need to ask. Better in what way?

- Better because there's less suffering being single?
- Is it actually less suffering or just *different* suffering?
- Doesn't a subpar relationship *also* produce suffering?
- Do we only prefer a relationship then because we suffer with someone else instead of alone?
- Why can't we suffer with a *friend* instead?
- What are we hiding from when we're unable to be single?
- Is it appropriate or honorable to use people as shields to hide from something?
- What healing are we postponing by not letting our wounds rest in the open air?
- Who is staying together better for?
- Those whose hands are full can receive no gift. What opportunities and gardens are passing us by?
- What opportunities are passing *our partners* by?
- If the split is going to happen eventually, does staying with them ultimately hurt their ability to negotiate for a mate in the future? For example, think of sexual economic repercussions. Does stringing a woman along and stealing her time hurt her chances of finding her best possible mate? Does stringing a man along and using his resources hurt his chances of finding his best possible mate? If so, the loving thing to do would be to break up and give them the best chance to negotiate and create true love.

These questions pull us away from self-interest and make us look in the mirror. Why are we staying in our relationship? Is it really for the complete benevolence of our partner? Or is the motivation for staying together mostly about ourselves? If our chief concern is ourselves rather than others, we may need to reevaluate our identities as Love Heroes.

"THEY'LL BE WHO I NEED THEM TO BE EVENTUALLY... THEY'LL CHANGE... THEY'LL COME AROUND..."

True love requires two people. *Not one person and a project.* If we love someone for who they *could* be instead of who they are now, we aren't in love with them. We're simply in love with the idea of them becoming someone else. More precisely, we're in love with *someone else*—an ideal we made up.

This excuse gives the sunk cost fallacy a run for its money in being the biggest reason for postponing breakups. In this excuse, we find couples who've been together for years shoving big disagreements under the rug. "*They'll come around to wanting kids eventually. I'll wait... They'll eventually change their mind about marriage... Their behavior won't always be like this... They'll be into sex someday... They'll come to believe in God...*"

The aftermath of this excuse is the woman staying with the man for 10 years, finally accepting that he won't marry her, and then leaving him. It's the man divorcing his wife because, 5 years into their marriage, she won't have sex with him. It's the woman breaking free of the man who promised for 5 years he'd quit his drug addiction and stop abusing her. These types of stories are tales as old as time.

Whatever is going to make people suddenly realize that our side of the big disagreement is clearly the right side, *it's not going to be us.* We've probably been around for years, so we're definitely not the catalyst. Their love for us is definitely not the catalyst. That decision isn't coming.

If it is coming, it will be the most unromantic, anticlimactic, and disingenuous thing we've ever experienced. "*We've been together for like 7 years, huh, so like, let's do the next thing you wanted instead of you leaving me...*"

In all likelihood, if they're going to change their mind, it's going to be when we threaten to leave the relationship. If behaviors and actions change only because of fear of the relationship ending, then it's certainly not from true love convicting their hearts. And *change that is not born of the heart is not lasting change.* Their frantic willingness to suddenly flip would simply be another proof that true love has evaded us.

That concludes all the myths we'll be busting. Next, we're going to explore what happens when someone breaks through these myths and decides to break up with us. How do Love Heroes take it?

Heartbreak Philosophy

While enduring rejection and heartbreak is never easy, there are some helpful perspectives that help us process them and increase the likelihood that we create true love.

Perspective #1: Breakups are *not setbacks*. They're the steps both parties take to say yes to the right relationship. Behind every no, there's a bigger yes. Failed negotiations don't mean true love is lost. They simply mean negotiation needs to be brokered elsewhere, and that there's a better fit. *That's progress*—not a step backward.

Perspective #2: We know a better fit is out there because one ambition of true love is to *be wanted and desired*. If someone doesn't want us, they've made it very easy for us to realize they're not the ones for us. We want someone who wants us. If they don't want us, by simple definition, *we don't want them either.*

Our hearts may take time to acclimate to this truth because they'll undoubtedly be tethered to the other person. But that connection will fade over time. Since we can describe love as a living, moving thing, we can say it has momentum or inertia. It'll take time to roll to a stop and for plants in the garden to wither.

Eventually, it'll resonate with us that while that person might have been truly wonderful, what we really want is someone who adores, loves, and wants us the way we do them.

Perspective #3: Failed negotiations and heartbreak in our greatest romantic endeavors *enhance future relationship security, commitment, and satisfaction*. The scars of our past carry lessons and character development that will 100% affect how we show up in our future relationships.

One lesson I learned from going to the ends of the earth,

Australia included, to write my love story was that I could look back and have zero questions or fantasies. I took every shot I could possibly take and attempted negotiations with essentially every candidate I found desirable. I tested my absolute limits of love by crossing the world, asking out professional athletes, and even shooting a shot into Selena Gomez's DMs. No stone is left unturned for me.

Without failure, we see no line marking where our potential stops, and no clear answer to what the universe is willing to give us. That leaves room in our minds for what-ifs. It can leave us open-minded about what's still out there to achieve. However, when we aim our highest, put in our maximum efforts, and achieve successful negotiations, security becomes the default position. Even when faced with additional outstanding options and potential fits.

When we've been tossed to the curb by our highest aspirations, we'll treasure the one who decided they wanted to negotiate with us and build a garden together. When we know we have the best treasure we could find, we'll treat that person with more respect, admiration, and love. That will affect how our partners show up and create a positive feedback loop, where either party would be foolish to abandon what they share.

Perspective #4: *An identity growing in love is still the ultimate aim.* Instead of planting our lives in an individual, we plant them in a transcendent purpose. This means that even when our relationships end, we still have an indispensable reason to move forward and thrive.

Now, as I conclude these perspectives, I must confess they don't suffice as perfect answers to overcome and heal from rejection. Unfortunately, there is no antidote to heartbreak. It's common for attachments to endure *years* after breakups.[i] So, if you're going through the trenches of heartbreak right now, these perspectives are by all means relevant, but there's also powerful grief you need to work through.

You may need to browse books on grief, learn about its landscape and how you specifically process it, give yourself plenty of time, get connected with a competent therapist, and lean hard into your support systems and community. Eventually, you'll draw meaning from it.

Heartbreak is simply a part of the Love Hero's Journey. You don't need to run from it. Rather, embrace it, and *make it count*. Let go and feel the fullness of brokenness and allow its emotions to flood your being. Attune yourself to what you're experiencing because at the center of this consuming darkness is where you learn the value of the dimmest light. Suspended in the abyss of heartbreak's waters, your identity enters its most fluid state. This is where you look for the sacred interconnectedness and the hidden well that is your birthright I mentioned in *Chapter 4*. At the end of it all, like the resurrected hero returning home with their reward, you'll emerge as a new creation.

But at this very moment, all I can offer you is my most heartfelt condolences and genuine encouragement. As a chaplain in a level 1 trauma hospital, I sit at the footstool of death and the void of fading existence with patients and families almost every other day. Fear, panic, devastation, loneliness, heartbreak, mourning, and grief are places I visit often. Trust that as I care for and see those facing the void, I care for and see you. I'm sitting with you in your pain and grief, and the loneliness they bring.

It may not feel like it now, but you will breathe again. *I believe* your sweetest breaths are still ahead. You have my honest faith that you'll create true love, dear reader. When the time comes, you'll find the seeds in your pocket and sprout a garden beyond your wildest dreams.

Smooth Transition... Heartbreak, Heartbreak, I'm All About It!

Finally, we reach the execution of the dreaded deed. We either know outright that *this is not it,* or we just know something isn't right, and we break up. Since most of this book has been about what we should say yes to in true love relationships, the rationale of breakups is easier to summarize.

Because instead of having to say, "This is what's wrong with you, me, and us," we can instead frame our rationale as: "*This is what we should say yes to, and we're not finding it together.*" Before we discuss how to construct our breakup rationale and message, though, we'll first examine the logistics of breaking up and dispensing rejection.

To begin, we arrive at our garden-collapsing, negotiation-abandoning verdict due to violated boundaries and unmet standards. Next, regardless of how long or how deep the connection we've made with someone is, when we're in a place where we're ready to call it quits, it's a Love Hero's duty to collapse a garden with compassion, respect, and kindness.

Why? For one, it's the identity of a hero to do the right thing and want what's best for everyone, not just the people we get along with. We're trying to make the *world* a better place. Plus, that sentiment discourages any escalation where they key our car, steal our pet gerbil, Jimmy, or set our house on fire.

Second, we don't know if our paths will ever cross again. They could be our boss one day, or the universe might unexpectedly rekindle our romance. Collapsing a garden graciously and compassionately is a heroic thing to do because it's largely an act of submission. Albeit a submission to attempt to give them what they want *with someone else.*

At the root of this submission, while we're looking to write our own love stories carefully, we're also concerned with how our partners' love stories go. If we can't create the love story that we genuinely want for them and ourselves, ending our relationship is an act of goodwill and submission. We're advocating for them to have another opportunity to create true love.

Even when they disagree while crying their souls out, if we're sincere and determined, we can walk away confident we did the right thing. If we put ourselves in their shoes, we'd want someone to feel more love for us than we feel for them now. In time, if they don't already, they'll see us in a light where we tried to do right by them. We didn't force them to change, give them an ultimatum, or waste their time. Sometimes, collapsing a struggling garden is really the most compassionate thing we can do.

So, logistically, how do we do it? We want to do it face-to-face at an appropriate location. A walk in the park or in their living space might be appropriate. If we're long-distance, do a video call to make it as personable as possible. These are human beings we're dealing with.

Preferably, we'd like some privacy where emotions can be processed freely through crying or productive conversation. So, probably not at a Costco or a family dinner. Then, if we can help it, we don't want to make any painful memories in places they're fond of. If they have beautiful childhood memories at Disneyland, we probably shouldn't dump them there.

Next, we want optimal timing. Of course, this doesn't mean good or convenient timing. There's no good time to break up, and it's rarely a frictionless experience. But there's certainly *bad* timing. Bad timing is when they're about to have major surgery, have just received a dire diagnosis, experienced a death in the family, or it's a major holiday or their birthday. Since Love Heroes partially understand breakups as setting the other person up for future success, we want to avoid staining any days that are important to them.

Sometimes bad timing is hard to gauge because some people just lead hard lives. They could just have perpetual financial burdens, mental health struggles, or stressful family dynamics. As long as the other person is near their baseline of well-being and they're not in a particularly vulnerable state, timing is "optimal."

Part of submitting, maintaining goodwill, and setting them up for future success is reasonably fulfilling any outstanding commitments we've made to them. Do we have a concert ticket that they bought us to their favorite band? Reimburse them for it. Promised to help them move in a couple of weeks? Look for a substitute.

Commitments like "I'll never leave you" should never have been stated, so you probably don't have to worry about learning your lesson there. That type of statement is an easy way to destroy people's faith in humanity and in the reliability of the opposite sex. Humble but confident promises may underwhelm, but at least we won't look like con-people in a getaway vehicle.

Last, when we let them go, *we let them go*. They're free to go establish another garden. They're released from all obligations to us. We're not asking them to pay for dinner or any other future expenses—not texting them for attention or to see how they're doing. We're not stringing them along as Plan B, not trying to cross paths with them, not competing with them to see who gets in a new relationship first, not staying in touch—*nothing*.

I know there are plenty of opinions on how to interact with an ex. So, to be clear, true love explicitly demands we omit exes from our lives because true love gardens have limited real estate. Where old roots get nourished, new ones cannot form.

If an ex casually continues trying to be a part of our lives, we need to clarify healthy boundaries with them. We clarify that it's in both parties' best interests to cut off communication and let the connection fade as much as possible for the sake of new connections. If needed, we can also emphasize that it's not due to any ill will or hatred.

Pretty straightforward, right? Give space for processing and mourning, be respectful, have their best interests in mind, keep our doable promises, don't pile the breakup onto other crises in their life, set them free from any obligations to us, and maintain healthy boundaries. Now, let's look at the rationale for breaking up.

♫ Tell Me Whyee It's Something of a Heartache ♫

The rationale for a breakup is that we know what we want to say yes to, and this isn't it. To have the courage to collapse a garden, *a Love Hero's desire for the other person to create true love without them has to be stronger than their fear of seeing the other person brokenhearted.* Our loving goodwill for their future has to be greater than our guilt of disenchantment and our fear of being alone.

In my experience, my most sincere breakup came in reading an honest letter I'd written her. I spent about 2 weeks, over 26 hours, drafting it. It may or may not be what you'd expect. There was no pointing of fingers about how flawed she was or assumptions of how right I was—no dramatic ultimatums or declarations of how we'd be better off without one another.

No, instead, it was a thorough analysis of what it meant to truly love someone, much of which you've already read about in this book. It was about how the picture of our relationship differed from the picture of true love and the roles we both played in making that picture.

I reflected on my mistakes, acknowledged her genuine care for me, presented evidence that she didn't truly love me, and offered an opportunity to say her piece. There was no rebuttal or denial. She simply didn't love me the way I seemed to love her. She didn't love me in "true love" fashion—she loved me in a "this works" fashion. And I bore no ill will toward her for it. I broke up with her not only because I wanted true love for myself but also because I thought the breakup would be a wake-up call for her to think about love differently and go create true love with someone else.

We can gather a few lessons from this experience. First, we don't need to cast blame. It's much simpler, less hostile, and more truthful to state that what we're looking for differs from what they're looking for. There's no need to express any superiority or inferiority and determine if someone's right. Being different is a perfectly acceptable reason for us to go our separate ways.

Instead of saying, "You're toxic, you yell too much, and you're insecure, so I'm leaving you," we can remain neutral and say, "You think it's okay to yell, lie, and manipulate, and I just don't feel the same way. I need my relationship to be honest and truthful. If those were truly part of who you were going to be in our relationship, they would've manifested by now. It'd be best if we went our separate ways so we can both find what we're looking for." And we'd say it in a gentle, kind, and respectful manner.

To enhance our neutrality, we'd be wise to reflect on the errors we've made and what we've learned from them. One issue this girl brought up to me some months beforehand was that she always felt like she was being watched and almost tested. It's only after writing the entirety of *Chapter 6,* years later, that I realized I *was* testing her. I had sensed she didn't truly love me. So, I kept litmus-testing her to observe any symptoms of true love, as I understood it.

Regardless, I admitted I was rather critical and apologized for not accepting her and for putting any pressure on her to change who she was. The fault I admitted was that I had no business trying to engineer her very being to be the right one for me.

We admit our faults because it's the loving thing to do. It raises the standard they should hold for themselves and communicates that we see them as worthy of respect and love. By doing so, we're increasing their odds of creating true love in the future because true love requires healthy boundaries and standards.

Whether they've wronged us or not, affirming a standard or boundary they should have is the right thing to do because Love Heroes have no true enemies. Even the harshest heartbreaks teach us lessons about what we don't want and the precautions we should take in the future. Both of those things help us grow, learn, and step toward true love. Anything and anyone propelling us toward true love is no enemy.

Next, we need to make it crystal clear that the breakup is well-thought-out. For those who've reached a significant level of soulful intimacy with their partner, I think processing thoughts through writing a letter and reading it aloud is a classy way to express sincerity and honesty.

Processing what's really behind our decision isn't only beneficial for us to learn what we want and need, but it also communicates that we genuinely respect and care for them. We wouldn't be so intentional with our decision if we didn't care.

With intentional thought, there's no "It's not you, it's me," or "Sorry it didn't work out, good luck out there!" There are no clichés. If we're sincere, our talking points or letter will start with something like "I want you to know I don't take this decision lightly..." and end with something like "It'd be best if we went our separate ways so we can both find what we're looking for."

In scenarios where there's something we can't quite put our finger on, we can say, "Something is off, but I don't have the capacity to find out what it is right now." There's no need to apologize or feel bad because, mostly, it just is what it is. We simply don't have the awareness to know why we're not desperately convinced to be in this relationship. But what we *do know* is that both of us deserve to be and feel wanted.

Finally, if our ultimate roadblock is a lack of physical attraction, it doesn't need to be stated explicitly. It's not going to be helpful to say, "I thought I could date someone who's not good-looking—I can't. I'm sorry, but it's over." Instead, we should use terms like "being disenchanted" or "not feeling a spark," while communicating that a spark is something we really treasure at this point.

If we're part of the majority who need physical attraction, then that's a perfectly acceptable reason to let someone go. Staying with someone purely because of our desire to be a good person makes the other partner a recipient of charity, not true love. It's much more loving to let them go find someone who will cherish them and be crazy about them!

Chapter's End

Overall, for significant breakups, I recommend drafting a letter on a phone or computer, then handwriting the final draft on paper. Write it with the intention of reading it to them. Once you do, allow them some time to process and respond, and then give them the letter.

I recommend letters because they're beneficial for both parties. It's good for us, the presenting party, because we won't miss key thoughts, get stumped, or simply forget everything we came to say. It's also good for the brokenhearted because letters allow them to reflect and better absorb our words.

When we're presenting our letters, we should be mindful of how personable we are. This letter isn't a script devoid of emotion or presence. We need to speak at an unrushed pace and make eye contact as much as possible to read, acknowledge, and empathize with their pain.

Breaking up is an uncomfortable and painful act, so being fully present is the least we can do. If we excuse ourselves from experiencing the negative aspects of the situation, we're acting more like cowards than heroes.

We should also be prepared for the possibility that they refuse to hear our letters. Some people may just prefer to make villains out of those who leave them, and that's their choice. Others simply don't want to be in the same space as us when they're breaking down.

Regardless, we should respect whichever way they wish to process, receive, or reject feedback and communication. If they refuse to listen, we don't need to say, "Well, fine then!" and proceed with insults. Whatever they need to do to cope with heartbreak, we need to give them the space to do so. Even if that means being scapegoated as a villain. Heroes gracefully do what they believe is right, even when others punish them for it.

Again, we just have to accept that breakups are a largely normal part of the journey to create true love. Finding the right person to create true love with only has to happen once. So, by default, failures will almost assuredly outnumber the one success.

Though sources and studies report different numbers, people typically go through 3-8 relationships before locking in with marriage. For me, it was 4, and essentially every married person I know has more than one ex. Per the evidence, breakups are almost an inevitable precursor to true love.

Breakup Letter Walkthrough

To close this chapter, I'll walk us through a template for a loving breakup letter, followed by an example breakup interaction. There are *five* basic elements in a loving breakup letter. If you can remember all these elements without a letter and would just prefer to freestyle the heartbreak appointment, that'd be perfectly acceptable. I just wouldn't trust myself to remember everything. To each their own!

As we begin our letter, we want to enter the right mindset. So, we'll ask ourselves a couple questions.

- "Who do you want to be when you're writing this letter?"
- "What character traits do you need to lean on when relaying your message?"

In the **first** element of our letter, we want to address them and *clarify our intentions*. For example,

> Dear Melbourne,
>
> Though it may be hard to hear and read, this letter isn't meant to rub anything in your face or point fingers. Rather, it's meant to give you answers I believe you deserve, and to help me articulate and share my thoughts about why our relationship won't work long-term.

Second, we *outline our rationale*—why it isn't working. Momentarily, you'll see some questions to help you determine your rationale. We might transition into this element with a story that brings one of our rationales to life, like, "I remember this one day you promised me you would stop drinking..." and then explain its theme in our decision.

Stories are powerful and meaningful because they're an opportunity for everyone to reflect and see the rationales play out in history. We could also say, "I first became concerned about our relationship when I noticed a difference in how we approach..." Or maybe, "the answers you deserve lie in our issues of..." Then, we continue listing our reasons for the breakup until we cover all the main ones.

- "What big disagreements do you see?" Remember, this includes perpetual small disagreements, which create contempt. If they still leave their jacket on our floor after we've told them 30 times, the disagreement is not about the poor gesture of leaving it there. It's about the *disrespect*

of ignoring our requests, desires, and standards.
Disrespect is a serious deal-breaker.

- "How would you word those disagreements as differences?" Again, this is not a finger-pointing thing of "you bad, me good." We are simply outlining our incompatibility. "You think this is acceptable, I don't."
- "What do you desire to learn about yourself outside this relationship?"
- "What change or growth have you wanted to experience throughout the relationship that's not possible with them?"
- "What self-defeating foundations in your relationship will always be there?" Like a cornerstone that pops out every other week, requiring you to put it back.
- "What kind of future do you want for them that you can't provide? "
- "What communication have we attempted that's been ignored?"

Third, we need to *say what part we played in the relationship's demise.* This is where we affirm the standards and boundaries we believe they should have, even though we didn't live up to them at some point. We apologize for any wrongs we partook in. "I should've communicated more," or "I didn't show up to pick you up when I said I would, and that led to a really nasty fight," or "I called you names that weren't true," etc. These confessions admit we didn't meet a bar that should've been met.

If our reasons don't make total sense, this would be the place to acknowledge it and take responsibility. If our romance killer was attraction, and we simplified it to "not feeling a spark," it's okay to acknowledge that it's not fair. It's okay to acknowledge that it doesn't make total sense, as long as we still emphasize the gravity of the issue. For example, "I know it may not make sense, but feeling a spark is something I need." Onto the questions!

- "What do you need to take responsibility for?"
- "Why aren't you willing to work through something?" For example, "Right now, I don't have the capacity to go through the necessary work, discomfort, and conflict it would take to get to a healthy place in our relationship."
- "What mistakes might you need to own up to?"
- "What could you have communicated better?"

Fourth, we express gratitude. No doubt, we've learned much about ourselves and what we want and need in a relationship. We couldn't have learned those things without them. We may have sour memories, but it's also pretty guaranteed we have precious, fond memories of laughing our bellies off and writing a beautiful snapshot of a love story. Those sweet memories will remain with us forever, as a part of us.

The purpose of this section is to, yes, express our gratitude, but also to set them up for success by bolstering their confidence to eventually get them back into the ring of love. The truth is, they do have something to offer. They will grow from this heartbreak and become better. It's the loving thing to do to help them succeed.

To start this section, we should clarify our intentions again because people could easily misinterpret it as an attempt to soften the blow. So, we can clearly state, "What I'm about to say next is not meant to distract from the pain, excuse me from causing any pain, or make me look any better in your eyes. I simply want to express my gratitude. Thank you for all the times you...how you treated me... stood up for me...encouraged me...made me believe...your patience..." The questions here are pretty simple.

- "What are you grateful for in the time you spent with them?"
- "What do you admire about them?"
- "What did they teach you about life and about love?"

Fifth, as we close our letter, we want to emphasize our sincere belief in a hopeful future. This is the shortest element of breakups. Transitioning from our gratitude, we simply state our faith in them to write a beautiful love story. It could literally be, "I know you'll create a beautiful love story one day."

Then, we sign our names. No endearing outro like "Love, Judas the Backstabber." We're trying to make this a clean break. That means we're leaving out any final nuggets of hope. We're extinguishing our reputation as romantic partners and emphasizing our role as just another human with a name.

- "What hopes do you have for them?"
- "How can you word those hopes as inspiring beliefs?" As in, "I know you'll find love one day," instead of, "I hope you'll find love…"
- "How do you want to inspire them? "

That's it for the elements of a breakup letter. I encourage you to make your letter as genuine as possible. If you want to use any content from here, put it into your own words as much as you can. Copying what I've written sort of defeats the purpose of writing an intentional letter. You got this!

Breakup Interaction Walkthrough

Now that we've written our letter, we'll cover the layout of the heavy interaction. The day of reckoning will be awkward, and the suspense will be silent but deafening. We won't passionately kiss them hello or longingly embrace them when we first see them because that'd be insincere and untrue of our intentions.

Right off the bat, they'll feel in their bones what's coming, and it'll be uncomfortable since there's no comfortable way to slip into a breakup conversation.

Regardless of how we open, "I need to talk to you… I have some thoughts I'd like to share… Let's go somewhere where we can talk," etc., the heartbreak to come is visible in our eyes and in our tone of voice. Yet the deed must be done.

Pushing through the discomfort, we must get to an appropriate and safe location and time with our letter in hand. They know what's here. They can feel it. We can feel it. We don't need to explain what's happening. We just need to *lead into* what's happening.

Step 1: Introduce the letter by saying something like "Delroy, there's no perfect way to have this conversation, but I want to have it because I respect you and I think you deserve proper answers. I didn't come to this conclusion lightly, and it'd mean a lot to me if you'd hear me out."

Step 2: Assuming they've given you either a nod, their full attention, or a verbal statement of understanding—really anything other than a rejection of what's happening—we can proceed with reading our letter while periodically keeping eye contact and being present with them in the pain. If they refuse to hear us out, we can just hand them the letter and be on our way.

Step 3: Give them time to respond and offer closing remarks. This is *not* an opportunity for them to talk us out of it. Whatever communication that could've saved the relationship should've been done already. Anyone who waits for hell to break loose in order to breathe life into their relationship certainly isn't someone who'll continually nurture it.

This response time is an opportunity for them to make peace with themselves and us in whatever way they need and/or an opportunity to set themselves up for healing. That could look like apologies, gratitude, agreement, criticism, questions, frustration, raised voices, etc. People process heartbreak in different ways, and we'd be kind to accept whichever way they process it.

We should understand, however, that we'll probably come across as the bad guy, or very well *be* the bad guy, *if we never communicated about any of the issues we bring up in the letter.*

Step 4: Hand them the letter, thank them for hearing us out, and then set them up for success with healthy boundaries. This doesn't have to be long, but it'll depend on how clear the boundaries we think they'll need are.

Most people will get the message if we simply say, "Thank you for hearing me out. To help us both move on and make room for other relationships, I'll be giving you your space and not communicating with you."

If they ever end up contacting us, trying to connect with anything other than strictly "business," then we can be more direct and say something like, "I don't think it's healthy to keep in contact, so I won't respond from here on out. It's not because I hate you or dislike you; it's just best for both of us. I hope you understand!"

Step 5: Prepare to say goodbye. Make sure the location is still safe and that they can reach their next destination safely. Leaving them alone in a park after dark isn't the move. We're breaking up with them—not leaving them for dead. They might want us to leave, and that's fine—we can oblige them. But we should also reason with them if the environment isn't safe.

It's okay to treat them like humans, and it's okay that they know we care about them. We did just write them an intentional letter after all. Just don't ask anything stupid like "Are you going to be okay?" They just lost a huge part of their support system—so, *no*. Part of rejection and heartbreak is *not* being okay, and that's okay.

Step 6: Say goodbye—awkwardly, most likely. No dramatic last kiss. Don't initiate any hugs, as they *really* may not want to be touched. If they request a hug, however, we can give it.

Goodbyes can be as simple as saying, "I'll let you get home," leading the way, and letting them leave with our letter. Or "Goodbye, Janice," and walking away. We've already said our piece, they've already asked their questions, and they know what to expect from us in the future because of the boundaries we set. They have closure.

The harshest yet easiest goodbyes are the ones where they force us to leave them alone in a rush, or they leave in a rush because they don't want to look at our faces. Read the room and their body language because they might view us as the plague and want to get away from us as soon as possible.

Or goodbyes can be as simple and pleasant as them saying thank you, getting up, leaving, and gesturing goodbye with a sincere yet failing smile.

Above all, plan ahead whenever possible so that once we've shared our conversation, we're not taking a 3-hour car ride or an 8-hour flight home together. Spare everyone the discomfort.

Step 7: Maintain the boundaries of a healthy breakup. No contact beyond what's absolutely necessary. Allow room for new gardens to form. Given they're most likely a standard non-crazed person, we probably won't have to arrange any restraining orders or deal with stalking. If we've stuck to the Love Hero weeding-out process, we've likely weeded out the wild ones.

The Goodbye to This Chapter

That's it! Obviously, the details I've covered about breakups require a period of methodical and critical thinking. Not all breakups allow for that. Sometimes, there's simply a spontaneous ending because of a big disagreement.

Nevertheless, consistent communication and relationship evaluation can heighten our awareness of potential breakup issues and prepare us to say yes to something different.

Which brings us to our final yes: the yes to happily ever after.

8

SUCCESSFUL NEGOTIATIONS

Google Maps steered me to a dead end in the middle of a backcountry forested road. Its confidence was unwavering as it advised me to forego any bridges and just drive into a river. My brain ignored that questionable advice. Knowing I was going to be late to my date, the car idled in an evergreen's shade, and my thumb hovered over the call button. But a lonely car approached in the distance. My finger froze in the dim, distant headlights.

A familiar face drove past me at snail velocity as we timidly scanned each other's windows. Red brake lights turned bright, then white, and our tires sheepishly backtracked, bringing our windows face to face. With the flip of a switch and an electronic whir, we let our guards down as the glass dropped. Separated by two steel doors and 4 feet of open air, a blushing, "Hi! Nice to meet you!" introduced us both.

Half-embarrassed, I explained our river predicament and volunteered another park in Wilsonville, Oregon, to be our picnic host. In agreement, we veered into its parking lot and greeted each other with googly eyes and a flustering embrace. Once I gathered myself, I did the same with my picnic supplies and, from a carrier in the passenger's seat, drew a secret weapon. Eleven weeks fresh out of the womb and twelve seconds straight out of a nap, Maddy lay ready to swoon.

Maddy, the Ultimate Secret Weapon of Mass Destruction and Slaying of Hearts

When Maddy scampered into my life, she was more than a dog. Years of searching for a Love Hero had passed, and she represented a significant outlet for my bottled love and affection. Any love she received, she'd gladly return to me and everyone else. We'd amplify love in the world together. My first lifelong love commitment was to a wonderful ball of fur, and she would happen to help me find my second.

Maddy only ever met three of my dates, but it was plain to see which one stood out to her because she nestled on her lap for a nap. That date was a cute and slender 5'7" girl with jawline-short brown hair and luminous honey brown eyes when golden-hour sunlight kissed her face. A modest light-grey dress danced around her knees, and I was out on a picnic with her in Wilsonville, Oregon.

Over fruit salad, jalapeño hummus, chips, and figs, her bread-and-butter seemed to be trading heart-centered questions. She failed to scream anything other than "Love Hero" and green flags. Our afternoon-long soulful exchange ended only when a nearby wildfire filled the air with smoke. It seemed fitting for the deep attraction and beacon of hope for love kindling in our eyes. But before our feet let us go our separate ways, they ushered us together in a heart-to-heart hug for a perfect goodbye.

Our next date signed us up for a bouldering gym, followed by dinner. The holds on the walls handed us opportunities for playfulness and seeing how we each handled challenges, failures, feedback, and perhaps new experiences. As a bonus, it was an innocent opportunity for us to wear athletic clothing. To say I liked what I saw would be an understatement. It was like Christmas with a sporty *Victoria's*

Secret special, but with much less skin. My hands would spot her falls and catch her, and we were both appreciative about the tension that touch built.

Our fingers eventually became noodles from the climbing, which led us to have another heart-to-heart over some pasta. Only this time, we dove straight into compatibility topics like religion and politics. We were truly cutting to the chase. Was this something real? Could it work? Or was this just a temporary thrill?

I think it was both her and my opinion that we knew we had to sacrifice the ideal image of a perfect mate at some point. So it might as well be now. We made the sacrifice, saw obvious minor differences, looked around, and nothing was on fire. In fact, we still liked each other *a lot* and were both still on a high.

A card swipe paid the dinner bill, and we headed back to the bouldering gym where she had left her car. Her hands wandered around her body for her keys, only to find a sense of panic. A quick phone call to the restaurant sparked simultaneous embarrassment and relief that her keys were left behind. Blushing and scrambling, she earnestly apologized. However, instead of frustration, gratitude sprang up in me. I'd get to savor more time with her as we rescued her poorly neglected keys.

After the rescue mission, as if to start a tradition, we shared another spellbinding hug, smiled like we were hiding a crush, and went our separate ways. In poetic fashion, one of her tires clambered over a curb, trying to pull out of the parking lot. Her brake lights beamed, her eyes darted around for any witnesses, and she poked her head outside her window. "Did you see that?! ...Nothing, never mind!" And she zoomed away to be immediately met with a red light. This girl might've been a hot mess in some ways, but every mess was hot and endearing to me. I couldn't wait to see her again.

In fact, I *only* wanted to see her again. So upon pulling into my driveway, I began messaging anyone else I was getting to know. Only after did I follow up with her. By that time, the message she thought she'd be receiving was an impending rejection. It turned out to be: "Sorry it took me a while to reach out! I was just messaging and closing all my other options because I only want to focus on you." She liked that. She liked that *a lot*.

On date three, Thai food filled our bellies at her apartment. After that, couch cushions sank us together while a show ran on her computer. As hormones raged, I busted a move as one does during "Netflix and chill." *That's right, I asked to hold her hand*. That move was accompanied by a hand-and-arm massage. I didn't quite get to see any ankle, but there was no need to rush.

By date four, we were in a relationship. About a month in, we met each other's families and exchanged "I love yous." With each passing day, we grew our relationship, introduced more friends, wrote new chapters, and created a beautiful love. An ol' COVID-pandemic relationship in a microwave.

One brisk autumn night, about 2 months into our relationship, we stayed at her parents' lake house in central Oregon. I grabbed some warm clothes and handed them to her. "Come outside with me!" I invited her. With the wonder of a child ready to hear a secret, she slipped on the oversized cozy gear and accepted my hand. Adventure was just past the sliding glass door.

Her arms wrapped around my arm as we walked onto the porch, down its paint-faded steps, and onto the pathway toward the dock. Scattered evergreen trees accompanied us toward the lake as moonlight beamed through their branches. Past the trees waited a sea of glass, demanding a pause of awe. Bundled together like a couple of penguins, we hobbled onto the time-frozen dock. "I want to show you something," I chirped, dropping onto my stomach. My face hovered over the water as I glanced up at her invitingly.

The moon looked at me with approval as I rolled up my sleeves and gestured that she do the same. For some wonderful reason, she was ready and willing to do whatever crazy thing we were about to do. A deep breath rushed into our lungs to brace for impact, and our hands gently pierced the surface of the surprisingly not-so-chilly water. I tipped my head to touch hers to see through her eyes. Ever so carefully, I guided her hands so as not to wake up the surface of the water.

Within seconds of surgical stillness, the moon's reflection became clear in her cupped hands. "I know people say I'll give you the moon when they're in love. But now, you're really holding it in your hands like no one else. It's yours to hold—our secret!" I playfully whispered, nudging my spirit closer to hers. Her eyes dropped the moon she was holding, turned to me with a twinkle in her eyes, and pressed her soft lips against mine.

Ten months is all it took to know it was time to put into law what was already done in heart—marry her. That meant asking for her mother's blessing, since she alone had raised her. So, on July 4, 2021, our families gathered to celebrate. Everyone shared pleasantries and gathered outside in my parents' backyard to eat. I kept scanning for the perfect moment to catch her mom alone. In the middle of all the socializing, I eventually saw her head back inside for more food, and I followed her in.

As if to whistle and look around, I rounded the kitchen island to join her as she spooned some dip onto her plate. My casual approach probably would've been smoother if I had actually bothered *to bring a plate*. Regardless, my mouth opened with a sincere voice as my fingers twiddled. "*Sooo...*" As we met each other's eyes, her plate stepped aside, her full attention locked in, and she immediately started crying. I half laughed, half choked on my voice, entirely lost what I was going to say, and then *I* started crying.

The only natural thing for us to do next was hug in tears, acknowledge the broken ice, and get ourselves together so I could give my little speech and ask for her daughter's hand in marriage. "Yes," quickly followed my speech, and we meandered to the front door to discuss ring details. My access to her daughter's Pinterest pages helped us narrow it down to the one. Size 5, radiant cut. Yellow gold, not white. I added it to the cart and shipped it to a friend's house in Hawaii. Our first big trip as a couple rapidly approached.

In the days leading up to it, her mom started buying her new clothes, taking her to the nail salon, and pampering her because she wanted her daughter to have the best vacation and look beautiful every day. Suspicious... but perhaps just generous. To be fair, as long as her mom didn't explicitly expose us all, it's typically pretty difficult to predict if someone would actually propose 10 months into a relationship.

Airplane wings carried us over the Pacific Ocean and set us down in a Hawaiian paradise on July 21. Her ring followed closely behind. Stepping out of our terminal, our host greeted us with a couple of Hawaiian leis—flowers strung into necklaces symbolizing love, friendship, celebration, and honor.

The car ride home held breathtaking vistas. Jungle mountains, vegetation-overgrown cliffsides, braids of vines, Albizia trees, and crashing waves hugged the Oahu highway winding to the North Shore.

The following day, my anticipation watched the package inch closer on the tracking map. While she knew I was expecting a package with a surprise, there was no reason to suspect it would be an engagement ring of all things. We neither shopped nor got her fitted for one.

My face glued to the window, the delivery truck pulled into view. I scurried out to retrieve the package and then gave the green light to prep for our "dinner and modeling" date. As she occupied the bathroom with curling irons, makeup brushes, and mirror checks, I broke out the glimmering ring. A geode ring box from Etsy replaced the manufacturer's ring box and held the ring like an oyster nesting a pearl. The geode's crystals were the perfect backdrop.

I hid any evidence, gathered my camera gear, and shoved an empty lasagna dish, some backyard flowers, a towel, and my hot-water-filled water bottle into my backpack. Everything was ready, and shortly thereafter, so was she.

Our dinner destination was a Thai food truck surrounded by waddling goats, chickens, and sheep. They were my first models of the night. The sound of the ocean massaged our eardrums and the tiring sun our skin. With our last bites, we waved goodbye to the livestock, returned to the car, and navigated to Keiki Beach in Turtle Bay.

Passing by beautifully unique trees, my camera shutter began chasing her beauty. "Oooo... Ahhh... YES! Give the people what they want! More attitude! You're teasing me!..." I cheered, hyping her up. The crashing waves and dropping sun seemed to chase her, too. A heart carved into a rock along the coastline called to us, letting us know that we were exactly where we should be.

It's a Sign

Amid my surveillance, I picked *the* spot—it was within shouting distance. No one else in sight. A boulder in place as a throne, nearly kissed by the crawling water. Our stroll continued until I invited her to sit down on said throne. "I have a surprise for you," I gushed. "I need you to close your eyes for a couple of minutes!" Wrapping a sweater around her eyes helped.

Like *Cars'* Guido at a racetrack pit stop, I blazed around her, sprinkling flowers from my backpack. The lasagna dish made its mark in the towel on the sand, warm water from my bottle formed a waterfall into it, and the ring was stowed out of view. Like pulling a final thread, the knot upholding her sweater came undone. "You can open your eyes now." Her eyelids parted to behold a beautiful sunset, waves crashing behind a man on one knee, scattered red flower petals, and a lasagna dish full of water. The dream.

Reaching for her feet, I lowered them into the dish's warm water and peered up at her, making soul-piercing eye contact. "I admire so much in you, Abbey. You are incredibly beautiful inside and out. I adore your story and the way you see people. You have a beautiful heart of compassion, warmth, and kindness. You make me want to become a better man every day, and your relentless willingness to give makes me want to give more." The precious feet in my hands called for careful attention. Like a paintbrush adoring a canvas, my fingers brushed water over her toes, rubbed her arches, and took their time in the priceless moment.

Continuing and gazing back up, "I love your family, I'm grateful for how they've contributed to the amazing person you are, and I want to have them in my life. I want to see your dreams come true—

to be a mother, to have a family, to make a home, to be a speech pathologist—all of it. I've never been more sure about anything or anyone in my life. And as I'm kneeling here washing your feet, I know I want to serve you for the rest of my life."

Her eyes were glued to mine, and I could tell she was hanging onto my every word. I resumed, "But in order for me to do that, you need to accept this rock." My spine angled as my hand reached under a folded corner of a towel. I pulled out what seemed to be an ordinary rock. Only it secretly opened. Still down on one knee, with the sunset in full blaze behind me, and tears building in her eyes, I took her hand and opened the geode ring box. Inviting her to build an ever-lasting garden with me, I said, "Abbey, will you marry me?"

She ever so sweetly nodded her head—heart and soul on full display—and I wiggled the ring on her finger. Flawless fit. The applause of the waves roared, and the gentle ocean breeze pushed us in for a kiss and a happily ever after.

Sometimes, negotiations do work out. We find someone we can continually create true love with. And that only has to happen *once*.

The Final Negotiation

We'll spend this chapter describing what successful true-love mating negotiations look like and a few tips on how to sustain them. In down-to-earth question form: *"How do we know we've reached successful true love negotiations beyond, 'You just know'?"*

This will be a very simple process. In a couple of pages, you'll be presented with a survey designed to help us determine if we're partnering with a viable candidate to create true love. Some survey components, like humor and music, we haven't discussed. So, as a quick explanation, I include humor because sharing similar senses of humor represents compatibility of play. Play is a key component in romance and in establishing and respecting boundaries.

Music requires a bit more philosophical depth and scientific explanation. The shorthand version is that there's something intimate about music—it exposes an innermost vulnerability of the human experience. We feel that, just as our musical tastes are judged, *we* are judged. Playing our most loved song only to have someone ask us to change it or turn it off, certainly wouldn't feel good. To connect through music taste is to connect on an intimate level.

The survey is also designed to measure the forces in our lives that create true love. If I had to guess, I'd say about 80% of true love is created and nurtured *passively*. One's philosophy of love narrates how they live and breathe love. That philosophy is what we've been working through this entire book—the Love Hero's Narrative and the identity of a Love Hero. The other 20% is actively learning and exercising technical relationship skills—things like precise communication, conflict resolution, defining and defending standards and boundaries, and continually reevaluating our mating negotiation strategies.

The reason I wrote so much about sleep, diet, and exercise is that so much of human behavior, interaction, and relationships passively revolves around the tiniest components of lifestyle. To illustrate this crystal-clear connection, a study was conducted over 21 days in which married couples were given blood glucose monitors and voodoo dolls representing their spouses. Every time someone felt aggressive impulses toward their spouse, they'd stab a pin into the doll.

The study found that those with low blood glucose levels inserted more pins into their dolls.[i] Glucose plays an integral role in providing energy throughout the body and maintaining healthy self-control. While low blood glucose is one pillar of diabetes, it can happen to anyone and cause dizziness, fainting, sweating, and *aggression*.

Calling back to *Chapter 5's* account of glucose spikes, low blood glucose often happens because of glucose spikes, which occur when we intake simple carbohydrates like white rice, cakes, white bread, juice—basically "glucose bombs." After the bomb goes off, like a mushroom cloud settling into dust, there's a lull in blood sugar called reactive hypoglycemia. In this study, the lull in blood sugar directly correlated with impulses of aggression toward one's partner.

Meaning, something as simple as food spiking our blood sugar could determine whether we aggressively pick a fight and stick a verbal pin in our partner. In turn, the more fights we pick and the more conflict we encounter, the less we may like our partner. The simple, repeated push over the edge by scoops of ice cream could stand between us and our best creation of true love. *That* is what I'm referring to when I say that as much as 80% of true love is created and nurtured passively.

True love ignites in our sleep, the way we eat, how much we move, the hobbies we practice, the habits we form, the way our tone of voice fluctuates, and more. In my experience, true love has *less to do with actively navigating complex problems and overcoming disagreements and more to do with preserving one's identity in the essence of infinite love.*

Abbey and I certainly still have our disagreements and arguments. We've argued about finances, morality, lack of communication, and feeling let down, but to date, after almost 6 years together, our biggest fight, with crying and all—though no yelling or name-calling—was about *shrimp. The crustacean.* We take comfort in understanding that putting in work will always be a fundamental part of a successful marriage. We know that creating true love is not *entirely* passive.

Dr. Jordan Peterson says, "If you are in a relationship and you have fewer than five positive interactions for every one negative interaction (below 5:1), the relationship will end—it's too negative. But if you have more than eleven positive interactions for every one negative interaction (above 11:1), it also ends."

Meaning, there's a sweet spot where some active conflict is actually *necessary* for satisfactory relationships. Peterson explains that the upper limit for positivity exists because while we want to be happy today, we *also* want to be happy decades down the line. So, we want someone who's going to push us beyond who and what we are now. The growing pains necessary for that push reside in conflict and argumentation. Hence, every time Abbey and I disagree, we know it's not just a brief inconvenience or pain, *but a vital component of our marriage's survival.*

In sum, both passive and active forces contribute to the creation of true love. Passive forces make up the majority. We've touched on both in this book. The following questions help us evaluate (1) how present those true-love-creating forces are in our relationship and (2) whether we've found an ideal candidate with whom we're creating true love.

If you answer every question with column 1, I believe you've found your golden goose and that you possess a powerful foundation on which to build and nurture a garden of true love. Otherwise, the test results are not intended as a judgment of you or your relationship. It may just mean that if true love is what you truly want, you may be missing some indispensable ingredients for creating it. You may need to select a new partner, adopt a new source of love, more fully embrace the Love Hero philosophy of becoming love itself, or some combination of those.

True love is a narrow path and a fragile art, and it's entirely possible to bounce in and out of "being in true love" depending on how we shift our priorities and how we choose to live. In fact, I'd say that's the *normal reality* for most couples creating true love. That's definitely been the case for me. Though I've always had a healthy relationship, there have even been times *while writing this book* that I've set aside the First Commandment, put writing productivity first, and fallen short of the conditions of true love.

This survey mainly serves to open our eyes. So, without further ado, take a stab at it. Hopefully, no stabbing of pins into dolls, though!

Moment of Truth Questions	1	2
Do they (1) add to and empower the meaning in your life or (2) detract and distract from it somehow?		
If someone said you were just like your partner, would you (1) be honored by it or (2) offended and embarrased by it?		
Do you feel like you (1) don't deserve your partner or (2) do deserve your partner? (Feeling like we don't deserve someone is akin to feeling like we are being given a privilege and a gift beyond what we could ask. No one receives a gift and says, "Oh yeah, I deserve this.")		
Do you (1) both have significant sexual attraction toward one another or (2) not?		
Do they (1) empower you and add to your peace or (2) seem to add burdens and steal your peace?		
Do they (1) gratefully see what you have to offer or (2) take you for granted?		
Do they (1) bring out the best in you and make you feel bigger or (2) dampen your spirit somehow and make you feel smaller, even if it's not malicious?		
Have (1) both you and your partner experienced a devastating heartbreak or (2) not?		
Would you be happy if (1) mini versions of them walked around as part of your life or (2) not?		
Are you more afraid of (1) being without them, or (2) simply being alone?		
Do they (1) add to a positive reputation for you or (2) taint your reputation?		
Do you (1) both consistently function within the stages of psychology mentioned at the end of Chapter 7's Supreme Ordeal section or (2) not?		
Do your senses of humor (1) mostly overlap or (2) not?		
Are you (1) both able to enjoy the same type of music or (2) not?		
Are you (1) both able to understand each other's primary mating-selection theories and negotiate "in their languages" or (2) not?		
Do you (1) both try to exceed standards beyond what the other person actively asks for or (2) not?		
Lastly and greatest of all, do you (1) both simultaneously and consistently prioritize developing in love above all else or (2) not? (i.e. the First Commandment, every choice hinging on the question, "What choice will best increase the odds that our relationship would thrive?")		

Table 6: True Love Litmus Test

As we review this litmus test, it's clear that these questions aim to concoct a preventive medicine for broken relationships. Preventive medicine stops problems from occurring and, therefore, disqualifies the need for repetitive *high*-stakes conflict resolution and healing.

If we lay a foundation of powerful, true-love-creating forces and a golden goose that loves nuzzling up against us, we're set to build and sustain a garden flourishing with true love. With the right boundaries and standards, and negotiations running smoothly, our relationships will undoubtedly be robust and resilient to any problems that come knocking.

Regardless of whether that set of questions revealed that you have your golden goose or not, we're going to move forward with discussing how to *preserve* successful mating negotiations. If we recall from *Chapter 3*, mating negotiations go on forever even if they're successful.

The deal is that once we find a golden goose, we keep it and cherish it. Even if it farts too much. For it is a timeless treasure spared from heaven in a decaying world and an everlasting flower bursting forth in a field of dust.

Golden geese who keep each other around benefit from longer lifespans and healthspans, and greater life satisfaction, purpose, financial prowess, emotional stability, goal attainment, impact on the world, personal growth, community building, resilience, sexual satisfaction, and more. Those are *a lot* of golden eggs worth keeping.

Sustaining Successful Negotiations with Technical Skill

Alas, we're going to spend some time focusing on technical relationship skills—the 20% of true love creation that isn't passive. Many resources and books address these skills, so I encourage all readers to dive deeper into these topics on their own time. My goal is *only* to highlight *lesser-known knowledge* and present my unconventional view on the spectrum of skills, tools, and knowledge available to us.

That being said, we'll skip straight to the fun part: sexual desire. Sex is fairly automatic towards the beginning of relationships and marriages in that there's little we have to do to get it going. It's exciting and spontaneous. With time, however, a few things happen: (1) the novelty wears off, (2) we don't truly try to understand the uniqueness of men and women, and (3) we don't take the time to understand our partners.

Sex loses some of its addict-like appeal and changes its frequency of occurrence. Hauntingly, sometimes, sex ceases altogether. According to sex author Tracey Cox, a whopping *30% of couples who've been dating for two years or more do not have sex at all*. Love Heroes do everything they can to embody and grow in *all* elements of love. That includes nurturing sexual vibrancy and consistency.

Technical Skill: Novelty in Sexual Desire

Referring to our romance equation from *Chapter 5*, we can deduce that the romantically spellbinding aspect of sex wears off when we're familiar with it. With familiarity comes comfort and repetition. Repetition defeats play, *spontaneity*, and *tension* building. Comfort is mutually exclusive with *leaving the comfort zone*. That's three components of exciting romance dead in the water.

It's not a sex-life death sentence, however. We can nurture novelty and romance without swapping out partners. As long as we choose a partner who's willing to work with us, there are several things we can do to revive novelty.

For starters, we can change our **environment**. Traveling to new locations can be enough to make things exciting. Go on vacations, simulate an X-rated episode of *Naked and Afraid* in the woods, spend a night in a local hotel, get in the back of a car out in the fields on the outskirts of Denver, Colorado—you name it. Switching the scenery is highly doable.

Another thing nurturing novelty is **preserving mystery** to maintain particular relationship dynamics. Relationships transform as we share information and unveil mysteries. For example, if someone knows an embarrassing story about us, we know it changes the way they see us, and it will ultimately transform our relationship. That's why there are some things we're only comfortable telling our parents, friends, or siblings. *Information transforms relationships.*

This means the type of information we share can determine the type of relationship we have. The mystery we maintain directs the relationship dynamic. Am I suggesting we keep secrets and feelings hidden from our one true love? Not exactly. I *am* suggesting we control the mystery, however.

Does he *really* need to know she has to trim a mustache? Does she *really* need to know how loud he can fart? Do they *really* need to know what their partner's face looks like when they're pooping?

Yes, these are vulnerable and normal things. But we must ask ourselves: does sharing this information support a growing romantic sexual desire? Odds are probably not. Unless you a freak. Then, respect. But novel sexual desire is typically full of mystery. For all we "know," the other people don't poop or have anything non-beautiful about them. They always smell wonderful, and their manicured appearance is miraculously just the way they naturally are.

Actions also transform relationship dynamics. While true love is a blend of all types of love, sibling love possesses a unique relationship dynamic that does *not* belong in true love. Even elements of parental love and relationship belong in intimate relationships. Though parents may always maintain the duty of being their children's home base for safety, security, affirmation, companionship, affection, and trust, children generally pass those roles on to their significant others. That's not the case with some sibling love.

We often treat our siblings the way we do because they often function as our hardcore guinea pigs for learning what socially acceptable behavior is. We can treat them this way because they can't really get rid of us. So, if we bicker with and disrespect our partner because we believe they can't get rid of us, or play around to their annoyance for the same reason, *we are in sibling territory*. If we regularly tell embarrassing stories about them for our own gain, *we are in sibling territory*.

For that reason, while farting in front of partners may be normal to many people, cultures, and countries, Abbey and I don't do it. We don't burp on purpose or engage in behaviors that could transform our relationship dynamic toward siblinghood. Though we play, we don't intentionally annoy each other or treat each other like the other can't get rid of us. *We don't want to be siblings.*

It's not that Abbey and I could never bear the thought of removing these mysteries or that we're unable to accept each other without the smoke screens. It's a fact that we both fart and go to the bathroom. We simply want to retain a specific relationship dynamic.

We don't typically break the fart barrier on a first date because it's considered rude. Not being rude means holding a certain level of respect for our romantic interest's standards. Preserving certain mysteries is how we maintain the standard of novelty.

So, we would be wise to understand how unveiling certain mysteries transforms our relationships and manage them accordingly. When we keep the mystery alive, novelty keeps breath in its lungs, and sexual desire benefits.

Next on the menu for sexual desire's longevity, we have foreplay. Traditionally, **foreplay** has essentially been known as anything sexual that isn't intercourse or oral sex. Meaning, sensual massages, kissing, flirting, dirty talk, gentle caresses, heavy petting—anything warming up to sexual activity. Something seldom thought of, however, is that *everything helps us warm up to sexual activity.*

What are the chances of both partners wanting to have sex three years into their relationship if they are annoyed with each other and feel neglected? When one partner gets caught in a backstabbing lie, what are the odds that the other person is going to want to jump their bones? If we make a fool of ourselves at a family gathering, what are the chances our partner gets turned on? The chances are near zero, if not *below* zero.

We simply don't want to reward and get closer to those who disrespect us, neglect us, annoy us, break our hearts, or ignite our rage. All of those things discourage long-term sexual intimacy. Reciprocally, being trustworthy, reliable, honoring our promises, and being thoughtful all endear us to the other person. We're much more likely to invite the touch of a gem-like person who delicately kindles our affections than someone we despise.

Hence, cleaning the dishes, remembering small details, getting them a drink when we get one, vacuuming the floor, giving them a hand rub, taking over one of their chores, taking care of our bodies, filling their gas tanks for them, charging their toothbrush, leaving them sweet notes—all are acts of foreplay. *Everything is foreplay.* Everything is an endearing or repellent action. Exerting foreplay in everything we do will nurture sexual desire.

Our next piece of wisdom comes from the phrase: "Distance makes the heart grow fonder." Throughout human history, mates never spent all their time together. Since humans survived through the patriarchy, women stayed home to look after the children and perform household duties while men went to gather and build resources for the family.

Nowadays, there's less separation. Many couples constantly share the same space and rarely live life apart. When we never leave our partner's side, *there's nothing to bring back.* There are no stories to tell, no updates, no missing or yearning for what's always around, and no individual challenges or growth. Temporary separation makes all these things possible.

As long as we can *maintain appropriate boundaries*, we *should* do things like taking a bros' or girls' trip away from our partners and nurture other positively influential friendships. Bringing back experiences and stories to tell is lucrative for fueling romantic desire we may not have even known was missing.

Time apart also reminds us to broaden our perspectives and see the world-scale narrative our true love gardens fit into. Our gardens are but a small plot of space, time, and energy in this world. They're not isolated structures. They require experience with external influences like water, symbiotes, oxygen, and day and night. Time apart is good.

Perhaps the easiest hack for stimulating sexual desire is **changing our appearance.** We could do this by wearing different clothes, working out, or even taking on a new challenge, such as a business venture or hobby.

When we're with our partners for a long time, we think we know them completely and can read them like a pre-K book. But when we're pleasantly surprised by a decision they make, a new hobby, or a commitment we never thought they'd make, it shakes our understanding of who they are.

When we shake understanding, mystery awakens. As mystery awakens, the known *shifts* to the unknown. Shifts and change mean *life* springs forth. As life runs its course, *growth* abounds. And where growth abounds, a *new creation is born*. There, we find novelty.

A new dress is a refresh of our appearance—an entrancing camouflage allowing others to view us in a different light. New hobbies or skills aren't simply a change in how we spend our time—they're commitments to putting ourselves in humble places to seek growth and expand our identities. Beginning a workout routine is evidence that we're trying to transition to a superior version of ourselves.

Whatever the case, changing appearance stimulates mystery and revives a sense of novelty. There's little mystery in who human beings are, but a great wonder in who they can and will become. With consistent change, who they become is an enthralling mystery revealed over a lifetime.

Altogether, these things make novelty follow like a shadow.

Technical Skill: Understanding Sexual Desire in Each Sex

A healthy goal for Love Heroes in sexual desire is to understand the opposite sex better than they understand themselves. It's healthy and significant because sex and its pleasures and benefits are a blissful gift we want to give.

My journey in understanding women meant studying female erogenous zones, educating myself about behavioral norms in the female menstrual cycle, learning to lean into either dominance or submission, and other technical sexual education topics. I won't bear all the eye-widening details, but we will walk through some of these ideas.

We'll begin with women understanding men because it's about as complicated as 1+1. Given the big assumption that they have a somewhat normally developed brain, that is. Now, it's not exactly uncommon for men to have sex-affecting brain complications. In the U.S., porn addiction claims 1-in-10 men,[ii] and that comes with real physical brain and body repercussions. Namely, they could be one of the 1-in-5 men over 20 years of age who experience erectile dysfunction.[iii]

Ignoring those complications to address most of the male population, however, a good principle for stimulating a man's sexual desire is to be feminine. For a man to write poetry in sexual acts, he needs to feel like a woman, and her beauty is worth protecting, adoring, losing himself to, and taking into his being. A woman emulating stark masculine energy will likely not awaken a man's full sexual desire.

The woman who doesn't know how to wield her feminine energy to make the masculine bend and sway destroys sexual poetry before it can begin. Embracing femininity is the key to bringing out masculinity's brawn, instinct, power, assertiveness, and sexual hunger.

I once watched a YouTube clip of a woman revealing how simple men really were in their desires. The woman proclaimed that when she flirts with guys, she simply comments on how big their hands are compared to hers.

She then invites the men to place their hands against hers for better comparison and again comments in amazement, "Oh my gosh, your hands are so huge compared to mine!" Her closing remarks were that men always react the same way: their brains go into caveman mode, essentially saying, "Woman small, soft, dainty, and we touch. Must protect! Oo-oo-oo ah!"

It's hilarious, but there's definitely merit in her approach. When women don't occupy masculine space and instead embrace their femininity, it gives men the opportunity to embrace their masculinity without shame. Encouraging a man's masculinity to stimulate sexual desire could be as simple as asking him, "What makes you feel like a man?"

If his vulnerable answers are entertained, like clockwork, his manhood takes flight, and he feels like the man he's likely been told to suppress all his 21st-century life. The feminine woman literally works a miracle, resurrecting something that was dead within him, and manifests herself as the exclusive key to his vigor. As his masculinity awakens to mesh with femininity, so too does his body wish to mesh. Besides that, women pretty much just need to get naked, follow instinct, and he'll be spellbound until he reaches his climax.

One should also be aware that factors outside a relationship and sexual experience can hinder a man's sense of manhood. Experiencing repeated failures, not measuring up to public expectations, being overly stressed, not getting enough sleep or water, and undergoing severe shame can all affect his sex drive in ways no small woman's hands could immediately remedy. Onto the more complex sex.

A thriving female sexual desire depends significantly on satisfying both mental and bodily needs. Ideally, a woman should be physically warm, not hungry, adequately rested, free of stress, and feel safe with their sexual partner. These factors holistically free her mind and put her at ease, allowing her to be fully in the moment. Once these foundational factors are met, women, as well as men, are subject to three types of sexual desire.

Sexual desire is either (1) spontaneous, (2) responsive, or (3) contextual.[iv] **Spontaneous desire** is always being ready and wanting to have sex. We don't need any romantic gestures—"just get over here and give me that thang!" Approximately 70% of men and 15% of women fall in this category.

Responsive desire is a type of desire that awakens in response to witnessing or experiencing sexual activity. Meaning, we could feel no ounce of desire whatsoever, but upon cuddling, kissing, touching skin, and removing some clothes, the mood sneaks up on us.

People with responsive desire may sometimes even feel no urge to have sex while their bodies tell a different story. Meredith Chivers, from Queen's University in Ontario, conducted a profound study on how people's bodies responded to diverse visual sexual stimuli.

Participants of the study watched tapes of people exercising naked, homosexual and heterosexual acts, solo masturbation, and Bonobo monkey sex. Men wore an apparatus around their penises, which gauged swelling. Women inserted a probe that measured vaginal blood flow and lubrication. Both sexes were given keypads to rate their arousal for each stimulus set.

Among the findings was that it took higher levels of sexual activity to arouse women. A curious thing, though, a wider variety of sexual actors aroused heterosexual women. Sexual activity from both sexual orientations and even bonobo sex aroused women, whereas men were not.[v]

Regardless of how low those women consciously rated their level of arousal on their keypads, their bodies were physically priming them for sex. Their bodies told a different story than their brains. Roughly 5% of men and 30% of women have this type of desire.

With 15% of women in the spontaneous category and 30% in the responsive, the remaining 55% fall into a mix of the two. That mix is contextual desire. In **contextual desire**, environmental conditions predominantly control sexual desire. So, consider situations like having a stomachache from being sick, having your kids sleeping in the adjacent room while the walls are paper-thin, or getting phone calls from debt collection agencies every 30 minutes. It'll really take something to get us going.

But with the right circumstances, like privacy, peace, and feeling good in our bodies, we'll be in the mood to get it on like Donkey and Dragon from *Shrek*! This category also includes the other 25% of men. Here, men will alternate between feeling like we need some convincing and feeling like we'll spontaneously explode if we don't immediately have sex.

Since most women tend to lean toward responsive rather than spontaneous desire, it'd be helpful for long-term sexual health to further explore how to stimulate female responsive desire. Physiologically, sexual desire is a deeply carnal hunger that naturally and gradually intensifies to a euphoric point where electrifying pleasure explodes throughout the body, rendering it unto a plane of consciousness out of our control. Also known as orgasms.

One utterly priceless way to stimulate female desire is to prioritize and program female orgasm into the base definition of what sex is. Meaning if the woman didn't orgasm, sex didn't necessarily happen. Although orgasms are certainly not everything, and connection should be the primary objective, women should have the same orgasmic incentive as men do. When orgasm is a consistent and normal part of their sexual experience, even if women don't feel like having sex in the moment, they can at least look forward to its pleasurable incentive.

To prioritize the female orgasm, we need to understand how women's progression toward orgasm differs from men's. For starters, women take more time to warm up to sex. A man can get an erection within seconds and be ready for intercourse. It takes about *25 minutes for a woman's body to be fully ready for painless and non-injurious penetrative sex.*

Even when women are fully aroused and lubricated, a 2018 study revealed that only about 18.4% of women orgasm by penetrative sex alone.[vi] That means if couples only ever have penetrative sex, with no other flips and tricks in the mix, 81.6% of women in relationships would never orgasm.

That's because the vaginal canal actually has very minimal nerve endings that gather pleasurable sensations. If it had any more, it'd make childbirth exponentially more excruciatingly painful than it already is. In fact, upon researching, I wasn't even able to find a number for how many nerve endings are in the vagina. The best I found was that the G-spot has about 32 nerve endings.

Meanwhile, we find that most of the female sexual nerve endings are actually directly *external* to the vagina in the clitoris. According to OHSU, the clitoris has somewhere over 10,000 nerve endings.[vii] For comparison, the entire penis has about 8,290 nerve endings.[viii] The clitoris isn't there just to look pretty.

I actually find its designated location to be a philosophical and poetic marvel. Women who orgasm are *five times more likely* to be satisfied with a sexual encounter.[ix] For a woman to have a satisfying sex life, her partner must fully embrace and connect with her on the feminine path of fulfillment we outlined in *Chapter 3*.

The masculine cannot simply do the same magic wand action with his hand every time to warm her up just for the sake of entering her to pursue his own pleasure. No, a man must go *out* of his own pleasure's way *and* devote his full attention to her to grant her the greatest sexual stimulation.

By doing this, he speaks, understands, and walks the ultimate powerhouse language of femininity: sacrificing for others and taking joy in their joy. He must take pleasure in her pleasure as he momentarily omits himself from receiving perhaps his most desired sexual stimulation.

Fully walking with a woman on her path of fulfillment is a profound connection made of vulnerability, empathy, and sacrifice. In his accompaniment, he quenches many, if not all, thirsts for attention yearning inside of her. Simultaneously, this act of sexual service also embodies the epitome of challenging masculine leadership, whereby one ultimately garners power and control for the sake of benefiting others. I believe that's what the anatomical design of female sexuality calls for.

Unfortunately, that call goes largely unprioritized, leading to an orgasm/pleasure gap. Heterosexual women have the lowest rate of orgasm per sexual encounter compared to all other sexual orientations.[x] Heterosexual men lead the way, having orgasms in essentially every sexual encounter—95% of the time. Gay and bisexual men follow at 89% and 88%. Lesbian women trail closely at 86%. Then, in the clear back, are bisexual and heterosexual women at 66% and 65%.

As a result, it's said that up to 50% of women aren't satisfied with how often they have orgasms.[xi] All we need to ask ourselves is what happens when we humans enjoy something? We tend to want to do it again. Therefore, men need to better prioritize the orgasmic incentive that would make a woman want to have sex again.

Prioritizing female orgasms requires education about the **female anatomy** and female orgasm psychology. Concerning anatomy and its role in the female orgasm, a good starting point is for men to ask: (1) What does the entire female sexual anatomy look like? (2) Where is the G-spot? (3) Where is the clitoris, and what does it look like structurally? (4) How might one perform oral sex well? (5) How might one combine penetrative sex and clitoral stimulation? (6) What other combinations are possible?

Knowing the female anatomy allows men to bring women's sexual desire to life and eventually experience orgasm. Capitalizing on this knowledge means strategic and playful yet romantic foreplay with sensual caressing and giving special attention to erogenous zones. Stimulating these senses helps women *settle into their bodies* and be fully present. Almost meditatively.

As a non-exhaustive list with guesstimated rankings, they are: (14) hair and scalp, (13) lower back, (12) forearms, (11), buttocks, (10) bottoms of feet, (9) lower abdomen, (8) ears, (7) pubic mound, (6) inner thighs, (5) breasts, (4) neck, (3) nipples, (2) clitoris, and (1) lips— kissing. Loving women in these areas is key knowledge for honoring and cultivating their sexual desire.

Men should also know **female orgasm psychology**. Women's orgasms highly correlate with *"body image, sexual assertiveness, sexual shame, and sexual pride."*[xii] **Body image** is basically a woman's relationship with her body. Does she like it? Is she confident or insecure about it? Does she believe it's attractive? Does she feel bad about the way she looks and have constant self-conscious thoughts? Is she living in the moment with whatever her body can and wants to do?

Sexual assertiveness is the ability to comfortably tell a sexual partner what they like, what feels good, and give sexual instruction and direction. **Sexual shame** represents the negative connotations one carries about their sexuality. Should they really be doing this? Does it go against their beliefs? What kind of person does this sexual act make them? What is the negative emotion or thought fighting against their ability to experience sexual pleasure?

Last, **sexual pride** is essentially the opposite of sexual shame, whereby one is actively resistant to shame and embraces everything about one's sexuality. Embracing what she actually wants, no matter how quirky or outlandish, without shame or embarrassment, is associated with more sexual satisfaction. To a certain extent, sexual pride is just a part of sexual assertiveness.

Having knowledge of both female sexual anatomy and orgasm psychology should empower men to better prepare to shift their priorities and make sex something women are exceedingly fond of. It should empower them to awaken a woman's sexual desire and satisfy her.

This shift might look like a culmination of extending foreplay with erogenous zones, delaying his own pleasure, or putting more effort into learning verbal foreplay. And hey, it's okay if dirty talk doesn't always go as planned. Sometimes, you text your wife in a group chat with your brother-in-law and his girlfriend: "Come home at 4. There are some things I'd like to do to you." *It happens*. To some of us. Definitely not me, though.

Shifting priorities could also take the form of performing oral sex, since it's part of the "golden trio" that increases the likelihood of female orgasm (Frederick et al., 2018). If that's the case, it should be done *safely* and be as *enjoyable* as possible. Per safety, it's crucial to know our partner's sexual history because oral sex carries risks of transmitting STIs, which can also lead to cancer. A little-known STI fact is that HSV-1, which is estimated to be carried by 64% of the world population under 50, *can be transmitted to the genitals.*[xiii] Manage the risk wisely.

Poor oral hygiene also affects safety, as it can dramatically increase the likelihood of transferring harmful bacteria. Consistent basic oral hygiene, like tooth brushing and flossing, is the best prep, though it *shouldn't* be done immediately before sex due to microcuts caused by bristles and floss.[xiv] It's best to wait an hour or more. Similar thinking should be applied to how what we eat affects the bacteria in our mouths.

As for enjoyment, if one experiences any obstacles, they can work with their partner to remove them *after* the sexual experience. By obstacles, I'm referring to things *both* men and women encounter, like smell and taste. Most obstacles are addressable through recent bathing, diets with healthy fats like avocados, nuts, and seeds, drinking lots of water, reducing sugar and caffeine intake, getting regular exercise, reducing stress, and cutting back on alcohol. If you're a woman, though, do *not* use soap down there.

Removing obstacles helps make oral sex enjoyable for both parties, making it something they both want to experience again. Or at least something they wouldn't mind doing again for the sake of their partner's pleasure. If it's within the scope of the couple's desire, a man prioritizing female soul-numbing orgasms addresses any obstacle hindering him from using the most effective tool in achieving her climax. He ensures his woman consistently receives the grand incentive to have sex.

Overcoming any type of sexual obstacle requires sexual assertiveness, which is a vital life skill that takes plenty of learning and practice. Learning and practicing this communication can be painful because sex is such an inherently vulnerable and deeply sensitive subject. It's not uncommon for sexual feedback to be taken personally and lead to shutdown.

Because of sex's intimate sensitivity, we'd do well to approach it with humility and always assume good intentions. When we're having sex, we don't know what it feels like for the other person. Only *they* know what feels better, and only they can give us direction to their greatest pleasure. It should be okay to admit that they know their senses and bodies better than we do. And if we really love them the way we say we do, hearing their requests should make us want to give them what they want even more.

Do we want them to feel uncomfortable asking us for things? Would we rather they hold their tongues from the very person they should rely on most for their needs? Then, we must put our pride aside. That's the receiving end.

As for the asserting end, when we give sexual feedback, there are a few simple rules to live by. These rules will propel us into a stronger and deeper sexual relationship. Ignoring them will lead to sexual hesitancy, hurt feelings, discomfort, anger, and shutdown.

The first rule we already sort of covered: if it *can't* be fixed in an instant, *don't* mention it *during* sex. If we want to suggest a slight change during sex, we should make sure it's presented in a positive light. So, for example: "Can you do that thing again, that drove me wild!" instead of absolutely killing the mood with, "Oh, stop that! That does nothing for me, you incompetent baboon!"

Second, we should *resist expressing disgust* and show grace. If something is off-putting the first time we try it, we don't need to shove our partners away aggressively and say, "That is never happening again!" Maybe it was just a poor set of circumstances that led to the dissatisfactory experience. Maybe they ate something weird that day. Maybe we had a bad day leading up to having sex. Or maybe our bodies were more sensitive than usual. Whatever the case, we want to assume a positive experience with sex and accept that circumstances could've just been amiss this time around.

Aside from that mindset, showing grace in sexual assertiveness can look like shifting our attention elsewhere. If it's their breath, kiss their neck. If it's their pits or another smell, Oh me—oh my—I'm so cold! Come get in the shower with me!"

As a last resort, it's okay to say we tried and want to give them what they want, but can't right now. Then, we can explain what's holding us back—shaving, bathing, bad breath, comfort zone limits, etc.—and express the openness and desire to try things again in the future.

The third and final rule is to do our best to prevent feedback from being needed. Prepare for sex like it's a job interview. We can reduce a lot of feedback by maintaining good oral hygiene, strategically avoiding smelly foods, staying fit, keeping ourselves well-groomed, smelling good, and getting enough rest. Whatever makes us most confident and increases the likelihood of our partners getting excited will make for a pleasant and electrifying sexual experience. Just don't overdo the prep so as to take all the spontaneity out of sex. Find what the right balance looks like for you!

The purpose of sexual assertiveness is to communicate what we need for the best sexual experience. We'll grow ever closer with our partners as we communicate and understand each other better, touch new vulnerabilities, and share transcendent pleasure.

Closing the conversation around orgasms, I'd like to clarify again that orgasm *isn't* the primary goal of sex. Outside of reproduction, *connection* is the primary purpose of sexual intimacy. Prioritizing orgasm for both partners is simply *strategic management of incentives* and motivations to have sex and connect. We're maximizing the likelihood we'll like each other.

Zooming back out to nurturing women's sexual desire, our last piece of wisdom lies in the menstrual cycle. As we may remember from biology class, when girls turn 12-15 years old, they get their periods, grow pubic and armpit hair, widen their hips, and develop breasts. This happens because their bodies develop into sexual maturity.

Upon sexual maturity, the female body begins releasing eggs to be fertilized by a male's sperm. Together, they eventually form a baby. An analogy for the menstrual cycle is a bakery. When eggs are freshly released during ovulation, it's like a bakery putting out fresh dough on the counter. If it's not baked within a certain amount of time, the dough will go bad and need to be thrown out. Similarly, when sperm doesn't fertilize an egg, the egg sits out, its vitality degrades over time, and the body eventually discards it.

This process of putting out fresh dough and throwing it out repeats until someone throws the dough into the oven before it goes bad. If they do that, then the bakery will have a sufficient supply of baked goods, and there's no reason to put out new dough. Similarly, if a woman becomes pregnant, there's no need to release new eggs because she'll have a growing baby.

Let's get more specific about how this helps in understanding women. This female "bakery cycle" is driven by hormone cycles that ultimately direct much of their lived experience. Using measurements of those hormones, we've been able to define four cyclical stages. To make the stages more memorable for everyone, I've developed an acronym: the **BABE cycle.**

The first stage is **Blood,** known as menstruation. The hormone progesterone is at an all-time low, as are estrogen, serotonin, and luteinizing hormone. As progesterone rests at an utter low, it causes blood vessels to constrict and cuts off blood flow to the endometrium—the cell lining of the uterus that fertilized eggs attach to. We'll come back to the endometrium.

Because blood flow is cut off from the endometrial cells, they get no oxygen and *die from suffocation*. Then, as if to shake off the dust, the uterus repetitively contracts like a cramping muscle to shed the dead cells, resulting in uncomfortable aches, bloating, and sometimes headaches. During the discomfort, women often experience heightened sensitivity to sounds, smells, and tastes. They also have low energy levels, need more sleep, and benefit from lower energy demand.

While low progesterone sponsors the strenuous *physical* symptoms, estrogen and serotonin drop together, producing *mental* symptoms. The drop in these two hormones manifests itself through mood swings, anxiety, and heightened sensitivity. These lead to uncomfortable irritability, which can resemble irrationality. Problems seem bigger and more overwhelming than they really are, patience is thinner than usual, and confrontation seems like a better option by the second.

There are some important things to note here. For women, knowing where they are in their cycle can help them understand why they may have heightened reactions or feel more overwhelmed than usual. Second, even though they aren't at fault for their intensified emotions, they're still responsible for their words and actions.

Men are to support women with this burden by taking what they say seriously, dissecting the merits, and standing their ground *when appropriate*. When a man shows he's dedicated to being reasonable, keeping himself accountable, and seeking what's right, he provides a sense of peace, control, security, and stability amid a wave of discomfort and chaos.

Still, it is *not at all* unlikely that a woman's calls to action and confrontations have merit. Oftentimes, disagreements get swept under the rug because they don't seem worth the trouble. This stage's shift in hormones is often enough to drive them to lift the rug, making them more likely to point out problems when they see them. According to the Gottman Institute, women bring up *80% of issues in relationships.*[xv]

Women somewhat serve as car dashboard warning lights. They're more sensitive to the vital issues under the hood that need to be brought to light. If the female menstrual cycle served no reproductive purpose, it would serve a *monumental* purpose and be a blessing in accelerating personal, emotional, and relational growth.

Besides working with women on the issues they bring to men's attention, the *Blood* phase is *not* an ideal opportunity for a man to seek blood or smoke. Enough issues can come up to be exhausting for women. This is *not* the time to bring *additional* stressors to their attention. That'll only add overwhelm.

What a man *can* do is get his things in order. He can add to her relief by ensuring everything runs smoothly around the home and by taking on more responsibility. He can be extra attentive to her needs, be a good listener, run her a bath, or give her a massage. In the days leading up to and during her period, he can help prepare meals for an anti-inflammatory diet. For example, as we mentioned earlier, consuming ginger root before and during the *Blood* stage can help reduce bleeding and pain.[xvi]

Basically, he can place her under as many comfortable psychological and physical circumstances as possible to prevent her from feeling the need to bring up issues. That concludes the dark, winter-like stage of *Blood*.

Next comes the spring-like stage, **Ascension**, known as the follicular stage. The second stage is called Ascension because estrogen and the happy neurotransmitter, serotonin, rise. During this stage, the body prepares to drop the egg—to set out fresh dough—and make a baby.

Since a woman's body isn't generating the endometrial wall for an egg to plant itself on, and there's also no wall to destroy anymore, progesterone levels stay low, and there's nothing causing her discomfort. As a result, she feels *phenomenal*, filled with energy! Being in a more positive mood, she's more open to adventure, motivated to get things done, confident, and has a stronger desire for sex. Ascension lasts for about *seven days.*

This is a good time for men to reopen hard conversations, as she'll be most receptive, emotionally resilient, and won't be as overwhelmed as she might during the *Blood* stage.

After *Ascension*, she drinks the goddess juice and enters the **Baby** stage. Whatever's in that juice makes her feel like *hot* shit. Her confidence, energy, and playfulness are spiking like she's on a suspicious drug, and her positivity is radiating. Her libido is on aggressive autopilot, persuading her to get pregnant and make a baby. At this stage, women are more likely to approach and be receptive to the men they're attracted to, engage in sex, and seem like joyous fountains of life. This lasts for about *two days.*

Last comes extended winter: **Exhaustion.** Some people like to describe this phase as fall just to fit the four seasons, but it's really more like winter. Progesterone levels rise to their peak, increasing blood flow to the endometrial lining of the uterus and forming a thicker foundation of cells so a fertilized egg can implant and grow into a fetus. So, women's bodies spend *a lot* of energy growing this wall to prepare for a baby. It's truly rather exhausting.

Being lower on energy once again, she feels fatigued, is once again more irritable and anxious, feels mildly bloated, is self-conscious of the way she looks, and benefits from the similar care and attentiveness she receives during the *Blood* stage.

Depending on several factors such as genetics, exercise, dietary habits, work-life, impulse control, and personality type, all physical and psychological manifestations of a woman's BABE cycle will vary in intensity and duration. Every woman is different. But both men and women should know how to best sexually relate to each other during this cycle.

Analyzing the BABE cycle, we can deduce that the *average* woman is only going to have reasonably spontaneous sexual desire during the *Ascension* and *Baby* stages—*9 days of the month, 32% of the time.* Outside of that time frame, they either may not want to have sex during the uncomfortable stages or may simply be in a more responsive state.

B.A.B.E. Cycle (~28 days)			
Blood (Menstruation) ~ 5 days	Ascension (Follicular) ~ 7 days	Baby (Ovulation) ~ 2 days	Exhaustion (Luteal) ~ 14 days
Progesterone ↓ Estrogen ↓ Serotonin ↓ LH ↓	Progesterone ↓ Estrogen ↑ Serotonin ↑ LH ↓	Progesterone ↑ Estrogen ↑ Serotonin ↑ LH ↑	Progesterone ↑ Estrogen ↓ Serotonin ↓ LH ↓
• Irritability • Confrontational • Lower mood • Low Energy • Uncomfortable • Winter-blues	• Increased energy • Positivity • Creativity and motivation • Increased libido • Upped confidence • Spring-time	• Peak energy • Peak positivity and mood • Maximum libido and fertility • "OMG I'm hot shit!" • Sunshiny Summer	• Irritability • Fatigue and overwhelm • Lower mood • Low Energy • Self-conscious • Extended Winter

Table 7: BABE Cycle Summary

Next, we can see how we men should carry ourselves during the BABE cycle. We essentially have a 9-day grace period of feeling less pressure to be at the top of our game. During the *Blood* and *Exhaustion* stages, our ducks need to be in a row because our shortcomings will be more apparent. Boundaries are taller, standards are higher, and both are more well-guarded.

So, to increase the odds we'll like one another, it's our responsibility to keep our things in order and be supportive by taking on more. The more we take on outside of her body, the better a woman can cope with what's going on inside of her body. That decreases the likelihood of conflict.

Summarizing everything we've learned in this section, the sexual desires of both men and women are comparable to intricate instruments. Men are akin to a whistle or a cowbell. You just kind of blow them or bang them, and they resound with joy. There aren't too many tricks.

Women are, as appropriately stated by J. D. Salinger, "...like a violin and all... it takes a terrific musician to play it right." Cumulatively, the sexual desire of women ebbs and flows on: (1) the BABE cycle, (2) having equal access to orgasm, (3) allowing time for their bodies to warm up and bloom for sex by attending to erogenous zones, and (4) having a stable, responsible, safe, and supportive mate who reduces her anxiety, stress, and awakens the light in her.

I encourage everyone to read books, listen to podcasts, and get more education pertaining to a thriving sex life and the differences between men and women. It's honorable and good to want to experience and connect with our partners more deeply, and it'll undoubtedly enhance our current and/or future relationship.

Technical Skill: Taking Time to Understand Sexual Desire in Our Partner

To close out this crash course in maintaining a healthy sex life, we must take time to understand our partners' sexual desire. We've gone through some general differences between men and women, but that's different from understanding *our partners*.

Sex is a very personal matter, and we can't do everything by the book. Every violin has a unique timbre, resonance, and richness. Cowbells and whistles can vary in pitch and volume. Bodies and senses of sexual desire are all unique, and the way they harmonize together is complex. Creating a satisfying sexual relationship amid this complexity requires continual *reflection, experimentation, and practice.*

By **reflection**, I mean asking the deeper questions of sex. What is our relationship to sex? Is it something we're battling shame about? Do we think it's a healthy way to connect? Is it enjoyable for us, or does it give us flashbacks from past abuse? Is it our primary form of stress relief?

What does sex mean to us? Is it something that makes us feel beautiful and desirable? Is it a cosmic binding of two souls? Is it an outlet for us to dominate and punish someone because we're angry at the world, a parent, or the entire opposite sex? Is sex an avenue of controlling our partner?

What does it mean to hold space for sex? Are we able to make eye contact and just get straight into it? Do we need to talk or cuddle before? Do we need to chill out and cuddle afterward, or do we just want to get on with our day? What sort of post-sexual activity do we need from each other?

What are we afraid to express with each other or afraid of being judged about? What would make us feel confident in our own skin? What level of stress can we tolerate to be open to sex? What sort of things do we need to change so we can like each other better and want to have sex?

By **experimentation**, I mean trying new things or testing the current boundaries. Which positions are most pleasurable? What sort of things do we like to hear? What romantic gestures do we like beforehand? What gets us in the mood? Where outside of the home would we be comfortable having sex? What playfulness-to-seriousness ratio do we prefer? Is any type of humor appropriate during sex? What frequency and duration of sex are we both happy with?

Are sex toys necessary? Which toys might elevate orgasms? What stimuli do they like to combine? Do they want to have sex during the *Blood* phase? How much time does it take to get aroused in each stage of the BABE cycle? What sort of measures do we need to take to make sex painless? How do sleep, diet, exercise, and other factors influence sexual desire? Is sex more natural in the morning or evening? What does it mean to have spontaneous sex?

By **practice**, I mean commitment to having sex to maintain connection and nurture true love. Is it getting easier to overcome when mishaps occur? Are we making sexual connection a priority? How can we keep sex as a priority? Are we becoming more in sync with what the other likes to maximize sexual chemistry? Are we getting better at reading the room and understanding how emotions affect our sexuality? How do we handle sexual rejection? How do we communicate our feelings about sexual rejection?

All these questions and their answers bring us to the end of our exploration of sexual desire's longevity. The reason much of this chapter is devoted to preserving sexual desire is that most of this book has been about the foundation of being a wonderful friend, a holistic person, and a smart relationship negotiator.

Without sex, however, all those things add up to us *just being friends*. Albeit beautiful, intimate friends—*just* friends. Friends negotiate how to relate to each other. They have boundaries, standards, and conflicts. They practice being good people and expressing love to one another. They're thoughtful, supportive, and help each other grow. *But they don't have sex.*

As an oversimplification, the difference between Love-Hero best friends and true-love soulmates is sex. Without sex, there's no true love because we aren't maximizing human connection, and that's what true love is. The only exceptions are perhaps disability or extreme old age, when physical limitations make sex difficult or impossible. Otherwise, if we want to create a garden of true love, sex is very much a part of it.

Onto the next skill.

Technical Skill: Expressing Gratitude

Recalling our earlier discussion of economics, value is determined by supply and demand. What is in short supply will demand higher prices. The valuation of human work ultimately involves *risk, technical ability,* and, perhaps most importantly, the *cost of time.*

Time is the one thing we can't get back. It's the one thing we must trade to learn and perform a skill, and to attain goods and services. We all trade in the currency of time.

When we think of value in terms of time, it's straightforward to see how much people truly give—especially in relationships. Great partnerships cumulatively save time. If we're driving together on a 4-hour road trip, that means one of us doesn't have to drive for 4 hours. The passenger can read, play a game, or engage in a productive conversation that meets both their needs for connection.

If one partner cooks, they may have to cut twice as much meat or vegetables, but the cooking and baking time is essentially the same. The cook probably takes on an extra 10 minutes of work but saves their partner anywhere from 30 minutes to 2 hours of meal prep.

When our partners do tasks for the team, they aren't just doing their part. They're actively *giving us life*—giving us more of life's ultimate currency and increasing our odds of success, fulfillment, and joy.

Furthermore, if our partners can do in one hour what would take us several hours, they're not only saving us time, they're saving us *exponential* time. They might also be doing a risky job we wouldn't want to do. Now, the task they're completing not only saves us time but also keeps us from facing danger.

If they're doing a task we don't know how to do, they're not only saving us the time of doing it but also the time of *learning* how to do it. Or maybe it's a task that couldn't possibly drain our souls more. The time they spend doing that task subtracts from the time we have to spend in misery or the mundane and allows us to give back in ways that give them life.

Mutual life-giving partnerships are a blessed miracle worthy of sincere celebration, and no fearsome obstacle should prevent us from expressing our gratitude.

There are things to be grateful for everywhere we look. "I appreciate the time you took to get ready... Thank you for pausing your game with your friends to come get me at the airport... The time you took to write me that note means a lot to me... Hot dang, you look sexy, get over here!... Birthing that child was no joke, you're my hero!!..."

"Thank you for doing the dishes and laundry... Thank you for reading to the kids so I could go lie down... Thank you for the massage and for sitting with me... Thank you for pushing me to stay consistent at the gym... Thank you for how hard you work to support the family... Thank you for all the little things you do to sustain the love we have..."

The thank-you list is endless, and we shouldn't underestimate its impact. Allen W. Barton, a researcher at the University of Illinois Urbana-Champaign, found that gratitude protected relationship well-being against conflict, ineffective argumentation, and even financial strain.[xvii]

We can always amplify thanks by combining those affirming words with other love languages. We could easily say thank you and give them flowers, chocolate, a dress, a note, or an accessory. Or we could use acts of service, make them a special meal, and express our appreciation. With physical touch, we could tell them thank you and give them a massage, a heartfelt hug, or the best sex of their lives. If we wanted to go the quality time route, we could even plan a spontaneous trip.

Because gestures of gratitude often involve sacrificing time to express appreciation for our partners' sacrifices, gratitude creates a feedback loop that ingrains positivity and love into the relationship. Gratitude also positively reinforces behaviors we like, validates our partners and their efforts, and creates mutual reputations of high regard.

Even if we think of and express gratitude late, hindsight gratitude is almost more meaningful because their actions affected us to the point that we had to go back, reprocess what happened, and thank them.

To be experts in expressing gratitude, we must practice it every day with everyone. Gratitude is a lifestyle and a trait foundational to identity, so it's not something we can reserve for one person. If we want its positivity to saturate our lives, we must express it to all and in every area of our lives. Only then will we have free rein over gratitude to nurture a garden of true love

Technical Skill: Ensuring Expectations Are Not Mutually Exclusive

Even though it happens all the time, we're somehow terrible at recognizing when we have contradictory expectations. Leaving them unresolved creates room for growing contempt and conflict.

For example, let's say a man wants both a hardworking, successful woman and a playful-spirited woman. Both desires typically repel each other because the characteristics needed for grinding to high success suppress play and lightheartedness. Meaning, if he wants to see her femininity blossom and spirit shine, he may need to accept that she should work less, be less monetarily helpful, and have more time to stay home and relax.

Maybe he wants a drop-dead gorgeous, dainty, manicured, feminine wife, but also an extreme outdoorsy adventure woman. While not completely mutually exclusive, these paint two strikingly distinct pictures of a woman. It'd take a human chameleon to bridge that gap. Not impossible, just improbable. Or maybe he even wants to have a family, but is unwilling to accept her body changing.

Perhaps a woman wants a man who works his butt off but expects all his attention and love to meet her emotional needs. Idolizing a work-obsessed man will lead to less quality time, fewer opportunities to nurture love, and the selection of harsher personality traits needed for success.

Resolving these scenarios and expectations requires intentional personal reflection, awareness, and communication. That communication could be: "Look, I know you love it when I'm this person. But then you also want me to be this person. I just need you to know I can't be both people you want."

Whatever the case, we can't have our cake and eat it too.

Technical Skill: Scheduling Proactive Negotiation and Goal Conversations

Since growth is a key component of the Love Hero identity, it's meaningful and beneficial to proactively reflect on growth and set growth goals. Uncomfortable conversations come up in everyday mating negotiations as we test, discover, rediscover, and develop new standards and boundaries. *Proactive* negotiation, however, involves making time to *seek* feedback and *plan* for growth. Thriving gardens require proactive nurturing, not just interventions when weeds start to overgrow or pests get out of hand.

While these conversations can feel unnatural and uncomfortable at first, it's important to remember that we're both imperfect humans moving toward what's right. We'll inevitably get on each other's nerves, yet we also need to respectfully collaborate with each other to develop in the right ways.

When we have these conversations, we should use the skills we learned in *Chapter 2* and come together with a peaceful heart. Our partners aren't obstacles or objects—they're lifelong allies. Simple body postures can hack our biology to help us maintain peaceful hearts and maximize our conversation's impact.

We can start by facing each other, palms up, as if we're about to receive something. Keeping arms close to our bodies and palms facing down are closed-body postures. Closed-body postures are instinctual survival stances. They make us smaller targets, allow us to wind up a punch in self-defense, and cover our vital organs. Meaning, they'll only amplify any instinct we have to defend ourselves emotionally as if we're in immediate danger. But we're not in danger. We're just putting our egos through a certain level of rebirth with these humble conversations.

Second, we can build and establish rapport and emotional resonance by looking into their left eye. If we're facing them, it's the right one, where our right hand is. Dr. Tara Swart introduced me to the neuroscience behind this. It's based on the mother-baby relationship.

Most people, and therefore mothers, are right-handed. When

we're holding a baby, our hand with the greatest fine-motor skill needs to be available to accomplish tasks. So, we hold our baby with our non-dominant arm. For most people, that's the left arm.

As we gently rock our babies in our non-dominant arms, they beam up at us with their gigantic eyes and heavy eyelids. We peer down at them and meet the eye that's furthest away from us, not pressed against our chest. It's a bit like reading a piece of paper. We won't hold it close to our chest—rather, we'll hold it out to get a better look. A baby's left eye is typically the one that's held out.

Eye contact throughout infancy is a powerful bonding mechanism between mother and child, and it's a key gateway to emotional understanding. When we look into someone's left eye, there's a 90% chance we're making eye contact with the eye their mothers repetitively looked into.

Though eye contact on its own is vulnerable, looking into someone's left eye partially replicates the emotional resonance of someone who cares for that person from the bottom of their soul. We resonate as someone who's a safe space, trustworthy, reliable, and wants the best for them. Which is absolutely true!

With the right body and heart postures, we'll be keen to create a space for asking questions and listening to one another. These conversations can happen once a month, once a year, or whatever works best. We should ask questions like:

- "What have I done lately that's gotten on your nerves?"
- "How would you like to be loved in the next week?"
- "What did you learn about yourself and your relationships in the last month?"
- "In what ways are you proud of yourself for nurturing our relationship?"
- "What do you wish you had done differently this week to enhance the health of our relationship?"
- "During what moments do you think I need to show more patience?"

- "What areas of your life do you feel you need more support in?"
- "How would you like to grow in the next year of marriage?"
- "How would you like to see our priorities shift?"
- "How can I listen better or help you feel more heard?"
- "What needs do we have that are being unmet right now?"
- "How are those needs in opposition to each other?"

The answers, reflections, and goals stemming from these questions help us manage current and future small- and medium-sized disagreements. They may start uncomfortably because of the self-sacrifice we're inviting. But as we witness how we hold each other's hearts, it brings us closer, cultivates a stronger foundation, and increases the likelihood that our relationships will flourish.

That concludes the less-conventional technical skills we'll cover for preserving true-love negotiations. As our journey together draws to a close, let's tie everything together.

THE BLUEPRINT OF TRUE LOVE

We opened this book by outlining the modern obstacle-ridden landscape that hinders the creation of true love. Common men and women stand discouraged and succumb to its challenges. Ultimately, only heroes have what it takes to overcome them.

The first part of this heroic identity is leaving behind any victim mindset. Victim mindsets rob us of autonomy because being a victim requires us to have a greater power ruling over us. One of the ways this mindset bleeds into romance is that it promotes the view that the *opposite sex is an oppressive force and enemy* preventing the creation of true love. However, if we choose to take ownership of our current circumstances, it would mean we no longer have oppressors. The less we attribute control over our lives to external sources, the more autonomy we have.

This shift leads Love Heroes to realize that many, if not all, of our frustrations and woes concerning love are misplaced and can be overcome. Historically, there have *always* been obstacles to true love—none of which have had all-powerful, controlling, and oppressive minds of their own. Modern obstacles include the food and pharmaceutical industries, social media, legacy media, sedentary lifestyles, gargantuan cultural and political shifts, and technological development.

Social psychology teaches us that people are a product of their environment. If we're frustrated and angry with the product, our issue should *really* be with the environment that produced it. It's here that we realize, if we have any view painting the opposite sex as an enemy, it's mostly because they're being scapegoated and blamed for the shortcomings of the world.

As we redirect our fight-filled energy toward overcoming the obstacles around us, our grace, compassion, and understanding extend to those who also hope to someday overcome their obstacles and create true love. We hush our hostilities and bitterness and center ourselves with a peaceful heart.

A hostile heart pushes people away, no matter how much hate-filtering we try to do. For true love to come into being, we must see *all* people as people. Only then will we be open to negotiating for a rich life partnership with a quality candidate and planting seeds of true love within them.

This negotiation for a life partnership occurs through several mate-selection theories simultaneously. By understanding each theory, we understand how we *and* others negotiate. As we negotiate, we're looking to exchange what we have for things we want, and we place unique demands upon each other. Those demands are our personal standards and boundaries, which we either inherit from family, attain by influence, adopt from culture, develop through personal preference, or perhaps gather from *Chapters 5 and 6*. These expectations represent our thresholds for successful mating negotiation and relationship satisfaction.

Failure to reach those thresholds is due to big disagreements: incompatible or irreconcilable differences in key standards and boundaries. That's when breakups occur. When we satisfy the standards and boundaries in each other's mate-selection theories, successful negotiation endures, and we create **functional relationships**. Yet functional does not capture the exceptional nature of true love, which *exceeds expectations*.

The unique theories, standards, and boundaries we use to negotiate represent our expression and understanding of love—they're manifestations of our definition(s) of love. Therefore, a love that exceeds all expectations requires a definition that transcends direct measurability. Its definition must be *alive—continually* transforming potential into reality and possibility into being.

This is why true love is so hard to put a finger on. The greatest potential of romantic love dances on the balance beam between two worlds. In one world, true love conquers quantifiable standards and boundaries that matter for the threshold of human relationship success. In the other, quantifiability is irrelevant because *its purpose is to escape and exceed anything quantifiable*. Its touch is true and real, but trying to measure it is like taking a picture just after the moment has passed. It's like artificial gravity, where finding a solid stance requires us to be rapidly moving. It's a ghost we can waltz with but cannot hold still. It's objective and transcendent at the same time.

But where do we get this definition of love? It must come from a source. The love we know was taught to us by the love we received. Sources of love channel love to individuals, impressing them with its concepts and ultimately sculpting their definitions of love. Being infused with particular definitions, individuals then become avenues for that love to enter the world.

Consequently, sources of love function as structures that shape the flow and expression of love, i.e., mate-selection theories. This means *all sources prescribe a narrative of love*, since narratives are sequential, cause-and-effect series of events. In short, narratives of love form by one being loved, learning love, and expressing that love.

Since characters are *parts* of narratives, sources *also* prescribe identity. The Christian source, and others like it, ultimately assign the identity of one who grows in perfection and goodness, imitating a source springing infinite love. This identity carries the responsibility to learn, respect, grow in, and negotiate using *all* mate-selection theories since they're all manifestations of love—*the collection of all potential means for benevolent connection.*

Altogether, infinite sources bestow a transcendent definition of love, the Love Hero's Narrative, the Love Hero identity, and the exclusive keys to creating true love. Accessing infinite sources and all they bestow requires that their love reach us, that we accept it, and that we experience changes in our life narrative and identity.

The full acceptance of new sources fundamentally necessitates a heart ready and willing to be reborn. That willingness is often synonymous with the involuntary experience of rock bottom. This is why changes in life direction and identity typically happen in the middle of, or *lead to*, life crises. Crises *force* us to reconcile old narratives, evidence, beliefs, and identities with new, perhaps contradictory ones. Without an urgent need for change, change typically happens very slowly, or not at all. Because if a song is sweet enough, we won't bother changing it. Only in rock bottom's vantage of humility are the loftiest heights in clearest view.

Heartbreak and rock bottom are the essence of what makes the search for and acceptance of infinite sources of love so challenging, counterintuitive, and unnatural. If we're not thrown into a place of heartbreak against our will, the only other option is to *put ourselves there willingly.* Both the intentional fracturing of identity and the severing of our tethers to reality induce life crises that push us to the edge of madness. And while self-inducing existential crises isn't exactly human nature, crises are usually an inevitable part of the human experience. If we don't run from them, they represent the Atonement with the Father/Supreme Ordeal stage of the hero's journey.

Here, a hero endures heartbreak as they battle the greatest power in their life. That greatest power, in true love's case, is essentially whatever commands the order of their universe. Whatever evidence, lived narrative, and identity found in that power dies. It becomes a milestone in their story as the hero makes peace with it and ultimately chooses a new greatest power—a new source or god—branding them with a new narrative, identity, and life.

The core truth is that only the crushed in spirit can be blessed with a radiant, harmonious love. For only in the death of self can we become no one and know how to be one with another. Only in the greatest darkness can one see the dimmest light, and in the most deafening silence, hear the secret heartbeat of the universe. Only there, at the brim of the great abyss and existence itself, is the sacred wisdom necessary for true love discovered.

The edge of that consuming void and failing desire to exist is where we meet the love that transcends the measurable bounds of reality and existence. The infinite and immeasurable source of love stands hand in hand with the inability to stand and the brokenness without measure. Only at the event horizon of this black hole are full terror and glory known.

The pinnacle of romantic love depends entirely on accessing this living, transcendent, and infinite source of love. This is why we define true love as "an infinite source of love maximizing human connection." An infinite source is the only means to provide connection in unlimited ways and to sustain the lifelong narrative of becoming the boundless epitome of love. Only then can we, and someone else with the same narrative, share love's highest potential.

Ideal true-love candidates won't only share the same trajectory to embody infinite love but also be at similar points in their developmental journey toward it. Mating negotiation cards are near-universal traits of desirability we use as leverage in negotiation. They also disclose where we are on our journeys as Love Heroes. The further we are on that journey of replicating a bountiful source of love, the more attractive cards we accumulate.

Among these attractive qualities, or "cards," as we've called them, are healthy bodies, emotional intelligence, romance, useful life skills, good hygiene, sobriety, having hobbies, and whatever else increases the likelihood we'll like each other and make our partners' lives easier and more enjoyable. And even though these cards are ultimately beneficial for our health and well-being, developing them often means defying social pressures, since societal norms tout personal gain and convenience.

A Love Hero's continual development of cards is made possible by the attunement to the secret heartbeat of the universe. That is, the ability to *see* love everywhere and in everything. This is the reward of experiencing death and rebirth: having emerged from the deepest darkness, they can make out the faintest light and note the contrast it casts on the world. They learn a sacred, unteachable attunement to love.

With this ethereal vision, they wander through diverse spiritualities, books, languages, cultures, places, and people, seeking the wisdom of love. Their bodies become tools to help others and gifts to love the ones who choose them forever. The smiles they offer strangers become grains of hope and energy that give them life. Whatever cards of love they find, they absorb them into their being and add them to their deck.

Continuously accumulating desirable, attractive cards builds an identity of love, establishing a positive feedback loop that exceeds expectations and creates a passive force that cultivates true love. Love Heroes serve each other as amplifiers of love, making mating negotiations increasingly successful, aligned, and resilient throughout time.

As we can see in *Figure 15's* illustration of the blueprint of true love, the Love Hero's Narrative is the process of transforming an infinite source's love into reality and directing its focus onto a romantic interest with whom one is engaging in mating negotiations. It's entirely possible to form successful and functional relationships without an infinite source. But without an infinite source, there's no Love Hero Narrative and no Love Hero identity. True love remains a hidden treasure and a lost paradise reserved for fables and myths.

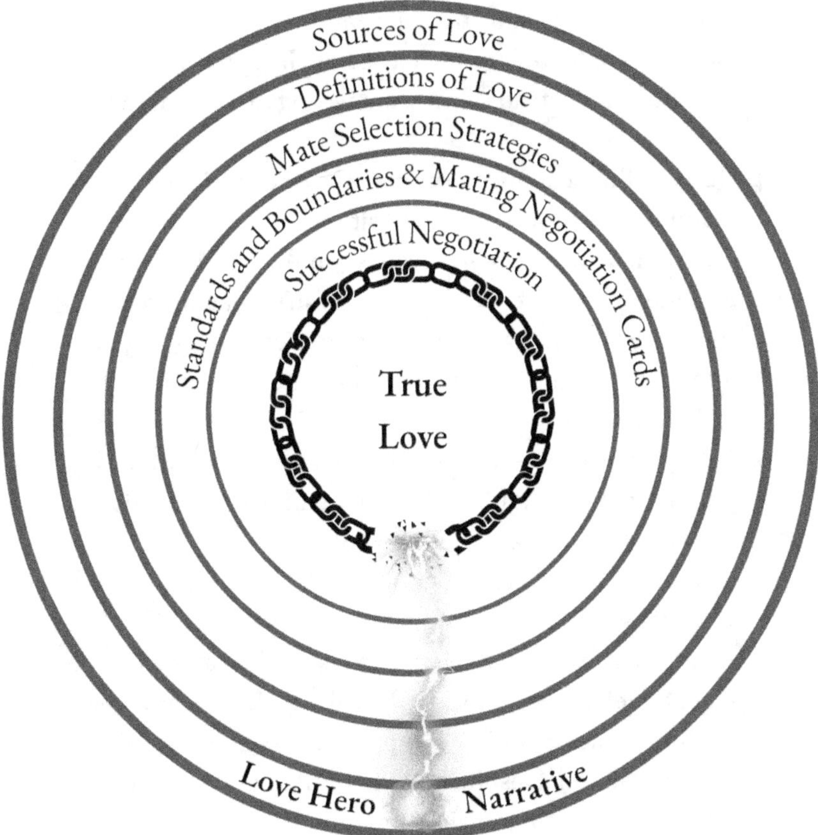

Figure 15: The Blueprint of True Love

Despite its cheesiness, the Love Hero identity has no shortage of heroic accolades. Based on what we've covered in this book, here's a non-exhaustive list of the heroic feats Love Heroes undertake:

1. Take radical ownership of circumstances to propel oneself out of victimhood and increase autonomy.
2. Actively learn and grow in all mating negotiation theories.
3. Realize "having it all" is not the point. There are finite resources to nurture a garden of true love. Abundance in one area of life demands the sacrifice of another. This often means that, if we want true love, we may be asked to sacrifice dreams of owning fancy cars, big houses, or fame.

Another way to frame this realization is to say we enter a stage where we unlearn what society has programmed us to value and instead select what we regard as vital to true love.

4. Resist influences, messages, people, or experiences leading us to despise the opposite sex. This requires us to maintain a posture of forgiveness, understanding, and to assume the best of people. This doesn't mean naivety.

5. Embrace true paths to fulfillment rather than giving in to attention-seeking endeavors, dopamine traps, and sedation.

6. Select a powerful source of love that carries a profound definition of love and assigns an identity and narrative of embodying infinite love. This could demand the abandonment of a religious, atheistic, or love-conflicting worldview and perhaps even trigger a life crisis.

7. Accept the reality that one may very well be alone for the rest of one's life. Embracing the call of a Love Hero means waiting to meet another compatible person who also accepts the call. Despite looking impossible odds in the face, one must remain vigilant and refuse to give up the love they dream of.

8. Set the embodiment of an infinite definition of love as their *top* priority.

9. Spend vast amounts of energy searching high and low for candidates of true love—even to the extent of going across the world.

10. Make every decision based on the question: "What action will increase the odds of relationship success and flourishing?" Such a framework bars self-destructive habits like smoking, drug abuse, video game addiction, porn, drunkenness—essentially any vice. In exchange, one would adopt habits that increase the odds of creating a garden of true love, such as healthy eating, exercise, plenty

of sleep, good hygiene, and the development of strong
support systems.

11. Experience repeated, disappointing rejection.

12. Dance on the line between play and breaking boundaries
    for the sake of vibrant living, humor, novelty, and
    romance. As we learn to dance on the line, we'll inevitably
    overstep and encounter awkward or hurtful moments.
    We'll sometimes be too vulnerable, be offensive to others,
    and test people's patience. It's all part of learning what's
    appropriate and what's not.

13. Experience heartbreak to the point of looking death itself
    in the eyes and being unfazed.

14. Take the best of the philosophies and traditions one was
    indoctrinated with, reconcile with them, and merge them
    with our new learnings and growth. This is making peace
    with the greatest power from the hero's journey.

15. Have a challenger's posture toward one's own ego,
    allowing them to seek what's right instead of who's right.

16. Intentionally purge one's flaws by diving headfirst into
    uncomfortable conversations that offer feedback.

17. Hold a deep desire to satisfy the needs and wants of our
    partners, even if they're somewhat contradictory to what
    we want in the moment—meaning submission.

18. Learn new skills and technical strategies to communicate
    effectively, foster a healthy sex life, and build a holistically
    thriving relationship.

19. Always honor the truth by keeping one's word, being
    accountable, and refusing to take part in lying and deception.

20. Reject and shatter other people's hearts in loving ways.

A Message of Doom

A professional overview of true love wouldn't be complete without an
honest disclaimer. I'm not sure I believe true love is possible for

everyone. Plenty of challenges litter the path to creating mere functional and healthy relationships. True love is also not everyone's deepest desire. If we don't want it, it's not something that's created by accident.

Most of all, however, we just live in an imperfect world. Multiple factors severely reduce the odds of true love's creation. Dark personality disorders, for example, make the mind a desolate, infertile, and brittle place to grow true love. These disorders stem mainly from genetic and environmental factors—*not* human choice. They're also not considered disorders that humans can completely eradicate from their personalities. We can notice those conditions within ourselves, consciously fight against them, and reduce their expression, but they may very well be a fervent thorn in our side forever, inhibiting us from true love.

Alternatively, being born at either end of the physical attractiveness spectrum can dramatically reduce our chances of creating true love. Being born unattractive decreases the number of interested mates. Being born perfectly attractive can actively impede personal development, discouraging interest from high-quality mates. One would also attract and possibly fall victim to members of the Dark Triad who use beauty solely for their own selfish gain.

Many factors affect how our imperfect world stands in the way of or almost outright disqualifies us from creating true love. Most of them occur by no fault of our own. Some people are simply born with more obstacles. Others will *let* their obstacles keep them from creating true love, and it will remain a fairy tale to them.

Unfortunately, more obstacles are on their way. Artificial intelligence will create artificial realities, immersive porn, and entice much of humanity into complacency and false paths of fulfillment. As AI chatbots and companions accept us for all we are, they'll help us settle into our delusions and comfort us as we distance ourselves from connecting with the rest of humanity.

Others will finish this book and be unwilling to do and give what it takes to create true love. They'll believe they can love out of their own sheer determination or go without embodying an infinite source of love. They'll believe they can get away with lies or foregoing growth and still have a beautiful, true-love story. *They will be wrong.*

Yet, with those sobering thoughts, I must admit, I'm not all-knowing for what obstacles an all-powerful source of love is capable of conquering in this world. While I can imagine circumstances that make true love's creation impossible, I am but a branch of my Source's vine, and only the vine determines what branches will become and what fruit they will bear. Infinite sources of love have a way of breaking through to people, calling them forth by name, and inspiring a rebirth.

Despite my doubts about who can access, understand, and manifest the blueprint of true love, they may very well be unfounded. True love in and of itself requires miracles. So, what's a little more miracle?

A Message of Hope

While there are so many terrible things plaguing the world right now and many obstacles that belie us, one thing emerges as a critical truth: true love has never been more accessible. The freedom we have to choose whom we love has never been paralleled.

Despite the landscape being more complex than ever, there have never been so many resources to better ourselves, learn new skills, and adopt fresh forms of love. We may not have cheap assets or easy living, but we *have* what we need, or we can *learn* what we need to create a true love story. There is a path forward, and we have the blueprint to create our hearts' desires.

And with that, dear reader, I'd like to acknowledge you for the critical thinking you've put into answering the questions I've posed for you in this book. I commend you for your growth and your openness to becoming someone you're proud to be. It's not a painless endeavor to change things about ourselves, but true love continually asks that of us.

I thank you for taking the time to hear me out. I hope someday I read or hear about how the Love Hero blueprint of true love inspired you to create a love so beautiful that it brought an overflowing joy into your life and established a beacon of love, radiating benevolence and inspiration to all around.

As you follow your destiny as a Love Hero, all will bear witness to the glorious source of love you've embedded yourself in. If you have a partner, you'll either see your relationship transform or dissolve before your eyes. It'll transform into a true love garden where you and your partner become each other's beloved unlikely heroes. Or it'll become a distant memory where you leave that relationship behind to start a new one capable of creating true love. Either way, a new life and narrative await.

If you're single and choose to live the Love Hero's arc, maybe you'll become someone you never could've dreamed of being, and maybe that'll carve a path to someone you never could've imagined meeting. Perhaps you'll meet the one who defied all odds to choose to be someone utterly magnificent for you.

Maybe you'll find the person to create a garden of true love with. A love that never gets old, even though your very bones do. A love that shines ever brighter, even as the world darkens. One that uplifts you as the nations around you fall. And one that gives you peace in a world at war.

Maybe... *Just*... Maybe... You'll meet your hero.

FROM THE AUTHOR

Everything you hold within these bindings was crafted over the span of 3 years and several thousand hours. From the cover to the illustrations to the exercises and, of course, the words, everything reflects the intentions of a heart forged over my 32 years of life. This book was born from more sacrifices than I can name or need to share. I suppose it wouldn't be a book of sacrifices and miracles if the author didn't sacrifice to share it.

Yet, my journey in sharing the blueprint of true love is only beginning. Beyond this book, I run a relationship-coaching practice and plan to host public speaking events as part of a *Love Hero* book tour. Due to the birth of my son in the few days prior to this book's publication, my coaching practice will be collecting a waitlist, and I plan to launch that tour at a later date. For official details, you can visit sourcetoheart.com or follow me on social media for updates. You can find links to my socials and sign up for my newsletter on the website.

Alas, if you've found significant value in this book, I'd be honored if you'd help me on my journey and mission to share true love with the world. Aside from being a Love Hero, leaving an online review, posting on social media, talking about *Love Hero* with family and friends, or gifting a copy are all tremendous ways to help. Your support means a lot!

To Creating True Love and a Beautiful World,
  Andrew

NOTES

1. The Modern Landscape of Romantic Relationships

i. Arnsten, A. F. T. (2009). Stress signaling pathways that impair prefrontal cortex structure and function. Nature Reviews Neuroscience, 10(6), 410–422. https://doi.org/10.1038/nrn2648

ii. Stop Abuse Campaign. (n.d.). *What does your ACE score mean?* https://stopabusecampaign.org/take-your-ace/what-does-your-ace-score-mean/

iii. World Health Organization. (2025, December 8). Obesity and overweight. https://www.who.int/news-room/fact-sheets/detail/obesity-and-overweight

iv. Food and Agriculture Organization of the United Nations, International Fund for Agricultural Development, United Nations Children's Fund, World Food Programme, & World Health Organization. (2025). The State of Food Security and Nutrition in the World 2025: Addressing high food price inflation for food security and nutrition. FAO. https://doi.org/10.4060/cd6008en

v. Macfabe, D. (2013). *Autism: Metabolism, mitochondria, and the microbiome.* Global Advances in Health and Medicine, 2(6), 52–66. https://doi.org/10.7453/gahmj.2013.089

vi. Wiertsema, S. P., van Bergenhenegouwen, J., Garssen, J., & Knippels, L. M. J. (2021). The interplay between the gut microbiome and the immune system in the context of infectious diseases throughout life and the role of nutrition in optimizing treatment strategies. *Nutrients, 13*(3), 886. https://doi.org/10.3390/nu13030886

vii. Recchia, F., Leung, C. K., Chin, E. C., Fong, D. Y., Montero, D., Cheng, C. P., Yau, S. Y., & Siu, P. M. (2022). Comparative effectiveness of exercise, antidepressants and their combination in treating non-severe depression: a systematic review and network meta-analysis of randomised controlled trials. *British journal of sports medicine, 56*(23), 1375–1380. https://doi.org/10.1136/bjsports-2022-105964

viii. Xu, F., Xie, Q., Kuang, W., & Dong, Z. (2023). Interactions between antidepressants and intestinal microbiota. *Neurotherapeutics,* 20*(2), 359–371. https://www.neurotherapeuticsjournal.org/article/S1878-7479(23)00084-3/fulltext

ix. Khan, I. F., De La Garza, H., Lazar, M., Kennedy, K. F., & Vashi, N. A. (2024). Effects of the COVID-19 pandemic on patient social media use and acceptance of cosmetic procedures. *The Journal of Clinical and Aesthetic Dermatology, 17*(3), 42–47. https://pubmed.ncbi.nlm.nih.gov/38495546/

x. Bhaimiya, S. (2025, December 21). AI was behind over 50,000 layoffs in 2025 — here are the top firms to cite it for job cuts. CNBC. https://www.cnbc.com/2025/12/21/ai-job-cuts-amazon-microsoft-and-more-cite-ai-for-2025-layoffs.html

xi. Bastani, H., Bastani, O., Sungu, A., Ge, H., Kabakcı, Ö., & Mariman, R. (2025). Generative AI without guardrails can harm learning: Evidence from high school mathematics. Proceedings of the National Academy of Sciences, 122(26), Article e2422633122. https://doi.org/10.1073/pnas.2422633122

xii. Kos'myna, N., Hauptmann, E., Yuan, Y. T., Situ, J., Liao, X.-H., Beresnitzky, A. V., Braunstein, I., & Maes, P. (2025). Your brain on ChatGPT: Accumulation of cognitive debt when using an AI assistant for essay writing task. arXiv. https://doi.org/10.48550/arXiv.2506.08872

xiii. Osterman, M. J. K., Hamilton, B. E., Martin, J. A., Driscoll, A. K., & Valenzuela, C. P. (2025). Births: Final data for 2023 (National Vital Statistics Reports, Vol. 74, No. 1). National Center for Health Statistics. https://www.cdc.gov/nchs/data/nvsr/nvsr74/nvsr74-1.pdf

xiv. Kramer, S. (2019). *U.S. has world's highest rate of children living in single-parent households.* Pew Research Center. https://www.pewresearch.org/short-reads/2019/12/12/u-s-children-more-likely-than-children-in-other-countries-to-live-with-just-one-parent/

xv. Gillespie, J., Shields, K., & Taylor, M. (2016, October 3). 40 facts about two parent families: Studies and statistics. GillespieShields [Blog]. https://gillespieshields.com/40-facts-two-parent-families/

xvi. Fry, R. (2023). *A record-high share of 40-year-olds in the U.S. have never been married.* Pew Research Center. https://www.pewresearch.org/short-reads/2023/06/28/a-record-high-share-of-40-year-olds-in-the-us-have-never-been-married/

xvii. Muise, A., Schimmack, U., & Impett, E. A. (2016). Sexual frequency predicts greater well-being, but more is not always better. *Social Psychological and Personality Science, 7*(4), 295–302. https://doi.org/10.1177/1948550615616462

xviii. Davey Smith, G., Frankel, S., & Yarnell, J. (1997). Sex and death: Are they related? Findings from the Caerphilly cohort study. *BMJ, 315*(7123), 1641–1644. https://doi.org/10.1136/bmj.315.7123.1641

xix. OHSU. (n.d.). *Benefits of a healthy sex life.* https://www.ohsu.edu/womens-health/benefits-healthy-sex-life

xx. Kucharz, E. J. (1988). Hormonal control of collagen metabolism: Part II. *Endocrinology, 26*(4), 229–237. https://pubmed.ncbi.nlm.nih.gov/3062759/

xxi. Grymowicz, M., Rudnicka, E., Podfigurna, A., Napierala, P., Smolarczyk, R., Smolarczyk, K., & Meczekalski, B. (2020). Hormonal effects on hair follicles. *International Journal of Molecular Sciences, 21*(15), Article 5342. https://doi.org/10.3390/ijms21155342

xxii. Jia, H., & Lubetkin, E. (2020). Life expectancy and active life expectancy by marital status among older U.S. adults: Results from the U.S. Medicare Health Outcome Survey (HOS). *SSM - Population Health.* https://www.ncbi.nlm.nih.gov/pmc/articles/PMC7452000/

xxiii. Murthy, V. (2023). *New Surgeon General advisory raises alarm about the devastating impact of the epidemic of loneliness and isolation in the United States.* HHS.gov. https://www.hhs.gov/about/news/2023/05/03/new-surgeon-general-advisory-raises-alarm-about-devastating-impact-epidemic-loneliness-isolation-united-states.html

xxiv. Holt-Lunstad, J., Smith, T. B., & Layton, J. B. (2010). Social relationships and mortality risk: A meta-analytic review. *PLoS Medicine, 7*(7), Article e1000316. https://doi.org/10.1371/journal.pmed.1000316

xxv. Cherlin, A. J. (1999). The marriage-go-round: The state of marriage and the family in America today. American Sociological Review, 64(3), 333–356. https://doi.org/10.2307/2657490

xxvi. Westervelt, A. (2018, May 26). Is motherhood the unfinished work of feminism? The Guardian. https://www.theguardian.com/commentisfree/2018/may/26/is-motherhood-the-unfinished-work-of-feminism

xxvii. Kahneman, D., & Deaton, A. (2010). High income improves evaluation of life but not emotional well-being. *Proceedings of the National Academy of Sciences, 107*(38), 16489–16493. https://doi.org/10.1073/pnas.1011492107

xxviii. Diener, E., Seligman, M. E. P., Choi, H., & Oishi, S. (2018). Happiest people revisited. *Perspectives on Psychological Science, 13*(2), 176–184. https://doi.org/10.1177/1745691617697077

xxix. Hill, P. L., & Turiano, N. A. (2014). Purpose in life as a predictor of mortality across adulthood. *Psychological Science, 25*(7), 1482–1486. https://doi.org/10.1177/0956797614531799

xxx. Stevenson, B., & Wolfers, J. (2009). The paradox of declining female happiness. American Economic Journal: Economic Policy, 1(2), 190–225. https://doi.org/10.1257/pol.1.2.190

xxxi. Wilcox, B., & Wang, W. (2023, September 12). Who is happiest? Married mothers and fathers, per the latest General Social Survey. Institute for Family Studies. https://ifstudies.org/blog/who-is-happiest-married-mothers-and-fathers-per-the-latest-general-social-survey

xxxii. Wolfinger, N. H. (2015, July 17). Want to avoid divorce? Wait to get married, but not too long. Institute for Family Studies. https://ifstudies.org/blog/want-to-avoid-divorce-wait-to-get-married-but-not-too-long

xxxiii. McErlean, K. (2021). The growth of education differentials in marital dissolution in the United States. Demographic Research, 45, 841–856. https://doi.org/10.4054/DemRes.2021.45.26

xxxiv. Hewlett, S. A. (2002). Executive women and the myth of having it all. Harvard Business Review, 80(4), 66–73. https://hbr.org/2002/04/executive-women-and-the-myth-of-having-it-all

xxxv. Dehingia, N., Raj, A., & Silverman, J. G. (2023). Violence against women on Twitter in India: Testing a taxonomy for online misogyny and measuring its prevalence during COVID-19. PLOS ONE, 18(10), Article e0292121. https://doi.org/10.1371/journal.pone.0292121

xxxvi. Coppolillo, E. (2025). Women who hate men: A comparative analysis across extremist Reddit communities. Scientific Reports, 15(1), Article 13952. https://doi.org/10.1038/s41598-024-81567-9

xxxvii. Worlddata.info. (n.d.). *Inflation rates in the United States of America.* https://www.worlddata.info/america/usa/inflation-rates.php

xxxviii. Hanson, M. (2025, September 23). *Average cost of college by year.* EducationData.org. https://educationdata.org/average-cost-of-college-by-year

xxxix. Cachero, P. (2023). *Supreme Court justices didn't face same student loan debt burden.* Bloomberg.com. https://www.bloomberg.com/news/articles/2023-02-28/student-loans-and-the-supreme-court-debt-is-up-2-807-since-justices-graduated xl. Monte, L. M. (2019, November 5). *"Solo" dads and "absent" dads not as different as they seem*. U.S. Census Bureau. https://www.census.gov/library/stories/2019/11/the-two-extremes-of-fatherhood.html

xli. Vigers, B. (2025, May 20). Younger men among the loneliest in the West. *Gallup News*. https://news.gallup.com/poll/690788/younger-men-among-loneliest-west.aspx

xlii. Cox, D. A. (2021, June 29). *Men's social circles are shrinking*. American Survey Center. https://www.americansurveycenter.org/why-mens-social-circles-are-shrinking/

xliii. Gelles-Watnick, R. (2023). *For Valentine's Day, 5 facts about single Americans*. Pew Research Center. https://www.pewresearch.org/short-reads/2023/02/08/for-valentines-day-5-facts-about-single-americans/

xliv. Fry, R. (2022, March 28). *Young women are out-earning young men in several U.S. cities*. Pew Research Center. https://www.pewresearch.org/short-reads/2022/03/28/young-women-are-out-earning-young-men-in-several-u-s-cities/

xlv. Kincaid, J. (2009). *OkCupid checks out the dynamics of attraction and your love inbox*. TechCrunch. https://techcrunch.com/2009/11/18/okcupid-inbox-attractive/

xlvi. Gerrard, B. (2021). *Why do women have the upper hand on Tinder?*. Medium. https://thebolditalic.com/the-two-worlds-of-tinder-f1c34e800db4

xlvii. Ueda, P., Mercer, C. H., Ghaznavi, C., & Herbenick, D. (2020). Trends in frequency of sexual activity and number of sexual partners among adults aged 18 to 44 years in the US, 2000–2018. *JAMA Network Open, 3*(6), Article e203833. https://doi.org/10.1001/jamanetworkopen.2020.3833

xlviii. U.S. Bureau of Labor Statistics. (2026, March 22). Labor force participation rate—High school graduates, no college, 25 yrs. & over, men (Series ID: LNU01327676Q) [Data set]. FRED, Federal Reserve Bank of St. Louis. https://fred.stlouisfed.org/series/LNU01327676Q

xlix. Joint Economic Committee. (2019). Long-term trends in deaths of despair (Social Capital Project Report 4-19). U.S. Congress. https://www.jec.senate.gov/public/_cache/files/0f2d3dba-9fdc-41e5-9bd1-9c13f4204e35/jec-report-deaths-of-despair.pdf

l. Hawrami, R., & Reeves, R. V. (2025, September 10). *Data spotlight: Suicide deaths among young men*. American Institute for Boys and Men. https://aibm.org/research/data-spotlight-suicide-deaths-among-young-men/

2. Preparing for Mating Negotiation

i. Bose, C. E., & Whaley, R. B. (2000). Sex segregation in the US labor force. In D. Vannoy & B. Hass (Eds.), *Gender mosaics: Social perspectives (Original readings)* (pp. 228–239). Oxford University Press.

ii. Gelles-Watnick, R. (2023). *For Valentine's Day, 5 facts about single Americans*. Pew Research Center. https://www.pewresearch.org/short-reads/2023/02/08/for-valentines-day-5-facts-about-single-americans/

iii. Steinberg, B. (2023, July 31). *Why people are becoming less attractive*. New York

Post. https://nypost.com/2023/07/31/why-people-are-becoming-less-attractive-facial-analyst/

iv. U.S. Department of Health and Human Services. (n.d.). *Overweight & obesity statistics*. National Institute of Diabetes and Digestive and Kidney Diseases. https://www.niddk.nih.gov/health-information/health-statistics/overweight-obesity

v. Healy, M. (2019, December 18). *By 2030, nearly half of all U.S. adults will be obese, experts predict*. Los Angeles Times. https://www.latimes.com/science/story/2019-12-18/nearly-half-of-us-adults-will-be-obese-by-2030

vi. World Health Organization. (n.d.). *Obesity*. https://www.who.int/health-topics/obesity

vii. University of Oxford. (n.d.). *Moderate obesity takes years off life expectancy*. https://www.ox.ac.uk/news/2009-03-18-moderate-obesity-takes-years-life-expectancy

viii. Cawley, J., Biener, A., Meyerhoefer, C., Ding, Y., Zvenyach, T., Smolarz, B. G., & Ramasamy, A. (2021). Direct medical costs of obesity in the United States and the most populous states. *Journal of Managed Care & Specialty Pharmacy*, 27(3), 354–366. https://doi.org/10.18553/jmcp.2021.20410

ix. Simon, G. E., Von Korff, M., Saunders, K., Miglioretti, D. L., Crane, P. K., van Belle, G., & Kessler, R. C. (2006). Association between obesity and psychiatric disorders in the US adult population. *Archives of General Psychiatry*, 63(7), 824–830. https://doi.org/10.1001/archpsyc.63.7.824

x. Moyer, C., Reoyo, O. R., & May, L. (2016). The influence of prenatal exercise on offspring health: A review. *Clinical Medicine Insights: Women's Health*, 9, 37–42. https://doi.org/10.4137/CMWH.S34670

xi. Schonfeld, Z. (2013, July). *Wives are cheating 40% more than they used to, but still 70% as much as men*. The Atlantic. https://www.theatlantic.com/national/archive/2013/07/wives-cheating-vs-men/313704/

xii. Schore, A. N. (2005). Back to basics: Attachment, affect regulation, and the developing right brain: Linking developmental neuroscience to pediatrics. *Pediatrics in Review*, 26(6), 204–217. https://doi.org/10.1542/pir.26-6-204

3. Negotiating with Mate-Selection Theories

i. Ackerman, C. E. (2023, April 19). *What is attachment theory? Bowlby's 4 stages explained*. PositivePsychology.com. https://positivepsychology.com/attachment-theory/

ii. Kennedy, J., & Kennedy, C. (2004). Attachment theory: Implications for school psychology. *Psychology in the Schools*, 41(2), 247–259. https://doi.org/10.1002/pits.10153

iii. Kirkpatrick, L. A., & Hazan, C. (1994). Attachment styles and close relationships: A four-year prospective study. *Personal Relationships*, 1(2), 123–142. https://doi.org/10.1111/j.1475-6811.1994.tb00058.x

iv. Mickelson, K. D., Kessler, R. C., & Shaver, P. R. (1997). Adult attachment in a nationally representative sample. *Journal of Personality and Social Psychology*, 73(5), 1092–1106. https://doi.org/10.1037/0022-3514.73.5.1092

v. Wedekind, C., & Penn, D. (2000). MHC genes, body odours, and odour preferences. *Nephrology Dialysis Transplantation, 15*(9), 1269–1271. https://doi.org/10.1093/ndt/15.9.1269

vi. Motaqhey, M., Ghanjal, A., Mastri Farahani, R., Ghabaee, M., Kaka, G., Noroziyan, M., & Fadaee Fathabadi, F. (2015). Sex differences in neuroanatomy of the human mirror neuron system: Impact on functional recovery of ischemic hemiparetic patients. Iranian Red Crescent Medical Journal, 17(8), Article e28363. https://pmc.ncbi.nlm.nih.gov/articles/PMC4586897/

vii. Acharya, S., & Shukla, S. (2012). Mirror neurons: Enigma of the metaphysical modular brain. Journal of Natural Science, Biology and Medicine, 3(2), 118–124. https://pmc.ncbi.nlm.nih.gov/articles/PMC3510904/

viii. Davenport, M. (2021, October 1). Revealing the logic of the body's 'second brain'. MSUToday | Michigan State University. https://msutoday.msu.edu/news/2021/10/logic-of-the-second-brain

ix. Ramírez-Uclés, I. M., & Ramírez-Uclés, R. (2020). Gender differences in visuospatial abilities and complex mathematical problem solving. *Frontiers in Psychology, 11*, Article 191. https://doi.org/10.3389/fpsyg.2020.00191

x. Vaillancourt, T. (2013). Do human females use indirect aggression as an intrasexual competition strategy? *Philosophical Transactions of the Royal Society B: Biological Sciences, 368*(1631), Article 20130080. https://doi.org/10.1098/rstb.2013.0080

xi. Gecewicz, C. (2018, October 1). *"New Age" beliefs common among both religious and nonreligious Americans.* Pew Research Center. https://www.pewresearch.org/short-reads/2018/10/01/new-age-beliefs-common-among-both-religious-and-nonreligious-americans/

xii. White, G. L. (1980). Physical attractiveness and courtship progress. *Journal of Personality and Social Psychology, 39*(4), 660–668. https://doi.org/10.1037/0022-3514.39.4.660

xiii. Reynolds, T., & Meltzer, A. L. (2017). Adopting a dyadic perspective to better understand the association between physical attractiveness and dieting motivations and behaviors. *Body Image, 22*, 48–52. https://doi.org/10.1016/j.bodyim.2017.05.001

xiv. Reynolds, T., & Meltzer, A. L. (2017). Adopting a dyadic perspective to better understand the association between physical attractiveness and dieting motivations and behaviors. *Body Image, 22*, 48–52. https://doi.org/10.1016/j.bodyim.2017.05.001

xv. Shaw Taylor, L., Fiore, A. T., Mendelsohn, G. A., & Cheshire, C. (2011). Out of my league: A real-world test of the matching hypothesis. *Personality and Social Psychology Bulletin, 37*(7), 942–954. https://doi.org/10.1177/0146167211409947

xvi. Dunkel, C., Nedelec, J., Linden, D., & Marshall, R. (2017). Physical attractiveness and the general factor of personality. *Adaptive Human Behavior and Physiology, 3*(1), 185–197. https://doi.org/10.1007/s40750-016-0055-7

4. The Love Hero's Narrative

i. Mueller, C. M., & Dweck, C. S. (1998). Praise for intelligence can undermine children's motivation and performance. *Journal of Personality and Social Psychology, 75*(1), 33–52. https://doi.org/10.1037/0022-3514.75.1.33

ii. Jauk, E., Neubauer, A. C., Mairunteregger, T., Pemp, S., Sieber, K. P., & Rauthmann, J. F. (2016). How alluring are dark personalities? The Dark Triad and attractiveness in speed dating. *European Journal of Personality, 30*(2), 125–138. https://doi.org/10.1002/per.2040

5. What to Negotiate With

i. Sundelin, T., Lekander, M., Sorjonen, K., & Axelsson, J. (2017). Negative effects of restricted sleep on facial appearance and social appeal. *Royal Society Open Science, 4*(5), Article 160918. https://doi.org/10.1098/rsos.160918

ii. Irwin, M., McClintick, J., Costlow, C., Fortner, M., White, J., & Gillin, J. C. (1996). Partial night sleep deprivation reduces natural killer and cellular immune responses in humans. *FASEB Journal, 10*(5), 643–653. https://doi.org/10.1096/fasebj.10.5.8621064

iii. Foundation for Traffic Safety. (n.d.). *Acute sleep deprivation and crash risk.* https://aaafoundation.org/acute-sleep-deprivation-and-crash-risk

iv. Williamson, A. M., & Feyer, A. M. (2000). Moderate sleep deprivation produces impairments in cognitive and motor performance equivalent to legally prescribed levels of alcohol intoxication. *Occupational and Environmental Medicine, 57*(10), 649–655. https://doi.org/10.1136/oem.57.10.649

v. Rasch, B., & Born, J. (2013). About sleep's role in memory. *Physiological reviews, 93*(2), 681–766. https://doi.org/10.1152/physrev.00032.2012

vi. UCLA Health. (2025, August 6). Early bird or night owl? How your chronotype affects your wellness. https://www.uclahealth.org/news/article/early-bird-or-night-owl-how-your-chronotype-affects-your

vii. Baron, K. G., Reid, K. J., & Zee, P. C. (2013). Exercise to improve sleep in insomnia: Exploration of the bidirectional effects. *Journal of Clinical Sleep Medicine, 9*(8), 819–824. https://doi.org/10.5664/jcsm.2930

viii. Giuntini, E. B., Sardá, F. A. H., & de Menezes, E. W. (2022). The effects of soluble dietary fibers on glycemic response: An overview and futures perspectives. *Foods, 11*(23), Article 3934. https://doi.org/10.3390/foods11233934

ix. Donaldson, M. S. (2004). Nutrition and cancer: A review of the evidence for an anti-cancer diet. *Nutrition Journal, 3*, Article 19. https://doi.org/10.1186/1475-2891-3-19

x. Kashefi, F., Khajehei, M., Alavinia, M., Golmakani, E., & Asili, J. (2015). Effect of ginger (Zingiber officinale) on heavy menstrual bleeding: A placebo-controlled, randomized clinical trial. *Phytotherapy Research, 29*(1), 114–119. https://doi.org/10.1002/ptr.5235

xi. Aldemir, M., Okulu, E., Neşelioğlu, S., Erel, O., & Kayıgil, O. (2011). Pistachio diet improves erectile function parameters and serum lipid profiles in patients with erectile dysfunction. *International Journal of Impotence Research, 23*(1), 32–38. https://doi.org/10.1038/ijir.2010.33

xii. Porterfield, C. (2023, January 26). *Just 28% of Americans are exercising enough, CDC says—and it's even lower in some regions.* Forbes. https://www.forbes.com/sites/carlieporterfield/2023/01/26/just-28-of-americans-are-exercising-enough-cdc-says-and-its-even-lower-in-some-regions/

xiii. Marshall, N. (2023, September 12). *Sitting for more than 10 hours a day linked to higher dementia risk.* The Independent. https://www.independent.co.uk/news/health/jama-university-of-arizona-dementia-society-england-b2409979.html

xiv. Matei, D., Trofin, D., Iordan, D. A., Onu, I., Condurache, I., Ionite, C., & Buculei, I. (2023). The endocannabinoid system and physical exercise. *International Journal of Molecular Sciences, 24*(3), Article 1989. https://doi.org/10.3390/ijms24031989

xv. National Institute on Drug Abuse. (2023, April 17). *What are marijuana's long-term effects on the brain?.* https://nida.nih.gov/publications/research-reports/marijuana/what-are-marijuanas-long-term-effects-brain

xvi. de Sousa Fernandes, M. S., Ordônio, T. F., Santos, G. C. J., Santos, L. E. R., Calazans, C. T., Gomes, D. A., & Santos, T. M. (2020). Effects of physical exercise on neuroplasticity and brain function: A systematic review in human and animal studies. *Neural Plasticity, 2020,* Article 8856621. https://doi.org/10.1155/2020/8856621

xvii. Palmer, J. A., Morris, J. K., Billinger, S. A., Lepping, R. J., Martin, L., Green, Z., & Vidoni, E. D. (2023). Hippocampal blood flow rapidly and preferentially increases after a bout of moderate-intensity exercise in older adults with poor cerebrovascular health. *Cerebral Cortex, 33*(9), 5297–5306. https://doi.org/10.1093/cercor/bhac418

xviii. Singh, B., Olds, T., Curtis, R., et al. (2023). Effectiveness of physical activity interventions for improving depression, anxiety, and distress: An overview of systematic reviews. *British Journal of Sports Medicine, 57*(18), 1203–1209. https://doi.org/10.1136/bjsports-2022-106195

xix. Rupp, T. L., Acebo, C., & Carskadon, M. A. (2007). Evening alcohol suppresses salivary melatonin in young adults. *Chronobiology International, 24*(3), 463–470. https://doi.org/10.1080/07420520701420675

xx. Zisapel, N. (2018). New perspectives on the role of melatonin in human sleep, circadian rhythms and their regulation. British Journal of Pharmacology, 175(16), 3190–3199. https://doi.org/10.1111/bph.14116

xxi. van Schrojenstein Lantman, M., Mackus, M., Roth, T., & Verster, J. C. (2017). Total sleep time, alcohol consumption, and the duration and severity of alcohol hangover. *Nature and Science of Sleep, 9,* 181–186. https://doi.org/10.2147/NSS.S136467

xxii. Pietilä, J., Helander, E., Korhonen, I., Myllymäki, T., Kujala, U. M., & Lindholm, H. (2018). Acute effect of alcohol intake on cardiovascular autonomic regulation during the first hours of sleep in a large real-world sample of Finnish employees: Observational study. *JMIR Mental Health, 5*(1), Article e23. https://doi.org/10.2196/mental.9519

xxiii. Evans, J. R. (2024, March 4). *Seattle leads the largest metros in alcohol spending, while Houston is at the bottom.* LendingTree. https://www.lendingtree.com/credit-cards/study/alcohol-expenditures/

xxiv. Royal, J., & O'Shea, A. (2024, March 5). *What is the average stock market return?.*

NerdWallet. https://www.nerdwallet.com/article/investing/average-stock-market-return

xxv. World Health Organization. (2023, January 4). *No level of alcohol consumption is safe for our health.* https://www.who.int/europe/news/item/04-01-2023-no-level-of-alcohol-consumption-is-safe-for-our-health

xxvi. Volkow, N. D., Baler, R. D., Compton, W. M., & Weiss, S. R. (2014). Adverse health effects of marijuana use. *The New England Journal of Medicine, 370*(23), 2219–2227. https://doi.org/10.1056/NEJMra1402309

xxvii. Brown, M. (2023, April 5). *The money behind marijuana.* LendEDU. https://lendedu.com/blog/money-behind-marijuana

xxviii. Urberg, K. A., Değirmencioğlu, S. M., & Pilgrim, C. (1997). Close friend and group influence on adolescent cigarette smoking and alcohol use. *Developmental Psychology, 33*(5), 834–844. https://doi.org/10.1037/0012-1649.33.5.834

xxix. Bearden, W. O., & Etzel, M. J. (1982). Reference group influence on product and brand purchase decisions. *Journal of Consumer Research, 9*(2), 183–194. https://doi.org/10.1086/208911

xxx. McDermott, R., Fowler, J. H., & Christakis, N. A. (2009, October 18). *Breaking up is hard to do, unless everyone else is doing it too: Social network effects on divorce in a longitudinal sample.* SSRN. https://doi.org/10.2139/ssrn.1490708

xxxi. Oral Health Foundation. (2022, November 2). *Bad breath is biggest barrier to landing your Valentine's Day date, reveals survey.* https://www.dentalhealth.org/news/bad-breath-is-biggest-barrier-to-landing-your-valentines-day-date-reveals-survey

xxxii. Regnerus, M., Gordon, D., & Price, J. (2016). Documenting pornography use in America: A comparative analysis of methodological approaches. *The Journal of Sex Research, 53*(7), 873–881. https://doi.org/10.1080/00224499.2015.1096886

xxxiii. Ahmed, F., Shafiq, M. Z., & Liu, A. X. (2016). The internet is for porn: Measurement and analysis of online adult traffic. *IEEE 36th International Conference on Distributed Computing Systems,* Article 88. https://doi.org/10.1109/ICDCS.2016.81

xxxiv. Winton, B. (2019, May 30). Disruptive innovation: Why now? ARK Investment Management LLC. https://research.ark-invest.com/hubfs/1_Download_Files_ARK-Invest/White_Papers/ARK%20Invest_052919_whitepaper_DI-Why-Now.pdf

6. What to Negotiate For

i. Brittle, Z. (2024, October 30). *P is for problems.* The Gottman Institute. https://www.gottman.com/blog/p-is-for-problems/

7. Unfit and Failed Negotiations

i. Chong, J. Y., & Fraley, R. C. (2026). The long-term stability of affective bonds after romantic separation: Do attachments simply fade away? Social Psychological and Personality Science. Advance online publication. https://doi.org/10.1177/19485506251323624

8. Successful Negotiations

i. Bushman, B. J., DeWall, C. N., Pond, R. S., & Hanus, M. D. (2014). Low glucose relates to greater aggression in married couples. Proceedings of the *National Academy of Sciences, 111*(17), 6254–6257. https://doi.org/10.1073/pnas.1400619111

ii. Grubbs, J. B., Kraus, S. W., & Perry, S. L. (2019). Self-reported addiction to pornography in a nationally representative sample: The roles of use habits, religiousness, and moral incongruence. *Journal of Behavioral Addictions, 8*(1), 88–93. https://doi.org/10.1556/2006.7.2018.134

iii. Selvin, E., Burnett, A. L., & Platz, E. A. (2007). Prevalence and risk factors for erectile dysfunction in the US. *The American Journal of Medicine, 120*(2), 151–157. https://doi.org/10.1016/j.amjmed.2006.06.010

iv. Nagoski, E. (2021). *Come as you are: The surprising new science that will transform your sex life.* Simon & Schuster.

v. Chivers, M. L., Seto, M. C., & Blanchard, R. (2007). Gender and sexual orientation differences in sexual response to sexual activities versus gender of actors in sexual films. *Journal of Personality and Social Psychology, 93*(6), 1108–1121. https://doi.org/10.1037/0022-3514.93.6.1108

vi. Herbenick, D., Fu, T. J., Arter, J., Sanders, S. A., & Dodge, B. (2018). Women's experiences with genital touching, sexual pleasure, and orgasm: Results from a U.S. probability sample of women ages 18 to 94. *Journal of Sex & Marital Therapy, 44*(2), 201–212. https://doi.org/10.1080/0092623X.2017.1346530

vii. White, F. (2022, October 27). *Pleasure-producing human clitoris has more than 10,000 nerve fibers.* OHSU News. https://news.ohsu.edu/2022/10/27/pleasure-producing-human-clitoris-has-more-than-10-000-nerve-fibers

viii. Tunçkol, E., Purkart, L., Eigen, L., Vida, I., & Brecht, M. (2023). Fiber counts and architecture of the human dorsal penile nerve. *Scientific Reports, 13*(1), Article 8862. https://doi.org/10.1038/s41598-023-35030-w

ix. Armstrong, E. A., England, P., & Fogarty, A. C. K. (2012). Accounting for women's orgasm and sexual enjoyment in college hookups and relationships. *American Sociological Review, 77*(3), 435–462. https://doi.org/10.1177/0003122412445802

x. Frederick, D. A., John, H. K. S., Garcia, J. R., & Lloyd, E. A. (2018). Differences in orgasm frequency among gay, lesbian, bisexual, and heterosexual men and women in a U.S. national sample. *Archives of Sexual Behavior, 47*(1), 273–288. https://doi.org/10.1007/s10508-017-0939-z

xi. U.S. National Library of Medicine. (n.d.). Orgasmic dysfunction in women: *MedlinePlus medical encyclopedia.* MedlinePlus. https://medlineplus.gov/ency/article/001953.htm

xii. McNichols, N. (2021, June 2). *The psychology behind the female orgasm: 5 key new findings about the female orgasm.* University of Washington, Department of Psychology. https://psych.uw.edu/news/3010

xiii. World Health Organization. (2025, May 30). Herpes simplex virus. https://www.who.int/news-room/fact-sheets/detail/herpes-simplex-virus

xiv. National Health Service. (2022, August 15). Sex activities and risk. https://www.nhs.uk/live-well/sexual-health/sex-activities-and-risk/

xv. Carrère, S., & Gottman, J. M. (1999). Predicting divorce among newlyweds from the first three minutes of a marital conflict discussion. Family Process, 38(3), 293–301. https://doi.org/10.1111/j.1545-5300.1999.00293.x

xvi. Kashefi, F., Khajehei, M., Alavinia, M., Golmakani, E., & Asili, J. (2015). Effect of ginger (Zingiber officinale) on heavy menstrual bleeding: A placebo-controlled, randomized clinical trial. *Phytotherapy Research, 29*(1), 114–119. https://doi.org/10.1002/ptr.5235

xvii. Barton, A. W., Lavner, J. A., Sutton, N. C., McNeil Smith, S., & Beach, S. R. H. (2023). The protective effects of perceived gratitude and expressed gratitude for relationship quality among African American couples. *Journal of Social and Personal Relationships, 40*(5), 1622–1644. https://doi.org/10.1177/02654075221131288

www.ingramcontent.com/pod-product-compliance
Lightning Source LLC
Chambersburg PA
CBHW071445140726
47997CB00005B/1594